Modern American Drama: Playwriting in the 1950s

DECADES OF MODERN AMERICAN DRAMA: PLAYWRITING FROM THE 1930s TO 2009

Modern American Drama: Playwriting in the 1930s
by Anne Fletcher

Modern American Drama: Playwriting in the 1940s
by Felicia Hardison Londré

Modern American Drama: Playwriting in the 1950s
by Susan C. W. Abbotson

Modern American Drama: Playwriting in the 1960s
by Mike Sell

Modern American Drama: Playwriting in the 1970s
by Michael Vanden Heuvel

Modern American Drama: Playwriting in the 1980s
by Sandra G. Shannon

Modern American Drama: Playwriting in the 1990s
by Cheryl Black and Sharon Friedman

Modern American Drama: Playwriting 2000–2009
by Julia Listengarten and Cindy Rosenthal

Modern American Drama: Playwriting in the 1950s

Voices, Documents, New Interpretations

Susan C. W. Abbotson

Series Editors: Brenda Murphy and Julia Listengarten

methuen | drama
LONDON • NEW YORK • OXFORD • NEW DELHI • SYDNEY

METHUEN DRAMA
Bloomsbury Publishing Plc
50 Bedford Square, London, WC1B 3DP, UK
1385 Broadway, New York, NY 10018, USA
29 Earlsfort Terrace, Dublin 2, Ireland

BLOOMSBURY, METHUEN DRAMA and the Methuen Drama logo
are trademarks of Bloomsbury Publishing Plc

First published in Great Britain 2018
Paperback edition first published 2021

Copyright © Susan C. W. Abbotson and contributors, 2018

Susan C. W. Abbotson has asserted her right under the Copyright,
Designs and Patents Act, 1988, to be identified as author of this work.

For legal purposes the Acknowledgements on p. vii constitute
an extension of this copyright page.

Cover design by Louise Dugdale
Cover image: Television Hour circa 1955 © Lambert/Getty Images

All rights reserved. No part of this publication may be reproduced or
transmitted in any form or by any means, electronic or mechanical,
including photocopying, recording, or any information storage or retrieval
system, without prior permission in writing from the publishers.

Bloomsbury Publishing Plc does not have any control over, or responsibility for,
any third-party websites referred to or in this book. All internet addresses given
in this book were correct at the time of going to press. The author and publisher
regret any inconvenience caused if addresses have changed or sites have
ceased to exist, but can accept no responsibility for any such changes.

A catalogue record for this book is available from the British Library.

A catalog record for this book is available from the Library of Congress.

ISBN: HB: 978-1-4725-7142-7
PB: 978-1-3502-1550-4
ePDF: 978-1-3500-1461-9
eBook: 978-1-3500-1462-6
Pack: 978-1-4725-7264-6

Series: Decades of Modern American Drama: Playwriting from the 1930s to 2009

Typeset by Fakenham Prepress Solutions, Fakenham, Norfolk NR21 8NN

To find out more about our authors and books visit
www.bloomsbury.com and sign up for our newsletters.

CONTENTS

List of Tables and Boxes viii
Biographical Note and Notes on Contributors ix
General Preface Brenda Murphy and Julia Listengarten xi

1 Introduction to the 1950s *Susan C. W. Abbotson* 1
   Domestic life 3
   Society 8
   Political events 13
   Popular culture 17
   Media 26
   Science and technology 33

2 American Theatre in the 1950s *Susan C. W. Abbotson* 39
   Introduction 39
   Notable playwrights of the decade 46
   Ethnic drama and plays of Otherness 54
   Key theatre practitioners beyond the playwrights 57
   Political drama 71
   African-American theatre 79
   Musical theatre 84
   Television drama 89
   Off-Broadway, Off-Off-Broadway, regional and college theatre 92
   Community and children's theatre 96

3   William Inge: *Come Back Little Sheba* (1950), *Picnic* (1953), *Bus Stop* (1955) and *The Dark at the Top of the Stairs* (1957)   Susan C. W. Abbotson   99

   Introduction   99
   Inge's theatre   103
   Come Back Little Sheba (1950)   106
   Picnic (1953)   110
   Bus Stop (1955)   114
   The Dark at the Top of the Stairs (1957)   119
   Conclusion   123

4   Stephen Sondheim: *West Side Story* (1957) and *Gypsy* (1959), with Collaborators Jerome Robbins and Arthur Laurents   Stuart Hecht   127

   Stephen Sondheim   127
   The collaborative process and musical theatre   130
   Jerome Robbins   131
   Arthur Laurents   135
   West Side Story (1957)   137
   Gypsy (1959)   146
   Conclusion   160

5   Alice Childress: *Florence* (1949), *Gold Through the Trees* (1952) and *Trouble in Mind* (1955)   Soyica Diggs-Colbert   165

   Introduction   165
   Childress's theatre   166
   Florence (1949)   168
   Gold Through the Trees (1952)   173
   Trouble in Mind (1955)   180

6 Jerome Lawrence and Robert E. Lee: *Inherit the Wind* (1955), *Auntie Mame* (1956) and *The Gang's All Here* (1959) Alan Woods 189
  Introduction 189
  Inherit the Wind (1955) 191
  Auntie Mame (1956) 201
  The Gang's All Here (1959) 205
  Conclusion 209

Afterword *Susan C. W. Abbotson* 211
  William Inge 211
  Stephen Sondheim 216
  Alice Childress 222
  Jerome Lawrence and Robert E. Lee 227

Documents: Popular Writings from the 1950s 233
  From 'The Spirit of the Age' in *Company Manners* by Leo Kronenberger (1955) 233
  From 'Introduction' to *The Power of Positive Thinking* by Norman Vincent Peale (1952) 239
  From *The Bride's Cookbook* by Poppy Cannon (1954) 241
  From *The Crack in the Picture Window* by John Keats (1956) 242
  From *The Vanishing Adolescent* by Edgar Z. Friedenberg (1959) 243
  From *100 Things You Should Know About Communism and Education* (1951) 244
  Extracts from House Committee on Un-American Activities hearings 1952–1956 245
  Theatre in the 1950s 250

Notes 257
Bibliography 283
Index 293

LIST OF TABLES AND BOXES

Tables

1.1: 1950s costs when the average annual income was $3,210–$5,010 4
1.2: Pulitzer Prizes for fiction and poetry in the 1950s 20
1.3: Hit movies of the 1950s 30
2.1: Longest-running Broadway dramas and musicals during the 1950s for each year of opening 41
2.2: Major theatre awards for plays and musicals during the 1950s 43
2.3: Tony Award-winning direction and stage design in the 1950s 60

Boxes

1.1: The story of Tupperware 7
1.2: Home ownership in the 1950s 11
1.3: Key figures of Cold War espionage 13

BIOGRAPHICAL NOTE AND NOTES ON CONTRIBUTORS

Susan C. W. Abbotson is Professor of Modern and Contemporary drama in the English department at Rhode Island College, USA. She is the author of several books, including *Critical Companion to Arthur Miller*, *Thematic Guide to Modern Drama*, *Masterpieces of Twentieth-Century American Drama* and *Student Companion to Arthur Miller*, as well as numerous essays in books and journals on a variety of playwrights that include Eugene O'Neill, Sam Shepard, Tom Stoppard, Paula Vogel, Mae West, Thornton Wilder, Tennessee Williams and August Wilson. She is currently editing a new collection of *Arthur Miller's Essays*, and is the Performance Review Editor for the *Arthur Miller Journal*.

Soyica Diggs-Colbert is an Associate Professor of African American Studies and Theatre and Performance Studies at Georgetown University, Washington, DC. She is the author of *The African American Theatrical Body: Reception, Performance and the Stage* (2011) and editor of the Black Performance special issue of *African American Review* (2012). Colbert is currently working on a second book project entitled *Black Movements: Performance and Politics* and an edited volume entitled *Do You Want to Be Well: The Psychic Hold of Slavery*. Her research primarily focuses on twentieth to twenty-first-century black drama, but her interests span the nineteenth to twenty-first centuries, from Harriet Tubman to Beyoncé, and from poetics to performance.

Stuart Hecht is Associate Professor of Theatre at Boston College, USA. He is editor of the *New England Theatre Journal*, an officer of the American Theatre and Drama Society, the Chicago Theatre History Project and the New England Theatre Conference's College of Fellows. Hecht has authored *Transposing Broadway: Jews, Assimilation and the American Musical* as well as several chapters and numerous articles on a variety of playwrights. He also appeared in the Peabody Award winning documentary, *The Broadway Musical: a Jewish Legacy*.

Alan Woods retired after four decades as a professor of theatre at Ohio State University, USA, where for a number of years he served as director of the Jerome Lawrence and Robert E. Lee Theatre Research Institute, an archive jointly administered by the Department of Theatre and the University Libraries. A former editor of *Theatre Journal*, his scholarship has appeared in all major theatre publications. Woods works in the professional theatre as a dramaturg, and was a founding board member of Senior Theatre USA. His own short plays for senior performers have been produced on every continent with the exception of Antarctica.

GENERAL PREFACE

Decades of Modern American Drama: Playwriting from the 1930s to 2009 is a series of eight volumes about American theatre and drama, each focusing on a particular decade during the period between 1930 and 2010. It begins with the 1930s, the decade when Eugene O'Neill was awarded the Nobel Prize for Literature and American theatre came of age. This is followed by the decade of the country's most acclaimed theatre, when O'Neill, Tennessee Williams and Arthur Miller were writing their most distinguished work and a theatrical idiom known as 'the American style' was seen in theatres throughout the world. Its place in the world repertoire established, American playwriting has taken many turns since 1950.

The aim of this series is to focus attention on individual playwrights or collaborative teams who together reflect the variety and range of American drama during the eighty-year period it covers. In each volume, contributing experts offer detailed critical essays on four playwrights or collaborators and the significant work they produced during the decade. The essays on playwrights are presented in a rich interpretive context, which provides a contemporary perspective on both the theatre and American life and culture during the decade. The careers of the playwrights before and after the decade are summarized as well, and a section of documents, including interviews, manuscripts, reviews, brief essays and other items, sheds further light on the playwrights and their plays.

The process of choosing such a limited number of playwrights to represent the American theatre of this period has been a difficult but revealing one. In selecting them, the series editors and volume authors have been guided by several principles: highlighting the most significant playwrights, in terms both historical and aesthetic, who contributed at least two interesting and important plays during the decade; providing a wide-ranging view of the decade's theatre, including both Broadway and alternative venues; examining many historical trends in playwriting and theatrical production during the decade; and reflecting the theatre's diversity in gender and ethnicity, both across the decade and across the period as a whole. In some decades, the choices are obvious. It is hard to argue with O'Neill, Williams, Miller and Wilder in the 1940s. Other decades required a good deal of thought and discussion. Readers will inevitably regret that favourite playwrights are left out. We can only respond that we regret it too, but we believe that the playwrights who are included reflect a representative sample of the best and most interesting American playwriting during the period.

While each of the books has the same fundamental elements – an overview of life and culture during the decade, an overview of the decade's theatre and drama, the four essays on the playwrights, a section of documents, an Afterword bringing the playwrights' careers up to date and a Bibliography of works both on the individual playwrights and on the decade in general – there are differences among the books depending on each individual volume author's decisions about how to represent and treat the decade. The various formats chosen by the volume authors for the overview essays, the wide variety of playwrights, from the canonical to the contemporary avant-garde, and the varied perspectives of the contributors' essays make for very different individual volumes. Each of the volumes stands on its own as a history of theatre in the decade and a critical study of the four individual playwrights or collaborative teams included. Taken together, however, the eight volumes offer a broadly representative critical and historical treatment of eighty years of American theatre and drama that is both accessible to a student first encountering the subject and informative and provocative for a seasoned expert.

Brenda Murphy (Board of Trustees Distinguished Professor Emeritus, University of Connecticut, USA)
Julia Listengarten (Professor of Theatre at the University of Central Florida, USA)
Series Editors

1

Introduction to the 1950s

Susan C. W. Abbotson

One common mythology about America in the 1950s was that it was a sterile conservative period of total containment during which a glib advertising industry forced its 'packaged' products on the cowed and gullible American populace, living in identical suburban homes, with identical nuclear families. Juxtaposed against this is a conflicting, kinder, image – captured in the *Leave it to Beaver*, *Father Knows Best* sit-coms of the era, and nostalgically recreated in later television (*Happy Days*) or movies (*Back to the Future* or *When Peggy Sue Got Married*) – that depicts the era as a golden ideal of possibility, freedom and fun, with happy families, diner hangouts, hula hoops and 3D movies.[1]

While neither view is totally incorrect, both remain oversimplifications, with reality lying somewhere between. Many saw the decade as a kind of American Renaissance, during which the nation could make a fresh start and be rebuilt. In 1959, the Union even gained two new states: Alaska and Hawaii. The decade saw several developments that would set the groundwork for the less authoritarian 1960s, and offer challenges to the moral restraints of the previous generation. While a semi-patriarchal family remained the social norm, more relaxed styles of parenting, the growth of a distinct youth culture, as well as the shifting status of women, ethnicities, cities, sexuality and religion, all contributed to profound changes in overall values and beliefs. As James Gilbert suggests, 'Attitudes towards a variety of cultural and social institutions changed rapidly,' and despite political intolerance, the 1950s saw some remarkable liberalization in the areas of civil rights and class mobility, as well as challenges to traditional thought regarding the social order.[2]

One undeniable truth is that the 1950s was a period of rising prosperity and 'conspicuous consumption' that created a lot of stress: to not buy American products was frankly un-American, and left one open to derision. Items labelled 'Made in Japan', for example, were considered little more than junk. Most felt the pressure to increase their quality of life and the compulsion to strive for an ideal over the real. The American Dream was tantalizingly glimpsed, as a widening middle class – in the throes of a massive economic, manufacturing and baby boom – were trying to redefine themselves as Americans. During the 1950s, American per-capita income tripled, even though not all shared in the general prosperity, and discrimination was still evident. While the percentage of low-income white families at least halved, this happened less among non-white families; and working women, especially, still encountered extensive prejudice.

Assisted by the GI Bill and increasing amounts of government funding, the 1950s saw higher levels of education and literacy that might suggest an opening out, but there was also a closing in and expanding anti-intellectualism, as the decade featured intense paranoia and anxiety, simplistic patriotism and a cautious passivity toward the trampling of certain constitutional rights. Fears of an impending nuclear holocaust caused great strain, along with fears (both justified and invented) of juvenile delinquents, communism, female sexuality and desegregation. It is hardly surprising the period also saw a tremendous growth in psychoanalysis and tranquillizers.

The British Empire had passed, and America had become the leading world superpower, itching to stretch its new muscles, with an economic boom and military-industrial complex to support this new imperial reach. As one commentator suggests, 'The 1950s was to be the first *authentically* American decade' and a swiftly modernized American image of freedom and prosperity began to spread, globally, enhanced by media that depicted the opulent American lifestyle with its air travel, two-car families, expanded highway system, vast supermarkets, fast-food, large-scale college education, vast corporations and growing managerial class.[3] Yet, for all of the drive to be number one, the decade also seemed to revere the centre: better to be middle class and middle of the road than to excel and become the nail that sticks out. Highbrow smacked of subversion and real Americans were down-to-earth folk. Vice presidential nominee Richard Nixon understood this trend as he played up his moderate origins and referred to himself as an 'ordinary American' in his Checkers speech of 1952, in which he denied accepting illegal campaign gifts but insisted that his family would keep the dog, Checkers, given to his children. This speech was heard or seen by around 60 million, mostly sympathetic, Americans and was an early example of the effective outreach that could be made through television, be it for socio-political engineering or consumerism.

Through the rise of national television, national advertising[4] and national restaurant, motel and store chains, there looked to be a growing uniformity – even homogenization – in the culture, as low- and high-brow tastes seemed to merge, but there were also disruptive trends that created new divisions, especially between the young and old. By the middle of the decade there was a growing feeling that mass media was standing between parents and their children as offspring began to look to the changing music, publications, television and movies of their peer culture rather than to their parents. Family, however, remained a central icon of the period and most public places underwent transformations to become more 'family friendly'. Thus, shopping centres, vacation resorts, restaurants and diners, service stations and sporting facilities (golf, bowling, ice-skating and roller-skating) were all redesigned to be more attractive to males, females, children and adolescents. A department store would now be sure to include clothing, appliances, hardware, sporting goods and toys within a single location to ensure that shopping became a family affair.

Domestic life

The dramatic rise in prosperity of the era was key to many of its developments, especially on the domestic front. While accounting for only 6 per cent of the world's population, by the mid-1950s Americans were consuming one-third of the world's goods and services.[5] Many families had extra cash to spend on new homes out in the suburbs that needed filling with new items, and the sale of lawn and porch furniture nearly tripled between 1950 and 1960. What were once considered luxuries were now available to almost all. According to the US Census, by the close of the decade 75 per cent of families owned at least one car, 80 per cent had a phone, 85 per cent a television and 96 per cent both electricity and a radio. While dryers, freezers and garbage disposals were scarcer, most middle-class homes had a washing machine, refrigerator and vacuum. Older values of hard work, thrift and delayed gratification were set aside in the face of consumer capitalism and the desire to 'keep up with the Joneses'. Mass marketing, built-in obsolescence and cheaper manufacturing using a variety of new materials encouraged people to spend. Everything had a new style; bright colours, bold patterns and geometric shapes were fashionable, and new synthetic drip dry or wash 'n' wear fabrics cut down on chores.

While 1950s designs were not *all* impractical, the look was often more important than comfort or practicality, and furniture took on strange new shapes and angles, often covered in rayon, vinyl or chrome. While much of the decorative plaster and plastic paraphernalia is nowadays viewed as 'kitsch', at the time they were a reflection of a buoyant culture that embraced novelty and exotic trends (often with Hawaiian, Mexican and Asian themes), albeit in a stereotypical fashion. With an emphasis on the happy couple, items often came in pairs – male and female – and, whether animals or people, were depicted as friendly and cute.

By 1955 there were 32 million children in the United States under 12, and, aside from Silly Putty or Play-Doh, most baby

Table 1.1 1950s costs when the average annual income was $3,210–$5,010

Loaf of bread	12 cents	Single home	$8,450–$12,400
Pint of milk	49 cents	Washing machine	$149.95
A dozen eggs	49 cents	21" B&W television	$148.95
Frozen chicken pie	19 cents	Chrome seven-piece dinette set	$99.50
Men's all-wool suit	$28.90		
Pair of denim jeans	$2.49	Pop-up toaster	$21
Women's skirt	$4.95	Car	$1,510–$2,200
		Gallon of gas	18–25 cents

(Source: http://www.thepeoplehistory.com [accessed 17 March 2016])

boomer toys were gendered; girls were put into housewife training with toy tin stoves, grocery carts, ironing boards and dolls (Barbie was first introduced in 1959), while boys had their Lionel trains (equipped with a rocket launcher car), Tonka toys, guns and cowboy suits. Disney's television series *Adventures of Davy Crockett* had 40 million viewers by 1954, and in 1955 Davy Crockett regalia had become a $100 million industry, spinning off songs, movies and tie-in products from peanut butter to pyjamas, with *Life* reporting a shortage of coonskin hats and other paraphernalia.[6] Such fads illustrate the rapid popularization of have-to-have items through modern communication. The themed lunch box would become almost standard for schoolchildren. The bicycle was also important for the younger generation to have, to show off and get around; Schwinn alone was annually selling half a million two-wheelers.[7] Children during this decade were generally allowed considerable freedom outside the home to explore their neighbourhoods and meet up with friends to play games like street hockey in urban centres, or baseball and football in the suburbs.

During the decade, milk started coming home in cartons, orange juice in a frozen concentrate, fresh vegetables were available year round and electric mixers, toasters and white bread in cellophane proliferated. While not all traditional cooking was eschewed, a growing food industry was moving middle-class homes, especially, away from fresh produce to perfectly designed meals created from frozen, dehydrated or canned goods.[8] Packaged food was marketed as a time saver, and 'ready-mix' became the go-to product, with frozen TV dinners in their oven-ready aluminium tray appearing in 1952. Fish sticks were introduced by Birds Eye that same year, and by 1953 had sold more than 7 million pounds, which rose to 30 million by 1954.[9] Such packaging led to sweeter, saltier and blander flavours, which began to become the expected flavours for many palates.

The rigours and dangers of the Second World War led many to desire a safe haven and more secure future, which was translated into domestic containment around a close-knit family. Americans in the 1950s married earlier, had more babies and divorced less frequently than in the 1940s or any subsequent decade.[10] Families usually dined together, went on outings together, socialized with neighbours, and girls stayed home until they married. The baby boom helped to sustain economic growth and foster a family-based domesticity in the rapidly expanding suburbs.

The 1950s might conjure up an image of a housewife vacuuming the spacious living room of her suburban home in high heels and pearls as her husband pursues a white-collar office career and clean-cut, obedient children attend school. Such is the public face of the era, but there was a split between public and private during this decade. Alan Petigny suggests that while, publically, many conformed to conservative middle-class ideals and quietly lived in suburbs with their large families, attending church and avoiding radical politics, conservatism was losing ground, and, privately, attitudes toward sex, parenting and religion were moving away from a traditional conservative framework.[11]

Courtship rituals certainly changed, as the goal of many high school girls became a desire to 'go steady' rather than casually date. The resulting intimacy must have led to more sexual activity, though the pressure to keep quiet about it remained. The Food and Drug Administration (FDA) would not approve the pill until 1960, but other contraceptives were available, and increasingly culturally acceptable. Before the war, most states had laws restricting advertising and dissemination of birth control tools, but by the close of the 1950s, only Massachusetts and Connecticut retained such restrictions, and planned parenthood was on the rise.[12] By mid-decade, drug stores – which had proliferated throughout the suburbs – openly displayed and sold condoms. When Alfred Kinsey's *Sexual Behavior in the Human Female* appeared in 1953, its readership was shocked by its claims that nearly half the country's women were having premarital sex, that 62 per cent masturbated and that around a quarter were having extra-marital affairs. But Kinsey's data was from earlier in the century, and while the period's growth in single motherhood certainly implies an increase in premarital sex, Petigny suggests that it was more an 'era of increased sexual titillation' rather than one of increased sexual activity.[13]

While there was increased sexual candour in music, movies, theatre and literature, a family-oriented culture prevailed. Family life was considered the bedrock of the society, and if one only looked to films, television, radio, comics and magazines of the day, one would assume that all of those families were firmly middle class. The 1950s saw a mix of stay-at-home moms and working women, but few questioned that women were responsible for the upkeep of the home and family. While nearly 50 per cent of wives worked for at least some period during their marriage, gender roles for the period remained fairly rigid – underscored by toys, cookbooks, magazines and the rest of the consumer culture – and only heterosexual relationships had societal approval.[14]

In 1963, in *The Feminine Mystique*, Betty Friedan would describe the previous decade's women as alienated and sickening from an imposed female domesticity, but her comments only covered a fairly well-off segment of the white middle class, and while not wholly wrong, her critique was incomplete.[15] Many women were limited, but challenges to those limits were on the rise;[16] husbands and wives were sharing more in family activities and decisions, including financial, and not all wives were quiescent and fully domesticated. Cooking and cleaning may have remained a woman's burden, women at work faced discrimination and there was a distinct lack of childcare support beyond family, friends and neighbours, but for every five males in the workplace the decade saw two women, also employed.

BOX 1.1: THE STORY OF TUPPERWARE

Invented in 1942 and initially sold in stores, Tupperware did not take off until the 1950s when it moved to a direct sales model using hostess parties. The product combined thrifty home economics with the excess of frivolous new designs, a contradiction that lay at the heart of much of 1950s consumerism. Spearheaded by Brownie Wise, the first woman to grace the cover of *Business Week* and an icon of possibility for other women, by the mid-1950s the Tupperware party had become a cultural hallmark of the era. While the sales model could be seen as exploiting women's networks and resources, and 75 per cent of the company's executive level management was male, it also allowed those same women a means of income, a culture of positive thought and self-empowerment, and a way to socialize in their new environment. The majority of American corporations at this time were 100 per cent male.

(Source: Alison J. Clarke, *Tupperware: The Promise of Plastic in 1950s America*, Washington: Smithsonian Institute, 1999)

In 1946, Dr Benjamin Spock had published his *Common Sense Book of Baby and Child Care*, and by 1952 sales had reached 4 million and it would continue to sell another million copies a year to the close of the decade.[17] Loved by parents and doctors alike, by 1960 nearly two-thirds of new mothers had read it, and 80 per cent of those owning it referenced it at least twice a month.[18] Spock emphasized positive reinforcement over stern discipline, urging talk and loving embraces over shaming or punishment. While Spock held conservative views that supported working fathers and stay-at-home mothers, his insistence that children are essentially good and could freely act out and copy their peers was permissive for the time and impacted on the way many 1950s children were raised. Discipline within the home was less stringent than is commonly supposed.

As church attendance rose, religious buildings were constructed and the Reverend Billy Graham drew massive crowds, it would appear that the era saw a religious revival, but religious piety was not necessarily on the rise, and many people's involvement in religion had become more social than theological: a stance against 'godless' communism. The growth of mantras such as Norman Vincent Peale's *The Power of Positive Thinking* (1952), with its de-emphasis on atonement, sin and guilt, symbolizes the increasing secularization of popular religion in post-war America, as temporal concerns overtook the spiritual. Most mainstream religions were relaxing standards over dancing, movies, drinking and make-up. The growth of interfaith marriages (especially between Protestant denominations), the secularization of Sunday as blue laws and 'Sabbath' observances were routinely defied as suburban-based stores began opening their doors in response to customer demand, and the rise in pastoral counselling from a psychological rather than devout standpoint, all indicate a reduction in religious conservatism. Indeed, conservatism in general was under threat from every side, and the seeds of the 1960s revolution were evident.

Society

Throughout the 1950s, American birth rates increased as death rates lowered. According to US Census estimates, the 1950s began with a population of around 151 million, rising to 179 million by 1960. This created a baby boom, with almost a third of the population being under the age of 14 by 1960. This rise was the second largest decade increase of the twentieth century after the 1910s. It was predominantly white, with a drop in the African-American population in the South and a rise of the same in northern and western regions (which helped to nationalize racial discrimination issues).[19] Couples were marrying younger than in any other Western nation: in 1957, ninety-seven out of every thousand girls between 15 and 19 had a child.[20] Meanwhile, between 1945 and 1960, the numbers of Americans over 65 rose by more than 50 per cent, with many being left behind by families moving to the suburbs as cities expanded to contain the growth. The population of rural America had declined to only 8.7 per cent of the country by 1960, and while more land was being cultivated, there had been a 30 per cent decrease in the number of farms, indicating a growing trend toward large-scale agriculture.[21]

The 1950s' workweek was a little over forty hours, and during the decade corporate profits more than tripled, average annual earnings more than doubled and the minimum wage rose above a dollar an hour (and was extended to include some trade and service workers rather than just manufacturing). Unemployment stood around 4.6 per cent, with continued military spending from both the Cold and Korean Wars to keep the economy vibrant. Many established companies, such as DuPont and General Electric, diversified to create huge conglomerates, investing abroad to create new markets. American business enterprises nearly doubled between 1945 and 1960, gobbling up natural resources and increasing US dependency on imported raw energy sources (particularly petroleum). While crude petroleum imports had been only 74.3 million barrels in 1945, this would rise to 371.5 million by 1960, even while domestic oil production nearly doubled.[22] While manufacturing jobs were on the rise, white-collar work also proliferated. William H. Whyte's *The Organization Man* (1956) considered the growing bureaucracy of corporations and how this impacted on workers, arguing for greater autonomy in the workplace to maintain creativity.

Part of this growth in white-collar positions was fed by the nation's higher levels of education and literacy. Total school enrolment was expanding and increased federal funding would be spent on school and college facilities, as well as on incentives and scholarships for promising students and faculty. Numbers of students in the 14–17 age range staying on through high school rose precipitously, and with the GI Bill, many who had not previously been able to afford college could now attend. College graduation more than doubled. Against unspoken fears that the Soviets would forge ahead, a 1949 report from the National Education Association had called for the transformation of the US education system, which had been judged too lax and insufficiently demanding.[23] In order to target aptitude, streaming replaced mixed ability classrooms, which helped intelligent lower-class children and girls to advance, but led to those who were not as intelligent in these groups being even more peripheralized. There was a drive to establish, particularly at the elementary and secondary levels, good citizenship programmes that taught democracy and increased devotion to public welfare.

During this period, education underwent expansion and restriction. Many textbooks were rewritten for school to offer a censored version of history in which Stalin was a villain, and other books were deemed politically or morally subversive and removed by education boards, PTAs and citizen groups (including works by Mark Twain, Bertrand Russell and George Bernard Shaw). Teachers had to take a loyalty oath or be suspended, and civil defence training was added to the school curriculum, with school drills that taught students to hide under their desks and cover their eyes at the first sign of an atomic flash. The National Defense Education Act, signed by President Eisenhower in 1958, shortly after the Soviets had launched Sputnik, displayed the country's educational agenda, earmarking federal funds for programmes deemed important to the nation's defence: specifically science, maths, foreign languages and technology.

Owning a house had become part of the American Dream, and whether it would be a suburban or trailer home, the upward bound were moving away from traditional urban neighbourhoods, leaving them to become enclaves of the poor. Some warned of mental health issues arising from a conformist suburban mentality they judged to be superficial, hollow and dangerously isolating.[24] Others feared overzealous mothering might result from women isolated in their new homes, leading to the emasculation of American men.[25] The fact was that suburban houses gave families more space and a better environment to raise children, even though it was often at the cost of leaving extended family behind. Not all neighbours were in competition, and individuality could be expressed in home decor; the suburbs were not as homogenized as some sociologists suggest.

The suburban population had grown to 30 million by 1953, and it was clear that a large proportion (as high as 87 per cent) of the country's growth was taking place in the suburbs. This was largely facilitated by low interest loans from the Federal Housing Authority to returning veterans, and easily accessible credit to others. An aspiring middle-class group of consumers centring on family evolved. Many saw suburbia, with its notions of containment, hygiene and growing affluence, as protection against a changing world of sexual liberation, female emancipation, communism and class conflict. By 1959, Vice President Nixon was able to boast to the Soviets that 31 million Americans owned their own home.

BOX 1.2: HOME OWNERSHIP IN THE 1950s

Levittown, PA, was the second of four sprawling subdivisions of that name built by William Levitt using assembly line techniques (the first was on Long Island). It featured thousands of three-bedroom ranch homes, raised at 150 a week, selling for $7,500 a piece. Part of the American Dream was to own a home, but demand caused shortages, and not everyone could afford even a modest suburban house. Thus, the permanent house trailer, at around $3,000 and set in one of the hundreds of trailer parks which were springing up on the fringes of American urban centres, became a viable alternative: better than a city apartment or shared space with relatives. The park rentals varied depending on what conveniences they offered, some even featuring churches and shops. The 1950s trailers tended to be sturdier and larger (up to 50 x 10 feet) with discrete rooms and full size appliances. However, despite the industry's efforts to improve the image of trailer parks, they never quite rose above the lower end of society, and a preference for the suburbs remained.

Meanwhile, youth culture was rapidly changing in terms of speech, styles, music, pastimes and mores, and the adult reaction to this was a mix of fear and curiosity. The public impression of a growing juvenile crime wave was exacerbated by a scaremongering media, which blew isolated incidents out of proportion. One 1959 poll showed that American citizens were more worried about juvenile delinquency than open-air atomic bomb tests.[26] In the past, young delinquents had sprung from urban deprivation, but now suburban affluence seemed to be providing the spark of rebellion, and many sought ways to salvage these new middle-class thugs. Articles and books, like Fredric Wertham's *Seduction of the Innocent* (1954), sought to try to understand new youth, often blaming films, comics and rock and roll for misbehaviour, along with working mothers and families broken by the previous decade's war. While there was a statistical rise in juvenile crime in the 1950s, this could be accounted for by the rise in numbers of youths, and that these 'crimes' included such misdemeanours as underage drinking, driving without a license or breaking curfew.

Even while many children still subscribed to their parents' values, the autonomy of youth over what they wore and whom they befriended/dated was growing. The ideal male required a dash of mischief so as not to appear too 'sissy', though the line was drawn at bullying. Sexual delinquency in girls was seen as potentially more dangerous, and necessary to curb. The growth of psychology led many parents toward leniency: having rules, but being flexible as their children 'found themselves'. There seemed an understanding that some rebellion was necessary for growth.[27] Adolescents also found themselves firmly in the crosshairs of marketing. More than a third of teenage boys in 1950 had after-school jobs – twice as many as in the 1940s – and due to increased prosperity they were allowed to keep their earnings. Weekly allowances were also on the rise, and most were free to spend their cash however they pleased. Movies, music, fashion and numerous products were targeted at youths, who by the close of the decade were spending $10 billion a year.[28]

While the period's prosperity provided optimism, this was also a time of great anxiety, over more than rebellious youth. The apparent onslaught of international communism and fears regarding an atomic war were endemic. Bomb shelter plans, like the government pamphlet *You Can Survive*, encouraged many to create personal or communal shelters, and many towns/communities developed civil defence societies, whose members would constantly monitor the skies for incoming missiles.

Political events

The United States had been wary of Russia since its 1917 Revolution, and the First World War's aftermath saw the arrest and deportation of numerous suspected political radicals from America, mostly accused of fomenting socialist revolution. However, the Depression spurred interest in socialist solutions and membership of the US Communist Party rose to 82,000 by 1939. The Second World War complicated relations with news of Stalin's evident hardline tactics as he turned the Soviet brand of communism into a totalitarian

BOX 1.3: KEY FIGURES OF COLD WAR ESPIONAGE

Alger Hiss: An American lawyer and government official, Hiss was accused of being a Soviet spy in 1948 but, under oath, denied all charges. More 'evidence' was produced leading to a conviction for perjury in 1950 and a ten-year sentence. He maintained his innocence to his death.

Klaus Fuchs: German-born physicist who lived and researched in Britain and America. In 1950, Fuchs confessed to supplying atomic information to the Soviets shortly after the war, receiving a fourteen-year sentence.

Julius and Ethel Rosenberg: An engineer and a secretary, both were charged in 1951 with espionage for passing atomic secrets to the Soviets. While other spies were given prison sentences, despite circumstantial evidence, the Rosenbergs were quickly convicted, and executed in 1953. Harder evidence later appeared to implicate Julius, but most historians feel Ethel was largely innocent.

state, purging competition and dissent within his own country, and forming a pact with Hitler. Then the Soviets joined the Allies after Hitler's invasion of their territories in 1941. President Harry S. Truman, taking office in 1945, deeply distrusted Stalin, and the Cold War grew from fears of communist infiltration into the United States, as the Soviets openly criticized American capitalism and detonated their own atomic bomb in 1949. Mainland China becoming communist in 1949, along with several prominent cases of espionage in the early 1950s, exacerbated concern.

As an investigative committee of the US House of Representatives, the House Un-American Activities Committee (HUAC) became permanent in 1946, tasked with investigating suspected threats of subversion or propaganda that attacked 'the form of government guaranteed by our Constitution'. Their target was anyone who exhibited communist sympathies or had – past or present – any communist connections. While communism was a legitimate threat, there were many who manipulated people's fears to serve a variety of other agendas. In 1950, the Department of Justice released a list of fascist, communist and subversive organizations, whose membership would violate the loyalty oath now demanded of federal employees and teachers. People were often called before HUAC on inconclusive evidence and, if they confessed to having at some time engaged in communist activities, asked to name names or be sent to jail for contempt. Even when investigations came up empty, many people's lives were subsequently ruined, as they lost employment or were blacklisted.

HUAC began by investigating government employees, but then turned their attention to the Hollywood film industry, starting with the 'Hollywood Ten', who were refused the protection of the first amendment regarding the right to free speech, and were sent to jail for sentences ranging from six to twelve months. Many subsequent witnesses turned to the fifth amendment, refusing to testify on the grounds that they might incriminate themselves, and while some received jail sentences (sometimes suspended), others were only fined. But the harsh treatment of the Hollywood Ten scared many into going along with whatever the Committee asked, and during the 1950s the entertainment industry became fiercely divided between those who gave names and those who refused. Over 300 actors, writers and directors were denied work in America through the informal blacklist that evolved. Some left the country to find opportunities, while others wrote under pseudonyms or the names of colleagues.

Senator Joseph McCarthy's involvement with the phenomenon that would bear his name began with a speech in 1950, during which he produced a piece of paper he claimed contained a list of known communists working for the State Department. This resulted in a flood of media attention. McCarthy would serve on committees covering government and military investigations into communist infiltration, but he did not serve on HUAC, although his scaremongering helped create the atmosphere that gave HUAC its credibility. After a 1954 documentary by newscaster Edward R. Murrow, in which Murrow challenged McCarthy and insisted, 'We will not walk in fear, one of another,' McCarthy began to lose public favour, but McCarthyism would last longer than its namesake, pressuring many to conform or lay low rather than become targets. In 1954, President Eisenhower reported that around 2,200 federal employees had either resigned or been dismissed, and surveillance would continue. Many suspected homosexuals were singled out as potentially subversive (arguably more prone to blackmail or extortion because of the illegality of homosexuality) during what became known as the 'Lavender Scare', as well as labour activists and those involved in civil rights.

US involvement in the Korean War was led by a similar desire to contain communism. The war began in 1950, when North Korean communist forces invaded South Korea. US troops led by General Douglas MacArthur under United Nations auspices came to the South's defence, driving the North back to its Chinese border. However, Chinese forces engaged and drove US forces back south. Without consent, MacArthur pushed back, but fearful that escalation might draw in the Soviets, Truman fired the general and limited fighting to Korean boundaries, resulting in a two-year stalemate. In June 1951, Congress lowered the draft age to 18 and extended the draft to 1955. The Korean War was bitterly divisive, with four million casualties and over 30,000 Americans killed before the 1953 armistice, and while the war ended, the situation remained unresolved.

With the catchy slogan 'I like Ike', Republican Dwight D. Eisenhower entered the 1952 presidential race, with Richard Nixon as his running mate, and heavily defeated Adlai Stevenson. Bringing many corporate leaders into his government, Eisenhower remained in office throughout the decade. Under him, the New Deal of the

1930s was generally maintained and social security was marginally strengthened, but no new social programmes were developed. Most poverty was ignored, and while conditions were less harsh than before, only a fifth of the poor got any government assistance. The general feeling was that welfare promoted dependency and the poor only had themselves to blame. One of Eisenhower's major contributions to national life was his creation of an interstate highway system through the Federal Aid Highway Acts of 1954 and 1956. He also directed federal funds into various science projects.

Fiercely anti-communist, soon after taking office in 1953, Eisenhower helped depose Iranian leader Mohammed Mosaddegh, who was trying to nationalize his country's oil, and in 1954 he initiated the overthrow of Guatemalan leader Jacob Arbenz Guzman, who was giving land to the peasants. In 1954, Eisenhower also signed a bill to add the words 'under God' to the pledge of allegiance (the following year, 'In God We Trust' would be added to all US paper currency), pushed through legislation to outlaw the Communist Party in the United States and first articulated the 'domino theory' in his description of the threat presented to the Free World by the spread of communism. The 'Eisenhower Doctrine', released in 1957, offered aid to Middle Eastern countries resisting communism. Eisenhower's response to civil rights was cautious, feeling change needed to be initiated at state level, but he was not inactive, signing a Civil Rights Act in 1957 to protect the right to vote. This was the first major civil rights bill since reconstruction, even if it was largely ineffective.

In 1900 there had been around one million Jews in the United States, but by 1950 this had risen to five million, which constituted almost half of the world's Jewry. Many would try to assimilate into a rapidly changing society, although anti-Semitism was on the decline, along with discrimination against other 'white' minorities (such as Catholics, Italians and the Irish) in the face of more pressing black civil rights and challenges to old Jim Crow laws. Although racism lost ground in the larger picture during the 1950s, Ku Klux Klan membership expanded, and at least 530 incidents of racial violence occurred in the South between 1955 and 1959.[29] White Citizens' Councils were formed to oppose integration, with one founder calling integration a 'communistic disease', in order to justify racist acts of intimidation as a patriotic duty.[30] Southerners, especially, believing a mythology of black men as sexual predators, remained paranoid over any mixing of the races. In 1955, an all-white jury acquitted the accused killers of fourteen-year-old African-American Emmett Till – lynched in Mississippi for reportedly flirting with a white woman. Colour segregation remained entrenched for much of the decade even in northern venues, but movement was afoot. In 1954 the Supreme Court ruling on *Brown v. Board of Education* struck down the evident sham of 'separate but equal' public schools. Little was initially done to follow this through, with Senator Harry Byrd, a Democrat from Virginia, even urging 'massive resistance' against the desegregation of schools. However, in 1957, after the government of Arkansas called the National Guard to prevent nine black students from attending Little Rock High School, the upsetting coverage provoked Eisenhower into sending paratroopers to protect the students and force the school to integrate. Several schools simply closed to prevent desegregation (as would Little Rock the following year), but thousands of black parents submitted applications for their children to attend all-white schools, and the National Association for the Advancement of Colored People (NAACP) filed dozens of suits, indicating an organized, non-violent refusal to give up on the political process. After Rosa Parks refused to sit at the back of the bus in 1955, the Montgomery Improvement Association, led by Martin Luther King Jr, called for a boycott of city buses – blacks made up 75 per cent of their fares – which lasted for 381 days. In 1956 the Supreme Court struck down segregation on public transport. It was clear that blacks were not content with the status quo and the civil rights movement was gaining momentum, with a charismatic leader in King. Boycotts could only work in places where blacks were allowed, so from 1955 onwards, sit-ins at various drugstores and restaurants became a popular form of action.

Popular culture

Music

The 1950s witnessed a huge transformation in regard to popular mainstream music, as the country drifted away from big band swing into novelty tunes and a new genre called rock and roll.

With new recording equipment and a wider selection of musicians, intrinsic changes occurred in how songs were written, arranged, performed and distributed. Records and radio disc jockeys (DJs) became the dominant means of musical distribution, and the younger generation took over determining much of the nation's musical production. High technical competence or the ability to 'write' music was no longer necessary to create a record, and recording equipment could be accessed in people's garages and storefronts. The industry developed sufficient flexibility to cater to every taste in a series of crossover styles, niche markets and short-term fads (including Mambo and Calypso). As music historian Alan Lomax declared in 1959, 'The record business has turned America into a musical democracy.'[31] Each week saw hundreds of new 'discs' being released, and record sales (predominantly to teens) rose from $213 million in 1954 to $613 million by 1959.[32]

Recording was 'big business', talent shows became prevalent as everyone sought to prove their star potential, and promoters could make money charging both the competing performers and their audience for entrance; record men scoured the streets for the next big celebrity.[33] Hits by unknown performers could be engineered, and the airwaves would spread the sound. Since talk radio had been largely superseded by television, most radio stations had switched to playing records to fill airtime, and the more popular DJs could make or break a hit. Listener requests could be fulfilled and playlists devised to suit local tastes. Although there was some initial exploitation,[34] many black performers increasingly found themselves in the same market as mainstream white performers, and previous musical categories splintered. Elvis Presley, whose run of hits was unprecedented, embodied what Albin J. Zak calls 'the era's haphazard convergence of musical dialects', with recordings that blended aspects of country, rhythm and blues and gospel.[35] The term 'rock and roll' initially surfaced as an alternative to 'rhythm and blues' (which was viewed as black), but what it meant did not fully gel until the 1960s. In the 1950s it embraced a motley collection of styles, full of raw excitement for the young, though often viewed as dangerous by the elderly.[36] Riots, hysteria or frenzied dancing at concerts, frequently suggestive lyrics and the increasing desegregation of music only served to deepen those fears. Live shows often faced bans or restrictions.

While the era saw the rise of plenty of new rock and roll stars aside from Elvis, including Bill Haley (whose 'Rock Around the Clock' became a youth anthem), Johnnie Ray, Jerry Lee Lewis, Chuck Berry, Little Richard and Fats Domino, many more 'acceptable' entertainers also had success, including established stars such as Frank Sinatra, Nat King Cole, Ella Fitzgerald, Dinah Shore and Perry Como,[37] and upcoming ones like Dean Martin, Rosemary Clooney and Jimmie Rodgers, albeit often with older listeners. Also, as the decade continued, it saw plenty of 'cleaner' young pop stars with more tolerable lyrics, such as Pat Boone, Buddy Holly or the Everly Brothers, along with the smoother sounds of young male 'doo wop' harmony groups promoted to counter the 'roughness' of those other stars.

Books, art and architecture

The 1950s was a fertile period for American writers, and book sales doubled due to a thriving paperback market filled with memorable sagas, such as James Jones's *From Here to Eternity* (1951), John Steinbeck's *East of Eden* (1952), Edna Ferber's *Giant* (1952), James Michener's *Hawaii* (1959) or Leon Uris's *Exodus* (1959). Self-help books, reflecting the optimism of the age, were also popular, such as Norman Vincent Peale's *The Power of Positive Thinking* (1952), which spent a record 98 weeks at the top of the *New York Times*'s bestseller list. Pulp fiction also had a heyday, pandering to people's anxieties, with tales of lesbianism, interracial sex and forbidden desire, presenting themselves as exposés to avoid the censor. Despite the fears expressed by scholars Lionel Trilling and Joseph Wood Krutch of anti-intellectualism,[38] all of the decade's Pulitzer winners for poetry remain well known, and while most of the Pulitzer-winning fictions delved into America's past, many popular novels of the era focused on contemporary youth, and made clear the growing rift between generations. J. D. Salinger's disaffected Holden Caulfield in *The Catcher in the Rye* (1951) would become synonymous with adolescent alienation and the first American anti-hero, while William March's sociopathic Rhoda in *The Bad Seed* (1954) and Vladimir Nabokov's sexually provocative *Lolita* (1958 in the United States) displayed the older generation's greatest fears. Other fears were also faced as Americans expressed ambivalence and self-doubt about their changing culture.

Table 1.2 Pulitzer Prizes for fiction and poetry in the 1950s

1950 *The Way West* by A. B. Guthrie (pioneer story)
1951 *The Town* by Conrad Richter (final book in a frontier trilogy)
1952 *The Caine Mutiny* by Herman Wouk (Second World War drama, about shipboard ethics)
1953 *The Old Man and the Sea* by Ernest Hemingway (set off Cuba, exploring the honour of struggle)
1955 *A Fable* by William Faulkner (commentary on war, set in France during the First World War)
1956 *Andersonville* by MacKinlay Kantor (Civil War prison story)
1958 *A Death in the Family* by the late James Agee (autobiographical story of hardship set in the early years of the twentieth century)
1959 *The Travels of Jaimie McPheeters* by Robert Lewis Taylor (wagon train saga)

No awards given for fiction in 1954 and 1957.
Poetry Prizes went to collections by Gwendolyn Brooks (1950), Carl Sandburg (1951), Marianne Moore (1952), Archibald MacLeish (1953), Theodore Roethke (1954), Wallace Stevens (1955), Elizabeth Bishop (1956), Richard Wilbur (1957), Robert Penn Warren (1958) and Stanley Kunitz (1959).

(Source: http://www.pulitzer.org/bycat [accessed 17 March 2016])

The country got to learn more about the Holocaust from John Hersey's fictionalization of the Warsaw ghetto in *The Wall* (1950) and the experience of a family in hiding in *Anne Frank: The Diary of a Young Girl* (1952 in the United States) – although Elie Weisel's harrowing *Night* would not be published in English until 1960. Ray Bradbury offered his dystopian view of a future where books are outlawed and television becomes dominant in *Fahrenheit 451* (1953), as well as advancing the genres of science fiction and horror with *The Martian Chronicles* (1950) and *The Illustrated Man* (1951). Isaac Asimov also published his influential science fiction *I, Robot* (1950), for which he created the term 'robotics', as well as his *Foundation* trilogy (1951–3). The dark violence of Flannery O'Connor's *A Good Man is Hard to Find* (1955) further chilled people, alongside Shirley Jackson's psychological thriller,

The Haunting of Hill House (1959). Sloan Wilson explored fears regarding conformity in the business world with *The Man in the Grey Flannel Suit* (1955), while Ayn Rand offered her negative view of government control in preference to unimpeded capitalism with *Atlas Shrugged* (1957), and Grace Metalious exposed the sexual underbelly of small town life in *Peyton Place* (1956).

First-person narratives predominated as Americans strove for self-awareness. In 1952, Ralph Ellison wrote his landmark *The Invisible Man*, in which he explained to the nation what it felt like to be black in America, and James Baldwin shared his view of American racism in *Go Tell It on the Mountain* (1953) and *Notes of a Native Son* (1955). America also saw the rise of the 'Beat Generation' counter-culture with Allen Ginsberg's bold and influential poem *Howl* (1956), Jack Kerouac's bohemian adventures in *On the Road* (1957) and William Burroughs's plummet into self-abuse: *Naked Lunch* (1959). The 1950s also saw the introduction of such notable writers as Saul Bellow, Philip Roth, Norman Mailer and Gore Vidal.

While young girls bought *Nancy Drew* and boys *The Hardy Boys*, both read E. B. White's *Charlotte's Web* (1952), which would become the bestselling paperback for children of all time and make the subject of death palatable for youngsters. The 1950s introduced even younger children to Dr Seuss with the now seminal (and subtly anti-authoritarian) rhyming books *Horton Hears a Who!* (1954), *How the Grinch Stole Christmas* (1957) and *The Cat in the Hat* (1957). For the older set, especially girls, there were plenty of teen guides, such as William C. Menninger's *How to Be a Successful Teenager* (1954), a conspiratorial blend of psychiatry and Dale Carnegie optimism, with chapters such as 'How to Live with Your Parents' (updated in 1958 to include chapters on alcohol and narcotics).

In the art world, differing styles of abstract expressionism by painters such as Jackson Pollock, Willem de Kooning and Robert Motherwell – members of an experimental group referred to as the New York School – were dominant. In paintings such as *Autumn Rhythm (Number 30)* (1950) and *Convergence* (1952), Pollock splattered his canvas, while de Kooning owed much to Picasso, with fractured images of subjects and surroundings in *Woman 1* (1952) or *Police Gazette* (1955), and Motherwell became known for the broad spaces and bold colour seen in such paintings as his *Elegy to the Spanish Republic* series, on which he worked throughout the decade and beyond.

Other artists found such art too self-absorbed and remote, and tried to connect more to the onlooker. In paintings such as *Number 61 (Rust and Blue)* (1953) or *Four Darks in Red* (1958), Mark Rothko used fields of colour to create a material presence. Meanwhile, Robert Rauschenberg's 'combines' – *Bed* (1955), with its use of a quilt, and *Canyon* (1959), with its controversial stuffed bald eagle – showed how he drew on innovative combinations of non-traditional art materials and objects that anticipated the evolution of pop art. Jasper Johns, on the other hand, often appropriated popular iconography and words into his designs, in such pieces as *Three Flags* (1958) and *False Start* (1959).

Architecture of the 1950s was generally large and spacious. In suburban neighbourhoods with plenty of land, the ranch style home became favoured by developers like William Levitt. The openness of such plans was influenced by Frank Lloyd Wright, whose cylindrical, swirling Guggenheim Museum, in New York, was completed in 1959. Regular house designs became more open plan; without servants, the door to the kitchen disappeared so the wife could maintain contact while in the kitchen, large family rooms replaced austere living rooms and patios for father's barbecue became common. The modernist 'International Style' remained influential, with the creation of numerous soaring corporate buildings with steel structures and glass walls, designed by such as Ludwig Mies van der Rohe, creator of the Seagram Building on Park Avenue (the world's most expensive skyscraper at the time it was completed in 1958). Other influential architects were Louis Kahn, with his monumental, monolithic designs, such as the Salk Institute, begun in 1959; and Eero Saarinen, with his neofuturistic expressionism and concrete shells, such as used on the Ingalls Rink for Yale University – commonly known as The Whale – which opened in 1958.

In more everyday realms, the glitzy 1950s diners were architecturally different from earlier railcar models that featured a basic counter. As the diner evolved from a male working-class eatery to a middle-income family restaurant, it needed to grow in size, adding booths and ambiance; designs became 'space age', with outside lights illuminating stainless steel siding, mirrors and large plate-glass windows to display the families having fun inside. Other family venues, such as bowling alleys and skating rinks, underwent similar refurbishment to create more exciting atmospheres and family friendly conveniences.

Sport, travel, leisure and fashion

More funds and leisure time led to rising interest in recreational and professional sports. Families looking for amusement flocked to the newly automated and refurbished bowling alleys, strapped on roller skates or ice skates, or grabbed a tennis racket. Hunting and fishing remained popular with the men. Professional golf became increasingly popular, and stars like Ben Hogan and Arnold Palmer helped create the idea that to succeed in business, men needed to play golf. With the creation of the Ladies Professional Golf Association in 1950, women joined men on the courses. Female athletes were also playing in the All-American Girls Professional Baseball League. Sports stars became one of the more diverse groups in the country during the 1950s, as ability finally outshone social status. Baseball, football and boxing made athletes, such as Jackie Robinson, Hank Aaron, Willie Mays, Jim Brown, Joe Perry and Sugar Ray Robinson, household names.

With sports now being televised, while the fan base grew, the number of minor-league teams decreased in baseball from fifty-eight to twenty-two. People watched the Summer Olympics in 1952 and 1956, with rivalry between countries exacerbated by the Cold War; in 1952 the United States beat the Soviets for medals but the tables were turned in 1956. In 1952, Rocky Marciano became world heavyweight champion, then retired four years later with a perfect record, the only such champion to do so. The New York Yankees won six of the decade's World Series, while the Cleveland Browns and Detroit Lions each won three NFL championships, but the 1958 Championship Game won by the Baltimore Colts in overtime became known as 'The Greatest Game Ever Played'.

While the possibility of air travel was growing, and railways still an option, with the new interstate highways, comfier cars, cheap gas and the speedy evolution of accessible motels and food chain highway restaurants, the favoured mode of travel in the 1950s was by road. The new highways moved people quickly, by-passed small towns and helped create central shopping malls. According to the US Census, car ownership by family rose from 54 per cent in 1948 to 77 per cent by 1960. While models were available for every age, income and class, the gas-guzzling cars of the 1950s mostly came in larger-than-life designs with massive grillwork, white-wall tires, outsize bumpers, tailfins that grew in size and height and lots of embellishments, including chrome trim. In 1949, Ford advertised its popular sedan as 'a living room on wheels' with 'sofa wide' seats, and in the 1950s cars got even bigger.[39] Annual sales of Ford station wagons – only 29,000 in 1950 – peaked in 1956 at 340,000, with the Country Squire model built in 1957 to accommodate nine passengers; Buick's Century Estate Wagon was 17 feet long. Travel games became a new business in order to keep the children occupied.

With a robust economy and increased paid vacation, most middle-class families went on vacation, and their preference was for a road trip. Educating their children as citizens, they would visit the country's renovated National Parks,[40] Western-styled towns or the new Disneyland. During its first month of opening in 1955, Disney's family friendly resort, filled with rides and performances, saw over 20,000 visitors a day. With new campgrounds and the refurbishment of existing ones, camper registration rose from 10 million in 1950 to 30 million by 1960.[41] Almost a third of those vacationing chose to camp, and gadgetry available to make the experience increasingly comfortable proliferated.

Highway gas stations featured clean restrooms and (instead of the free dishes or stemware with gas purchase one could get at the local gas station) gave away free maps with travel tips. There were even special guides for African-American travellers so they could avoid motels and restaurants that would refuse service. The development also of drive-ins, both restaurants and movies, further emphasized America's love affair with its cars.

Aside from family vacationing, new recreational sports, movies, television and plenty of family friendly restaurants within middle-class budgets, other leisure time activities for the older set included bingo and scrabble, and for the youngsters, sock-hops, pyjama parties and hot rod racing. Even though it remained illegal in most states, bingo became a national craze in the 1950s. In 1955, Bill Davidson claimed, 'Americans pay nearly a billion dollars a year to play the game – more than they pay to watch baseball, football, basketball, and boxing combined.'[42] Most games were run by veterans' groups or Catholic churches, which made shutting them down problematic. Scrabble was introduced in the late 1940s, but by 1952 its makers were selling 400 sets a day and it had become America's favourite board game, while Canasta won at cards.

Teenagers met up at dance socials, such as bunny-hops or sock-hops (so-named as everyone removed their shoes), where a DJ would spin records and they could try the latest dances. Girls were especially keen on sleepover pyjama parties where they could swoon together over the latest teen idol, while boys preferred to swoon over fast cars. In the 1950s, hot rodding became a way young men could display mechanical prowess, physical courage and independence. It became a symbol of the thrills of youth culture; any junk car could provide a base, then parts would be added to create a unique vehicle that could be raced. As its popularity increased, as a safety measure, the National Hot Rod Association was created to bring cars off the streets onto tracks, turning a rebellious act into a controlled sport.

In terms of fashion, husbands headed to the office with a tie and a smart suit of wool or Dacron, still with a hat. Sportswear for men became big business for a leisure conscious population, and two-tone colour combinations or tropical/tribal prints were considered especially stylish, as well as cabana sets for the beach. Designs for both men and women became increasingly playful, with a variety of collar and pocket designs, and 'Western wear' proliferated for all ages.

The Second World War had influenced women's clothing, which now allowed for trousers and shorter hair, but many women still commonly wore skirts or dresses. The pinched shirtwaist dress and ensemble outfits with matching jackets were popular, and designer fashions (especially those of Dior, Chanel and Givenchy) were available to more of the populace. A great variety of fabrics were used, including the synthetics Nylon and Rayon, with solid colours that were embellished with lace, beadwork or rhinestones, or bold prints. Hips and busts tended to be accentuated by either full or tight skirts and bras designed for maximum uplift, such as the famous conical bullet bra, along with a tight sweater for emphasis. Slips were usual, along with girdles to hold up stockings (as pantyhose was not yet invented), and accompanying stylish nightgowns were fancy bed jackets. Working women often adopted skirt suits made from the same material as men's suits, and for leisure women wore capri pants, pedal pushers or Bermuda shorts. 'First Lady Pink' became the hue for everything from dresses to bathroom fixtures as pink became a fad, initially as the favourite colour of Mrs Eisenhower, then later in combination with black as Elvis's favourite combination.

Teen styles tended toward tight blue jeans, although some schools initially banned them as inappropriate. However, clever advertising by Levi Strauss, featuring respectable students heading to school in their jeans, helped soften the image, and jeans soon became common casual wear for adults, too. Over the 1950s, Levi Strauss doubled their net worth.[43] Decent boys wore crew cuts, two-tone gabardine jackets and sometimes a bowtie, while the more dangerous ones adopted ducktail hairstyles, T-shirts and a leather jacket. Good girls put on poodle skirts with matching scarf, sweaters and saddle shoes, while 'bad' girls paraded leopard skin prints and high heels. All wore sunglasses to show the abundance of leisure time and that everyone was star material!

Media

During the 1950s, television swiftly dominated mass media and became the ultimate purveyor of mass culture in the country, impacting on films, radio, newspapers and theatre.

Radio and television

At the start of the 1950s there were over 2,000 licensed radio broadcast stations, but radio networks and advertising were moving to television, and network programming for the radio dwindled as shows were converted to the new medium. Stations had to become more self-reliant, and records became an invaluable means of filling up airtime. Playlists were designed to be responsive to local tastes, and the public reacted well. Charismatic DJs such as Bill Randle or Alan Freed,[44] hosting these new shows, became celebrities themselves and highly influential in making the new pop stars of the era, as well as adept at selling related products. While the rest of the family was watching television, millions of adolescents began listening to pop tunes on the radio. By 1959, there were 156 million radios in the country (many of them now portable), which was over three times the number of televisions owned at that time.[45]

In 1950 television sets could receive only twelve channels, from two to thirteen. These were VHF frequencies, but signal converters enabling UHF channels became available later in the decade. In 1953, *TV Guide* began publication with a circulation of 1,562,000. Early televisions needed to 'warm up' and adjustments were necessary to stop the screen rolling or having interference. Passing cars could leave white streaks across the screen. At the start of the decade, a little over five million American homes had a television set, but by 1959 that number had risen to 42 million – around 80 per cent of American homes – and some had more than one.

With the laying of coaxial cables and microwave relays coast to coast, transcontinental television service began in 1951 with President Truman's address to the United Nations. Now broadcasters did not just read the news, but showed film clips of events and live-action scenes to make the news feel more real. Most news shows only ran 15 minutes, but others provided more depth. Journalist Edward R. Murrow turned his radio newsmagazine show *Hear It Now* into *See it Now* and viewers could tune into *Meet the Press* or *Face the Nation*. There were also documentary series such as *Industry on Parade* or *Americans at Work*, educating people about the benefits of industry. *Omnibus* was a 90-minute arts and culture show that elevated the mainstream with opera, ballet, world culture and science shows, and series like *Calvacade of America*, bookended with advertisements promoting its sponsor's corporate values and products, screened 'biographical dramas' of famous people.

Television became the most effective advertising medium ever invented and the cost of advertisements rose fivefold over the decade. Advertisers targeted men as husbands and fathers, and women as wives and mothers (outside interests only encouraged if the housework would not suffer – filling ads with labour saving devices). In 1947, the total revenue of television networks was $1.9 million, but by 1957 this had risen to $943.2 million, and Americans, on average, were watching over five hours of television a day.[46]

Television of the 1950s introduced daytime programmes geared to women at home, such as *Search for Tomorrow* (debuted 1951),

Guiding Light (radio debut in 1937, but moved to television in 1952) or *As the World Turns* (debuted 1956). These were dubbed 'soap operas' because of the number of cleaning advertisements they included. Also cartoons or entertainments like *The Howdy Doody Show* and *The Adventures of Rin Tin Tin* for the children and sporting events for dad proved instantly popular. Variety shows, such as *Texaco Star Theatre*, hosted by Milton Berle, and others led by such figures as Red Skelton, Sid Caesar, Dinah Shore, Jack Benny and Ed Sullivan, as well as anthology dramas – *Pulitzer Prize Playhouse, Studio One, Robert Montgomery Presents* or *Playhouse 90* – were big hits. As the decade advanced, drama shows began to lose ground to sit-coms, such as *Make Room for Daddy, The Adventures of Harriet and Ozzie, Leave it to Beaver* and *Father Knows Best*, which reflected a rosy, unrealistic and limited view of middle-class life – predominantly comfortable, white suburbanites – which many wrongfully assumed to be the norm.[47] *The Phil Silvers Show* or *I Love Lucy* were a little zanier, though equally positive. As the music craze mounted, lots of teen-targeted shows like *Teenage Dance Party, Teen Hop* and *American Bandstand* were also added to the roster, the last becoming equally popular with parents.

A sign of the times was that many television shows featured squeaky-clean heroic protagonists, such as Superman, Mighty Mouse or Buck Rogers, who would consistently defeat the evil geniuses against whom they were pitted, although these would keep returning so they had to stay on guard. Set in the twenty-first century, *Captain Video* ran from 1949 to 1955, and its hero fought off villains with the help of his Atomic Rangers and hi-tech devices that allowed him to see through objects and shoot radioactive rays. This not-so-subtle Cold War analogy was exacerbated by 'Video Ranger Messages' that warned viewers against those who wanted to destroy America and trample its flag.

Cowboy heroes like Hopalong Cassidy, the Lone Ranger and the Singing Cowboy, Gene Autry – who created the 'Cowboy code' to promote moral values – remained popular. Moved in from the movies, along with *Lassie*, these and new western characters were created in popular shows such as *Gunsmoke* and *Maverick*. Even by 1959 television westerns still accounted for a quarter of programming and attracted a third of the television audience, with eight of the top ten shows being westerns.[48] Filled with heroic figures defending plucky settlers from the bad guys, these offered escapism from suburban life or organizational work, and as some suggest, reasserted 'masculinity in a domesticated family culture'.[49] Aside from its *Davy Crockett* franchise, Disney was serving up its popular *Disneyland* anthology series that included everything from cartoons like *Dumbo* and *Mickey Mouse* to live action stories or documentaries like *Survival in Nature*, *Man and the Moon* or *Our Friend, the Atom*, and the hugely popular Mickey Mouse club debuted on afternoon television in 1955. Other well-liked shows were *Arthur Godfrey's Talent Scouts* (that had also transferred from the radio) and the game show *The $64,000 Question*, which later became embroiled in quiz show scandals of the era that led to many shows being cancelled, after it was revealed that a number of them were rigged, with popular contestants being fed answers or given questions suited to their expertise. The end of the decade saw popular new crime dramas like *Perry Mason* and *Dragnet*, and the premier of the far edgier and often satirical *Twilight Zone*.

Film

Post-war US cinema hit three major roadblocks in the 1950s: changing economics, HUAC and television. The Supreme Court's decision to apply the Sherman Anti-Trust Act to the motion picture industry meant the demise of the old studio system that had allowed assembly line production and guaranteed venues. To break the studios' monopoly on production, distribution and exhibition, they were forced to divest themselves of their theatre chains, and to save costs many began filming abroad (especially for the series of blockbuster biblical epics that ensued); this also helped with marketing in other countries. This was not all bad, as it made space for more independent films, but the overall market was dwindling.[50] HUAC's spotlight on the industry restricted creativity, with care being taken to present the mainstream agenda, and television also severely reduced audiences.

While many great movies were made during this decade, television took a huge bite out of sales. Some movies tried to emulate television, embracing a more episodic structure with family themes. Others fed into the anxieties of the age, with shadowy film noir worlds of moral perplexity and paranoid fantasies of invasion and (mostly atomic) mutation. Film, however, could do some things television could not: present grand spectacle and be less restricted regarding content after the Production Code was weakened following the retirement in 1954 of its watchdog, Joseph Breen. Budgets for special effects increased, as studios spent more money on fewer projects to try and ensure a hit, and various innovations were sought to attract audiences; of these, only 3D and Cinemascope might be considered somewhat successful, although 3D had pretty much vanished by 1954 as it was hard to stock the special glasses, and people complained of headaches. AromaRama, with its accompanying scents – *Behind the Great Wall* (1959) featured seventy-two – was considered too gimmicky.

While the eight major studios released 320 films in 1951, they only screened 184 in 1960.[51] Consumers were asked to pay less for a movie ticket than for other forms of recreation, with an average

Table 1.3 Hit movies of the 1950s

Oscar for Best Movie	Popular genres
1950 *All About Eve* 1951 *An American in Paris* 1952 *The Greatest Show on Earth* 1953 *From Here to Eternity* 1954 *On the Waterfront* 1955 *Marty** 1956 *Around the World in 80 Days** 1957 *The Bridge on the River Kwai** 1958 *Gigi* 1959 *Ben Hur*	**Biblical:** *Quo Vadis* (1951); *The Robe* (1953); *The Prodigal* (1955); *The Ten Commandments* (1956). **Hot Rod:** *Hot Cars* (1956); *Hot Rod Girl* (1956); *Hot Rod Rumble* (1957); *Dragstrip Girl* (1957). **Rock and Roll:** *Shake, Rattle, and Roll* (1956); *Don't Knock the Rock* (1957); *Go Johnny Go!* (1959). **Science Fiction/Horror:** *The Thing from Another World* (1951); *The Day the Earth Stood Still* (1951); *Them!* (1953); *Invasion of the Body Snatchers* (1956); *Forbidden Planet* (1956); *The Fly* (1958). **Teen Crime:** *Teenage Crime Wave* (1955); *The Delinquents* (1957); *Juvenile Jungle* (1958). **3D:** *Bwana Devil* (1952); *House of Wax* (1953).

**Produced by independent companies.*

(Source: http://www.imdb.com [accessed 17 March 2016])

price of 52 cents in 1950 (when a baseball game averaged $1.54). This stayed steady throughout the decade (even dropping to 25 cents in 1954 after the amusement tax was dropped). In 1950 there were over 17,000 indoor cinemas and 2,000 drive-ins, but by the end of the decade 5,000 indoor theatres had closed, although drive-ins had risen to 5,000. As the decade advanced, studios began selling their movies to television to stay in the black, and some even produced television shows.

In a narrower market, films needed to be made for those most willing to attend, and in the 1950s this increasingly became the younger set rather than the multi-generational audiences of the previous decade. Teenagers preferred to escape home and swap television for the big screen,[52] and the industry responded with a slew of movies featuring teens, catering to their tastes. *The Blackboard Jungle* (1955) caused controversy with its depiction of juvenile delinquents in New York City, but also made Bill Haley's 'Rock Around the Clock' an anthem for youth. Filmmakers discovered that teen pictures such as *Rock Around the Clock* (1956) were far less expensive to make than popular musicals like *Guys and Dolls* (1955) or *The King and I* (1956), and made as much money. They tended to portray rock and roll from a teen perspective as a fun-loving youth rebellion against intolerant adult authority: more about music than plot. Non-musical movies featuring the young tended to depict either unredeemable rebellious youths or angst-filled teens looking for direction, such as in two of the period's most iconic movies: *The Wild One* (1953), which spawned a spate of teen crime movies, and *Rebel without a Cause* (1955), which led to numerous hot rod drag-racing films. In the first, Marlon Brando famously answers the question, 'So what are you rebelling against?' with 'What d'ya got?' In the second, a bewildered James Dean struggles to find himself, as weak parents fail to give him proper direction. Sandra Dee's *Gidget* (1959) was typical of lighter romantic comedies being marketed to the young by the close of the decade.

Singing stars Elvis (for the edgier crowd) and Pat Boone (for the more straight-laced) became vehicles for a series of bestselling movies, but sensational horror and science fiction also became popular among the young (often analogous to the period's 'red scare', with aliens and monsters replacing communists). While playing into the communal fears of nuclear power and science gone crazy (lots of mutant monsters caused by radiation), many of these were so over-the-top they were humorous rather than scary. In most studio-produced films, people are saved by the government and its military machine, while the independents tended to blame government overreach for the problem, and have scientists save the day. Advertising rhetoric for movies was often overblown to increase the sense of titillation, excitement and danger, and controversial topics would be speedily sensationalized for the screen.[53] The lapse between news events and movie release grew incredibly short. After Sputnik was launched in October 1957, *War of the Satellites* opened coast to coast in April 1958. After the under-ice voyage of the *Nautilus* submarine in 1958, producers raced to register the title *Atomic Submarine*.

Big stars were important to attract audiences, and the main box-office draws throughout the decade were John Wayne, James Stewart and Gary Cooper. In the early years, comedy teams Bob Hope and Bing Crosby, and Dean Martin and Jerry Lewis, did well, and after the latter split, Lewis continued to attract customers. Randolph Scott and Betty Grable were also popular at the start of the decade. Glenn Ford and William Holden became box-office gold by the middle years, but by the close, different types, including Frank Sinatra, Cary Grant, Debbie Reynolds, Elizabeth Taylor and Rock Hudson, were leading the polls. Actresses Doris Day and Susan Hayward went in and out of fashion, and Marlon Brando, Marilyn Monroe and Alan Ladd all had their moments in the spotlight.

Newspapers, magazines and comics

As the reliance on television for news grew, newspapers dropped in circulation and many were closed. The speed with which events were broadcast reduced newspapers' ability to get a scoop, and photographs paled next to film footage. To save money, many papers printed packaged news without questioning its veracity, and most increased levels of non-news features. However, print media also saw new life in terms of magazines and comics. People had more leisure time to read and welcomed publications that spoke to their specific interests, from *Good Housekeeping* to *Science and Mechanics*. Women's magazines, filled with cooking, sewing and fashion guidance, did particularly well, and the decade's circulation of such stalwarts as *Reader's Digest* and *Sports Illustrated* steadily rose, from 148 million to more than 190 million readers. *Playboy*'s first issue in 1953 featured Marilyn Monroe as cover girl and nude centrefold, and drew surprisingly slight public admonishment. There were plenty of men who welcomed its titillating fantasies – and at least half its readership was married. Meanwhile, new magazines aimed at teens (*Dig*, *Teen World*, *Modern Teen*, etc.) sold well: unlike the magazines previously aimed at this age range that had spoken with adult voices offering guidance, these addressed the teen as a peer – by 1952, *Hot Rod* magazine claimed 500,000 in circulation.

While the 'golden age' of superhero comic books was ending, sales of crime, romance, western, horror and science fiction comic books reached a peak in the mid-1950s, with an estimated 90 per cent of children reading them. New superheroes, such as *The Flash* or the reincarnated *Green Lantern*, began to appear later in the decade. This 'silver age' of comics would continue developing into the 1960s. Some edgier publications, such as EC Comics' *Tales from the Crypt* (1950) and *Weird Science* (1950), featured graphic violence, sexuality and social critique. Feeding on contemporary interest, *Psychoanalysis* (1955) featured a hero battling human neuroses in a series of emotionally ravaged clients, and *MAD* magazine hit the stands in 1952 with its juvenile brand of satire. Comic strips began the decade as fairly conservative – for example *Peanuts* (1950), *Beetle Bailey* (1950), *Dennis the Menace* (1951) and *Hi and Lois* (1954) – with central characters who were intrinsically decent, if not exactly perfect, but earlier strips, such as Walt Kelly's *Pogo* (1948) and Al Capp's *Li'l Abner* (1934), continued to be more challenging.

Science and technology

Science, including an increasing respect for the social sciences, held great promise for Americans in the 1950s. Psychology in particular had a tremendous surge. Therapy made great advances during the war years and by the 1950s membership of the American Psychology Society saw a sixfold increase. More importantly, the general populace had faith in new techniques promulgated by psychiatrists like Carl Rogers, and the decade witnessed a dramatic increase in clinical treatment. Where Sigmund Freud had described people as messily conflicted, Rogers took a more humanistic approach, insisting that people had an internal mechanism that automatically impelled them toward self-improvement and psychological healing. His 'client-centred' therapy was less about diagnosis or preaching, and introduced the therapist as a guide or facilitator who would listen empathetically and help the client toward self-realization.[54] One in six Americans admitted to consulting a psychiatrist during the mid-1950s, and most were not for particularly severe problems.[55] Psychiatry had entered the popular consciousness, and everyone knew about neuroses, maladjustment and the inferiority complex.

The 1950s also saw the rise of psychotropic drugs (initially developed by the military for use against the enemy), not just for severe cases of mental illness but to medicate the relatively normal. In 1955 the FDA approved the tranquillizer Miltown. Its first month only brought in $7,500, but word spread, and by the year's end monthly sales were exceeding $200,000. By 1956, an estimated 30 million prescriptions for tranquillizers were written and by 1957 that rose to 40 million, 'accounting for four of the top ten prescriptions written by doctors'.[56] Within ten years of its release, 25 per cent of American adults admitted having taken it.[57] Drug treatment would eventually displace psychoanalysis as the dominant psychiatric paradigm.

Psychology de-emphasized faith and began to explore guilt in a more secular light: another indication that traditional constraints were loosening. Alcoholism, for example, became viewed as a disease rather than a weakness, and one that could be cured with the proper support. Alcoholics were transformed from moral failures to victims. While 1950s psychology did not instigate any transformation in gender roles, in lauding ideas of self-actualization and questioning traditional authority, it laid the groundwork for future cultural revolutions.

As president, Eisenhower was a big supporter of technology, and the government spent more on natural science than the private sector did. This meant that government decisions played a big role in shaping the direction of US scientific research. To ensure US military technology was more sophisticated than that of potential enemies, Eisenhower helped create the Defense Advanced Research

Projects Agency (DARPA). Although much of its initial research was missile defence and nuclear detection, other projects on communication systems would eventually lead to the development of the internet, and they would also sponsor research into artificial intelligence. Eisenhower also bolstered science education in the country via the National Defense Education Act shortly after the Soviets launched Sputnik, the first human-made satellite to successfully orbit Earth.

While Edward Teller ostentatiously warned television audiences that with the launch of Sputnik the United States had lost 'a battle more important and greater than Pearl Harbor',[58] the government downplayed the achievement, pointing out they had been concentrating on more important military missiles rather than satellites. But they were quick to create their own satellite. After the ineffective launch of *Vanguard* two months after Sputnik, in 1958 the United States was successful with *Explorer*. Data from this satellite led James Van Allen to discover intense radiation surrounding the Earth that would later be named the Van Allen radiation belts. Later that same year, Eisenhower would also create the National Aeronautic and Space Administration (NASA), which began the 'space race' with the Soviets. By the close of the decade, government allocations for scientific research and development had risen to 10.1 per cent of the Federal Budget (back in 1940 it had been less than 1 per cent) and continued to grow.

Some of the decade's technological landmarks included television remotes in 1950, when Diners Club also issued the first credit cards. In 1951, UNIVAC, the first computer, was marketed to businesses, albeit with limited capabilities, as well as the introduction of power steering and sugarless chewing gum. In 1952, US detonation of a hydrogen bomb was reported and 'Don't Walk' signs were installed in New York City. In 1953, colour televisions and Corvettes went on sale. The launch of America's first nuclear submarine came in 1954, and in 1955, Coca-Cola appeared in a can, and the first pocket transistor radio was sold. In 1956, transatlantic phone cables went into operation, mothers could buy disposable diapers and non-stick frying pans, and videotapes and recorders were invented. In 1957, a nuclear reactor plant opened for production of electricity, and 1958 saw the invention of the microchip and the first domestic jet-airline passenger service begun by National Airlines between New York City and Miami, with transatlantic flights soon to follow. The year 1959 saw the launch of the first US weather station in space. This was a fruitful decade of invention and innovation for an evidently progressive society, despite its conservative reputation.

Inventions in the music business totally changed how records were made and marketed, which would alter not just how music was made, but also who made it. Cheaper sound recording equipment let virtually anyone set up their own studio, and electronic effects allowed for manipulations of sound never before imagined. Higher fidelity, greater durability and more flexibility had long been goals of record production, restricted to 78-rpm shellac discs. With new vinyls and improved technology, CBS Record Company introduced a 12-inch, 33⅓-rpm long playing record in 1948 that was instantly popular. RCA followed this in 1949 with a 7-inch 45-rpm record with a snap-in plastic insert – known as a spider – that would make it compatible with the new 33⅓-rpm players. This 'single' record proved even more popular – its flexibility and size lending it particularly to the growing jukebox industry – and by 1954, assisted by a boom in new musical trends, more than 200 million had been sold. By 1958, 78-rpm was abandoned.

Developments in man-made fibres and plastics changed packaging, containers, furniture and clothes. Automation and miniaturization, made possible by transistors that had appeared in 1948, helped reduce production costs and create new growth companies, such as IBM, Polaroid and Xerox, as well as whole new markets. The availability of cheap energy allowed numerous homes to switch from coal heating to oil or gas. By 1950, 94 per cent of rural homes had electricity, and through telephones and radios were as connected to common consumption patterns as urban dwellers. While television had begun mostly in urban centres, a flood of new stations from 1954 to 1960, following the termination of an earlier freeze on station licenses, made television nationally available (though most shows had urban/suburban settings rather than country, unless they were depicting the West of the previous century). With all the new electronic devices, the decade's use of residential electricity quadrupled. The built-in obsolescence of most electrics and machinery ensured that customers would be returning for more (and there was a subsequent rise in the amount of things heading to the landfill).

On the medical front, infant and maternal mortality continued to decrease, and in 1952 the United States successfully used a mechanical heart machine during surgery. Also, in 1954, Boston saw the first successful organ transplant (of a kidney from one twin to the other), and in 1957, US Surgeon General Leroy Burney became the first federal official to publicly identify cigarette smoke as a cause of lung cancer. New antibiotics were developed, as well as antihistamines to help with allergies, and vaccines for whooping cough and diphtheria. However, the medical advance that affected the most lives came from Jonas Salk. Offering relief for many parents fearful of the crippling disease that claimed children by the thousands every year, trials for his polio vaccine began in 1954 and would soon be available to everyone. He would nobly refuse to patent the vaccine to ensure wide dissemination. Composed of a 'killed' virus that needed to be injected, it would be replaced a few years later by an oral vaccine controversially developed from a 'live' virus that was considered more effective, though it possibly caused some new infections. The 1950s was clearly a decade of great advancement and innovation in almost every scientific and technological field. These developments also did much to drive the economy to even greater highs.

2

American Theatre in the 1950s

Susan C. W. Abbotson

Introduction

The 1950s has been described as an 'unsettling and aberrant period' in America's history, due to the effects of that era's prominent red-baiting and McCarthyism, the actions of HUAC and fear of an oncoming atomic apocalypse.[1] Beneath a fire notice warning patrons it was illegal to light a match within the auditorium, many 1950s playbills still carried a note from Herbert R. O'Brien, Director of Civil Defense, which read, 'In the event of an air raid alarm remain in your seats and obey the instructions of the management.'[2] It was a period of political paranoia that evokes anger and shame in many present-day Americans, but the widespread fear of subversion ran deeper than McCarthy's rants, and 1950s Americans feared more than communists and nuclear fission.

This was an age during which the forces of political and social conservatism were fighting for the soul of the country against what they saw as dangerously radical liberals and those unfit to call themselves American. Battle lines were being drawn between the privileged and those who saw themselves held on the periphery not just by political affiliation, but also by gender, sexual preference and/or race. Drama became a means of expression for the growing liberal voices of the nation, voices that called for greater equality, while acknowledging the seemingly unbridgeable inequities of the time. The 1950s saw a set of American playwrights fully engaged in what Christopher Bigsby describes as 'the realities, the illusions and values of their own society', and due to America's post-Second World War rise in stature they were also able to influence more than be influenced by playwrights from abroad and to begin making what would become an indelible mark on the international stage.[3]

The 1950s was the period during which American drama truly came into its own, both at home and abroad, undergoing a fundamental transformation. John Gassner views mid-century American theatre as experiencing 'one of the most eclectic phases of its history'.[4] Many playwrights were engaged in experimentation, drawing on different theatrical styles and ideas from home and abroad to create a variety of engaging theatrical hybrids. Admiring what he saw as American playwrights' widespread embrace of psychology,[5] which he saw as being behind this 1950s rise in critical respect, David Sievers wrote that 'it must be clear to the most worldly of drama critics that the United States need no longer apologize for its drama and look enviously to the British, French or Italian'.[6]

Changing post-war finances had driven up the cost of producing a play to ten times that of pre-war rates. The break-even point for a Broadway production had risen to around 200 performances for a play and 300 for a musical. In the past, plays had often been able to make a decent profit by touring for a few months, but these costs had risen, too, and the 1950s saw a drastic decrease in touring productions even as Broadway costs continued to rise. Some theatres that had hosted touring productions began mounting their own shows, thus spurring the growth of regional theatre. Larger cities slowly developed their own equivalent to Off-Broadway.

Despite increased financial concerns, there would be a series of what would become seminal productions written by old and new playwrights. New acting styles, new stage designs (both in the shape of the theatrical space itself, with a growing interest in theatre-in-the-round and thrust stages, and in the innovative sets being placed on those stages) and new styles of direction all kept the theatre scene vibrant. Traditional living room dramas in three acts on a proscenium stage became increasingly uncommon. Off-Broadway was viewed as a less-expensive alternative to Broadway, while

Off-Off-Broadway began to take on Off-Broadway's earlier investment in experimentation. Professional regional theatres swiftly grew in stature, quality and numbers. Important theatre could now be experienced at an increasing number of venues beyond the narrow terrain of Broadway. For all of its sociopolitical troubles, the 1950s can be seen as heralding a golden age for American drama and musicals, as American theatre became acknowledged as a field worthy of greater notice and respect.

Out of the 730 productions that opened on Broadway during the 1950s, 165 ran for more than 150 performances, and of that number only twenty were imports from abroad, about the same as the previous decade. The highest run among the imports was achieved by the musical revue *La Plume de Ma Tante* (835 performances), Agatha Christie's courtroom drama *Witness for*

Table 2.1 Longest-running Broadway dramas and musicals during the 1950s for each year of opening

Year	Drama	Run	Musical	Run
1950	The Happy Time	614	Guys and Dolls	1,200
1951	The Moon is Blue	924	The King and I	1,246
1952	The Seven Year Itch	1,141	Wish You Were Here	598
1953	Teahouse of the August Moon	1,027	Can-Can	892
1954	Witness for the Prosecution	645	The Pajama Game	1,063
1955	Inherit the Wind	806	Damn Yankees	1,019
1956	Auntie Mame	639	My Fair Lady	2,717
1957	Look Homeward, Angel	564	The Music Man	1,375
1958	Two for the Seesaw	750	La Plume de Ma Tante	835
1959	The Miracle Worker	719	The Sound of Music	1,443

(Source: http://www.ibdb.com [accessed 17 March 2016])

the Prosecution (645 performances) and the French farce *Affairs of State* (610 performances). Americans wrote an overwhelming majority of the plays that scored on Broadway, and of these, 39 were straight dramas, eight of which ran for over 600 performances. Aside from the ones noted in Table 2.1, other dramatic successes of the decade were *Tea and Sympathy* (712 performances), *Cat on a Hot Tin Roof* (694 performances), *The Tenth Man* (623 performances) and *The Diary of Anne Frank* (717 performances).

Fifty-one of those plays that ran for more than 150 performances were American comedies, eight of which ran for more than 600 performances. In addition to those noted in Table 2.1 were *The Fourposter* (632 performances), *The Fifth Season* (654 performances), *Anniversary Waltz* (611 performances) and *No Time for Sergeants* (796 performances). Another fifty-five were American musicals (only two musicals were successfully imported that decade, and both were revues). Of those musicals, nineteen ran for 600 or more performances, with *My Fair Lady* taking the lead at 2,717 performances, a record to be held for another eight years until *Hello Dolly* (2,844 performances) and *Fiddler on the Roof* (3,242 performances) in 1964. Prior to *My Fair Lady*, only two Broadway productions had longer runs: the drama *Tobacco Road* (1933; 3,182 performances) and the comedy *Life with Father* (1939; 3,224 performances).

Despite a prevailing view that the 1950s saw a dumbing down of theatrical offerings as producers aimed for profit over artistry, this seems to be a largely unsubstantiated claim given the statistics. There were about as many serious productions of homegrown drama in the 1950s as there had been in each of the previous two decades and would be in the following. The misunderstanding may be due to the clear lack of enthusiasm for foreign fare. Over the decade, recent European developments in theatre, including Bertolt Brecht's 'epic' *The Good Woman of Setzuan* (1956),[7] Friedrich Dürrenmatt's macabre satire *The Visit* (1958), Eugène Ionesco's absurdist *The Chairs* and *The Lesson* (1958) and Samuel Beckett's existentialist *Waiting for Godot* (1956) and *Endgame* (1958), had brief showings both on and off Broadway. But despite critical admiration, the plays' theatricalisms, existential nausea and muted hope for humankind did not particularly engage the American public. Plays by Jean Anouilh and Jean Giraudoux also impressed, but few sought to emulate. It is also interesting to note that 1950s productions tended to run longer, with only 175 closing with fewer than fifteen performances. In the

Table 2.2 Major theatre awards for plays and musicals during the 1950s

Year	Tony Best Play	Tony Best Musical	Pulitzer Drama	NYDCC Award Best Amer. Play	NYDCC Award Best Musical	Outer CC Award Best Play	Outer CC Award Best Musical
1950	The Cocktail Party	South Pacific	South Pacific	A Member of the Wedding	The Consul	The Cocktail Party	The Consul
1951	The Rose Tattoo	Guys and Dolls	No award	Darkness at Noon	Guys and Dolls	Billy Budd	Guys and Dolls
1952	The Four Poster	The King and I	The Shrike	I Am a Camera	Pal Joey	Point of No Return	No award
1953	The Crucible	Wonderful Town	Picnic	Picnic	Wonderful Town	No award	Wonderful Town
1954	The Teahouse of the August Moon	Kismet	The Teahouse of the August Moon	The Teahouse of the August Moon	The Golden Apple	The Caine Mutiny Court-Martial	Kismet
1955	The Desperate Hours	The Pajama Game	Cat on a Hot Tin Roof	Cat on a Hot Tin Roof	The Saint of Bleeker Street	Inherit the Wind	Three for Tonight
1956	The Diary of Anne Frank	Damn Yankees	The Diary of Anne Frank	The Diary of Anne Frank	My Fair Lady	The Diary of Anne Frank	My Fair Lady
1957	Long Day's Journey Into Night	My Fair Lady	Long Day's Journey Into Night	Long Day's Journey Into Night	The Most Happy Fella	Long Day's Journey Into Night	My Fair Lady
1958	Sunrise at Campobello	Music Man	Look Homeward, Angel	Look Homeward, Angel	Music Man	Look Homeward, Angel	Music Man
1959	J. B.	Redhead	J. B.	A Raisin in the Sun	La Plume de Ma Tante	The Visit	No award

NYDCC: New York Drama Critics Circle (critics writing for metropolitan New York publications).
Outer CC: Outer Critics Circle (out-of-town newspapers, national publications and other media beyond Broadway).
(Sources: http://www.tonyawards.com/en_US/history/ceremonies/index.html, http://www.pulitzer.org/bycat, http://www.dramacritics.org/dc_pastawards.html and http://outercritics.org/awards/ [all accessed 17 March 2016])

1940s, with only sixteen more overall openings, 330 had closed before reaching fifteen performances.[8] Still, costs had risen precipitously and it had become harder for any play to make a profit, and producers were less willing to take risks.

The majority of the Tony, Pulitzer, New York Drama Critics Circle and Outer Critics Circle prize-winning productions from the 1950s are still commonly produced today, several of which are now considered seminal classics. These were the major drama awards of the era as the Drama Desk awards did not begin until 1955, and it would not be until the 1960s that American playwrights would make a concentrated showing in their nominations. Aside from O'Neill's *The Iceman Cometh* in 1956, no other American play won this award during the 1950s.

The Obie Awards were created in 1956 to bring attention to some of the better Off-Broadway efforts, although they took a few years to develop. In 1956, Lionel Abel won best new play for his classical story of *Absalom*, and in 1957 Louis Lippa won the same for *A House Remembered*, a convoluted story about an Italian immigrant family in which the sons vie for control as they deal with their father's death. While categories were expanded in 1958, several had no award, including best new play, although Word Baker's Off-Broadway production of Arthur Miller's *The Crucible* won best revival. In 1959 the best new play went to Irish playwright Brendan Behan's *The Quare Fellow*, set in a Dublin prison, addressing issues of homosexuality and the death penalty.

During the 1950s, Broadway became an even more upper middle-class venue, with less than 10 per cent of attendees identifying themselves as 'working class', and ticket prices averaging eight times those for movie attendance.[9] Higher ticket prices drove some away and altered the dynamic and demographics of a typical audience. A casual look at the advertising in 1950s playbills reveals a series of luxury items being marketed to wealthy patrons, who were predominantly middle aged, conservative and white. This was the audience to which any writer of Broadway plays still had to cater. Also, with the disappearance of so many newspapers as readership dropped in favour of radio and television news and entertainment, power came to be concentrated in the hands of a smaller group of critics who could often make or break a show.

Bruce McConachie suggests that the previous decade's reliance on radio and telephone for communication provoked a move toward greater abstraction and allegory in 1950s theatre as playwrights moved away from realism, and audiences were more willing to accept such innovation, just as the onset of television would change the writing styles of the following decade.[10] The introduction of flashbacks and stream-of-consciousness so often utilized in radio drama certainly gave 1950s playwrights more options. Cold War politics also created a societal sense of 'us' against 'them' that led people to question who/what the 'us' might mean. When accusing so many of being un-American, a clear idea of what it meant to *be* American was necessary, and many playwrights of the era tinkered with this definition through dramatic explorations of national concepts of law and order, regional difference, family, religion, sexuality and gender roles. As George Jean Nathan opined in 1953:

> Our younger playwrights are by and large a more seriously inclined lot than their counterparts used to be. World conditions, ideologies, politics and other such concerns occupy their attention in much greater degree than ever they did in the past and the situation is reflected in their dramatic efforts.[11]

Even comedies began to have a more serious edge and farce appeared to be on the decline.

There was a growing concern among writers of the 1950s regarding ethical aspects of American life in the years following the cataclysmic Second World War and America's rise into the world spotlight. The anxieties of the age had led to major invasions into personal liberties and there was dissent regarding the propriety of this. Many of that period's writers had grown up during the Great Depression, which led them toward more socialist agendas and a keen interest in those on the margins; they were more than happy to expose inequities that lay beneath the country's prosperous veneer. In some, a darker understanding began to emerge that everyone is capable of evil, that truly unselfish goodness was a rare commodity and that we are often our own worst enemies.

Despite continued strands of mainstream conservatism, there seemed an opening up of what might be openly discussed, partly provoked by the growth in psychoanalysis and partly by a general sense of optimism in the country's potential as the economy and population boomed, revivifying, for many, the American Dream. Family concerns and issues of social injustice that might prevent the acquisition of happiness and prosperity were treated with increasing candour as the decade proceeded. A key goal was to uncover what exactly it meant to be American, and a tension arose between those looking to past traditions and those wanting to create something new rather than settle for the status quo. Knowledge of the atom bomb and the Holocaust had changed forever how honest people could view themselves, and as Bigsby suggests, 'American notions of the autonomous self, secure and morally inviolable, seemed suddenly more difficult to sustain.'[12] Dramatists were keen to explore the newly exposed fictions of small town America, individual decency, personal responsibility and caring families, against the potentially self-destructive realities of materialism, conformity and self-concern.

Notable playwrights of the decade

O'Neill, Miller and Williams

When Eugene O'Neill had won the Nobel Prize in 1936 he was considered America's leading playwright, but during the 1940s his career had languished. Although O'Neill died in 1953, the 1950s saw a rejuvenation of his career, with posthumous Broadway productions of *Long Day's Journey into Night* (1956), which ran for 390 performances, and *A Touch of the Poet* (1958), which ran for 284 performances. Both were plays he had written during the 1940s, but with their psychological complexity and emphasis on family relations seemed well suited to the '50s zeitgeist. Filled with what Bigsby views as 'self-conscious performers', we meet characters predominantly caught in spiritual inertia, kept alive only by their stories.[13] These suggest a new direction for O'Neill, one less concerned with experimentation of form – as they are almost conventional realism aside from the density of the language – but with the hopelessness of hope. Bigsby suggests that O'Neill may have glimpsed the same 'vortex of absurdity' as Beckett, and was similarly critiquing the efficacy of language itself as his characters vainly pile up words to create barriers against their fears.[14]

The critical success of *Long Day's Journey* and *Touch of the Poet* also led to a revival of *A Moon for the Misbegotten* on Broadway and a landmark Off-Broadway revival of *The Iceman Cometh* with Jason Robards that ran for 565 performances. Both plays had been largely overlooked during their 1940s airings. The 1950s even saw successful musical versions of *Anna Christie* and *Ah, Wilderness!*, respectively retitled *New Girl in Town* (431 performances) and *Take Me Along* (448 performances), each with music and lyrics by Bob Merrill. Gassner considers the 1950s to have possibly been O'Neill's greatest decade.[15]

Arthur Miller, who had risen to star status after his seminal 1949 play *Death of a Salesman*, continued to address central social concerns of the day with plays that spoke bravely to power and explored group mentality. However, partly due to the cautious nature of the period, he was far less successful with 1950's *An Enemy of the People* (thirty-six performances), 1953's *The Crucible* (197 performances) and the 1955 one-act versions of *View from the Bridge* and *A Memory of Two Mondays* (149 performances). All together these four plays only ran for half the performances of *Death of a Salesman*.

Addressing key socio-political concerns of the period, *Enemy* focuses on the dangers of mob mentality, while the semi-autobiographical *Memory* reveals the lower-class lives of a collection of immigrants working in an auto-parts factory, caught in a social and economic trap, yet pulling together with a tender and surprising camaraderie. It offered, Miller noted, a countervailing idea to 'McCarthy's time, when even the most remote conception of human solidarity was either under terrific attack or forgotten altogether'.[16] *The Crucible* and *View* (in both its 1955 one-act and 1956 two-act versions) more directly addressed Miller's concerns regarding the bullying behaviour of HUAC and the morality of whether one should or should not inform. Bigsby points out how Miller's 'language of mutual responsibility and personal identity' was at odds with the period's mass consumerism.[17] As the decade unrolled, Miller seemed to become more and more at odds with America, and uncertain as to whether he could counter her growing intolerances.

Stunning the world with his 1956 marriage to movie star Marilyn Monroe, who consequently seemed to usurp much of his time and energy, the 1950s is often seen as a period of low output from Miller. However, although he produced no plays between 1956 and 1964, he did write an extended 'Introduction' to his *Collected Plays* that was published in 1957, which has become, along with many of his other writings about theatre, seminal to understanding the directions American theatre, and Miller's own, took during this period.[18] Each of his dramas, Miller declares, 'was begun in the belief that it was unveiling a truth already known but unrecognized as such'. For Miller, the playwright's job is to allow each audience member the opportunity to see his/her connection to others, 'to make man more human, which is to say, less alone'.[19]

Tennessee Williams's ability to stun audiences with his tortured but salacious portraits of outsiders searching for love on the periphery of society seemed to win him continued popularity, perhaps because they were, with one exception, less overtly political (and quickly became popular movies featuring star performers). His plays were increasingly shocking, with growing references to abortion, castration, cannibalism and sexual activity. Brooks Atkinson wrote of the new 'streak of savagery' he saw in Williams's work of the mid-1950s, and David Krasner suggests that Williams was offering a deliberate challenge to 'the bland moral certainty of the Eisenhower era, portraying characters risking ostracization to express their nonconformity' and effectively confronting American materialism, McCarthyism and homophobia through his collection of dreamers and overly sensitive individuals.[20]

The Rose Tattoo (1951; 306 performances), *Cat on a Hot Tin Roof* (1955; 694 performances), the Off-Broadway showing of *Suddenly Last Summer* and *Something Unspoken* as the double bill, *Garden District* (1958) and *Sweet Bird of Youth* (1959; 375 performances) were all strong showings for Williams, while *Camino Real* (1953; sixty performances) and *Orpheus Descending* (1957; sixty-eight performances) were largely rejected. This could, however, be viewed as Williams's most prolific decade, and each play can be viewed as unique, showing Williams's continued desire to change how theatre was done.

Unusually upbeat for Williams, Atkinson found *Rose Tattoo* 'imaginative and tender. The loveliest idyll written for the stage in some time.'[21] Not all critics agreed, but in this Sicilian folk comedy in which the widowed Serafina finds a new lover and lease on life, Williams showed a much lighter and brighter side than revealed in his previous creations. *Cat*, on the other hand, seemed a return to an earlier Williams, perhaps with deliberation in order to guarantee a hit: something of which Williams was also accused by his rewriting of the third act at director Elia Kazan's behest to bring back Big Daddy, soften Maggie and make Brick have a clearer change of heart. Yet the play still addressed quite forcefully the mendacities of modern life filled with callous, exploitative relationships, and it gave Williams the hit he so badly wanted.

The coy treatment of whether or not *Cat*'s Brick is homosexual, as the family wrangles over Big Daddy's imminent death and their own inheritance, seems tame next to the atrocities depicted or spoken about in *Suddenly Last Summer* and *Sweet Bird of Youth*. *Suddenly*, and its tale of a young girl about to be lobotomized to prevent her from talking about her cousin's homosexuality and cannibalistic murder by a group of street boys in Cabeza de Lobo, clearly reflects Williams's own psychoanalysis and continued guilt over the time when his mother sent his sister Rose for a lobotomy while Williams was away at college. *Sweet Bird*, with its range of self-centred monsters, from aging movie star to racist politician, and the broken central relationship between Chance and Heavenly, seems a bleak treatise on an increasingly selfish and corrupt American culture.

The comic strip mentality of *Camino Real* and its array of grotesques made it the most controversial show of 1953. Williams saw the nation's growing obsession with communism and wealth equally dangerous and sought to satirize both in this play about a naïve American wanderer, Kilroy, who gets momentarily caught up in a bizarre nightmare of a town filled with tyranny and corruption. Having the central character invade the audience space was highly innovative, and John Lahr suggests, 'Nothing quite as poetic and visually playful had ever been tried on Broadway.'[22] Kazan deliberately directed it as if it were a dream, feeling that it 'should set new limits of theatrical license and freedom'.[23] Critics were not prepared for such experimentation and Walter Kerr called it, '[t]he worst play yet written by the best playwright of his generation'.[24] The play also featured Williams's first unambiguously homosexual character in a Broadway production.[25]

Orpheus Descending, Williams's rewrite of his early failure, *Battle of Angels*, about a vagrant who shakes up the lives of unhappy women trapped in a small town, but who ends up being destroyed by a mob, was again rejected, although it fared better in a 1959 Off-Broadway production. Despite the complaints of critics, Gassner noted, 'no one could mistake the play for a work of a mediocre playwright, for it had profound imaginativeness'.[26]

New playwrights

If we add together the performance totals of all of Williams's 1950s output, including two collections of one-acts that were also produced, the total number of performances only comes to 1,587, which falls short of one new playwright whose series of hit plays in the 1950s remains an extraordinary feat. Between *Come Back, Little Sheba* (1950), *Picnic* (1953), *Bus Stop* (1955) and *Dark at the Top of the Stairs* (1957), William Inge totalled 1,614 performances. While this is less than the run of many musicals (seven of which during the 1950s ran for more than 1,000 performances), it is a substantial number for drama. While Williams continued to depict the miserable lives of non-conformists, Inge seemed to depict the equally miserable and lonely lives of conformists.

Inge presented images of ordinary Americans who lived outside the main urban areas, and, through his portraits, challenged the old idealized image of small-town America by depicting such places as filled with frustration and limitation. His work centres on Midwesterners, never previously considered to be good subjects for art, but through them he draws out the difficulties of living and surviving in a country that promised much and often delivered so little. Thomas Adler correctly views Inge as 'the most significant dramatizer of the Midwest',[27] but Inge was also a keen observer of human psychology on a wider level. His plays introduced audiences to characters who eloquently represent the growing fears of the period regarding identity and fulfilment, especially among women. His quiet studies of desperation are uniquely illustrative of a culture that for all its rhetoric of inclusion was forever creating outsiders, by class, gender or sexual preference.

Inge's plays allow audiences to better realize the difficulties faced not just by the great minds of society, but by the common folk on its periphery. He also, as Adler rightly suggests,

> managed to broach topics whose currency would not become widespread in the American theater until almost three decades later, providing compelling portraits of those who were marginalized as outsiders for their difference, be it racial or sexual, and of women who found their channels of fulfillment severely circumscribed by stereotypical notions of what should be allowed the feminine. In many of his insights, Inge wrote ahead of his time.[28]

Aside from Inge, the 1950s saw several other newer writers have their biggest Broadway successes, including George Axelrod, Jerome Lawrence and Robert E. Lee, John Van Druten and Arthur Laurents. Axelrod scored with two imaginative comedies that delve into popular psychoanalytical theories of the day: *Seven Year Itch* (1952), which ran for 1,141 performances, and *Will Success Spoil Rock Hunter?* (1955), for 444 performances. In both, men have their sexual fantasies apparently fulfilled, but then are safely brought back to the fold by the close. Axelrod teases us with sexual situations, but nothing too risqué is allowed to take place and sentiment wins out over satire. In *Seven Year*, Richard gets over his mid-life crisis and fantasies about a neighbour to run back to his wife, and in *Rock Hunter* the devilish agent is defeated as Mike settles for moderate success and George gives up his enchanted hold on the desirable Rita. As Gerald Weales asserts, 'commercial comedy is designed to seem outrageous and to be comforting'.[29]

Lawrence and Lee also sold a lot of tickets with *Inherit the Wind* (1955) at 806 performances and *Auntie Mame* (1956) at 639 performances. *Inherit*'s relation of the trial of a teacher who had had the audacity to teach evolution at a Tennessee school in the Bible belt spoke directly to issues of free speech, while *Auntie Mame* was both a celebration of a free spirit and satire of the restricted American upper class. These, and Axelrod's plays, would be turned into highly successful movies, although the Axelrod ones would be drastically rewritten for the screen. Lawrence and Lee were notable in that they achieved success in multiple genres, including straight plays, comedy and musicals. Hence, it becomes difficult to define their style, but Alan Woods suggests their work is 'linked by thematic concerns ... the right of the individual to personal fulfillment and the expression of an individualized approach to life'.[30] The degree to which people could exercise rights to personal development free of societal oppression was central to 1950s culture, but while Lawrence and Lee had their characters frequently defy authority, it was always done non-violently.

Van Druten's comedy about modern-day witches, *Bell, Book and Candle* (1950), racked up 233 performances and his adaptation of Christopher Isherwood's Berlin experiences, *I Am a Camera*, another 214. Druten's play turned Julie Harris into a star, although the musical version, *Cabaret* (1966), would become a far bigger hit. Laurents had moderate success with his bittersweet romance between an American secretary and Italian shopkeeper in Europe – *The Time of the Cuckoo* (1952) – that ran for 263 performances, but scored much better with his books for *West Side Story* (1957) and *Gypsy* (1959), the lyrics for which would also bring Stephen Sondheim to the fore.

Several good writers began writing for television but then moved to Broadway in the second half of the decade. Both William Gibson and Paddy Chayevsky scored big with two shows apiece: Gibson giving us *Two For the Seesaw* (1958) and *The Miracle Worker* (1959) that together ran for 1,469 performances; and Chayevsky's *Middle of the Night* (1956) and *The Tenth Man* (1959) that together ran for 1,100 performances. *Two for the Seesaw* (1958), Gibson's first stage hit, was a bittersweet comedy about a damaged couple attempting to connect in the big city. It is unusual in that the male protagonist, Jerry, is not very sympathetic, Gibson showing him taking advantage of the lonely Jewish dance teacher, Gittel, with whom he has an affair while undergoing divorce, but then dumps. His final return to his wife may be a moral victory, but feels less than a happy ending. Gibson's next play, *The Miracle Worker* (1959), an expansion of his 1957 television version, would become his most famous. Recounting the relationship of teacher Annie Sullivan and her deaf and mute student, Helen Keller, it is less an uplifting look at the overcoming of handicap than an exploration of the power of words and love. As Adler suggests, 'The vocation of teaching becomes the medium through which the human form is shaped and perfected.'[31]

Chayefsky's first staged play was an adaptation of his television piece *Middle of the Night* (1956), about an older Jewish garment manufacturer falling for his young secretary while she is undergoing an unpleasant divorce and having to overcome the disapproval of his family. Chayefsky better fleshed out the characters for a later film version, and that would become more successful. For *The Tenth Man* (1959), his first piece directly written for the stage, he allowed himself a wider focus and more characters than in his smaller television pieces. As John Clum suggests, 'No longer satisfied with telling touching stories about average people, Chayefsky began to dig deeper, to try to lay bare the spiritual malaise that cripples many modern men.'[32] In this loose adaptation of S. Anski's play *The Dybbuk* (1925), Chayefsky has the man need the exorcism rather than the girl – not of a spirit, but of the scepticism that is holding him back from loving another. Also, moving the tale from Eastern Europe to Long Island enabled him to explore the changing conditions for Jews in the United States, with both faith and tradition feeling challenged by a modern society filled with uncertainty and insecurity.

A number of other playwrights had what would turn out to be their only major hit during the 1950s, including Carson McCullers's *Member of the Wedding* (1950) at 501 performances, John Patrick's *The Teahouse of the August Moon* (1953) for 1,027 performances, Frances Goodrich and Albert Hackett's *The Diary of Anne Frank* (1955) for 717 performances, Anderson's *Tea and Sympathy* (1953) for 712 performances, Archibald MacLeish's *J. B.* (1958) for 364 performances and Lorraine Hansberry's *A Raisin in the Sun* (1959) for 530 performances. Each of these plays also contributed something unique to the stage, and a host of interesting new character types. Based on her earlier book, largely a close study about the relationship between the moody 12-year-old Frankie struggling to connect to the world of adults, her younger cousin John Henry and Berenice, an African-American housekeeper, McCullers's *Member* was high on talk and contained minimal action, especially in the first two acts that are staged in a small kitchen. This led Weales to suggest it might be 'the most obvious structural innovation in the recent American theatre', although he found the third act, which moves outside and features Frankie being accosted by a soldier and John Henry's death, too melodramatic.[33] But *Member* also offered audiences a delicate portrayal of outsiders in its focus on a black woman and two young white children, characters usually kept on the periphery of any narrative. Its success surprised Harold Clurman, who had directed, and led to his 'renewal of faith in the sensitivity and awareness of our New York theatregoing public'.[34]

Interestingly, a fairly high proportion of plays in the 1950s were taken from other sources, and *Teahouse* was adapted from the novel by Vern Sneider. During the United States' post-Second World War occupation of Japan, Captain Frisby is instructed to impose American democratic and capitalist values on a small Okinawa island town, but gets seduced by the natives. A happy compromise for all is reached by the close, and while there is some cultural insensitivity in its depiction of Okinawans, some viewed it as encouraging tolerance and interracial relationships. Based on Anne Frank's wartime diary, recounting how she, her family and neighbours hid from the Nazis, though somewhat sentimentalized,

The Diary of Anne Frank was an early play that gave voice to the recent plight of the Jews in Europe. An original story, *Tea and Sympathy*, broke several Broadway taboos regarding sexual orientation and related prejudice with its plot about a young boy suspected of homosexuality, later seduced by a housemaster's wife to restore his self-esteem.

As a verse drama on a religious theme, *J. B.*'s lengthy run at the ANTA Playhouse, and procurement of the Pulitzer Prize, was quite the coup, the responsibility for which should be shared with its director, Kazan, and stage designer, Boris Aronson. It presents the biblical Job as an American businessman undergoing a series of afflictions, from a car accident and sex crimes to the atom bomb. Using psychiatry, theology and Marxism, we see Job finally accepting guilt but not necessarily God, as he continues on in resignation rather than faith. A chilling commentary on a growingly complex capitalist society, McConachie views the play as conveying how the material abundance of the era had lulled Americans into a false vision of themselves as God's elect and, through Job's series of losses, critiques the smugness of those who had thought such abundance their due.[35]

The 1950s also witnessed Gore Vidal's first hit play, another import from television, *A Visit to a Small Planet* (1957), which ran for 388 performances. In it, a warmongering alien, who has left his own planet (which has no work, sex, death or birth) out of boredom, turns the Cold War into a military conflict. While the television version ended in war, the Broadway one was softened, as a young girl prevents it. There were also important plays by Michael Gazzo, *Hatful of Rain* (1955), and Jack Gelber, *The Connection* (1959), both referencing the growing drug culture. This decade also saw the rise of Horton Foote's career, as his plays began to get more notice, and the launch of Edward Albee with his first American production.

Ethnic drama and plays of Otherness

The decade also saw works by playwrights including Alice Childress, William Branch, Louis Peterson, Ossie Davis and Lorraine Hansberry that asserted the growing presence of an

African-American theatre responding to the inequities of the period. A committee had been formed between Actor's Equity, the League of New York Theatres, the Dramatists Guild, the Negro Actors Guild and the NAACP to try to increase African-American employment in Broadway shows, combat racial stereotyping in the theatre and encourage upcoming African-American writers. Most African-American plays of the period tended to deal with creating a positive identity for blacks in society to counter offensive mainstream stereotypes. However, rather than offer depictions of 'successful' African-Americans – the tendency in 1940s films that featured a number of black doctors, nurses and businessmen – they dealt more closely with the psychology of blackness within the country and tried to offer realistic everyday portraits rather than simplistic solutions to the educational, economic and social problems being faced by African-American communities.

While Asian-American drama had made minor inroads since the 1920s, the 1950s saw little being produced. Elizabeth S. Kim points out that while 'shifting geopolitical currents yielded enormous Broadway and Hollywood interest in representations of Asia and Asians through Western lenses' – Richard Rodgers and Oscar Hammerstein II's *The King and I* (1951) and *Flower Drum Song* (1958), John Patrick's *The Teahouse of the August Moon* (1953), Paul Osborn's *The World of Suzie Wong* (1958) and Leonard Spigelgass's *Majority of One* (1959) – 'Asian-American playwriting entered a period of relative dormancy'.[36] Furthermore, these productions rarely cast an Asian actor in any lead role.

Suggesting reasons for the lack of plays written by Asian-Americans during the 1950s, Kim hypothesizes that disenfranchised Japanese-Americans were diverted by a need to rebuild their lives and communities after the Second World War, and the political turbulence in Korea and Vietnam led many Asian-Americans 'to rewrite their perpetual outsider status through "quiet assimilation" into the mainstream'.[37] However, Asian-American drama would begin to flourish in subsequent decades, at the same time that Latin-American drama would begin to proliferate. During the 1950s, the craze in Latin music led to its inclusion in various set pieces in the era's musicals, but one of the few mainstream representations of Latin-American characters on stage would be the Puerto Ricans in *West Side Story* (1957). Arthur Laurents and Stephen Sondheim at least created sympathetic characters, but this exploration of the immigrant Latin-American experience remains fairly cursory and stereotypical.

It was not just ethnicity that attained greater visibility on that era's stages, but also other peripheral sections of the population. The anxieties of the period led to what McConachie describes as a proliferation of 'driven, anxious figures and narratives that pitted apparently weak characters against seemingly overwhelming odds'.[38] Bigsby writes of the period's 'insecurity about national identity and social cohesion' that drove Americans to try to define themselves mostly by purging what they saw as *not* American.[39] Such endeavours created a growing sense of alienation, especially in those already seen as being on the edge of society. Numerous such figures can be found in plays of the period, including bohemians who fall outside the capitalist system, homosexuals who are disallowed and other individuals cut off from the larger society by unpopular politics or morality.

David Savran sees the negative references to homosexuality in Williams's plays as revealing 'the impossibility of its revelation during the 1940s and 1950s as anything other than the "ugly truth"'.[40] However, this might be due more to Williams's own view of sexuality than to its being the only response of the period. While plays like *Cat on a Hot Tin Roof* and Robert Anderson's earlier *Tea and Sympathy* (1953) may reveal the homophobia of the era, as Brick bitterly scorns the idea of his own homosexuality and the schoolboy Tom Lee swiftly switches his affection to the teacher's wife to affirm the status of heterosexuality, this is not the full story. While muted, there were more positive representations, or at least less demonized depictions, of homosexuality seeping into 1950s drama, such as the harmless and amusing gay men in Wolcott Gibbs's hit comedy *Season in the Sun* (1950). Audiences were also introduced to the humanized homosexual protagonist of Augustus and Ruth Goetz's adaptation of André Gide's *The Immoralist* (1954), who marries to try to 'cure' his proclivity, but has an affair with an Arab houseboy.[41] There was also the lonely but decent Virgil in Inge's *Bus Stop*, the openly bohemian characters of John Van Druten's *I Am a Camera* (1951) and the homoeroticism of Louis Coxe and Robert Chapman's adaptation of Herman Melville's *Billy Budd* (1951). While still cautiously depicted, unsurprising given the continued illegality of homosexuality in the States, images of same-sex desire in drama began to feel less condemnatory or villainous.

Key theatre practitioners beyond the playwrights

While many felt that in writing such plays as *A Streetcar Named Desire* (1947) and *Death of a Salesman* (1949) Williams and Miller had intrinsically changed American drama, the impact had come not from just their scripts, but from the incredible productions that director Elia Kazan and designer Jo Mielziner had created, and which the chosen actors had brought to life. Frank Rich insists that Mielziner's design for *Salesman* 'influenced every major production of the play for the next half-century'.[42] Creating a landmark play has always been about more than simply writing a great script; it also depends on finding the right production team. The 1950s seems the era that began to acknowledge this by often placing the names of director or actors above that of the playwright in theatrical posters and advertising.

Dynamic directors such as Kazan and Josh Logan were much sought after, each balancing their talents between the stage and screen, each style informing the other in interesting ways. Both became fairly notorious for the demands they made on the playwrights with whom each worked, often requiring substantial rewrites to satisfy their vision of the play. The rise of integrated musicals also brought a number of other important directors, including George Abbott and Jerome Robbins, opportunities for success. Scenic design was also changing, and bold designers such as Aronson, or the subtler, but just as innovative, Mielziner, became precious commodities to enhance a written script. During the 1950s, the old single-set presentation of a single room gave way to more intricate stage designs, often using symbolic scenery and more complex stage machinery. This allowed playwrights far greater scope in how they could present place, time and even state of mind.

Aside from championing American writers, the Group Theatre, formed back in 1931, had adopted a naturalistic style of acting, based on the theories of Constantin Stanislavsky, by which actors learned to become their characters from the inside out, by tapping into their inner emotions to reach a sincere and spontaneous performance. Referred to as The Method, and popularized by the charismatic performances of such actors as Marlon Brando, James

Dean, Ben Gazzara and Kim Stanley, by the 1950s this had become the preferred style of performance on both stage and film, and for many actors, a way of life. It was a style that seemed to fully suit the self-absorption of the age. Two of the original Group Theatre members, Lee Strasberg and Stella Adler, ran acting schools in the 1950s to disseminate their slightly different opinions of the best Method.

Strasberg took over direction of the Actor's Studio from Cheryl Crawford, Kazan and Robert Lewis in 1951. Expanding what had begun as a free workshop for gifted stage performers into an influential and controversial acting school, Strasberg added his own psychoanalytical ideas to Stanislavsky's teachings; where the Russian had asked actors to search their memories for clues as to how to respond in an acting situation, Strasberg asked them to delve deeper into their subconscious: not to *think* but to *feel* the part. As McConachie suggests, 'Strasberg's desire to privilege the actor's subtext over the author's subtext gets at the possibilities for narcissistic expression inherent in Method acting' and creates another aspect against which period playwrights often had to fight to maintain their sense of their text.[43] In 1955, Marilyn Monroe would leave Hollywood to enrol, and become Strasberg's prize pupil. Adler's Acting School, meanwhile, deciding that Stanislavsky had intended a more reasoned approach, advised actors to use their imaginations rather than personal memory, to more safely create roles and to avoid being subsumed by their characters.

Acting stars of the era, especially those in musical theatre, such as Ethel Merman, Gwen Verdon or Mary Martin, would guarantee ticket sales and sometimes dictate changes in the play they were performing, such was their influence. Some stayed predominantly in the theatre, like Uta Hagen, Helen Hayes and Alfred Drake, or switched between the theatre and film, such as Henry Fonda, Jason Robards Jr, Eli Wallach, Julie Harris, Mildred Dunnock, Maureen Stapleton and Shirley Booth. Others used their theatrical success as a springboard to the big screen, including Marlon Brando, Paul Newman, Warren Beatty, Shelley Winters and Audrey Hepburn.

Important stage directors

As John Kendrick explains, 'In the 1950s, the old separations between acting, song and dance in musical theatre faded, and were replaced by a greater fluidity in the staging and structure of musicals.'[44] To that end, directors such as George Abbott, Jerome Robbins and Josh Logan began to get more involved in the development of new musicals, and would put their creative stamp on these productions. As actor, writer, producer and director, Abbott had been working in the theatre since 1913[45] and by the 1950s he had achieved tremendous stature and would encourage such new creative forces as Bob Fosse and Robbins. Best known for his deft hand with comedy and musicals, he was revered for his ability to craft hit shows with swift pacing and solid construction. Over the 1950s he would direct 15 shows, mostly musicals, including *Call Me Madam* (1950), *Wonderful Town* (1953), *The Pajama Game* (1954, with Robbins), *Damn Yankees* (1955), *New Girl in Town* (1957) and *Fiorello* (1959). For all of these, except *Wonderful Town*, he also wrote the book, which had become an integral part of the period's musicals, which needed to have strong story arcs rather than just feature a collection of sketches.

While Robbins had mostly worked as a choreographer in the 1940s, he had first directed in 1945. In the 1950s he would help doctor several shows with Abbott, Logan and others, such as *A Tree Grows in Brooklyn* (1951), *Wish You Were Here*, *Wonderful Town* and *Silk Stockings*, choreograph for the New York City Ballet and shows such as *The King and I*, as well as direct several successful musicals of his own, including *The Pajama Game* (with Abbott), Mary Martin's *Peter Pan*, *Bells Are Ringing* (1956), *West Side Story* and *Gypsy*. Coming from the world of classical ballet, Robbins often made dance an intrinsic aspect of his musical productions, with as much importance and impact as the script and score. Consequently, revivals of his shows frequently maintain his original design. Building on the work of Agnes DeMille, who had created Laury's memorable dream sequence ballet in *Oklahoma!* (1943), Robbins created the narrative dance and oriental styling of the 'Small House of Uncle Thomas Ballet' for *The King and I*, as well as the memorable 'March of the Siamese Children' and 'Shall We Dance'. Kendrik suggests that the choreography Robbins created for *West Side Story* shaped 'the entire show as one nonstop

Table 2.3 Tony Award-winning direction and stage design in the 1950s

Year	Play/Musical	Director	Play(s)	Designer
1950	South Pacific	Josh Logan	The Innocents	Jo Mielziner
1951	Guys and Dolls	George S. Kaufman	The Rose Tattoo The Country Girl Season in the Sun	Boris Aronson
1952	The Shrike The Fourposter Stalag 17	José Ferrer	The King and I	Jo Mielziner
1953	Picnic	Josh Logan	Wonderful Town	Raoul Penè Du Bois
1954	Ondine	Alfred Lunt	Ondine The Teahouse of the August Moon	Peter Larkin
1955	The Desperate Hours	Robert Montgomery	House of Flowers	Oliver Messel
1956	The Matchmaker	Tyrone Guthrie	Inherit the Wind No Time for Sergeants	Peter Larkin
1957	My Fair Lady	Moss Hart	My Fair Lady	Oliver Smith
1958	Sunrise at Campobello	Vincent J. Donehue	West Side Story	Oliver Smith
1959	J. B.	Elia Kazan	A Majority of One	Donald Oenslager

(Source: http://www.tonyawards.com/en_US/history/ceremonies/index.html [accessed 17 March 2016]) choreographic event'.[46] While *Gypsy* was not a dance show, Robbins helped build its characters through the vaudeville and burlesque dances he created.

Josh Logan entered the theatre as an actor in the 1930s, but swiftly turned to directing, finding moderate success in 1938 with Paul Osborn's comic play about the role death plays in life, *On Borrowed Time*, the Rodgers and Hart musical *I Married an Angel* and Maxwell Anderson and Kurt Weill's musical *Knickerbocker Holiday*. During the 1940s he directed several hit shows, all for which Mielziner did the stage and lighting designs. These were mostly musicals, including *By Jupiter* (1942), *Annie Get Your Gun* (1946), *Happy Birthday* (1946) and *South Pacific* (1949); he also did well with the naval comedy *Mister Roberts* (1948), which ran for 1,157 performances. In the 1950s, Logan continued to work predominately with Mielziner and would direct eight new productions and two revivals, beginning in 1950 with his own translation of Chekhov's *Cherry Orchard*, *The Wisteria Trees*, relocated to Louisiana and starring Helen Hayes.

Critics viewed Logan as a crowd-pleaser who tended not to seek out provocative or avant-garde theatre, but he was a skilled theatrical craftsman, who directed with great emotional force. Only two of his 1950s productions were musicals, the summer camp frolic *Wish You Were Here* (1952) and the tumultuous romance *Fanny* (1954). Harold Rome wrote both, and both were hits, the first running for 598 performances and the second for 888. The comedies *Kind Sir* (1953) and *Blue Denim* (1956) fared less well, but *Picnic* (1953), *Middle of the Night* (1956) and *The World of Suzie Wong* (1958) were all dramatic hits, and his work in the '50s represents the peak of a prestigious career. Like Kazan, Logan also had success in Hollywood, with film versions of *Picnic* (1955), *Bus Stop* (1956) and *South Pacific* (1958). He would also frequently assist with both writing and production on the material he was directing.

Another successful director during the 1950s was Robert Lewis, who had begun as an actor in the 1930s with the Group Theatre, alongside Kazan. By the 1940s he had switched to direction and had his first success with *Brigadoon* (1947). While an early and firm supporter of Method Acting, Lewis felt that actors needed to prepare for a role both internally and externally, and directed accordingly. Over the decade he directed twelve productions, including: the hit comedies *The Happy Time* (1950) and *The Teahouse of the August Moon*; the musical *Jamaica* (1957) that brought Lena Horne and Ricardo Montalban to fame; and the most successful British import of the decade, *Witness for the Prosecution*. He was also the director for Arthur Miller's translation of Ibsen's *An Enemy of the People* (1950) and Truman Capote's comedy *The Grass Harp* (1952).

Possibly the best known and most influential director of the decade was Elia Kazan, not only in theatre but also on film. He was particularly skilled at drawing out intensely realistic and edgy performances from the actors he employed, actors often unknown until he projected them into stardom, as he preferred to work with people who would take his direction without demur. With a reputation for being the best actors' director, he worked closely with them, often becoming close friends, and was largely responsible for making stars out of Marlon Brando, Rod Steiger, Karl Malden, James Dean, Julie Harris, Carroll Baker, Eli Wallach and Natalie Wood. Kazan would energize his productions with lots of stage business, creating countless mini-climaxes to engage the audience and maintain a constant sense of onstage movement. He also chose only material he found interesting to direct, and that tended to lean toward the new and the provocative. He had little interest in musicals or the classics.

Kazan had begun directing in 1935 with the Group Theatre, for whom he had also acted. In 1942 he began to get noticed with the comedies *Cafe Crown* by Hy S. Kraft and *Skin of Our Teeth* by Thornton Wilder. He would continue to direct two plays a year, including the major hits *A Streetcar Named Desire*, *All My Sons* and *Death of a Salesman*, through which he made a permanent mark on American theatre, thereafter working almost exclusively on straight drama. Like Logan, Kazan often worked with Mielziner as his stage and lighting designer, but also Aronson, Peter Larkin and, for *Camino*, the prolific but short-lived Lemuel Ayers (who had previously designed *Oklahoma!*, *Kiss Me Kate* and *High Button Shoes*).

Kazan began the 1950s with a revival of *Streetcar* with Anthony Quinn and Uta Hagen, followed by eight more productions: George Tabori's *Flight Into Egypt*, *Camino Real*, *Tea and Sympathy*, *Cat on a Hot Tin Roof*, *The Dark at the Top of the Stairs*, *J. B.*, *Sweet Bird of Youth* and a revival of Sean O'Casey's *Shadow of a*

Gunman. Nearly every one was a major hit, while at the same time he was also directing blockbuster movies in Hollywood, including *Streetcar* (1951), *Viva Zapata!* (1952), *Man on a Tightrope* (1953), *On the Waterfront* (1954), *East of Eden* (1955) and Tennessee Williams's *Baby Doll* (1956). During the 1950s alone he would win a Tony (*J. B.*), an Oscar (*Waterfront*), two Golden Globes (*Waterfront* and *Baby Doll*), Cannes Film Festival Awards (*East of Eden* and *Viva Zapata!*) and more awards at the Venice and Berlin film festivals, as well as five Best Film awards from the British Academy (*Streetcar, Zapata, Waterfront, East* and *Baby Doll*), strongly asserting America's dominance in that arena.

Kazan's decision to name names to HUAC was controversial, but driven by his disgust at what communism had become under Stalin, and his need to work in Hollywood and abroad. It cost him his previously close friendship with Arthur Miller and several others, although Tennessee Williams would continue to demand his services throughout the decade, feeling that he needed Kazan's magic touch to produce a hit.

Important stage designers

The Tony Awards for scenic designers began in 1947, and an individual designer would often be nominated for more than one show in the same year. The award went to specific shows rather than all that had been nominated. Leading scenic designers of the 1950s were clearly Boris Aronson (out of twenty-seven show designs during the decade, he achieved thirteen Tony nominations and three named wins), Jo Mielziner (a stunning forty-seven shows, with eleven Tony nominations and two wins), Oliver Smith (thirty-four shows, twelve Tony nominations and two wins) and Peter Larkin (twenty shows, eight Tony nominations and two wins). As Atkinson explained in a 1954 article, it is not the function of stage designers to decorate or embellish, but to 'serve the theatre like directors by translating the author's ideas into the vernacular of the stage'.[47]

Born in 1898 in Russia, Boris Aronson left in 1922 to explore the world, and after a brief stop in Berlin, came to America to find work in the Yiddish theatre district. Years ahead of mainstream American theatrical thinking – which had yet to discover Stanislavsky – he initially struggled to have his work understood and often toned things down to find employment. Eschewing living room plays, he preferred epic dramas that required complex and hopefully asymmetrical stage sets filled with obstacles to better challenge an audience. His non-realistic designs suited themselves particularly to musicals, where they were allowed freer reign. He joined the Group Theatre in the 1930s as they began to explore Russian theatrical ideas, and would create twenty-one Broadway designs during the 1940s. However, it was in the 1950s that Aronson began making his artistic mark. He worked with several leading playwrights over the decade and won Tony Awards in 1951 for his sets for Wolcott Gibbs's comedy *Season in the Sun*, Clifford Odets's *The Country Girl* and Tennessee Williams's *The Rose Tattoo*.

Influenced by the Russian designer Vsevolod Meyerhold,[48] and his anti-realistic challenge to Stanislavsky's realism, Aronson developed a 'constructivist' style that attempted to interpret rather than copy real life, to bring out a play's inner essence. Avoiding flat painted scenery, he worked to produce three-dimensional sets filled with odd angles and partial obstructions to avoid the conventional box design. He liked to obliterate the 'fourth wall' so that the audience could be drawn into the scene by being deliberately shown its workings. Often incorporating stairs, platforms and ladders, he frequently created several levels on stage to offer actors greater range of movement. His purpose in constructing a set was to: 'permit varied movement for the actor; dramatize the emotion of each scene; by its organic fusion of forms and color, be beautiful in its own right'. 'A set,' he insisted, 'must possess compositional and synthetic beauty.'[49]

While Laurents's *The Bird Cage* (1950), about a man who gains hold of a tawdry nightclub through nefarious means and tries to frame his partner when it runs into financial trouble, had not been successful, Harold Clurman called Aronson's ambitious set for it 'the most original and striking of the season – an illustration of how the discoveries of modern art can be made to serve both the functional and atmospheric problems of a many-scened play without striking an audience as too obviously stylized'.[50] Aronson had used exposed poles, mirrored walls, abstract cityscape, revolving platform and partial curtains to cover sections of the set. The outdoor cabin scene he created for *Season* was more realistic, but fully three-dimensional and filled with ramps and steps for the actors to move around. For *Rose Tattoo*, he used painted sets but in an unrealistic manner. He made the deepest sections light rather than dark to generate an ethereal glow, and included a large apron to allow the play to flow toward the audience, behind which was an earthy and colourful landscape to underscore the play's celebration of sexuality.

Aronson created another complex design for Williams in 1957, for *Orpheus Descending*. To reflect two different moods, the set could be both opaque and transparent: the first to convey the enclosed drug store, but when lit up it was able to refract wider possibilities. Over the decade he also worked on *The Crucible*, *A View from the Bridge* and *A Memory of Two Mondays*, *Bus Stop* and *A Loss of Roses*, *I Am a Camera*, *J. B.* and, his biggest commercial success, *The Diary of Anne Frank*. In all of these he tried to create something unique to his vision, though was not always allowed.

Miller had liked Aronson's initial forbidding and mysterious designs for *The Crucible*, but the director, Jed Harris, had rejected them in favour of more conventional sets that emulated Dutch interiors, to give the play the feel of a classic. After Harris left the production, Miller removed most of the scenery and used black velours, but the static feeling Harris had established was too endemic to save that production. Aronson was given more freedom to create a basic unit set that could accommodate both *A Memory of Two Mondays* and *A View from the Bridge*, two short plays set in different time periods and in different styles, with the first being intimate and poetic, set completely indoors, and the other overly dramatic with a need for exteriors. Inspired by painter Paul Klee's luminous abstract designs, Aronson filled the set of *Memory* with windows and atmospheric light, while for *View* he added broken Greek pillars to imply tragic forces, against a backdrop of a restless sea with an open-backed apartment in the foreground, with a circling metal stairway.

Often inspired by the artistry of others, Aronson's design for *Bus Stop* was based on Edward Hopper's painting *Nighthawks at the Diner* (1942). He was able to convey within a single set both the warm interior of the diner and the dark, threatening exterior, with a storm shown through both a large plate-glass window to the rear and by a cutaway roof. *Anne Frank* called for more than a dozen settings, but the director, Garson Kanin, asked for a single set without revolves, platforms or the downing of lights on one section to emphasize another. Offering almost a cross-section of the building, Aronson filled the stage with small compartments, each with its own representational clutter to convey character, in which small details would be changed to show the passage of time. The cutaway roof showed a cyclorama of the streets beyond, based on views from the top of Amsterdam's cathedral, to allow for a contrast between the beautiful city beyond and the narrow lives inside, with their lack of privacy and containment.

But Aronson preferred bigger designs that created a more fantastical environment. *J. B.*, and its director Kazan, offered him that chance, and was, as Frank Rich asserts, 'to many, the most significant achievement in American theatre design since the Mielziner sets for *Death of a Salesman* and *Streetcar Named Desire* a decade earlier'.[51] Kazan wanted to set this allegorical play within a modernistic circus that could convey a mix of fear and pleasure. Aronson eliminated the house curtain and painted the proscenium black to blend the set into the auditorium and persuade the audience they were inside the tent with the performers. The stage contained a variety of steps and platforms on which the actors could move and initially contained no visible tent but a collection of ropes by which the tent was raised and later collapsed. Kenneth Tynan described it as 'one of the most majestic' sets he could recall. 'It prepares the heart for events of towering grandeur and cosmic repercussion.'[52] While many found fault with the play, the staging was an undivided success. Aronson would go on to design sets for musicals such as *Cabaret*, *Fiddler on the Roof* and *Zorba*, as well as several Stephen Sondheim musicals, for which he would win many more awards.

Jo Mielziner came from a very different background to Aronson and understood that sometimes less was more. Influenced by the earlier designer Robert Edmond Jones, who called for more delicate creations, Mielziner used subtle nuances of light and shade to create a sense of aesthetic unity. Indeed, Mielziner would often begin with his lighting design, and loved to use windows to introduce additional lighting on the actors. Designer Oliver Smith describes Mielziner's sets as a combination of architecture and lighting, whereas he saw Aronson's as combining architecture and painting:[53] a far more solid approach. Aronson certainly enjoyed being turbulent and off-kilter in his more expressionistic and bolder designs, but Mielziner's designs revealed a cinematic sensibility, and his sets were famed for a flexibility and ingenuity that allowed for a variety of moods and movement. His use of lighting, especially, allowed him to achieve numerous, swift scene changes and create an easy flow.

Mielziner was a prolific designer throughout the 1930s and 1940s and seemed to be able to work on any kind of production from Shakespeare to musicals. His work in the 1940s, particularly, had firmly established him after the successes of *Streetcar* and *Salesman*. He had won the Tony Award in 1949, not only for *Death of a Salesman* but also for *South Pacific*, *Anne of the Thousand Days*, *Summer and Smoke* and *Sleepy Hollow*. By the 1950s, Mielziner was the foremost stage and lighting designer, as well as the most prolific, designing 47 Broadway productions (including five musicals). His intent was always 'to "design with an eraser" (his favorite aphorism) so that a play's poetry could be released into a theatre space like a genie out of a bottle'.[54] His frequently abstract, skeletal and minimalistic scenography had moved stage design away from the detailed minutiae of realism that had previously dominated. Using scrims, transparencies, lighting and the forestage in new ways, he was able to offer audiences interiors and exterior on the same set, creating a greater sense of fluidity in both time and space. This not only provided a better flow for plays that wanted to move among a variety of locations, but also for those that wished to show more effectively a shift in psychological gears.

Mielziner would win Tony Awards for William Archibald's *The Innocents* (based on Henry James's ghost story, *The Turn of the Screw*) and *The King and I*. In *Innocents* he created a shadowy twilight filled with giant shadows, and spotlights on the actors to create a wonderful sense of foreboding. For *King and I* he created an evocative Asian shadow-play motif for the 'Small House of Uncle Thomas' number, with two pairs of gigantic golden tassels framing the stage. To convey the King's fascination with the West, he included deliberate Western touches in the furnishings and designs, and a backdrop image of Brooklyn Bridge. Mielziner used a similar backdrop for *A Tree Grows in Brooklyn*, behind its grim evocation of the seamier side of the city.

For the musical *Guys and Dolls* he also used backdrops to establish the time, place and mood, effectively creating what Atkinson admired as 'the counterfeit glamor of the joints and street scenes'.[55] Incorporating lots of scrims and abbreviated sets that slid on and off stage, he accommodated the musical's seventeen scenes in a fashion that Atkinson praised as deceptively simple and effortless.[56] Mielziner's favourite scene was his design for the crap game in the sewers under the city, with its striking ladders. His scenery for *Can-Can*, inspired by the artwork of Toulouse-Lautrec, offered a series of dazzling poster-art paintings, including an aerial view of Paris, filled with bright colour and strong contrasts, that even the critics applauded.

For nearly every 1950s production he directed, Josh Logan hired Mielziner to work his magic. For *Wisteria Trees*, Mielziner filled the grand living room with broken lattices and water-stained ceiling and walls to indicate its evident decay. He also provided the giant onstage swimming pool Logan had wanted for *Wish You Were Here*. In *Picnic*, he developed a single set that depicted a worn, weather-beaten house with a sagging rear porch that seemed realistic, but was able to capture many of the nuances of Midwestern life without too much actual detail. His work on the film version of this in 1955 would be his only movie experience. For *The World of Suzie Wong* his Hong Kong settings were more intricate, with comic-book style features that almost overpowered, but suited the play. *Fanny* was another large production that included a full-rigged ship!

Sometimes a production needed a more realistic design, and Atkinson praised how Mielziner's set for *Tea and Sympathy* 'contrasted the loneliness and insecurity of a schoolboy's life with the permanence and comfort of the quarters where the housemaster lives with his wife. The intervening corridor emphasizes the gulf that separates the homeless boy from the adult householders.'[57] Using a single set to accommodate all the scenes, Mielziner had elevated the boys' dorm room and made it smaller to create this effect, adding the connecting anteroom to offer a buffer between the two environments. But a musical like *Gypsy*, with its twenty-two scenes, needed more flexibility. Using every stage trick, he incorporated drops, travellers (curtains), scrims, props, wagon stages and projections. For the number 'Rose's Turn', he opened up the entire stage, pulling down fake drops and paraphernalia to place Ethel Merman against a lit backdrop filled with shadows and light. For the railroad scene he used another drop to suggest an infinite perspective, enhanced by the tracks below and wires above.

Mielziner liked to try new ideas. For the many scenes of *The Lark* (1955), he used no solid or realistic scenery, but designed a series of low platforms randomly placed against a cyclorama – a fabric curtain at the rear held tight on a frame – on which he could project different designs, from a church's rose window to a vibrant pattern of blue fleur-de-lis (for the throne room) to prison windows. To create the impression of Joan of Arc's cell, he had a row of guards holding upright poles, through which light was shone to create the effect of bars with the shadows. For *Look Homeward, Angel*'s multiple scenes, he created a skeletal boarding house with a small turntable within that offered two alternate scenes. All the walls were made of scrim which he could light to render solid or transparent, to suggest even more settings. Even when a show flopped, his designs often still won praise, such as the surreal series of slide projections he used for *Miss Lonelyhearts*, a 1957 stage adaptation of Nathanael West's novel. Filled with bold colours, symbolism and distorted angles, projected onto a muslin backdrop, they evoked various interior and exterior locations and, according to Atkinson, 'caught the tone of the story more concretely than anyone else. His wide towering surfaces, bizarre planes and torn-off glimpses of particular places capture the mad incantation of the story.'[58]

Mielziner also designed the sets for two of Williams's 1950s offerings: *Cat on a Hot Tin Roof* and *Sweet Bird of Youth*. For *Cat* he used a raked stage, thrusting into the audience to allow the characters a point of connection. Above this he floated a ceiling at the reverse angle to focus the audience's gaze on the central bed. Non-existent walls were represented by strips of material hung to emulate the columns of a Southern mansion, and jalousies, moonlight, fireworks and the storm were projected onto a backdrop. For *Sweet Bird*, he created a wide setting with luminous backgrounds and menacing lighting to emphasize the plight of the characters on stage. Toward the end of the decade one of Mielziner's dreams came true when he was contracted to help design not just a production, but an actual theatre, for the projected Lincoln Center, along with architect Eero Saarinen – a project that would take him well into the 1960s.

Similar in his aesthetic to Mielziner, with designs that were more delicate than the bold compositions of Aronson, Oliver Smith had achieved success with a string of musicals in the 1940s that included

On the Town and *Brigadoon*, and would consolidate this in the 1950s, creating the designs for such productions as *Paint Your Wagon, Candide, Jamaica, Flower Drum Song, My Fair Lady, West Side Story, Destry Rides Again* and *The Sound of Music*. The last two of these also won him Tony Awards. In the 1950s he would also work on the production designs of the memorable film versions of *Oklahoma!* (1955) and *Guys and Dolls* (1955). His work extended beyond musicals, and during the 1950s he also designed sets that gave 'substance to the dark but humorsome moods' of *In the Summer House*,[59] switched between an upscale New York hotel and Hollywood office for *Will Success Spoil Rock Hunter?*, recreated a 1958 Virginia living room for *A Visit to a Small Planet*, and displayed a playful array of modern Americana for *Auntie Mame*.

Through designs that combined painting and the architecture of a set, Smith was good at conveying the changing moods of a production. Atkinson felt that the sky blue curtain covered in random fish and kites used at the start, the Chinese style print of the Golden Gate bridge as a backdrop and the 'suggestions of intricate Chinese designs in the room décor' gave *Flower Drum Song* a 'gorgeous appearance'[60] and also helped convey the influence of tradition on San Francisco's Chinese immigrants. For *Destry Rides Again* he created an amusingly gaudy and nostalgic set in his depiction of the Last Chance Saloon. For the more tragic *West Side Story* he provided distinctive abstract designs of a stark tenement street, but kept the staging minimal.

Peter Larkin began designing in the 1950s shortly after graduating from the Deerfield Academy and Yale – it would be his most successful decade in a decades-long career that would later move into film and television. Looking deeply into the scripts of the plays on which he worked, and often incorporating almost cartoonish graphic effects, he created the Tony Award-winning sets for *Ondine* and *The Teahouse of the August Moon* in 1954. Atkinson admired the way in which Larkin's teahouse design provided 'a light though formalized background against which the architecture of the performance acquires substance and beauty. Although details of the teahouse are realistic, the toy moon and the general tone of scenic improvisation keep the performance droll.'[61] Of *Ondine*, Atkinson praised the final act's 'ominous storybook terrace' that 'raises the macabre judges to a level where they dominate the story'.[62]

In 1956, Larkin would win another Tony for the 'ingenious and elaborate' set he created for *Inherit the Wind*, which presented a two-level arrangement that conveyed the idea of an entire country town, again commended by Atkinson,[63] and for *No Time for Sergeants*. For *Sergeants*, Atkinson once more lavished approval, calling Larkin:

> the hardest working laborer in the production. He has had to design enough scenery for a bountiful musical comedy, and he had had to make it progressively wilder in style to match the tone of the story. He has not only solved the scenic problem like a craftsman, but has contributed some comic gusto of his own to the frenzied second act. The scenery goes beyond routine illustration.[64]

Larkin would work again with Lawrence and Lee on *Only in America*, as well as the successful thriller *Dial 'M' for Murder* and the musicals *Shangri-La* and *Peter Pan* (with Mary Martin), for which he also designed the subsequent television productions.

Political drama

The post-war 'Red Scare' and machinations of the HUAC hearings largely dominated 1950s politics. Those subpoenaed to testify in front of HUAC had no actual trial where they could be proven innocent. They were routinely denied the opportunity to make any kind of statement or would be silenced if they tried to rationally state their position. There was neither judge nor jury, and those called were not allowed to cross-examine their accusers or present a defence; just the fact that you were testifying led most to assume you were a communist conspirator, which, even if you cooperated, might lose you your job or lead to the harassment of both yourself and your family at school, work or in the neighbourhood. The hearings themselves were a kind of drama for public consumption, for as Eric Bentley suggests:

> HUAC carefully dramatized the act of informing for purposes of waging political warfare: to intimidate some, to encourage

others, and so on. It was theatre, or, if you like, ritual: a rite of purification that would also put the fear of God (HUAC's man in Heaven) into the as yet unpurified.[65]

Given the power of HUAC to ruin a person's life and career, while many felt the tyranny of the blacklist, few felt it wise to offer a direct challenge as a new round of 110 subpoenas was sent out in the spring of 1951, followed by another round in 1953 focused on those involved in radio, television and theatre in New York. Those in receipt were urged 'to avow their Communist pasts, acknowledge that they had seen the light, and (as proof of regeneracy) provide the Committee with the names of others who had strayed'.[66] It was dangerous to be too outspoken against this powerful committee; to be critical of American values from any standpoint was considered 'Un-American' and, therefore, suggestive of communism. Thus, in the early part of the decade many dramatists seemed to steer away from the political, producing instead what Barry Witham refers to as 'wistful and inoffensive' melodramas that dealt with psychologically troubled individuals.[67]

But while the increasing interest in psychiatry helped create many such plays, Cold War concerns about communist infiltration and atomic apocalypse, as well as the loss of American liberties under the pall of McCarthyism, still coloured much of the decade's drama. While the theatre was less targeted by HUAC – whose energies focused on artists involved in the mass media of film and television – and theatrical blacklisting never became official on Broadway as it did in Hollywood, as Brenda Murphy insists, 'the show business investigations had a tremendous effect on American drama and theatre between 1947 and 1960', becoming a 'persistent subtext' in many plays of the period.[68]

Some plays were deliberately inoffensive, but not all theatre practitioners played it safe; several refused to stay silent and forcefully addressed social and political issues of the day. Ossie Davis began his first foray into playwriting with the one-act *Alice in Wonder* (1952) that he expanded the following year into *The Big Deal*. It was based on his experiences defending Paul Robeson, who had been targeted by HUAC, and portrayed a black television producer who is asked to testify and feels torn between loyalty to his friends and keeping his job. While its reception was muted, it had a reasonable run at the New Playwrights' Theatre. Off-Broadway was clearly more welcoming to political plays, such as Robert Ardrey's *Sing Me No Lullaby* (1954) about an eminent mathematician who feels he has to leave the country and go to China to escape HUAC. Ardrey followed this not so subtle polemic against the demands of political conformity in the United States with *Shadow of Heroes* (1958), about a Hungarian writer wrestling against the thrall of communism, to expose the dangers of any political fanaticism that impinges on the rights of an individual.

Other playwrights were not so lucky. Howard Fast had tried to stage *Thirty Pieces of Silver* (1951) – a chilling narrative of a low-level Treasury Department employee who is pressured to inform on a friend and subsequently loses everything – but could not find an American producer willing to take it on. It played well abroad and would be published in 1954, but it was too direct a statement against HUAC to find a US production, even Off-Broadway. Albert Maltz's *The Morrison Case* (1952), a hard-hitting tale about unfair blacklisting at the Brooklyn Navy Yard, could not even find a publisher.[69]

Among plays that could be staged in the United States, some supported the need for fear by depicting a real communist threat or the need to accept an authoritarian stance, while others eloquently exposed how American civil rights were being obliterated out of paranoia and self-concern, albeit sometimes indirectly through analogy. Even a supposedly light comedy such as Van Druten's *Bell, Book and Candle* can be seen as commenting on HUAC's activities in its pointed references to bewitching and witch hunts.[70] The plays of Lawrence and Lee also provide fodder for an insightful exploration of that era's socio-political trends with their consistent stance against limiting individual freedom.

Despite a popularity that might belie the sedition behind depictions of an irrational trial and corrupt politicians, in a period during which, under the Smith Act, a person could be prosecuted for conspiring to advocate subversive ideas, such works as *Inherit the Wind* (1955) and *The Gang's All Here* (1959) keenly illustrate the impact of that period's politics. Fictionalized reenactments of the Scopes monkey trial and the events surrounding the nomination and presidency of Warren G. Harding allowed Lawrence and Lee to pass meaningful commentary on current events. Though set in the past, these plays passed contemporary comment on restrictions regarding free speech and thought and the vagaries of the HUAC administration with its self-serving politicians. Though Eisenhower was popular, his presidency was marred by charges of corruption among his underlings, and *Gang's All Here* was able to expose the increasing moral, emotional and personal difficulty any US president now had to face: a timely and cautionary warning in the run up to elections for the next president.

On the side of authority, plays such as Sidney Kingsley's adaptation of Arthur Koestler's *Darkness at Noon* (1951), Coxe and Chapman's *Billy Budd* (1951) and Herman Wouk's adaptation of his own book, *The Caine Mutiny Court-Martial* (1954), assert either the reality of the dangers of communism, or that under possible threat the dominating authority, however harsh, needs complete obedience to maintain safe order (the ship of state becoming a literal ship in each of these latter renditions). Depicting the fate of Rubashov, an Old-Bolshevik brought before Moscow's show trials, at which revolutionaries were forced to publically abase themselves before being executed, Kingsley's *Darkness at Noon* dropped the book's more subtle anonymities to become a melodramatic and propagandistic weapon against Russian communism, showing the darkest horrors of the Stalinist regime.

Meantime, *The Caine Mutiny Court-Martial* depicts the trial of Steve Maryk who has led the crew to mutiny against an evidently paranoid Captain Queeg to save their ship from imminent danger. However, although Maryk is acquitted, his own lawyer's commentary in the aftermath makes it clear that the crew had been disloyal and acted too hastily against a war hero and putatively inviolable figure of command. Thus the play ultimately advocates an authoritarian stance in Queeg's favour. In this depiction of individual conscience against institutional authority, democratic values of freedom against national security, intellectual against military response and the capacity of judicial hearings to be manipulated, *Caine* created what Murphy calls 'a major ideological touchstone in the mid-fifties' and 'a safe cultural site for battles over several of the issues that were polarizing Left and Right'.[71] The plot of *Billy Budd*, by which the innocent title character accidentally kills the evil Claggart who has tormented him since arriving onboard ship, but is hanged by the Captain to preserve order aboard the ship, again carries the suggestion that at times law and order must supersede justice for society to remain intact. It also underlines that resistance to authority exacts a price.

Saul Levitt's *The Andersonville Trial* (1959) is based on the trial records of Captain John Wirz who had overseen the Confederate prison camp in Andersonville, Georgia, in which prisoners had been treated abominably. Murphy suggests this was Levitt's response to *Caine Mutiny*, in its suggestion that Wirz's blind obedience to authority, though putatively legal, was morally wrong.[72] By obeying the orders of his superiors, Wirz helped to kill thousands of prisoners and he is found guilty of conspiracy and hanged. Despite the fact that he was only following orders, he is held morally accountable, as would be many of those who had followed orders at the Nazi death camps.

Among those who wished to argue against authoritarianism, as Murphy points out, an 'aesthetic strategy' was developed, 'firmly grounded on the representation of recognizable historical events'[73] that would allow for an indirect commentary on the current times; thus, writers utilized historical analogy rather than direct address. This would allow an author plausible deniability of any political implications, even while an audience would be sufficiently aware to make the connection. Using a trial structure for such plays' action became an ironic commentary on the nature of the HUAC hearings that were effectively trials in which it was impossible to mount any defence as they had no jury and were often pursued with little hard evidence. The trial of Socrates, the Inquisition and the Salem witch trials, in particular, lent themselves to explorations of scapegoating and the social persecution of those with anti-establishment opinions.

In *Barefoot in Athens* (1950), Maxwell Anderson presents Socrates as an unyielding democratic voice against a communist-style totalitarian Sparta that executes him after a brief trial. But by having Socrates' greatest crimes be his intellectual inquisitiveness and refusal to accept authority blindly, the play's ultimate message appears double-edged as a critique of both communism *and* the anti-intellectualism and strong-arming apparent in HUAC.

Noting how Joan of Arc and Galileo became popular figures to portray on both stage and television in the 1950s, Murphy suggests that Joan, who refused to back down from her religious convictions, came to represent the 'unfriendly witness' or 'victimized innocence', while Galileo, who renounced his astrological beliefs to avoid punishment, was a 'cultural symbol of choice for cooperation with oppressive political institutions and pragmatic recantation of one's beliefs'.[74] In 1951, George Bernard Shaw's *Saint Joan* (1923) was successfully revived by the Theatre Guild (with Uta Hagen in the lead) and again in 1956 by Phoenix Theatre. Also, just as Arthur Miller seemed to rehearse in *The Crucible* what he would later testify to HUAC – in John Proctor's declaration that he would not name names and bring trouble on another person – so did Lillian Hellman allow Joan to echo her earlier refusal to name names in her 1955 translation of Jean Anouilh's 1952 play, *The Lark*, in which Joan is tried, condemned and executed for her faith. Hellman also altered other dialogue to more clearly critique McCarthyism, and changed the close to reveal how those who sought to execute Joan regret their actions and acknowledge their error.

Hellman's pointed 1953 revival of her 1934 play *Children's Hour*, in which two women's lives are ruined by malicious innuendo, had also contained a clear stab at the way HUAC was destroying people's lives through its dubious accusations. She would again mockingly connect the Inquisition to HUAC in her libretto for *Candide* (1956), in which the title character and others are sentenced to die on spurious evidence. The letter that the playwright sent to HUAC in 1952 had declared, 'I am ready and willing to testify ... as to my own opinions and my own actions, regardless of any risks or consequences to myself,' but she refused to answer questions about other people, even if legally compelled. 'To hurt innocent people,' she continued, 'whom I knew many years ago in order to save myself is, to me, inhuman and indecent and dishonorable. I cannot and will not cut my conscience to fit this year's fashions.'[75]

As Adler has suggested, Anderson's *Tea and Sympathy* can also be viewed, like Hellman's revival of *The Children's Hour*, as a warning of the dangers caused by careless insinuation, as the boys spread rumours about Tommy and one of the school instructors. The resultant suffering undergone by sensitive young Tommy speaks to 'the prevailing atmosphere of the witchhunt unleashed by the McCarthy hearings'[76] and the ways in which it unnecessarily destroyed so many innocent people's lives. The young faculty wife, Laura, defends Tommy by pointing out how people wrongly make targets out of others they simply do not like, without any real proof against them, and we learn that the instructor also loses his position without any hearing or chance to face his accusers.

The best known play of the period that called the machinations of HUAC into question was Miller's *The Crucible*. As Atkinson's review acknowledged, 'Neither Mr. Miller nor his audience are unaware of certain similarities between the perversions of justice then and today.'[77] Prior to writing *Crucible*, Miller had translated Henrik Ibsen's *An Enemy of the People* to act as a commentary about how truth-tellers could be persecuted by corrupt politicians and easily persuaded mobs. As he explained in his preface, he wanted to address a concern he saw as 'the central theme of our social life today … Simply, it is the question of whether the democratic guarantees protecting political minorities ought to be set aside in time of crisis' and 'whether one's vision of the truth ought to be a sense of guilt at a time when the mass of men condemn it as a dangerous and devilish lie'.[78] Depicting a protagonist who is pilloried for trying to expose the poisonous waters the town's spa is peddling clearly indicates Miller's opinion. As Adler suggests, working on *Enemy* 'helped crystallize Miller's thinking about the dilemma of the morally aware and committed citizen who sees his community embarking on an immoral social position'.[79]

In *Crucible*, Miller did not create a one-to-one analogy between the Salem Witch trials and the HUAC hearings, but it was impossible not to understand his message regarding the self-serving corruption in both arenas. Murphy suggests that Miller's strategy in *Crucible* was more effective than either direct realism or satire, and that the play's power is rooted in the inevitability of its parallelism 'because it was the spectator who constructed its meaning in the context of contemporary events'.[80] Although *Crucible* was more historically accurate than many of Shakespeare's plays, it was rejected, by some, as being untruthful, and by others as making an unfair analogy. These now seem mere strategies to try to discredit its authority. The relative success of *Crucible* gave others license to offer their own indirect commentaries, such as Louis Coxe's *The Witchfinders* (1956), a more fictionalized rendering of the seventeenth-century scapegoating. After attending the British production of *Crucible* in 1956, the playwright John Arden later asserted that the play 'moved the theatrical re-creation of history forward in one great stride of English language, and thereby made it as important a vehicle for enacted ideas as were Brecht's not dissimilar and roughly contemporary plays'.[81]

The morality of naming names is an important aspect of *The Crucible*, and Miller's close friend of the time, Kazan, needing to save his career, but also justifying his decision by claiming communism to be a real threat that needed to be rooted out, had named names in 1953. Kazan's 1954 movie, *On the Waterfront*, scripted by Budd Schulberg, who had also given the committee the names they demanded, is clearly an attempt to justify their decision. The central character, dockworker Terry Malloy, is driven to inform against a corrupt union boss, Johnny Friendly, against the unspoken law of the dockside that insists they protect their own against the police. Through his obviously honourable actions and subsequent beating at the hands of the thugs he is exposing, Stephen Whitfield suggests the creators are trying to 'convert a Judas figure into a Christ symbol'[82] and gain pity for the informer as a scapegoat who is intrinsically virtuous.[83]

Many critics viewed the shortly following *A View from the Bridge* (1955 one-act; 1956 two-act), with its depiction of an informer clearly damned for his 'betrayal', as Miller's response to *On the Waterfront*. Miller denied the rebuttal as Eddie was not a political informer, but admitted he had not liked the way in which *Waterfront* had portrayed the act of informing. Adler suggests that *View* 'even more than *The Crucible* ... provides a testament to the savagery of the McCarthy years, as it focuses on branding someone as "other" and on betraying the outsider to the authorities'.[84] In 1956, shortly after his engagement to Marilyn Monroe made him front-page news, Miller found himself subpoenaed to appear before HUAC. Refusing to name names, he was cited for contempt and given a $500 fine and thirty-day suspended sentence. Two years later his conviction was overturned on the grounds that the questions he had been asked served no legislative purpose.

Unlike the politics of McCarthyism, dramas that addressed the United States' involvement in the Korean War were sparse, and the few that were produced tended to address its effects on those soldiers who returned. Michael Gazzo's gritty *Hatful of Rain* (1955) ran for 389 performances, dealing with the fortunes of returning soldier Johnny Pope, whose stay in a military hospital has led to a secret addiction to morphine, and explores the problems this causes. *Time Limit!* (1956), by Henry Denker and Ralph Berkey, had a respectable run of 127 performances and featured a court case against returning prisoners of war accused of collaborating with their North Korean captors, exploring the complexities of conscience under such brutal conditions. Plays about the Vietnam War would not appear until later decades.

African-American theatre

During the Second World War many African-Americans had fought for their country in what was seen by many as a fight for democracy against fascism, only to return to a country still racially segregated. The decade's drama saw what Harry J. Elam calls an 'emerging black demand for equality and protest against segregation and second-class citizenship'.[85] The 1950s was certainly the age during which civil rights in America began to take real hold, and we see the emergence of a stronger African-American consciousness, reflected in the development of more mainstream and outspoken African-American drama, initially Off-Broadway and in other smaller theatres, but by the end of the decade on Broadway itself.

Among important African-American plays of the decade were William Branch's *A Medal for Willie* (1951) and *In Splendid Error* (1954), Louis Peterson's *Take a Giant Step* (1953), which also brought fame to actor Louis Gossett Jr, and Loften Mitchell's *A Land Beyond the River* (1957). In *Medal*, a black mother draws attention to national discrimination and the hypocrisy with which African-American soldiers were being treated when she refuses the medal her son is being posthumously awarded for war bravery. Suggesting a parallel between pre-Civil War racial-political struggles and the contemporary situation, *Splendid Error* relates a meeting between John Brown and Frederick Douglass, in which Douglass unsuccessfully tries to persuade Brown from rebellion, and then wonders, after Brown's execution, if he should have been more supportive.

In *Giant Step*, Peterson, meanwhile, offers a powerful picture of separatism through the story of a young black man growing up in a predominantly white middle-class neighbourhood. Exposing Broadway's middle-class white audiences to the implications of their own innate racism, aside from the insidious racism meted out by teachers, classmates and neighbours, his protagonist also faces pressure from his own parents to assimilate, and an underlying self-hatred of his own blackness. Mitchell's *Land Beyond* depicts a black couple joining the legal fight against school segregation in the South. Despite the declining health of the wife, they survive intimidation that includes threats and the burning of their home; the play makes a forceful argument for racial justice.

Though not a mainstream production, Charles Sebree and Greer Johnson's *Mrs. Patterson* (1954), about a young black girl who dreams of growing up to be a rich white woman (and which helped establish Eartha Kitt's reputation), also made a mark, though it would be the first play by a new writer, Lorraine Hansberry, opening in 1959, that would bring African-American drama fully into the spotlight. *A Raisin in the Sun* took Broadway by storm and ran for 530 performances. Hansberry became the first African-American woman to have a play produced on Broadway, as well as the first to win the New York Drama Critics Circle Award, and it would be the longest running play by a black writer for a quarter of a century.

While *Raisin in the Sun* (1959) may be the best known African-American play of the decade, it was the earlier work of Alice Childress – as actress, activist, director and playwright – that did much to pave the way for African-Americans to become more involved in serious drama in mainstream theatre, and which made Hansberry's success largely possible. Having begun in the theatre as an actress, Childress began writing plays because she saw too few decent roles being written for black actresses, and she had characters usually confront their white antagonists on stage, to encourage interracial casts. On the Committee for the Negro in the Arts she fought for union rights in theatres and was a founding member of Sojourners for Truth and Justice, a radical black women's civil rights group that campaigned against lynching, the rape of black women by white men, Jim Crow, South African apartheid and sexism.

Both a feminist and ardent socialist, Childress's work centres on the shifting personal, political, social and familial demands black women, especially, faced in America, as they entered the civil rights and Black Power movement periods. Despite their veneer of comedy, she used her plays to encourage protest and political commitment and present authentic representations of black life on the stage, drawing attention to the limitations of the American Dream for black people following the Second World War. The black and white women in her first play, *Florence* (1949), convey through movement and dialogue the vast social and psychological divide the nation's segregation policies inevitably enforced. Childress had written a column for Paul Robeson's newspaper, *Freedom*, from the point of view of a black maid called Mildred, based on her Aunt Lorraine. This comical but enlightened commentary on black lower-class life and black–white relations of the period affirmed African-American human value and dignity. While she later collected these pieces into the book *Like One of the Family*, she chose a similar character, featured in Langston Hughes's short story collection *Simple Speaks His Mind* (1950), to adapt into her next play, *Just a Little Simple* (1950). In this, Childress called attention to the disenfranchisement of black citizens that impacted on their domestic and political belonging. Hughes followed this dramatic lead, creating a seemingly light-hearted musical for his Simple character in 1957, *Simply Heaven*, that nonetheless contains an underlying social agenda conveyed through such ironic moments as Simple's dream about being the first black to lead white Mississippi soldiers into war, or a domestic worker iterating her strong racial pride.

In Childress's other plays of the 1950s – *Gold Through the Trees* (1952) and *Trouble in Mind* (1955) – she continues to explore racial and gender division and to advance possibilities for future African-American drama. With *Gold Through the Trees*, a drama that chronicles the black protest movement against civil disobedience from South Africa to America, and back to South Africa, she became the first black woman to have a play professionally produced with Equity actors on a New York stage.[86] The montage-style structure of the play – blending poetry, music and historical events into a political critique – is also an innovation for the time. While working at *Freedom*, Childress met and collaborated with Lorraine Hansberry. An FBI report suggests that the two authors collaborated on an untitled black history programme for a Negro History Week celebration held on 12 February 1952. Hansberry was also sent to review Hansberry's *Gold Through the Trees*, and wrote that 'Alice Childress seems to know more about language and drama than most people who write for theatre today, *Gold Through the Trees* is probably the most worthwhile and entertaining show currently running in New York.'[87] In a later piece, Hansberry also praises Childress's acting, declaring her to be 'unquestionably one of the finest actresses in the theatre on or off Broadway'.[88]

In its relation of a mixed-race cast, rehearsing a fictitious lynching play, *Trouble in Mind* challenges theatrical black stereotypes and Broadway itself, in its story of African-American actress Wiletta, who eventually refuses to appear in what is clearly a racist production in its black depictions. For its Off-Broadway run, producers ironically persuaded Childress to write a happier ending to make the play less confrontational, in which the other actors leave with Wiletta and the racist director rewrites the play to bring them back. Also, several speeches expressing the black actors' anger were cut. Childress disliked these changes as she felt they let the director character off the hook and implied that whites could fix the problem. She refused to allow this version to be played on Broadway, and consequently it was never produced there. Her preferred ending, which is the one she would later publish, has a bleaker close as Wiletta voices her criticisms with the certainty she will be fired. Childress wanted to convey the realistic consequences of such behaviour.[89] She also refused to portray black women as downtrodden, suffering or victimized, but as autonomous, dignified human beings, regardless of their profession. As she explains, 'I attempt to write about characters without condescension, without making them into an image which some deem more useful, inspirational, profitable, or suitable.'[90]

Some scholars have suggested that Hansberry muted the script of *A Raisin in the Sun* in order to get it produced, and that may be possible. There was one early version set aside, which showed the Younger family in their new home with a far more militant Mama/Lena patrolling with a loaded gun for protection. Earlier drafts had also featured Walter in a much smaller role, while the version produced on Broadway turned him into a more sympathetic hero. However, Hansberry was more political than often credited – her FBI file was as full as most engaged writers of the period – and while her plays may not seem confrontational on the surface, it is because their feminism and political nature is more subtly embedded.

Rather than strike audiences as combative, as much drama from 1960s' African-American playwrights would become, *A Raisin in the Sun* spoke as much to white audiences as black, for as Bruce McConachie suggests:

Hansberry used the specific language, cultural habits, and social situations of a particular ethnic group to suggest the dilemma of many groups at a similar stage of history. From her Popular Front perspective, the African American experience of the Younger family could be both particular and universal.[91]

Much about the Younger family was also at odds with common black and female stereotypes, and the play's success established the fact that African-American dramatists could successfully write for the Great White Way. As James Baldwin noted at the Philadelphia tryouts, 'I had never before in my life seen so many black people in the theatre. And the reason was that never before, in the entire history of the American theatre, had so much of the truth of black people's lives been seen on the stage.'[92] It was also the first play directed on Broadway by an African-American director, Lloyd Richards, who would do much to advance other black playwrights, and it launched the careers of several black actors, including Sidney Poitier, Claudia McNeill and Ruby Dee.

In the middle of a population boom that created a shortage of housing, a central racial conflict of the era was over where to live. As urban space became increasingly tight, African-Americans were largely unwelcome in the new suburbs, and zoning laws were frequently racially motivated and caused much dissent. Aside from the overt legal segregation occurring in the South, many African-Americans were suffering even worse with urban blight and ghettoization in the North. Hansberry's family suffered discrimination trying to get themselves a decent home, and she was personally familiar with the situation she created in *A Raisin in the Sun*. As Krasner suggests, 'Hansberry's observations on housing, class divisions within the black community, the generational conflicts, the struggle for economic empowerment, and the desire for human dignity while living in a money-driven society shape the play's social message of critical participation.'[93] This was a message that could be seen in other plays of the period, as many Americans found themselves faced with the dilemma of how to achieve upward mobility in their careers and personal lives, though these remained more problematic achievements for African-Americans. As their name suggests, the Younger family are full of vitality and potential, and Hansberry allows us to hope their drive and restlessness may lead to greater things.

It is important to note that none of the women in Hansberry's play are entirely traditional for their time: Mama may be patient, stoic and loving, but she has a stronger sense of pride than stereotypical black mothers of the day; Beneatha opts for career over a husband; and Ruth is prepared to have an abortion rather than bring another child into poverty. While these women do not take on leadership roles or fight for liberation themselves, they help foster the men's resistance to racism, and so have a role to play in the struggle for equality. Also, by presenting audiences with such a realistically drawn African-American family, Hansberry was directly challenging the underpinnings of American racism against which this ordinary family strove to find their American Dream.

Musical theatre

In the 1950s, Broadway musicals, spurred on by an abundance of creative talent, public demand and a booming economy, became a major part of American culture. Songs from each new musical soared to the top of the music charts, and many of the musicals created during this period would form the core of musical theatre repertory for several decades. While stars of earlier musical theatre, such as Irving Berlin and Cole Porter, would continue to write into the 1950s (and have moderate success), their work was overshadowed by the popular duo Rodgers and Hammerstein, who seemed to have devised a winning formula during the 1940s, with hits like *Oklahoma!* (1943), *Carousel* (1945) and *South Pacific* (1949).[94] This formula became known as the 'integrated' musical, in which all the elements of the show align into an integrated whole, and for which the 'book' became increasingly important. As Ethan Morrden suggests, 'the 1940s introduced the notion and the 1950s exploited it'.[95] Realistic well-developed characters, strong narratives full of romance and humour, and songs that helped build characterizations and advance the storyline seemed to produce hits out of even mediocre musicals, but in the hands of masters they flourished.

During the 1950s, Rodgers and Hammerstein continued to succeed with *The King and I* (1951), which ran for 1,246 performances, and their final collaboration, *The Sound of Music* (1959), which ran for 1,443 performances, although *Me and Juliet* (1953), *Pipe Dream* (1955) and *Flower Drum Song* (1958), comparatively, fared less well.[96] Building on the nation's fascination with Eastern culture, *The King and I*, based on Anna Leonowens's real life experiences tutoring the royal family of Siam in the 1860s, turned Yul Brynner into a star. *The Sound of Music*, also set on foreign shores, relates the experiences of the Austrian Von Trapp family, in the tale of a young nun leaving her calling to marry the widower for whose children she has been caring. The family then escapes from the Nazis rather than become complicit in their takeover. Amid the admitted sentimentality, Hammerstein is quietly condemning those who take the easier path and do not resist. As Kendrik suggests, the pen of Hammerstein 'had turned the once innocuous Broadway musical into a potent dramatic form, and had turned lyrics into essential dramatic tools'.[97]

Alan Jay Lerner and Frederick Loewe, utilizing the same winning formula as their colleagues, built on the success of *Brigadoon* (1947) with the more moderate *Paint Your Wagon* (1951), about the lives and loves of people in a Gold Rush mining camp. It ran for only 289 performances, but their record-breaking *My Fair Lady* (1956) clocked up 2,717 performances. Based on Shaw's *Pygmalion* (1913), it relates the growing romance between a confirmed bachelor and the young cockney girl he trains to pass as a lady. *My Fair Lady* has been called 'the perfect musical'[98] and is filled with examples of flawless story–song integration, such as 'The Rain in Spain', which illustrates the first breakthrough in Eliza's development, or Professor Higgins's 'I've Grown Accustomed to Her Face', which conveys his understanding of the growth of his feelings for Eliza.

Other successful creations of the period that followed a similar design were Richard Adler and Jerry Ross's two major hits, *Pajama Game* (1954) and *Damn Yankees* (1955). The first depicts the now familiar trope of romance between opposites, this time between a factory superintendent and union rep as a strike looms, and the other is a modern retelling of the Faust story, set in the world of baseball. Both were energized by the innovative and sexy choreography of Bob Fosse and the deft comic direction of George Abbott. Harold Rome also had a series of moderate hits with *Wish You Were Here* (1952), set in a Catskills resort with its gimmick of a full size swimming pool on stage; *Fanny* (1954), a tempestuous story of a French girl separated from her love but eventually reunited after being pressured into marrying an older man; and *Destry Rides Again* (1959), based on the classic 1939 western about a peace loving sheriff contending with a sexy madam. Meredith Wilson would also have a major hit with *The Music Man* (1957), about a phony travelling salesman whose scheme gets thwarted when he falls in love with the local librarian. It ran for 1,375 performances, and its more traditional underpinnings helped it beat *West Side Story* for the Tony Award.

Yet another writer who recognized the importance of building a musical around a good 'book' and who had had his first success toward the close of the 1940s with the period comedy *Where's Charley?* (1948) was Frank Loesser, who also had two major successes during the 1950s. The first was *Guys and Dolls* (1950), built from characters that had appeared in Damon Runyon's stories of the New York underworld. It relates the budding romance between a free and easy gambler and an uptight female Salvation Army sergeant, and ran for an impressive 1,200 performances. The second was *Most Happy Fella* (1956), based on Sidney Howard's Pulitzer Prize-winning play *They Knew What They Wanted* (1924), though omitting its political, labour and religious references. It relates a romance between an older man and a young woman, and ran for 676 performances. In it, Loesser blended operatic arias with upbeat pop songs to create an original and effective mix that may have fared better had it not been somewhat overshadowed by that same year's *My Fair Lady*. Loesser also wrote the memorable music and lyrics for the Danny Kaye film biography, *Hans Christian Anderson* (1952).

In 1955, NBC broadcast a live performance of the sold-out musical version of *Peter Pan*, which had opened on Broadway the previous year. Directed by Jerome Robbins, with Mary Martin playing Peter, more than 60 million viewers were estimated to have watched, which Thomas Greenfield suggests was a 'harbinger of future interactions between television and Broadway'.[99] It was so successful that NBC repeated the experience in 1956. Some musicals began to be developed directly for television, including Rodgers and Hammerstein's *Cinderella* (1957). Its broadcast reached more than 107 million viewers, though it would not be produced on Broadway until 2003. Another interesting avenue of income for several Broadway composers, including Harold Rome,

Adler and Loesser, came in the form of writing jingles, while others allowed versions of songs from their musicals to be used in advertising. Timothy Taylor explains how 'In 1955, only 5 percent of TV commercials featured original music, but by 1960, about 85 percent employed music.'[100] This helped bring many songs from musicals, and their creators, further into the common zeitgeist.

As the only principal conductor of the New York Philharmonic to write for Broadway musicals, Leonard Bernstein created some of the most ambitious musical theatre scores, blending classical, jazz and pop into distinctive productions. His score for the 1953 hit, *Wonderful Town*, about bohemians living in Greenwich Village, included an aria, a comic duet, innovative jazz and a wild conga. He would also pen Broadway's last self-proclaimed 'comic operetta', *Candide* (1956), for which Lillian Hellman wrote the book. However, his vital score for 1957's *West Side Story* that included the pure operatic strains of 'Maria' and 'Somewhere', alongside the vaudeville of 'Gee Officer Krupke', the Latin sound of 'America', the hit ballad 'Tonight' and several jazz compositions, may have become his most memorable.

The decade began with the overpowering influence of Rodgers and Hammerstein, whose ideas were much emulated, but it also saw the beginnings of others who worked hard to make musical theatre an even more serious form. Stephen Sondheim had studied under Hammerstein, but would take his art in a very different direction. His work would ultimately change the Broadway stage forever through his development of a new kind of musical theatre that presented even deeper psychological characterizations, shunning sentimental romance or complacent reassurances, to address more complex social issues. Though related to the integrated musicals of Rodgers and Hammerstein, Sondheim's 'concept musicals', that were built around an idea rather than a traditional narrative, would heavily influence the future style of musicals throughout the world. While he only wrote the lyrics for *West Side Story* (1957) and *Gypsy* (1959), these early 1950s works foreshadow a new and powerful kind of American musical theatre.

Andrea Most suggests that we consider *West Side Story* as an attempt to rewrite the musical to reflect deep disillusionment over the optimistic liberal ideals the genre was invented to express.[101] As the violence spirals and the young hero lies dead, it certainly reflects a more pessimistic and deterministic worldview than most preceding musicals. Laurents's treatment of the Romeo and Juliet story turns it into a disturbing racial conflict, and beneath the jokey surface, a song like 'Gee, Officer Krupke' explores the environment of the juvenile delinquent and how adult misunderstanding too often reduces them to stereotypes. The musical had become a socio-political statement, and Sondheim's lyrics were deemed profoundly original. As composer Bernstein exclaimed when Sondheim joined the creative team, 'I went wild, I thought he was a real, honest-to-God talent ... the lyrics didn't sound like anybody's lyrics by any means.'[102]

West Side Story also stood out for its clever amalgam of high and low culture: an urban rumble inside a Shakespearean play with jazz inflected music and balletic choreography created by the talented Jerome Robbins who used dance to create atmosphere and develop characterizations. Robbins insisted on an eight-week – rather than the standard four-week – rehearsal schedule, to ensure quality and have time to work with raw young talent unused to singing and dancing. Consequently, the production had a youthful energy, and John Chapman's review asserted that 'The American theatre took a venturesome forward step ... a bold new kind of musical – a juke-box Manhattan opera – the skills of show business are put to new tests – as a result of a different kind of musical has emerged – a perfect production.'[103] With a hugely successful movie version in 1961, and repeated revivals, it has become one of the most popular musicals of all time. Sondheim admits the characters in the musical could be more fully developed, but explained, 'It's not about people. It's a way to tell a story. What was best was its theatricality and its approach to telling a story in musical terms.'[104] What Bernstein, Laurents, Robbins and Sondheim had jointly achieved was an innovative way in which song, music, dance and dialogue could blend together to create a new fluidity

More acclaimed today than when first presented, *Gypsy* gave the ultimate musical comedienne, Ethel Merman, a more serious role as the monstrous show biz obsessed mother of the famed burlesque stripper Gypsy Rose Lee. Sondheim's impactful lyrics for the show, filled with elegant and daring phrases, contained more subtext than was usual for musical numbers, allowing the characterizations to become darker and more complex, such as in the searing 'Rose's Turn' in which Rose Hovick exposes the unpleasant fierceness of her jealousy and ambition. Laurents views Sondheim as the 'best

Broadway lyricist, past or present' in the way each song, permeated with dramatic action, feels like a 'one-act play'.[105]

The 1950s also saw the first hit of Jerry Bock and Sheldon Harnick with *Fiorello!* (1959). It ran for 795 performances and reflected an increasing choice in musicals of more serious material. A fictionalized version of the life of Fiorello H. LaGuardia, while celebrating his eventual victory in becoming Mayor of New York, it also offered a cynical exposure of political corruption. In 1960, this would tie with *The Sound of Music* for the Tony Award for Best Musical and would be one of only a few musicals to win a Pulitzer Prize. The couple would go on in the next decade to write the blockbuster *Fiddler on the Roof* (1964), based on Sholem Aleichem's tales about a Jewish family trying to survive in 1905 Russia, which would be the first musical to pass the 3,000-performance mark.

As Laurents would later insist:

> The musical, you must remember, is America's most distinctive contribution to the theatre, and though it's the most popular form of theatre in this country, it is a form that has been lacking in content and in artistry. Its potential is largely unexplored. There is no reason that the musical must be trivial to be entertaining and successful.[106]

The groundwork of Sondheim and others in the 1950s provided the impetus to create American musicals that could no longer be considered trivial. Musical plays were now as popular as musical comedy, and revues had virtually disappeared, moving to nightclubs and coffee houses.

Television drama

Television programming has had a huge impact on American and world culture. Many critics have dubbed the 1950s as the Golden Age of Television. Initially, TV sets were expensive and so the audience was generally affluent. Television programmers knew this and they knew that serious dramas on Broadway attracted this audience segment. So, the producers began staging adaptations of Broadway plays or classic and popular novels in the television studios, and all the networks had at least one hour-long weekly programme that featured drama. Many of these plays were also broadcast live and would bring several important actors to wider attention, including Paul Newman, Joanne Woodward, Eva Marie Saint, Walter Matthau and Martin Balsam. Later, writers like Paddy Chayefsky, Reginald Rose and J. P. Miller wrote original plays specifically for television. Their plays – *Marty*, *Twelve Angry Men* and *Days of Wine and Roses* respectively – all went on to become successful movies. Chayefsky referred to the television play as 'the scorned stepchild of drama' and felt it was never given its proper due, even while, he insisted, it 'may well be the basic theatre of our century'.[107] He would later move toward Broadway, and finally to Hollywood.

At the start of the decade there were several programmes that specialized in producing drama. The quality of many of these shows was reflected in their winning Primetime Emmy Awards. In 1951, *Pulitzer Prize Playhouse* was recognized for their first season, which included *You Can't Take It with You*, *The Magnificent Ambersons*, *Abe Lincoln in Illinois*, *The Silver Cord*, *Mary of Scotland*, *Alison's House* and *Our Town*, and in 1952, *Studio One* was recognized for the quality of its anthology drama. After this, the Emmy Awards were dominated by the burgeoning sitcoms and comedy revues, such as *I Love Lucy* and *Make Room for Daddy* or *The Red Skelton Show*, *The Phil Silvers Show* and *The Jack Benny Show*, although such anthology series as *Omnibus*, *Robert Montgomery Presents*, *The U. S. Steel Hour*, *Playhouse of Stars*, *Philco-Goodyear Television Playhouse* and *Playhouse 90* all had some recognition.

In 1954, a cooperative organization was formed by a group of upcoming writers, including Chayefsky, Tad Mosel (*Other People's Houses*, 1953), Horton Foote (*The Trip to Bountiful*, 1953), N. Richard Nash (*The Rainmaker*, 1953) and Robert Alan Aurthur (*A Man is Ten Feet Tall*, 1955), to write and promote serious television drama. Others writers, including Reginald Rose, Gore Vidal (*Visit to a Small Planet*, 1955) and Rod Serling (*Requiem for a Heavyweight*, 1956), were also finding opportunities to improve the level of television drama. Many of these plays would be later adapted for Broadway production and/or film. The names of these playwrights became known to millions through this growing media

(Chayefsky even had his own fan club), and most of them were able to publish their television scripts, suggesting their permanent worth.

Reginald Rose produced three influential television plays in the mid-1950s that responded to the country's growing concern over juvenile delinquency: *Crime in the Street* (1956), *Twelve Angry Men* (1957) and *Dino* (1957). Rose felt that the physical abuse of children, especially where fathers beat their sons, was a major contributor to delinquency and teen crime. While the most famous of his plays, *Twelve Angry Men*, centres on the trial of an adolescent youth charged with killing an abusive father, it concentrates on the varying responses of a jury to this crime. The other two focus more closely on the criminals and their crimes. *Crime* takes a sociological approach and features a settlement house worker in a dead-end urban environment trying to reclaim warring gang members. Three of these are unredeemable sociopaths, and their plot to kill an old man even causes their fellow gang members to baulk, but it is the overall environment that provides the largest hurdle. In *Dino*, Rose takes a psychological approach. Dino Manetti kills an old warehouse guard, but his psychiatrist later reveals that this was an Oedipal substitute for Dino's abusive father.

Paddy Chayefsky's early works focused on poor immigrant characters, pleasant but lonely working-class types, who live in colourless urban settings and seek something better. 'Through careful rendering of character and milieu', Clum suggests that Chayefsky's plays 'explore what lies underneath a relationship' rather than simply depict the relationship alone.[108] This gave his dramas a depth, despite the brevity of the genre. His language recreates authentic urban speech in turn both prosaic and eloquent, making him something of a 1950s Clifford Odets, only less political.

Chayefsky produced 11 plays for the *Philco-Goodyear Television Playhouse*, only one of which was an adaptation of another work (which was the more common approach to television drama). *Marty* (1953), about a lonely butcher looking for love, would become one of the era's best known small-screen dramas, especially after being turned into an Oscar-winning movie in 1955. Other plays were *Printer's Measure* (1953), about facing the march of progress in a print shop; *The Bachelor Party* (1953), about a young man uncertain about embracing the mature roles of husband and father; and *The Mother* (1954), about an older widow fighting for independence from her daughter through employment. Each play was marked by its realistic depiction of the mundane lives of working-class people, whose lives usually found improvement through the discovery of love. Such intimate, everyday portraits and small-scale dramas were well suited to the television medium, especially as more urban and middle-class people began to watch on their 12" black-and-white screens.

Sadly, the boom in television drama was short-lived as networks reduced time spent on original plays, preferring to produce more lucrative and formulaic comedies, adventure serials and quiz shows, as their audience grew less highbrow. Many of the better writers moved to Broadway or Hollywood, though Rod Serling would stay to create the influential *The Twilight Zone* anthology series that began airing in 1959. Neil Simon, whose comedies would make him the hottest new playwright on Broadway in the 1960s, began by writing for television rather than the radio, as many of the successful writers of the '40s and '50s had done. Weales suggests that despite its frequent realism, television drama, with its imaginative range of location and time, not only helped spread ideas about 'nonrealistic staging' (already being influenced by cinematic techniques), but also led to 'the concomitant shattering of the strict act structure'.[109]

Off-Broadway, Off-Off-Broadway, regional and college theatre

While Broadway bounced between meaningful drama and pure entertainment, there remained some genuinely oppositional theatre Off-Broadway, as the decade advanced.[110] In 1949, the newly formed Off-Broadway Theatre League negotiated a special contract with Actors' Equity to allow Equity actors to perform at reduced rates. This allowed the theatres to become more professional and commercial, and able to be reviewed by the *New York Times*.[111] Even major writers of the period, such as Williams, premiered or had revivals of their work – for example Miller, Wilder and O'Neill – at Off-Broadway venues, which helped increase the importance of such theatres. Often a producer would find it more profitable to keep a hit play running in the smaller Off-Broadway venue than to try to move it onto Broadway; a production of Kurt Weill and Bertolt Brecht's *The Threepenny Opera* stayed open at the Theatre de Lys for seven years. The number of Off-Broadway theatres expanded during the 1950s, but the price to mount a play there also rose, which began to discourage would-be producers in taking any risks, and the number of productions would contract in the 1960s.

In 1950, Guild Theatre was renamed the American National Theatre and Academy, or ANTA Playhouse, committing itself to non-commercial drama from home and abroad, and other such groups would spring up in subsequent decades. As a not-for-profit theatre, Circle-in-the-Square, established by José Quintero, Theodore Mann and others in 1951, worked essentially as a regional theatre within the boundaries of New York City, producing unusual or contemporary productions and several important revivals. Artists Theatre ran from 1953 to 1956 as a subscription theatre with limited runs and gave several new writers an outlet. Although most of these would become better known as poets – including James Merrill, John Ashbery and Frank O'Hara – Lionel Abel's *Absalom* (1956) would be the first Obie winner for best new play.

The Phoenix Theatre opened its doors in 1953 and produced many important revivals of foreign writers, including Chekhov, Strindberg, Pirandello and Schiller, as well as introduced American audiences to works by Brecht and Ionesco. Joseph Papp's Free Shakespeare in the Park also began in 1956, to introduce classic plays to the masses. Founded to produce experimental works by Julian Beck and Judith Malina in 1947, Living Theatre moved around the city during the 1950s, at first producing experimental drama from abroad, but eventually turned to homegrown playwrights such a Jack Gelber, whose 1959 play *The Connection* caused a major dramatic stir.

Of Living Theatre, Julian Beck once asserted, 'Our aim was *to increase conscious awareness, to stress the sacredness of life, to break down walls.*'[112] The group wanted 'to reach the audience, to awaken them from their passive slumber, to provoke them into attention, to shock them if necessary, and ... to involve the actors with what was happening in the audience'.[113] Joseph Chaikin, who would become a driving force behind the experimental Open

Theatre during the 1960s, joined Living Theatre in 1959. While Beck and Malina had initially been attracted to Brecht's ideas, during the 1950s they began to view Antonin Artaud as a better model. Where Brecht had sought to alienate his audience through a theatrical distancing, Artaud wanted to make his audience intimately feel each performance on a gut level. This is what they attempted in *The Connection*.

Kenneth Tynan called *Connection* 'the most exciting new play that off-Broadway had produced since the war',[114] and Henry Hewes judged it 'the most original piece of new American playwrighting in a long, long time'.[115] Finely crafted, though ostensibly improvised, this presentation of a group of down-and-out addicts waiting for their next fix against a background of jazz and violence, including someone overdosing on stage, was described by other critics as tasteless, disgusting and deeply depressing. However, as Ruby Cohn suggests, it 'became a clarion call for the theatre of the 1960s, thriving as it did on drug indulgence, racial commingling, group improvisation, and erosion of barriers between actors and audience'.[116] The intent had been to show these addicts as thinking human beings, and not simply dismiss them as evil. Having disturbed both theatrical and social conventions, *Connection* would lead the way for other experimental works by Gelber (*The Apple*, 1961), as well as Jack Richardson (*The Prodigal*, 1960; *Gallows Humor*, 1961) and Edward Albee, whose exploration of isolation and dehumanization in a materialist society, *The Zoo Story*, would open at the Provincetown Playhouse in 1960 (alongside Beckett's even bleaker *Krapp's Last Tape*), beginning an award-winning career that would last well into the twenty-first century.

However, while the earlier smaller theatres of Off-Broadway had begun as venues for the avant-garde, in the 1950s many were now becoming cheaper alternatives to try out plays for Broadway and seemed less willing to take risks. But avant-garde theatre would continue to thrive in a number of regional and college theatres, as well as the gradual development of Off-Off-Broadway, with its smaller theatres containing fewer than 199 seats. This began toward the close of the decade, with the opening of Joseph Cino's Caffé Cino in 1958, and the rise of performance art. Though viewing what he did as art rather than theatre, Allan Kaprow's *18 Happenings in 6 Parts*, presented in New York in 1959, revolutionized the practice of performance art and created a new theatrical genre: the happening – a spontaneous improvisational performance that tried to capture, on a symbolic level, the aesthetic of everyday experience.

Combining a Zen Buddhist drive for enlightenment, Artaud's insistence on the physical tangibility of any production, and the ideas of Jerzy Grotowski (who advocated actors co-creating the event of theatre with its spectators) and avant-garde composer John Cage, who challenged definitions about musicianship and musical experience, Kaprow tried to avoid breaking what he saw as the barrier between art and life. The audience was often invited to participate in the show as the non-scripted action is presented 'with no more meaning than the sheer immediacy of what is going on'.[117]

While the Little Theatre Movement had been gradually proliferating across America since the start of the century, regional theatre, that (once established) would feature resident professional troupes, really began to take off after the Second World War. In 1947, Margo Jones and Nina Vance, respectively, created Theatre '47 in Dallas and the Alley Theatre in Houston. In 1950, Zelda Fichandler started the Arena Stage in Washington, DC, and Herbert Blau and Jules Irving opened the avant-garde Actor's Workshop of San Francisco in 1952. The success of these would encourage many more regional theatre groups to form across the nation – including the Milwaukee Repertory Theater (1954), Chicago's Court Theatre (1954) and the Dallas Theater Center (1959) – theatres that would serve their communities first and foremost. Some would allow Broadway producers to try out their productions prior to taking them to New York, but many would also develop their own playwrights who could then take their successful pieces to Broadway.

Most regional theatres would create subscription seasons to help support themselves and would perform both classics and new plays. Several artistic directors, like Margo Jones, who was a missionary for theatre-in-the-round, built stages that offered alternatives to Broadway's predominantly proscenium arch designs. As Gwen Orel points out, foundation and government support, which had become increasingly available during this prosperous period, helped enhance 'the stability of regional theatre as a viable professional alternative to Broadway theatre. Beginning in 1959 the Ford Foundation began awarding three-year matching grants to the

Alley, the Workshop, and the Arena, enabling them to hire Equity actors for full-season contracts.'[118]

Community and children's theatre

The 1950s also marked a massive expansion in both community and children's theatre groups throughout the nation. The Depression and the Second World War slowed the development of new theatres (and closed some down), but a burst of new activity occurred after the war, fuelled by ready funds and an increased desire for social recreation. In 1959, Robert Gard and Gertrude Burley estimated that there were about 3,500 full-scale community theatres in the United States, producing on a continuing basis, *and this number would swiftly rise to* 18,000 by 1962.[119]

Unlike the Little Theatre Movement, whose aim was mainly to bring theatre to the people, amateur-volunteer community theatres were more centred on having the people intricately involved in creating their own theatre. An early form of this would be pageants that could involve hundreds of people, but as they evolved, many of these community theatres would simply mount regular plays, only with a local, non-professional cast and crew. In 1958, the American Community Theatre Association was formed to foster standards of excellence for production, management, governance, community relations and service, and this would later become a division of the American Theatre Association as community theatres continued to proliferate across the country. One 1968 survey asserts that community theatre 'engaged more people in theatrical activity, albeit part-time, than all the rest of the American theatre put together, including schools and colleges'.[120]

Children's theatre differs from adult in its objectives and audience. Initially it had been more of an amateur endeavour, but encouraged by social workers and educators as having beneficial possibilities – at both individual and community levels – it had become a more concerted movement in the 1930s. At the start of the 1950s, between 200 and 300 permanent children's theatre groups were operating, but they were demanding 'better scripts, better direction of plays and a better understanding of the child audience'.[121] With an increase in demand, and plenty of government funding, children's theatre would make giant strides forward during the 1950s after Winifred Ward established the Children's Theatre Committee in 1951 – to become the Children's Theatre Conference in 1952 (as a division of the American Theatre Association) – covering 16 regions (including Canada), each with its own organizational structure, to promote children's theatre and encourage high standards of production. A newsletter was created to circulate information, and membership was pulled from schools, colleges, Junior Leagues, community theatres and professional companies.

The Junior League established a drama library for scripts, sets, costumes, props and lighting equipment. In 1956, named after a popular children's playwright (who mostly adapted fairy stories and classic literature), the Charlotte Chorpenning Cup was established to recognize on an annual basis an outstanding children's theatre playwright. In 1958, the Children's Theatre Foundation was formed to head up special projects and services, primarily through funding graduate students to get involved in significant children's theatre research, and provide funding for speakers and for delegates to travel. Several colleges, such as Emerson, Northwestern University and the University of Tulsa, developed children's theatre groups, and many community theatres added a specific children's theatre branch.

Nellie McCaslin lists the details of 27 dedicated children's theatre organizations established in the 1950s across the country, most of which were still operating in 1987 when her book was published.[122] Some, like the New England Theatre Guild for Children, founded in 1955, tour schools and mount performances at public venues such as aquariums, hospitals and colleges. Using professional performers, they tend to adapt fairy tales and childhood classics into 45-minute participation plays. Others, like New York's Paper Bag Players, founded in 1958, use simple props, uniform garments, mime and improvisation to create original works. Several, like the San Francisco Mime Troupe, founded in 1959, specialize in mime, and New York's Young Audiences began in 1952 with just music, but later branched into theatre. Tufts University Magic Circle, established in Boston in 1955, tries to involve children in every aspect of their productions. In 1958, the Zeta Phi Eta-Winifred Ward Award for Outstanding Achievement by a new children's theatre company that had survived for at least four years was established, to encourage further growth.

3

William Inge: *Come Back Little Sheba* (1950), *Picnic* (1953), *Bus Stop* (1955) and *The Dark at the Top of the Stairs* (1957)

Introduction

Born in 1913 in Independence, Kansas, to Maude and Luther Inge, William Motter Inge grew up immersed in small-town life. His parents' marriage was not the happiest: his father, a travelling salesman for the family's dry-goods business, was none too faithful on the road. His mother would let out rooms to unmarried female schoolteachers to make ends meet. As the youngest of five – one sister died at the age of three – Inge was the family 'baby', spoiled by his mother and older siblings. The eldest two, Lucy and Luther Boy, were fairly outgoing, but Luther would die from blood poisoning when Inge was seven.

With a mostly absent father, his older brother dead and surrounded by females at home and school, his biographer, Ralph Voss, suggests this may have instigated the deep sensitivity Inge later displayed toward his female characters.[1] He felt closest to his sister Helene, who, like himself, was more introverted and somewhat smothered by his mother. Never outgoing, but affable, he tended to stay apart rather than be left out. Key to this was his growing realization that he was gay, a sexuality he accepted but was not inclined to act upon. As Robert Alan Aurthur explained, 'Bill carefully disguised his homosexuality. To a Midwestern boy faggotry was at the very least a terrible embarrassment.'[2] However, as Voss suggests, Inge's 'severely closeted homosexuality influenced his muse, affected his characters and their conflicts, and imbued his creations with an undercurrent that is an additional key to today's endurance of his works'.[3] Though he could never accept himself, Inge's works are filled with the acceptance of others. As Arthur McClure suggests, one of Inge's great strengths was his 'compassion for and understanding of the lives of small town people' and his 'basic attitude toward them is fondness, rather than hatred or contempt'.[4]

Like many other writers, Inge could not wait to get away from his place of birth, but then spent much of his early writing career recreating that life in his work. His formative small-town experience and life as a perennial outsider would feed his dramatic vision. Putting on plays with the neighbourhood children, with a scrapbook of well-known actors and love of recitation, he initially thought he would pursue a career in acting. However, lacking sufficient self-confidence and funds, he needed to find paying work after his 1935 graduation from the University of Kansas. After stints as both a radio announcer and working on a road gang for the Kansas State Highway Department, he went into teaching, a profession to which he occasionally returned but in which he was never fully comfortable.

Inge taught both English and drama, first in 1937 at a high school in Columbus, Kansas, and then at Stephens College in Columbia, Missouri, from 1938 to 1943. At this point he was offered a post at the *St. Louis Star Times*, replacing a younger writer who had been drafted. Working as their art, music, book and theatre critic, he would stay with them for nearly three years, writing hundreds of reviews. Voss claims that while Inge tended to be a fairly genial reviewer, he 'nonetheless often felt when covering plays that he could have produced better work than what he was reviewing', and became convinced that he should try.[5] In 1945 he asked a fascinating new playwright, Tennessee Williams, for an interview.

Williams was visiting his mother in St Louis shortly before the Chicago tryouts of *The Glass Menagerie*, and came to Inge's own apartment. They struck up an instant friendship, and were possibly even lovers for a brief period, although a growing rivalry, as Inge's plays outdid his mentor's, would eventually sour their relationship. Inspired by *The Glass Menagerie*, in a later interview Inge confessed, 'I had met genius. It was the most beautiful play I had seen in years.'⁶ Voss explains the result of Inge's response: 'Williams had fashioned this marvelous and wonderful play out of the raw material of his own life, out of his family, out of his emotions, and Inge knew he could do the same.'⁷ He took three months to write the semi-autobiographical *Farther Off from Heaven* and shared it with Williams. Williams set him up with his own agent, Audrey Wood, who disliked this play, but would adore his next: *Come Back, Little Sheba*. In *Sheba*, Inge focused on a childless older couple similar to the sister-in-law and her husband who had appeared in *Farther*. Williams also introduced Inge to theatre producer Margo Jones.

In 1947, Jones produced *Farther Off from Heaven* at her Theatre '47 in Dallas, Texas, to moderate success. Inge also had an early version of *Picnic*, called *The Front Porch*, mounted in St Louis by the Morse Players, although he was unhappy with the production, feeling it was too heavy-handed. Meantime, Wood had persuaded the Theatre Guild to underwrite a tryout of *Come Back, Little Sheba* in Westport, Connecticut. By 1950, *Sheba* was ready for Broadway.

At 191 performances, *Sheba* had an impressive run for an unknown playwright – though to maintain this, the director, Daniel Mann, and some cast members took pay cuts. Lead actors Sidney Blackmer and Shirley Booth both won Tony Awards, each for the first time, and after a 1974 revival, John Simon suggested the play 'may ring truest of all depictions of addicts in American drama during the previous twenty-five years'.⁸ The New York Drama Critics Circle voted the play a narrow second to Carson McCullers's *A Member at the Wedding* for that year's best play, and named Inge the most promising playwright of the season. Wood sold the movie rights for a reported $150,000, and it was published by Random House.⁹ Inge was an instant celebrity, and with each subsequent play and its following successful film, his prestige would grow.

Three years later, Inge's next Broadway play, *Picnic*, was an even bigger hit, with a run of 477 performances. Leading critic Brooks Atkinson approvingly asserted that 'Inge seems to have no personal point of view, but only knowledge of people and an instinct for the truth of the world they live in.'[10] The director, Joshua Logan, won a Tony, two of the actors, Eileen Heckart (Rosemary) and Paul Newman (Alan), got acting awards from *Theatre World*,[11] the play gained the New York Drama Critics Circle and Outer Circle (non-New York critics) selections for best play, tied with *The Crucible* for a Donaldson Award, and Inge took home a Pulitzer. Initially written with six different sets, and the character of Madge staying home and losing both the men who had courted her at the close, Logan persuaded Inge to make changes to create what he saw as a more dramatically pleasing production. Action was to be concentrated on a single set, designed by Jo Mielziner, and Madge would follow the exciting young Hal. Wanting a success, Inge reluctantly agreed to the alterations, but would later publish his preferred version, as *Summer Brave* (1962).

Inge's next hit was *Bus Stop* (1955), directed by Harold Clurman. Expanding it from a shorter piece, 'People in the Wind', Inge created even more of an ensemble play than *Picnic*, although the subsequent movie version, directed by Logan, would cut two characters (the Sheriff and Dr Lyman) to focus more on Bo and Cherie. Inge, however, had intended it to be an exploration of many different kinds of love, including homosexual.[12] It ran for 478 performances and was nominated for four Tony Awards, including best play, but lost to *The Diary of Anne Frank*. Atkinson saw in the play a greater 'intellectual and artistic maturity' and insisted, 'Having written a wonderful play two years ago, William Inge has now written a better ... Out of a rather ordinary situation Mr. Inge has put together an uproarious comedy that never strays from the truth.'[13]

The Dark at the Top of the Stairs, a revision of his earlier *Farther Off from Heaven*, continued Inge's winning streak, with a run of 468 performances and five Tony nominations, though an historical piece about Roosevelt, *Sunrise at Campobello*, beat it for best play. Atkinson declared this 'Mr. Inge's finest play. Although the style is unassuming, as usual, the sympathies are wider, the compassion deeper and the knowledge of adults and children more profound.'[14] All of Inge's 1950s hits were made into equally successful movies, with box-office stars such as Burt Lancaster, William Holden, Marilyn Monroe, Robert Preston and Dorothy McGuire, which were likely seen more widely than the plays themselves. However, Inge had no control over any of the screenplays, and was quite upset by several changes imposed to make these more palatable for movie audiences.

Inge's final play of the 1950s, *The Loss of Roses*, introduced a young Warren Beatty, but fared less well, closing after twenty-five performances. However, even this was made into a movie in 1963, retitled *The Stripper*. Inge had begun drinking at college, as a means of alleviating his depression and social reluctance, but he soon became an alcoholic. He did not seek treatment for this until 1948, when he joined Alcoholics Anonymous and sought psychiatric help, which also introduced him to prescription drugs. He would be in and out of therapy for the rest of his life. As his insecurities increased he would return to drinking and drugs. Intensely lonely, but fearful of contact, it was possibly only the therapeutic aspect of his writing that kept Inge alive so long. Aside from an Oscar-winning screenplay in 1961 for *Splendor in the Grass*, Inge would never have another success, and committed suicide in 1973.

Inge's full life story reflects a long history of insecurity and mental illness. Voss writes of Inge suffering from 'bouts of depression and insomnia' as early as his twenties, and he would suffer from these throughout his life.[15] Even at his most successful, Inge was never content. For him, success was a double-edged sword: he craved it, yet constantly feared its loss to the point he could never fully enjoy it when it occurred. Both agoraphobic and claustrophobic, he found it difficult to find comfort anywhere. Coupled to these phobias was his knowledge, but disapproval, of his own homosexuality, which led him to maintain distance from anyone who tried to get close. He imposed on himself a lonely life of isolation, becoming a spectator rather than player of life. Intriguingly, we see many of these 'spectator' figures appear in his work: characters intrigued by life, but fearful of getting too involved.

Inge's theatre

A majority of theatregoers during the 1950s preferred to spend their money on musicals and light comedy, rather than straight drama. But during the decade, Inge had unprecedented success with four hit plays in a row. Collectively, these had 1,614 performances, over a hundred more than Tennessee Williams would achieve with five plays over that same period. Perhaps it was the veneer of gentle humour or the underlying kindness toward his characters that won Inge his audience, but it was one that would turn away from him in the 1960s when his work became darker.

Inge's first four plays take place in small Midwestern towns, but they are hardly nostalgic visions to feed a patronizing cosmopolitan idea of uneducated, small-town life; indeed, in *Bus Stop* he even mocks such attitudes by exposing the supposedly educated Dr Lyman as unaware of what state he is in, and having Elma point out the cultural aspects of a Midwest that is bereft of neither art nor culture: there may be rodeos and more restricted opportunities for women, but there are also symphony concerts and Shakespeare. Playwrights prior to Inge, if they paid any attention to the Midwest at all, either depicted it as a small-minded place of monotony or celebrated its wholesomeness apart from decadent urban lives. Inge refused both models and showed an authentic Midwest, with both its positives and its negatives.

While on the surface, Inge's characters seem gentler than the outrageous ones we meet in Williams's plays, there are several unsettling events even in these early plays that show the comic veneer to be deceptive, and speak to more serious issues. A husband attacks his wife with a hatchet, women are abducted or abandoned, an old man seduces a young girl, a young man commits suicide and we witness much abuse of alcohol. However, Inge does not allow his audience to get as outraged as they might at such excesses in other plays. This is partially because of the surrounding humour that helps deflate concern, but also due to Inge's insistence that nobody is truly evil or totally self-concerned. It is this compelling compassion for his characters that made his plays so popular, and makes even wife-beaters and paedophiles sympathetic. As actress Ellen Burstyn suggested, after playing Mrs Potts in a revival of *Picnic*, 'I think Inge truly loved all his characters, understood them, felt for them, forgave them their foibles and flaws ... He did for them what he could not do for himself. He allowed them to be themselves.'[16]

While it later became a common error to view Inge's work from the 1950s as nostalgic paeans to a by-gone small-town era predating that decade, at close inspection these plays are totally redolent of 1950s life. Inge was able to effectively evoke the repressed fears and desires hidden beneath the surface conformities of the decade, which insightfully foretell the upcoming sexual and social revolution of the next. As Jeff Johnson argues, Inge undermined expected gender roles 'for the purpose of politically and socially destabilizing social norms'.[17] Inge's plays also reflect the era's obsession with psychiatry, filled with references to 'inferiority complexes', psychiatric cures for alcoholism and depression, and almost case study characterizations. In 1955, David Sievers complimented the plays for their ability to draw on Freudian insights 'without succumbing to the obvious or the trite' and admired how Inge could 'extract ever fresh and original patterns of human relationship from contemporary life and ... view with psychological as well as aesthetic perception the life around us'.[18]

Inge's plays may have out-of-the-way Midwest locales, but they are filled with contemporary references, issues and concerns, including alcoholism (as sickness rather than weakness), the changing roles and needs of women and modes of sexuality, adolescent insecurities and the growing generation gap. Beneath his genial surface lie portraits of dysfunction and rebellion that speak directly to the decade, with an end goal of asking for acceptance and tolerance of those depicted. The frequency of specific period references within Inge's plays belies any charge of nostalgia; even Madge's fantasies of becoming a spy or contributing to medical research are timely in a Cold War period of increased medical research.

Of the plays set in the 1950s, *Sheba* references Kinsey's 1948 *Sexual Behavior in the Human Male*, atomic worries and Tarzan,[19] while *Picnic* has characters discussing Carson McCullers's *The Ballad of Sad Café* (1951) and Picasso (at a peak of international fame in the 1950s), as well as hot rods, couples 'going steady' and listening to pop music on the radio. In *Bus Stop* the popular amateur contests of the era are discussed, as well as the cabaret star Hildegard, who appeared in many television specials of the decade; Bo appears in tight blue jeans and a leather jacket, and owns a 24"-screen colour television; and Marlon Brando in *Julius Caesar* (1953) and Burt Lancaster both get referenced. Younger characters' dialogue in all the plays is strewn with 'hip' phases of the day, from 'goon' to 'I don't dig', and they wear T-shirts and drink cans of beer.

As a writer, Inge was able to present images of ordinary Americans who lived outside the main urban areas, and several great roles for women. His work centres on Midwesterners, never previously considered to be good subjects for art, and through them he managed to draw out the difficulties of living and surviving in a country that promised much and often delivered so little. His quiet studies of desperation are uniquely illustrative of a culture that for all its rhetoric of inclusion was forever creating outsiders, by class, gender or sexual preference. Thus, his plays allow an audience to better realize the difficulties faced, not just by the great minds of society, but by the common folk on its periphery. As R. Baird Shuman explains, 'Inge was the first successful playwright to examine the Midwest with psychological insight into what small-town life on the plains and the prairies did to people', and by delving into its 'sociological uniqueness' he was able to present 'with astounding veracity and authenticity the oppressive banality, the utter commonplaceness of the lives of his characters'.[20]

In Inge's plays, problems are not neatly solved as for him that did not reflect reality. While directors often imposed pat endings on his work, he himself resisted. His early plays are intensely realistic, with dialogue that effectively captures the cadence of Midwestern speech. He fills them with open-ended characterizations and numerous young characters that allow for the possibility of hope but also keep that future uncertain. Characters are offered opportunities for love and happiness, but he allows no guarantees. We do not see how long his couples will last as he only depicts the beginnings of relationships. Through his characterizations, Inge challenges traditional notions of success, ambition and morality, and, as McClure suggests, 'tells us that we should accept our own nature and shape our lives from it', however modest that life should turn out to be.[21]

Come Back Little Sheba (1950)

Living in a run-down Midwest community, 'Doc' Delaney and his wife of twenty years, Lola, are surviving a past that constantly threatens to tumble them back down. It involves an early marriage due to pregnancy, the subsequent loss of that child and the possibility of any more, the husband's loss of ambition and subsequent alcoholism and the wife's loss of self-respect. Tensions begin to rise since Lola's pet dog, Sheba, has gone missing, and their young college student lodger, Marie, has taken up with a hot new lover, Turk. While Lola finds joy in Marie's dalliances – quietly and indiscriminately watching her with both lover and regular boyfriend, Bruce – she also feels nostalgia for her own youth. She spruces up herself and the house ready for Bruce's visit. Doc, meanwhile, fuelled by a crush on Marie and seeing her with Turk, goes on a bender.

Marie is enjoying herself with Turk, but once the wealthier and more dependable Bruce arrives and proposes, she swiftly leaves college and the Delaneys to join her fiancé. Doc returns still drunk, and after verbally abusing his wife and breaking their best dishes, attacks her with a hatchet; it is evidently misdirected anger at what he feels is Marie's betrayal of his idea of her innocence when she slept with Turk. Lola calms him and gains the assistance of Ed and Elmo, two of his Alcoholics Anonymous (AA) sponsors, to get him locked up to dry out.[22] Offered no support from her own parents, she is left alone, and waits until the penitent Doc returns home a week later, when they declare their mutual need. She accepts the fact that Sheba will not be returning, and they plan to get a bird dog so Doc can take up hunting.

This first success for Inge juxtaposes a middle-aged couple, each battling deep regret, against a modern thinking threesome of the younger generation, whose attitudes toward sex and gender roles reflect the changing culture in which they all live. We are led to compare the lives of the older couple against those of the young, though not necessarily to take sides. While there was no shortage of shotgun marriages in the 1950s, the greater availability of condoms allowed women to have sex prior to marriage with greater impunity, as Marie seems eager to do. Doc's view of women is clearly dated, insisting that they should not work once married, and prior to that they must stay innocent and virginal. His literal mystification[23] over Marie's behaviour shows just how far out of touch he has become. He married Lola because he felt he had to, not only because she was pregnant, but because he had slept with her.

Doc gave up his dream of medical school to settle down with Lola and become a chiropractor, and they lost the baby due to their fear of using a regular doctor for the delivery as Lola had been impregnated out of wedlock. Falling prey to alcoholism in disappointment over his life, aside from setting up his office, Doc has squandered a substantial inheritance on alcohol and given Lola a miserable time. All of it was, he admits, his own fault: '[I]f I'd used my head and invested it carefully, instead of getting drunk every night. We might have had a nice house, and comforts, and friends.'[24] In more recent years he has discovered AA, which has allowed him to reach a more peaceful equanimity in between bouts of falling off the wagon. As the play begins, he has been sober for a year. This resolve, however, becomes shaken by his growing feelings toward Marie. Caught between a sense of protective paternalism and sexual lust for this eighteen-year-old lodger, after getting evidence of Marie's dalliance with Turk, Doc goes out drinking. When he finally returns home he explodes into a drunken rampage and abuse of his wife (calling *her* 'slut' and 'whore'[25] even though she has never slept with anyone other than him). Lola nevertheless sticks by him, and by the close they seem to rekindle a love for one another.

Lola has developed a tendency to let housework slide, as she has let her body slide, which makes her a putative villain in the eyes of her husband (who has to get his own breakfast), her energetic neighbour Mrs Coffman (with her seven children and dislike of dirt and disorder) and the audience (who have been fed a diet of idealized middle-class homes through magazines and television). Lola's home is decorated without taste: just a '*cheap pretense at niceness and respectability*' that looks '*awkward*', and Lola is dressed in a '*lumpy kimono*' and '*dirty comfies*'. Their lodger, by contrast, '*wears a sheer, dainty negligee and smart feathery mules*'[26] and is obviously a creature prepared for the modern age, with, we discover, modern mores and concerns. Doc is bothered by the fact Marie has to study biology for college, but that is surely a sign of the times: women's lives and knowledge are starting to expand. Part of his attraction is the vibrancy and cleanliness she exudes next to his slovenly wife, blindly referring to her as 'clean and decent' and 'sweet and innocent',[27] but he is partially to blame for the way Lola is.

Without children or work (which Doc has disallowed), Lola is lonely and bored. Her listening to racy soap operas on the radio[28] is similar to her calling after her missing dog: a means of searching for something more satisfying in life. With an unsteady income due to her husband's drinking, she has taken in a lodger, and lives in fear of when Doc will drink again and become abusive. Her panic when she discovers the whiskey missing, repeated stage directions indicating her fear when he enters the room, swift enlistment of his AA sponsor Ed and silence when they take him away to be locked up tell us that he has a history of violent drunkenness and his sobriety has only ever been tenuous. Ed and Elmo know what to do as this has happened before and they anticipate Doc's tricks to escape, showing us a more unflinching portrait of an alcoholic than depicted in the more romanticized version, *The Lost Weekend* (book 1944; film 1945).

Despite her husband's alcoholism, there is love between them, as we can tell by their interplay over card tricks, past recollections and Doc's ability to resist his violent impulses on being asked by his wife to recall their past: 'You said I was the prettiest girl you ever saw. Remember, Doc! It's me! Lola!'[29] But this love appears atrophied at the play's start, as each goes through the motions. He calls her 'Baby' and she refers to him as 'Docky' and 'Daddy' to indicate the infantilizing nature of their relationship – it is little wonder she dreams of her lost youth and chances. Their relationship seems to have halted at the point she lost that baby. She has never been allowed to properly mourn, and they are unable to communicate with each other on any meaningful level. She chats with the postman (kindly giving him a toy for his children), the milkman and her disapproving neighbour, Mrs Coffman, but feels in a rut. Her drive to clean up for Bruce's arrival is sincere, and lasts through to the end of the play. It wins her Mrs Coffman's approval and may help in her relationship with Doc, as she seems to be bolstering his masculinity at the close, making him breakfast and allowing him to replace her baby-substitute – the fluffy little Sheba – with a more macho bird dog. Perhaps by acknowledging their mutual dependency they can move forward? Inge allows for that possibility, even as we also realize part of this accommodation is Lola becoming a more stereotypical wife, and there is no guarantee Doc can stay sober.

The easy lives in this play belong to the young, especially the object of Doc's regard, Marie. Totally self-concerned, Marie is oblivious as to how far she upsets Lola when she mocks her dancing, and when she returns shortly after Doc has attacked Lola, she is so full of her own news, she does not notice the disarray and Lola's exhaustion. Deeply practical, Marie is far more worldly than the sweetly naïve Lola. When Marie explains to Lola, 'Bruce and I had a very businesslike understanding before I left for school that we weren't going to sit around lonely just because we were separated', the romantic soul of Lola finds the news *'a serious disillusionment'*.[30] Marie was just enjoying herself with Turk – even using him, as he declares 'I'm nuts about you'[31] – while she has no intention of staying with him and fully controls their relationship. However, given Turk's physicality, posing semi-naked as Marie draws him in the living room, he is depicted as eye-candy who can no doubt swiftly seduce another girl with his athletic prowess, and we are not encouraged to sympathize. Bruce is as practical and unromantic as Marie, and obviously a better match: 'Do we have to eat by candlelight?' he complains, 'I won't be able to see.'[32]

The play is structured around Lola's dreams that demand psychoanalytical analysis. At the start, Lola dreams of taking her dog Sheba for a walk and losing her because she was moving too fast. It is unclear how long Sheba has been gone, but Lola still calls for her from the porch (especially after witnessing the vibrancy of Marie's life and loves). Sheba operates as a symbol of everything Lola feels she has lost over the past twenty years, and this includes her child, her youth and any chance of a different or better existence. At the close her dream has changed to reflect a new understanding. She realizes it is no use bemoaning things lost. In the new dream, Doc becomes her hero, throwing the javelin (a fairly blatant penis substitute) further than young Turk, and then she discovers the dead body of her dog in a muddy field, but Doc will not allow her to grieve over it. As she relates this, we see her coming to terms with their past life together and reaching an acceptance, finally, of what they have to look forward to: just each other.

Picnic (1953)

The action takes place around the back porch and yards of two small-town Kansas houses filled with women. The environment is deliberately ordinary and friendly, backed by a *'high sky of innocent blue'*.[33] Flora Owens, with her two daughters – Madge the town beauty and Millie the town brains – and an aging spinster teacher, Rosemary Sydney, inhabit one, while Mrs Helen Potts and her invalid mother reside in the other. Vagabond Hal Carter arrives in town to look up his old college chum Alan Seymour, a local rich boy, in the hopes of a job. His arrival causes ructions as he pursues Madge who has been going steady with Alan. Mrs Potts is feeding Hal in exchange for some odd jobs, which brings him into this circle of women, who all feel the attraction, but none more so than Madge. While she likes Alan, there is none of the passion she feels at first sight of Hal, and she cannot resist.

Everyone is preparing for the town's Labor Day picnic. Rosemary, outspoken and feeling her age (around forty), is tiring of dining out with her fellow spinster teachers, finding independence lonely and unfulfilling. Simultaneously prudish and flirty, she cuts a brash figure. Disapproving of Madge's behaviour, after getting a little tipsy from the bootleg alcohol her boyfriend Howard has brought along, she also flirts with Hal and is upset and vindictive when rejected by the young man. She and Howard are supposed to take Madge to the picnic, but go elsewhere to talk, leaving Madge behind. Rather than go to the picnic, Madge and Hal head elsewhere to have sex.

Later that evening we witness Rosemary pleading with Howard to marry her, and his reluctant agreement. Their departure the next day is interspersed with the breakdown of relations between Madge, Alan and Hal over what has happened. Hal had intentions of settling down, but Alan sets the police on him and he has to leave. Alan declares he is also leaving at his father's suggestion that he should attend graduate school. Hal asks Madge to join him, and even though it is implied that Alan will forgive her and return, she decides to pack her bag and follow Hal. In her risky decision to go to Hal, as Mrs Potts points out, she will be repeating her mother Flo's life: being tied to an irresponsible man, but unable to resist the pull of love – a decision that the play implies is the better choice.

Flo's love for her husband had made her feel weak and dependent, which broke them apart as she resisted, becoming mean and demanding. This led him to drink, other women and eventual abandonment. Thus, in resisting she had limited her own life. She loves her children and wants Madge to marry Alan and have a life of comfort, but Madge cannot settle for comfort over passion. As Mrs Potts reminds Flo, 'You don't love someone 'cause he's perfect.'[34] Love, for Inge, is wonderful but dangerous, as it makes you vulnerable; it was something he never dared let himself feel but he allows it in his characters. In her youth, Mrs Potts had eloped, but her mother had forced her to annul the marriage and return home. She made the opposite choice from Madge and her life was thereafter contained, being forever at her demanding mother's beck and call, with the most excitement being the annual Labor Day picnic. However, although Mrs Potts gave up her husband, she kept his name, and while she stays with her mother, she is clearly one of the more open and tolerant figures in the town despite her history. She has found a way to accept her solitary lot, and while she has no man of her own, she still asserts the pleasure of having one around.

The play's central catalyst, Hal Carter, is an ambiguous character and early example of the anti-heroes that would soon populate the culture. '*Exceedingly handsome*'[35] in a T-shirt that is off and on to display his body and his 'bad boy' image, all of the women in the play are attracted to him, whether or not they approve. Though not entirely insensitive, he is at times brash and boastful, making us unsure how much to believe of what he tells us, and whether or not we should even root for him and Madge.[36] Alan tells us how unpopular he was at college and how he did not like him at first, but then got to know him and became close friends. To gain our sympathy, Inge gives Hal a disadvantaged life – a father who drank himself to death, a mother who took his inheritance and pushed him away, an uncomfortable college experience and not much luck since – and he seems genuinely desirous to settle down and taken with Madge, despite his history with other women. He has to leave to avoid jail, as Alan has set the police on him out of revenge for taking his girlfriend, but he seems to have felt a real connection with Madge and asks her to join him with sincerity.

Inge makes it clear that Hal and Madge are well suited. When they dance together '*their bodies respond without touching*'[37] and they are both inflicted with beauty over brains, yet a desire to achieve something in life. Hal does not seduce Madge, as much as she is drawn to him from the moment she sees him. It is she who initiates their first kiss, flattered by the way he opens out to her. While she is ashamed of having slept with him so quickly, it is an attraction she cannot deny, and she tells him 'it's no more your fault than mine'.[38] Alan hardly sees her as human – underlined by his repeated refrain regarding whether or not she is real

– and seems only attracted by her looks. Hal's relation to the train that both brings and takes him away, next to Madge's wistful confession, 'Whenever I hear that train coming to town, I always get a little feeling of excitement', and the way she is drawn to the sound of the train whistle, *'there is a train whistle in the distance, MADGE hears it and stands listening'*, further connects them.[39]

A repeated refrain of the play is that all Madge has are her looks. She did not do well at school and currently works at the local dime store. She is not as intelligent as her sister Millie, who has a college scholarship, decides to never fall in love (we see her literally chase off boys with a stick) and to write books that will shock the world. But Madge has ambition, too, and not for the fairy-tale life one might expect, but to make an impact by being a successful spy or contributing to medical research. While she likes Alan, it is clear she is not enthusiastic and would rather follow her heart than wealth. Alan is also something of a 'square': he listens to classical music, never tries to do more than kiss her and does whatever his father tells him. As Flo points out, 'Alan is the kind of man who doesn't mind if a woman's bossy,' which makes him seem weak rather than forward thinking.[40] He is no match for Hal, reinforced by the sneaky way he tells the police Hal stole the car he loaned him, and then when he tries to hit him, Hal just pins him down and refuses to fight.

Against the interactions of this younger generation struggling to make the right choices, Inge complicates matters with the contrapuntal characterizations of Rosemary and Howard. Rosemary adds humour through her grating but jocular coarseness and evident hypocrisies. She complains that Hal's naked torso is improper while taking a good look, she tells off Madge for flirting while she forces herself on Hal, she tells Howard off for bringing liquor then takes a swig of it herself and she frequently praises female independence before begging Howard on her knees to marry her in a comic inversion of the expected proposal situation. We get additional humour out of Howard's evident reticence over being trapped. It is evident that the older generation that this couple represents holds no answers, but exudes a similar fear and bewilderment as their younger counterparts. For all their talk of independence, Rosemary and her single teacher friends would each prefer to have a permanent man in the picture and not have to work (Rosemary quits her job as soon as she has a ring on her finger). After being gently spurned by Hal, who is nonplussed by her flirtation (and upset by her mean-spirited recriminations), Rosemary is forced to realize she is no longer young and must either embrace the single life wholeheartedly or get Howard to marry her. She chooses the latter, which he resignedly accepts in the hopes that being a married man will increase his business, but their future together is as tenuous as that of Hal and Madge.

Bus Stop (1955)

Beginning in a fairly typical 1950s diner, with counter and tables, we first meet the middle-aged owner Grace and her young teenage waitress Elma Duckworth preparing for a late-night bus delayed due to a blizzard. The local sheriff, Will Masters, checks in on them. The bus's arrival brings the driver Carl, who will end up in Grace's rooms for the night; Dr Gerald Lyman, an aging, alcoholic teacher with a penchant for young girls, who will flirt with Elma; and a nightclub singer, Cherie, who is panicked about her abduction by a young cowboy, Bo Decker. Will assures her of his protection.

Bo and an older cowboy companion, Virgil Blessing, had fallen asleep on the bus, but enter next. Bo is full of bluster and enthusiasm, with Virgil trying to act as a calming force. Just 21, Bo has fallen for Cherie, and since she slept with him, assumes they should now marry and is taking her back to his ranch. She finds his manner overpowering and is trying to escape. Locked in by the storm and putting on a brief 'talent show' between them, this group undergoes a series of changes. While reciting *Romeo and Juliet* with the innocent and gullible Elma, Lyman realizes he is behaving badly and cancels his appointment to meet her in Topeka. Once the sheriff has beaten Bo in an offstage fistfight, Virgil persuades his companion to be more gallant and tender toward Cherie. This wins her approval and consent to continue on, and Virgil, seeing that Bo has a new partner, lets them go without him. At the end, the blizzard has abated, and so have all the conflicts it brought with it into the diner.

Bus Stop is a treatise on love, featuring an ensemble array of lovelorn characters trying to understand what that four-letter word might entail, and who in the end is deserving. Just a casual look at the characters' names underscores Inge's intent. Cherie is French for 'dear one', and her obvious partner is Bo in its assonance with 'beau' – meaning male admirer. Because he 'lies' to himself and others, Lyman will never find love, whereas the more giving Grace will at least find satisfaction. Young Elma, close to Alma, meaning soul, might suggest youthful purity and longing, but Elma itself means 'God's protection'. Protection here is afforded by the older Will Masters who benignly watches over them all (though punishing when due) and ensures the rightful outcomes. He has both will and mastery, and one cannot doubt he has a loving wife at home waiting for him. Virgil will, of course, assist his friend to find the love of his life, as Dante's Virgil led him to Beatrice, and be left alone in 'limbo' once the job was done.

As Grace implies when telling her about discontent with her ex-husband Barton, love is about more than the sexual act: 'makin' love is *one* thing, and bein' lonesome is another'.[41] Cherie may not be the brightest, but she puts her finger on the answer when she supposes, 'ya gotta feel he *respects* ya'[42] (187). For love to work, it must be mutual, and there needs to be respect on both sides. While this may not be attainable for everyone, and people certainly marry without it – as even Cherie supposes she may end up doing – it is not something to waste. In the growing complexity of modern life, Inge sees a tendency in people to be too wary for love, as Lyman fears:

> Maybe we have lost the ability. Maybe Man has passed the stage in his evolution wherein love is possible. Maybe life will continue to become so terrifyingly complex that man's anxiety about his mere survival will render him too miserly to give of himself in any true relation.[43]

For Inge, love means giving yourself to another, as a selfish man like Lyman cannot do. In his heart, Lyman knows this, which is why he drinks. Warning away the young girl he tried to seduce, he explains, people need to be 'strong enough inside themselves to love ... without humiliation ... I never had the generosity to love, to give my own most private self to another, for I was weak.'[44] Lovers, as Virgil tells Bo, even if he cannot do it himself, need to take a chance by letting down their guard and showing the other their vulnerability. When Bo follows this advice, reducing himself to tears in front of her, he swiftly wins Cherie's heart.

Despite her past – sexually active since 14, singing in a sleazy nightclub and wearing skimpy clothing – 19-year-old Cherie is meant to be *'fragile'*, with *'the appeal of a tender little bird'*.[45] After a tough childhood, forced to leave school at 12 to help in the home, then losing touch with most of this family during the floods and hoping to make it famous as a singer with little talent, Cherie has a good heart and just wants to find love. Even though she angrily turns on Bo and tells him she would like to see him being pounded by another man, she sobs when it actually happens. She has tried to reinvent herself as 'Cherie' but does not even know what the name means, and Bo's inability to say it correctly – he calls her Cherry throughout – suggests his dislike of pretension, or even an ironically inverted implication of virginity. When they are finally honest with each other – she tells him she has slept with other men and he confesses she was his first – they begin to see each other differently. As in *Picnic*, where Inge inverts gender with a woman on her knees proposing to a man, here we have a woman drawn to a man because she took his virginity. When Bo asks permission to kiss her and does so tenderly, they discover that necessary mutual respect that will allow them to happily marry.

Bo's initial antagonism toward the older Will, in particular, suggests a rebellious youth trying to assert himself against authority (he even has the jeans and leather jacket). An energetic and bombastic figure, he boasts of his Montana ranch, multiple rodeo wins, 24" colour television, huge appetite and multiple women. While the first three are true, his appetite and experience with women prove to be mere bravado. He is so full of life it is unsurprising that the spiritually deadened figure of Lyman draws away. Bo's enthusiasm for Cherie is equally enormous, but makes her feel overwhelmed and claustrophobic. Luckily, Bo has older men watching out for him, as both Virgil and Will give him solid advice. Will teaches him about humility and the selflessness that comes with not assuming everything is there just for you. He gets Bo to look at events through the eyes of others, and leads him to apologize with sincerity. Virgil, who has protected and advised Bo since his parents died, does so patiently and gently, suggesting he should treat Cherie with greater respect and tenderness.

At 21, Bo is something of an open book, and while his initial possessiveness of Cherie veers close to abuse, he is saved by his naiveté as he dejectedly admits, 'I just never realized ... a gal might not ... love me.'[46] Inge often has characters behave badly, but soon allows us to forgive them by showing us they were not aware they were behaving badly, and by having them show remorse. Bo is a decent guy, and, for the penniless Cherie who is looking for a life change, quite a catch. He does not drink or smoke, and she admits early on that he is 'awful *cute*' and she finds him sexually attractive.[47] Having grown up among cowboys, many of whom have talked disrespectfully about women, Bo has no real experience of how to behave, but he seems to learn his lessons well, even giving Cherie his jacket to keep her warm as they leave together. At this point she has taken over from Virgil as his calming voice of reason.

Virgil is quiet, gentle and unassuming, the total opposite of Bo. As his name suggests, Virgil Blessing is essentially a good man, and, just like Dante's Virgil, acts as a kindly and knowledgeable guide for Bo, also able to reprimand him when necessary. They could be a couple, but that Bo is heterosexual. Virgil loves Bo, if only platonically, and, even though he knows he is talking himself out of the picture, does all he can to mend things between Bo and Cherie. Of the varied performances given in the diner talent show, it may be ironic that Virgil's is the only one that is actually any good, but stage directions indicate the others are unaware of their limitations: another reason, perhaps, to view them with pathos.

Grace is happy without her husband, and content to have a casual sexual relationship with the bus driver Carl when he passes through, to alleviate her loneliness. Their relationship has a mutuality that makes it feel right, regardless of their marital state (it is possible that Carl may be married). While decent and kindly, looking out for Elma and respected by Will, it feels odd that she pushes Virgil out into the cold at the close. Perhaps Inge does this intentionally to his liminal homosexual to show how much of a pariah society viewed such people: one reason Inge was never openly gay and an emblem of his own sense of isolation. As Virgil responds to Grace saying he will be left out in the cold, 'Well ... that's what happens to some people,'[48] Bo wonders if looking after him had prevented Virgil from settling down, but this does not seem true. Virgil admits to preferring the simple company of men, and has always been uncomfortable around women, but he wants more for Bo. Virgil's line, 'A long time ago, I gave up romancin' and decided I was just gonna take bein' lonesome for granted,' comes straight from Inge's own heart.[49]

As a representative of the law, although the sheriff is '*somewhat forbidding*'[50] he is also dependable and astute as he looks out for the women, accepts Grace's affair with humour rather than condemnation, ensures Elma knows the truth about Lyman without embarrassing her and protects Cherie from Bo (even while suspecting all along they are well suited, and informing her that Montana is fine). He understands the give and take of life, knows no one is perfect and brings comfort to those around him: he takes coffee to the road workers, gives Bo solid advice and makes sure the young man holds no grudge for being beaten in a fight.

Though young, Elma has a similar sense of balance. Intelligent but naïve, she does well at school and enjoys higher culture, which Grace suggests may be keeping the boys aloof. She is flattered by Lyman's attention and not at all suspicious of his intent, although when she discovers what this is she is not too bothered, explaining, 'it's nice to know that someone *can* feel that way'.[51] Her lack of horror further alleviates the potential for our objection to the paedophilic Lyman.

Lyman is the closest we get to a villain, and even he redeems himself by backing away from his liaison, admitting he is a fake and suggesting a desire to do better. In his fifties, Lyman is beginning to fray, but is not yet totally disreputable. We see the danger he poses to Elma long before she does. Quoting Shakespeare and speaking of his three failed marriages with engaging self-deprecation, were it not for the fact that he was hitting on an underage girl he might be considered charming (foreshadowing Nabokov's Humbert Humbert in *Lolita*, published in Paris in 1955, but not in the United States until 1958). He tells us that he travels 'around from one town to another just to prove to myself that I'm *free*'.[52] It becomes evident that the opposite is true and the constant movement only highlights the entrapment he feels from his guilt as a failed human being, with three bad marriages and a dangerous predilection for youth. His self-deprecation is a means of criticizing himself before others can do so. While intoning Romeo's lines he comes to a moment of self-recognition as if this young couple's true passion has made him face his own predatory ways, after which he drinks himself into a stupor to avoid doing any harm and to escape again from this unpleasant truth. He knows he is caught in a downward spiral but simply cannot stop himself. He considers trying psychiatric treatment, though we should doubt the seriousness of his intent.

The Dark at the Top of the Stairs (1957)

Not set in the contemporary period, this is a semi-autobiographical piece that explores divisions in Inge's own family, and his childhood concerns from the 1920s. Despite the different time frame, it exhibits similar themes and messages regarding tolerance and honesty that we see in the earlier plays. In the living room of a small house in small-town Oklahoma, we meet the Flood family. Rubin works hard to maintain his household, but is feeling the pressure as his line of work – selling horse harnesses – is becoming outmoded. His wife, Cora, maintains the house, coddles the children (who appear to hate each other) and complains about their lack of ready cash. Reenie is their painfully shy teenage daughter, and 10-year-old Sonny is a definite 'mommy's boy'.

About to leave on a business trip, Rubin is troubled by his son's inability to prevent the neighbourhood boys from bullying him without his mother's help, and his wife's dissatisfaction over their income. Thinking he will not notice, Cora has bought Reenie an expensive dress to attend a party to force her out into society. When Rubin learns of this, as well as his wife's suspicions that he is having an affair, he becomes so angered that he hits his wife and runs off. Though Reenie is concerned, Sonny is glad to see his father depart. Cora invites her sister Lottie, along with husband Morris, to dinner, hoping to wrangle an invitation to live with them. However, her sister is reluctant, and we learn her marriage is in a worse state than that of Cora, as she and her husband, aside from surface pleasantries, have no real relationship.

Cora manages to get Reenie to accompany her arranged date – a young Jewish boy called Sammy Goldenbaum – to the dance, but Reenie's lack of self-confidence leads her to abandon him there. She later learns he was insulted by their anti-Semitic host, and, unable to find his date, ran off to a hotel where he committed suicide, urged on primarily by a letter he had just received showing his mother's callous neglect. The family is horrified to hear this news, but meantime, Cora has realized she needs to distance herself more from her son and get her husband back. Rubin returns, repentant, and with news he has found himself a new job. They speak more honestly to each other to reach a better understanding, and the play ends with not just Cora and Rubin reconciling, but also the warring siblings.

This is small-town Midwest where rumours fly (did Ralston really shoot himself in the foot to gain the insurance money?) and no one can keep a secret. The Floods live in a 'goldfish bowl' and of course Rubin will find out about the dress and Cora will know when he has seen Mavis Pruitt. The township is full of bigotry and ignorance – against Jews, Catholics and women like Mavis who refuse to conform. This is, after all, why Inge had to leave his hometown, as he had secrets he wished to keep. Existence in a small town, Inge shows, is not the innocent sweet idyll one might expect.

The play's central metaphor is again relayed in its title, an image Inge requests to be constantly present onstage '*as though it holds some possible threat to the characters*'.[53] There is deliberate irony in that '*possible*', as it turns out that all of the family's fears – of isolation, connection, poverty and loss of respect – are manageable by the close of the play, as Cora mounts those stairs toward her husband, and her children happily attend a movie together. Through love and honesty, the family have reconnected in more positive ways, and it is those outside this group – Lottie, Morris and Sammy – who end in darkness, as the shallowness of Lottie and Morris's marriage has been revealed and Sammy commits suicide. Once they have relinquished their petty differences, the Floods' household is based on love, and that has made all the difference. The opening description foreshadows this outcome: '*despite the moodiness of shadowy corners ... there is an implied comfort and hospitality*'.[54] Despite being set in the 1920s, the play closes with a 1950s image of a contented nuclear family.

There are further aspects that make it a 1950s play, with several jokes and references to psychiatry, and Cora's suggestion that 'Kids don't just "get over" things, in some magic way. These troubles stay with kids sometimes, and affect their lives when they grow up.'[55] Also, Reenie's schoolfriend Flirt's comments on her differences of opinion with her father evoke the growing cultural generation gap of that decade. While references to major 1920s movie stars Rudolph Valentino, Thomas Meighan and Norma Talmadge abound, Gloria Swanson and Jackie Coogan are also included, as they began in the 1920s but were still very popular in the 1950s. While nothing undercuts the play's historical setting, its strong message of conformity conveyed by Cora reflects a particularly 1950s concern: 'People distrust you if you don't play the same games they do, Sonny. It's the same after you grow up.'[56] While this suggests a darker aspect of 1950s culture, it is balanced against Inge's continued insistence on tolerance as Cora warns her children: 'There are all kinds of people in the world. And you have to live with them all. God never promised us any different. The bad people, you don't hate. You're only sorry they have to be.'[57]

Sammy becomes the official scapegoat of this society as that archetypal outsider, the Wandering Jew. He cannot change who he is, and his fear of loneliness and desire to belong dominate his life. While the Floods try to be tolerant, even they are ignorant regarding Judaism, thus emphasizing Sammy's separation. While Sammy enjoys socializing, he explains to Reenie how every time he goes to a party, 'I have to reason with myself to keep from feeling that the whole world's against me.'[58] His fears come true with the public rejection he receives at the Ralstons' party. He knows he is an outsider, yet Inge takes pains to show that he is far more friendly, thoughtful and engaging than Flirt's rather unpleasant (but socially acceptable) date, Punky Givens. Sammy plays with Sonny and is able to calm the boy's tantrum, he draws out the shy Reenie for a time, remembers the favours he promised her brother and senses straight away that Reenie is a far nicer person than the self-involved Flirt. His desire to be inclusive is demonstrated by his openly inviting Sonny to join them. His flighty mother, who continuously rejects him by sending him to a series of boarding schools, has only increased his sense of alienation – she does not even attend his funeral. She is the polar opposite of Cora, who takes too much interest, and her coldness makes Cora's overzealous mothering seem preferable.

Reenie may be shy, but she is not ignorant. She knows that Flirt is just using her, and her qualms about going with Sammy are not because he is Jewish, but because she would be uncomfortable with anyone. While she understandably finds her petulant brother annoying, she is a sensitive soul and loves her family. She worries over the expense of the dress and when her parents fight. Both Reenie and Sonny keep the wider society at arm's length, but while Reenie finds it intimidating, Sonny seems to find it simply repugnant, aside from his idealized film stars.

Many have noted Sonny's similarity to the young Inge – a boy smothered by his mother, who collects movie star pictures, likes pretty things and desires to perform: a 'speckled egg'[59] as Cora suggests to denote his difference. Sonny may not lack courage to fight the bullies – he sees himself as somewhat superior – but moreso he likes his mother to help as it proves her affection. His father is distanced, but this is mostly Sonny's fault, as he holds him at bay. His Oedipal rivalry[60] causes him positive delight when his father walks out and Cora turns to him. But Cora finds the strength to resist playing Jocasta, and turns her son adrift. While he is initially resentful, unlike Sammy, with whom he had felt a connection, Sonny is able to rebound and rise above his meagre years to claim a necessary independence. He has been quietly observing and knows how grown-ups behave. Smashing his piggy bank he declares, 'She's not going to boss me for the rest of my life.'[61] The shock of Sammy's death also leads him to draw closer to his sister and father, so he is not left alone.

Cora is more refined than her husband and from a moneyed background, but she loves him. Her love, however, can be smothering for all the family, as it manifests in a belittling jealousy toward her husband as she tries to bully him in the same way she bullies her children when she is not using her disempowering protectiveness against them. She envies her richer friends, which causes a rift in her marriage, but we are meant to excuse her for this as she was pampered as a child, her husband has not been fully honest with her and once he is she accepts the situation without complaint. She is also, despite her initial intolerance toward her own family, by the close, the greatest voice of tolerance in the play.

Though a little panicked over his growing obsolescence as a harness salesman, Rubin remains a vital man and has a spirit that allows him to survive with hope for the future as he finds himself a new career in selling farm machinery. As Cora reminds Sonny, 'He and his family were pioneers. They fought Indians and buffalo, and they settled this country when it was just a wilderness.'[62] He has the vibrancy and sense of purpose poor Morris lacks. Morris ambles aimlessly around the neighbourhood to escape his bothersome wife (to whom he has never given an orgasm and has not slept with in the past three years). Rubin got Cora pregnant within two weeks of dating and they still have regular sex. Also, unlike Morris, Rubin insists on 'being the man' in his own house; however, he also becomes willing to be more forthright with his wife. The third-act conversation they have, in which they reveal their worries to each other, allows each to see the other's point of view (similar to Cherie and Bo in *Bus Stop*) and allows them to reach a better understanding. She sees his fears about being able to properly provide for her, and he sees she is willing to accept less and be more supportive.

Money is important to these people – and not just to have enough, but to have more. Lottie still resents Cora for getting all of their family inheritance, as well as for her children and more vital marriage. Lottie is both ridiculous and insensitive, with her crazy ideas about Catholics, advice to Sammy to convert to Christian Science and the way she constantly puts words in her husband's mouth. But even Lottie, by the close, wins our sympathy, after she and Cora, too, have an honest heart to heart, and we learn of her soulless marriage, as she repents and offers to take Cora in.

Conclusion

Inge's four hit plays of the 1950s helped America reach a better understanding of not just the lives of Midwesterners, but ordinary people throughout the nation. His writing clearly hit a cultural nerve, making him the most attended playwright of the decade, and as Albert Wertheim asserts, 'Perhaps Inge's greatest achievement as a dramatist was to bring sexual matters to the stage in such a way that they were neither grotesque nor obscene but could be discussed in a theatre so as to illumine the private lives of the spectators.'[63]

While less attention has been afforded the potentially queer aspects of Inge's plays than his more outspoken contemporary Williams, there has been some recognition of how Inge incorporates the homosexual gaze toward characters like Turk, Hal and Bo: the first two especially, given they are directed to remove their shirts and each literally pose for someone to sketch them. Both Sammy Goldenbaum and Virgil have been recognized as the homosexual Other, and Hal has been viewed as a 'gay hustler'. Inge seems prescient in the way he so frequently destabilizes sexual and gender boundaries, granting agency to many of his female characters and softening the male. Robert Patrick also points our attention to the 'wistful, intellectual, alienated child or teenager' in Inge's work, such as Millie and Sonny, as 'little signature figures of the silent lonely gay' who, like Inge, would never find contentment in a world that denied them their true sexuality.[64]

As Inge explains, his drama was drawn from personal experience and offers 'some view of life that is peculiarly mine that no one else could offer in quite the same style and form'.[65] His work is unique and creative in ways too frequently overlooked, such as his attempt in *Picnic* and *Bus Stop* to present a group dynamic rather than centre on isolated protagonists. 'I regard a play as a composition rather than a story,' he explains, 'as a distillation of life rather than a narration of it.'[66] When viewing Inge's work, one should consider the overall texture and pattern rather than separate out single characters or moments for analysis. His work is character- rather than plot-driven, but his whole network of characters needs to be studied to get the full picture. Similar characters between plays are spun in different directions, to offer alternative outcomes. These echoes allow for the complex world of Inge to grow in dimension to a universal level that transcends its Midwest origin.

Inge's plays often feature women who are dealing with a man who has left them – Flora, Grace and Mavis Pruitt – and they manage fine without men by taking in lodgers, or finding work. There are also those whose husbands do not *physically* leave, but in staying the wives have subsequently suffered more, such as Lola and Lottie. Inge's men seem often prone to violence or overpowering forcefulness – Doc and Rubin, or Hal and Bo – as if they need to take the frustrations of their positions as men in a changing society out on the world; each also regrets his aggression. Rubin and Hal both describe a need to make their own way in the world for their own self-respect and the understanding that no one is going to give them what they want. Hal could also be seen as a version of Turk (posing for Millie as Turk did for Marie), and Bo wins the heart of Cherie as Hal did Madge by being entirely open. Meanwhile, Madge does the opposite of Marie in following her heart over a comfortable existence with a wealthy young man, while Cherie gets the best of both worlds: a man she loves who also happens to own his own ranch.

The list continues, for Mrs Potts is an older version of Lola in her kindness and the way she gets joy from watching young couples come together. Grace is a mix of Flo and Rosemary: like Flo, her husband has abandoned her but she has no children, and like Rosemary at the start, she enjoys her independence (as long as she has the occasional visit from Carl). Lottie is also like Rosemary, with the same lively brashness and crudity, full of herself and her own opinions. She bullies her husband Morris as Rosemary does Howard, even while she feels a similar dependency. But at least Lottie declines to dance with a young man, and like Lola, accepts her waistline and her age. There are also echoes of the alcoholic Doc Delaney in Dr Lyman, though the latter has had more sexual experience and let down; both drink to drown their disappointment with how their lives have turned out. In some way, Bo might reflect a younger version of Doc Delaney in his naïve certainty that he needs to marry any girl with whom he has slept, and Rubin and Cora were another shotgun wedding like the Delaneys, with a baby on the way. Elma is an echo of Millie – both intelligent, cultured young girls who have ambition, though while Millie decides to eschew the complications of love, Elma is longing for a relationship. Reenie is another version, shyer than Millie, but similarly having more brains than beauty and equally fearful of love. What ties all of these characters together is Inge's central understanding of 'the human need for love' and what Voss views as the playwright's central message: 'to accept life and make the "very best" of' whatever life might offer.[67] A message of comfort for the age of anxiety.

4

Stephen Sondheim: *West Side Story* (1957) and *Gypsy* (1959), with Collaborators Jerome Robbins and Arthur Laurents

Stuart Hecht

Stephen Sondheim

Born in 1930, Stephen Sondheim was a decade younger than his *West Side Story* collaborators. Though also gay and Jewish, Sondheim came from greater affluence and family angst. He attended military school, prep school and later Williams College, where he studied classical music with composer Milton Babbitt and wrote his first staged musicals. But his greatest education came from Oscar Hammerstein II, father to a schoolfriend of Sondheim's in Doylestown, PA, where newly divorced and socially ambitious Foxy Sondheim moved with her teenage son.

Hammerstein had a personal and direct influence on his son's young childhood friend, for whom Hammerstein became surrogate father and mentor, providing both a stable household and a stolid role model. Sondheim accompanied the Hammersteins to attend the latest Rodgers and Hammerstein openings, and sought to emulate the elder man. He began to write musicals of his own and asked Hammerstein to vet them. Hammerstein paid Sondheim the compliment of taking his work seriously and dissecting his work ruthlessly, which both men understood to be the path toward excellence and success. Both Foxy Sondheim's and the Hammersteins' social connections opened doors to Sondheim after graduation, as well as those of some college chums. He was an avid partygoer and expanded his circle of friends and contacts. He got a job in New York City writing television scripts and meanwhile composed words and music to what was to be his first Broadway musical, *Saturday Night*.[1]

Saturday Night was based on a script written by the brothers Epstein, the same duo who had written the screenplay to the film classic *Casablanca*. It was a romance set in the 1920s just before Wall Street crashed. As such it offered little of the substance audiences would later expect from the author's more mature work. One can see from this how important Sondheim's experience with *West Side Story* and *Gypsy* would prove in his growth and development. *Saturday Night* did not reach Broadway because its producer unexpectedly died, leaving Sondheim and his show adrift.[2]

Sondheim hesitated to accept Arthur Laurents's offer to write lyrics for *West Side Story*. It was his ambition to write both words and music; in fact, he favoured music over words. It was Hammerstein who counselled him to accept, pointing out the opportunity that working with top-notch talents like Robbins and Bernstein would mean to his ongoing training and development. Sondheim consequently accepted the offer.[3]

Hammerstein's work had set the stage for the musical's Golden Age. Sondheim would in turn prove the lynchpin between the first and second halves of the twentieth-century musical. The lessons he learned from Hammerstein greatly influenced his writing and career. Sondheim remembered his friend Burt Shevelove's comment that he thought Sondheim's entire career was an effort to write an effective ending to *Allegro*, a show Hammerstein had written from scratch, which was unorthodox in form and serious in tone, and which proved an unexpected flop. The teenage

Sondheim attended *Allegro*'s opening alongside the Hammerstein family and hence had a personal investment in that show's history. Furthermore, in *Allegro* Hammerstein experimented with an abstract plot presented thematically in a montage fashion, elements Sondheim would himself use repeatedly in his future musicals.[4]

Sondheim never worked directly with Hammerstein, though he consulted him often. He did, however, attempt to write lyrics for an increasingly bitter, insecure and then-alcoholic Richard Rodgers, as a posthumous favour to his mentor. Their *Do I Hear a Waltz?* proved tortuous to create as well as a commercial and artistic flop. While Sondheim benefitted early in his career from Hammerstein's support, he himself would not enter the Broadway scene until the mid-1950s, only a few years before Hammerstein's death. Sondheim never forgot Hammerstein's lessons, and struggled with them and occasionally against them when shaping his own shows and songs. Though he had some success finally writing words and music for *A Funny Thing Happened on the Way to the Forum* (which he dedicated to Hammerstein), Sondheim would not break through really until 1970 with his show *Company*. *Company* launched Sondheim's artistic dominance of the American musical in the 1970s, 1980s and 1990s in particular. It is safe to say that, in his heyday, Sondheim's musical theatre efforts and accomplishments eventually paralleled those achieved by his mentor Hammerstein some thirty years earlier: both men strove to stretch what constituted the musical form and both sought to bring thoughtful and provocative subject matter to the Broadway musical stage. Hammerstein began his Broadway career in the early 1920s; his protégé Sondheim would continue to write successfully for the musical stage well into the 1990s, perhaps beyond, an acolyte, perpetuating his mentor's example through to the end of the twentieth century and on into the twenty-first.

Curiously, Sondheim defines the musical's 'golden age' as ending in 1960, a half-decade earlier than is commonly used to mark this era's end. As 1960 also marked the death of Oscar Hammerstein, perhaps Sondheim's definition reflected a personal sense that that era matched the pinnacle of his mentor's own contributions and greatest success, from *Oklahoma!* (1943) to *The Sound of Music* (1959). Once Hammerstein was gone, so too were the sorts of shows that proved emblematic of that era.[5]

The collaborative process and musical theatre

Because plays are written to be performed, their impact, shape and meaning are defined in part by the elements of production. Directors can tilt meaning simply by whom they cast, as actors' personalities and biases colour their portrayals: hence the audience understanding of that character in situation. If it is indeed the case that theatre is a social art, with collaborators elaborating on the germ offered by the playwright, this collective dynamic is especially true of musical theatre where a finished work is the product of composer, lyricist, book author and choreographer/director especially. The boundaries of who did what often blur, especially when a show is most successful, leaving audiences with what appears to be a synthesis in which each and every element combines into an artistic whole in which no one element can be removed without toppling the entirety.

While in more recent years we have seen more conscious efforts to mix historical periods and styles, such as the use of rock and roll to tell the story of Andrew Jackson's 'bloody' career, this is a deliberate break with a more narrative tradition that sought unity of production, in which all the musical's elements were shaped in harmony in an effort to create a consistent onstage reality and tell a realistic tale. But there is nothing all that new about recent anachronistic tales: in the 1920s, for instance, the team of Rodgers and Hart created *A Connecticut Yankee*, a show whose humour depended upon historical anachronisms. Yet it was the same Richard Rodgers who two decades later teamed with Oscar Hammerstein to aim toward more artistically integrated musicals bent primarily on telling a story rather than merely spotlighting stars. The striving toward realism that corresponded with notions of unity is no longer absolute. The 2015 musical *Hamilton*, for example, featured a mixed race cast playing multiple historical characters, relying on colonial era clothing and props to define historical period, but was otherwise more an exercise in the eclectic and the deliberately and self-consciously theatrical. Some of this aesthetic freedom would grow out of the work of Stephen Sondheim in the 1970s and 1980s, along with the Brechtian influenced work of director Harold Prince. But during the musical's

Golden Age, realism ruled, even if the characters paradoxically and unrealistically broke out into song, with dance, words and story aesthetically aligned.

The twenty-year run of Golden Age musicals arose from several generations of theatre artists, as one group influenced the next and often overlapped. It started with *Oklahoma!* in 1943. Composer Richard Rodgers had previously partnered with lyricist Lorenz Hart; lyricist and adapter Oscar Hammerstein II had worked most notably with composer Jerome Kern and, with Kern, already stretched the possibilities of musicals into integrated terrain with their *Show Boat* (1927). In this case, 'integrated' means that *Show Boat* dealt with racial issues and featured an integrated cast, but it also revolutionized the musical form by aiming to create three-dimensional characters, with a strong narrative storyline, which wove together music with dialogue, with songs that reflected and commented upon the action of the play itself. Yet it was not until *Oklahoma!* that this book musical template became the dominant norm, replacing the often light-hearted, improbable musical comedies and revues of the previous few decades.

Stephen Sondheim emerged as part of the 1950s Broadway scene as a lyricist for *West Side Story* and helped top off the decade by again writing lyrics to another classic, *Gypsy*. He has described working on both shows as a sort of apprenticeship that formed the foundation for a career in which he would dominate American musical theatre, especially in the 1970s and 1980s. But during the 1950s, Sondheim should be viewed as a junior member of a collaborative team of musical theatre artists – from whom he learned, as well as to whom he contributed. As we shall see, the make-up of the group varied: aside from Sondheim as lyricist, it included at one time or another director/choreographer Jerome Robbins, the writing team of Betty Comden and Adolph Green, author Arthur Laurents and composers Leonard Bernstein or Jule Styne.

Jerome Robbins

The ongoing driving figure central to the collaborative teams that produced both *West Side Story* and *Gypsy* was Jerome Robbins. Over the course of two decades, Robbins spearheaded a string of significant musical productions that essentially corresponded to this Golden Age of Broadway musicals. Robbins did not begin that era, but his work spanned those same years. Jerome Robbins's first Broadway effort was *On the Town* in 1944, less than a year after *Oklahoma!*'s debut, and his last major show was *Fiddler on the Roof* in 1964, thereby closely matching that era in his own personal output.

Yet the work of Robbins and those with whom he chose to work differed in tone and outlook from the dominant musicals of this era. Theirs was a blend of high culture with the popular, often embracing subject matter that ran counter to the nation's more conservative, conformist societal norms of the post-war years. While Oscar Hammerstein II's work with Rodgers preached inclusive liberalism, shows like *Oklahoma!*, *Carousel*, *South Pacific* and *The King and I* were intended to reach a broader national audience, not just appeal to the generally more open-minded New York crowd. Their shows often featured unconventional romantic relationships, sometimes interracial, that would be conveniently resolved through a character's death, thereby ultimately preserving 1950s notions of homogeneity and wholesomeness. It is interesting to note that Rodgers and Hammerstein's greatest works appeared in the years before and after the height of McCarthyism and HUAC. Their last great success, *The Sound of Music* (1959), appeared near the decade's end, after the worst of the Red Scare witch-hunts was over.

The overwhelming popularity of *Oklahoma!* forced others to follow the 'musical play' model of Rodgers and Hammerstein during those years, often with remarkable results. Yet such shows often lacked the ethical bite of Hammerstein, content instead with only pleasing. Robbins and company also adhered to this form, but tended to use it to promote a liberal social awareness. They sought to infuse classical musical and dance elements into the Broadway musical form in order to improve it, to expand its quality and range, much as they sought to spotlight social issues and concerns.

Jerome Robbins worked with a range of artists on a variety of shows during his Broadway career, yet his most important and perhaps finest work centred on his collaborations with a core of theatre artists, who were members of his own generation and who largely shared his artistic and societal sensibilities. Robbins's first passion was classical dance and his ambition led him to work with

George Balanchine for what was to become the American Ballet Theatre. He joined the company as a dancer, but aspired to become a choreographer.[6]

Offered an opportunity, Robbins assembled a list of possible ideas for dances. In one of these he described a short dance about three sailors on leave in wartime New York City. 'Fancy Free' debuted in 1944 and proved a smash hit. Robbins revolutionized existing classical dance norms by weaving together ballet with 1940s popular dances, for a story set in then-contemporary urban America. His dance developed alongside music written by another unknown, composer Leonard Bernstein, whom Robbins recruited for the project. Bernstein's music matched Robbins' dance to perfection, similarly forming a hybrid of classical and current with theatrical flair and youthful exuberance.[7]

At the suggestion of scenic designer Oliver Smith, Robbins and Bernstein quickly set about to transform 'Fancy Free', expanding it into a Broadway show. Bernstein turned to Betty Comden and Adolph Green to write the lyrics and book. Bernstein had befriended Green while both were teenagers attending the same summer camp. Green later became an actor and, while auditioning around town, met another aspiring actor, Comden. Banding together they added two men and a still-teenaged Judy Tuvim (later Judy Holliday) to form a cabaret act that they called The Revuers. They wrote skits and songs, often light parodies of current events and trends, and performed often in Greenwich Village during the late 1930s and early 1940s. Occasionally, when their accompanist was unavailable, Leonard Bernstein would take over at the piano. So now Bernstein invited his old friends to join in the collaborative fun to help shape what became *On the Town* (1944). Comden and Green also performed in the show.

As Carol J. Oja has noted, *On the Town* not only reflected the creative foursomes' youth and exuberance, but also their shared political ideals. Much like the old Broadway chestnut, the 1890s' *A Trip to Chinatown*, *On the Town* featured a travelogue tour of New York City. But this 1940s version portrayed the city as now diverse, and, without any fanfare, featured a mixed cast. Playing Miss Turnstiles was Sono Osato, a Japanese-American whose father was then living in a California internment camp, even as her brother fought in the US Army. Osato was described as 'exotic', which was then often used to characterize non-WASP-looking starlets and models. While not as prominent, the *On the Town* cast also included several African-American dancer-singers, a practice unheard of at the time. *On the Town*'s touring company was not racially mixed, suggesting that the producers believed that what played in New York City would not play to less tolerant national audiences beyond.[8]

On the Town launched the Broadway careers of all four of its creative team, who then went on to work in combinations with other artists through the decade. In addition to designing classical dance, Robbins became in hot demand as a Broadway choreographer and director; among many projects, in 1951 he choreographed *The King and I*, most notably expressing the team's liberal views in his Siamese-style ballet version of *Uncle Tom's Cabin*. In the early 1950s Bernstein also returned to Broadway, working again with old pals Comden and Green to create *Wonderful Town*, another ode to New York City. Around the same time, Jerome Robbins decided to 'perform solo', singing names to appease HUAC, betraying friends and colleagues to preserve his own career.[9]

While Robbins's testifying alienated many, he still found acceptance among his circle of artists and friends. In the early 1950s he was in a romantic relationship with actor Montgomery Clift who had been approached to act in *Romeo and Juliet*. Robbins had the idea of transforming the Shakespeare play into a Broadway musical and placing it in contemporary New York City. The blend of past and present, of mixing cultures and creating another hybrid of high culture with the popular was very much in line with what he had previously done in *On the Town*. He turned again to Leonard Bernstein and the two formulated the idea of a modern-day *Romeo and Juliet* but with New York's teenage Irish Catholics at war with the city's young Jews; they planned to call it *East Side Story*. There are elements of this early idea sprinkled about the *West Side Story* score, such as the very opening when one gang member enters accompanied by what could only be described as the orchestral equivalent of a ram's horn (*shofar*), traditionally blown at Rosh Hashanah to trumpet the arrival of the Jewish New Year. But the two men put this project aside until Robbins later read of the rise of Puerto Rican immigrants in New York and, like so many before and since, instances of gang violence. Robbins brought this to Bernstein's attention who liked that it meant he could compose another strain of music, this with a decidedly Latin beat. Thus *East Side Story* would be transformed into *West Side Story*.

Bernstein was simultaneously writing a light operetta with Lillian Hellman (book) and Richard Wilbur (lyrics) based on Voltaire's classic, *Candide*. Whereas Bernstein's music was light and bubbly (according to Stephen Sondheim), Hellman's script was a heavy-handed attack on McCarthyism.[10] It seemed ironic that Bernstein composed an anti-HUAC piece while at the same time collaborating with Robbins, who had so recently named names! Musically, some material Bernstein originally intended for *Candide* wound up in *West Side Story*, and vice versa, despite the sharply contrasting settings, styles and stories.[11]

Arthur Laurents

Brooklyn-born Arthur Laurents (nee Levine) attended Cornell and later New York University before writing scripts for the radio. Drafted into the army, Laurents spent the Second World War in Astoria, New York, authoring training films with the likes of director George Cukor and actor William Holden, important connections into theatre and film. Immediately after the war, Laurents's first play, *Home of the Brave*, the story of a psychologically damaged GI, was produced on Broadway. Though gay, Laurents had a romantic relationship with ballet dancer Nora Kaye and, through her, met Jerome Robbins. In 1948, Laurents first worked with Robbins to develop *Look, Ma, I'm Dancin'!*, which ran half a year on Broadway and cemented their professional relationship.

Throughout his career writing for stage and screen and also directing on Broadway, Laurents promoted left-wing issues and explored gay and gender rights, but especially favoured the conflicts and pressures of the normative versus the deviant, arguing heavily for the rights of the latter. Perhaps his most revealing creation was the film *The Way We Were* (1973), which traces the unlikely romance between a handsome, conventional WASP (played by Robert Redford) and a strident, outspoken socialist Jew (played by Barbra Streisand), with sympathies going toward Streisand's character.[12]

Because Comden and Green were unavailable, Robbins instead recruited Arthur Laurents at a Los Angeles poolside party, inviting him to write the book to *West Side Story*. Bernstein was originally going to write the show's lyrics, but while attending a party in New York City, Laurents ran into a young, still unknown author of his acquaintance named Stephen Sondheim. Apparently, Laurents smacked his own forehead realizing that Sondheim could be involved in the project, and invited him on the spot. It is unclear just how Bernstein felt about this, but he welcomed the young man into their collaborative mix, willing to share authorial credits.[13]

Stephen Sondheim did not work alone. Even though he eventually did reach a point in his career where he wrote both words and music for his shows, Sondheim relied heavily upon working collaboratively. It was more than a question of having a supportive circle of like-minded artists; Sondheim has noted that he was dependent especially upon the book writer to provide the characters, plots and themes upon which he could subsequently elaborate through his lyrics and tunes, as he acknowledged in a 2010 interview:

> The sorts of musical I write are narrative musicals. Even when there's no story line they're about character. It's something I learned from Oscar Hammerstein. So it depends on the librettist. Every show I've ever done starts with the librettist. We talk a lot, and the characters, the songs; everything comes out of, from, the librettist. In a sense a songwriter for this kind of show is as much of an interpreter as the conductor is, or a musician is, or an actor is. The librettist makes something out of nothing; the songwriter, and the director and the actors, they make something out of something.
>
> Now, a songwriter, because I'm also creating out of nothing, in a sense, is partly a creator. But I don't create out of whole cloth. Somebody has invented a story and characters, and I contribute to that story. Sometimes when we talk I make suggestions that are picked up or used, but still it's his or her work. And so, it's not inspiration, it's working with somebody who's invented a story.[14]

Over the years, Sondheim has worked with a string of librettists. It began with Arthur Laurents; later came Burt Shevelove and Larry

Gelbart, George Firth, Hugh Wheeler, James Goldman, James Lapine, John Weidman and David Ives. Sondheim also spoke of wanting to write with British playwright Peter Shaffer, which did not come to fruition. But Sondheim's literary apprenticeship, working on both *West Side Story* and *Gypsy*, came from working directly with Arthur Laurents in this capacity, perhaps laying the groundwork for his future authorial collaborations.[15]

Sondheim came to admire Laurents's skill as a librettist, noting the writer's ability to craft characters, language and scenes with a tempered efficiency, adept at getting the point across clearly while setting up and leaving room to allow the given song to maximize its emotional effectiveness. It was Laurents who condensed Shakespearean material into the stuff of contemporary teen gangs, such as 'from womb to tomb'. This in turn gave Sondheim the characters and idiom to explore and elaborate thereby making his own contributions.[16]

West Side Story (1957)

Two rival teenage street gangs in 1950s New York City. The Jets are made up of self-styled Americans, and the Sharks are comprised of recent Puerto Rican immigrants. No longer a Jet, Tony falls in love with the Puerto Rican Maria, both hoping to escape the mean streets and forge a new, better life. The Jets' leader is Riff, Tony's best friend; the Sharks are led by Maria's brother, Bernardo, whose girlfriend is Anita. The two gangs plan a rumble that Tony attempts to stop, but in the confusion Bernardo kills Riff, and an enraged Tony retaliates by killing Bernardo. When Maria learns Tony killed her brother, she first pushes him away but then realizes she still loves him. Maria has been promised to Chino, who plans to avenge Bernardo by killing Tony. Maria persuades Anita to warn Tony to stay away. When Anita goes to the soda shop to do so, Jets' gang members assault her. In a rage she lies, saying that Maria is dead. With nothing to live for, Tony goes to the rumble where Chino shoots him dead, though not before Tony sees Maria is still alive. Maria mourns over Tony's body, and when the gangs threaten to fight, Maria takes Chino's gun and threatens them all, causing an end to their rivalry and cycle of violence.

Sondheim has said much about working with Leonard Bernstein on *West Side Story*. Certainly Bernstein had a flair for language and no doubt hoped that working on *West Side Story* would replicate the collective youthful joy he had found a decade earlier working on *On the Town*. It seems that Laurents and Sondheim were game, though the material here was far more challenging and serious. Also, in the years since *On the Town* (and naming names for HUAC), Jerome Robbins had grown increasingly defensive and insecure. He wanted perfection and despaired or ran away when that seemed unattainable. Robbins's obsessed insistence and often-ruthless means short-circuited any chance of a return to the joyous working conditions experienced a dozen years earlier.[17]

Robbins famously terrorized the cast and co-creators of *West Side Story*. Wanting to maximize its impact, he divided the cast in two, with rival gang members forbidden to cross the stage into the other gang's territory. He demanded a realistic intensity from his actors, even as he himself designed highly stylized movements as their choreography. Carol Lawrence played Maria and remembered that when things grew too intense it was Bernstein who would pull the cast to him at the piano and have them simply sing, letting off steam in the process. Other times Robbins would stand directly behind Bernstein at the keyboard, seemingly massaging the composer's shoulders, almost willing music to flow from him. But Robbins could be caustic and was the one person whom Bernstein feared. Following one performance on the road, before opening on Broadway, Robbins interrupted Bernstein, who was conducting the orchestra in the pit, and ridiculed sections of music, correcting the maestro on how it needed to be improved, thereby humiliating him publically. Rather than fight back, Bernstein followed Robbins's dicta, trusting Robbins's talent and theatrical know-how, even if stung by his abrasive methods.[18]

Sondheim has said that Bernstein favoured 'purple prose': extravagantly emotional, highly poetic phrases that matched his soaring musical score. But that was not Sondheim's temperament or taste. Sondheim aimed for greater authenticity, akin to the lessons of Oscar Hammerstein, and was by his nature more sceptical and reserved, as well as highly disciplined about writing for specific meaning. Sondheim was never sold on phrases he wrote that were insistently endorsed by Bernstein. For instance, in the song 'Tonight' he has Tony and Maria sing how 'the world is just an address' which Sondheim later challenged as being too abstract and philosophical for teenage street-kid characters. He also subsequently mocked the repetition of the name 'Maria' in the song of that name, finding it essentially specious even if it matched Bernstein's emotional melody. As the show evolved, so too did Sondheim's confidence and understanding; it was later in the process that he made his special mark with the songs 'America' and 'Officer Krupke'. Right before *West Side Story* opened, Bernstein generously removed his own name as co-lyricist for the show, thereby giving full credit (and more royalties) to newcomer Sondheim.

Jerome Robbins and Leonard Bernstein sought, with *West Side Story*, to blend what they viewed as the 'long hair' (high culture) with popular culture. Hence Robbins used classically-based dance to express gang life, just as Bernstein blended classical refrains with then-current jazz. Through their efforts they hoped to make *West Side Story* into a more sophisticated musical than that which had come before it, moving the form itself toward greater heights. Curiously, neither they nor Sondheim considered *West Side Story* a success, believing it failed in this mission. Nor was it a commercial stage success. In fact, the show only began to make money after its film version appeared several years later and it thus reached a larger viewing audience. But even after this success, Sondheim still thought the show fell short, that it portrayed characters and situation in two-dimensional terms, that it lacked the necessary subtlety or depth. In contrast, in 2007 an elderly Arthur Laurents came up with the idea to direct a revival of the show, this time having the Puerto Rican characters sing their songs in Spanish, translated by Lin-Manuel Miranda. Laurents felt this gave the show greater authenticity and power; it ran on Broadway for over two years.[19]

The 1950s in America is remembered as an era of homogeneity and domesticity. As had happened following the First World War, post-Second World War America experienced a reactionary turn, though exacerbated by fear of the atomic bomb and communist territorial aggression under Stalin. It was the height of the Cold War and at home the House Un-American Activities Committee (HUAC) ruthlessly sought to ferret out traitors and, in doing so, polarized the nation. Nativist fears translated to persecution of those who seemed 'different' (ideologically, ethnically, religiously, lifestyles) and implicitly demanded conformity to traditional WASP, middle-class values. Eisenhower's presidency is remembered for fostering peace and building the economy, but by the decade's end he warned of a rising 'military-industrial complex'. It became the era of the 'organization man', of gray-flannel-suited, interchangeable corporate clones, of smiling television suburban stay-at-home moms who baked while wearing high heels and with a string of pearls accompanying their apron strings. No more Rosie the Riveter or mention of civil rights, only a litany of families blithely negotiating pre-fab situations.

Broadway musicals pretty much fell into line. Mid-1950s shows include *Kismet*, *The Pajama Game*, *Plain and Fancy*, *Silk Stockings*, *Damn Yankees*, *Bells Are Ringing*, *Peter Pan* and *The Music Man*, a blend of down-home Americana and fantasy and, for the most part, lily white and uncontroversial. And as wonderful a show as *My Fair Lady* is, note how creators Lerner and Loewe eliminated the unromantic, politicized ending of George Bernard Shaw's *Pygmalion*, the original play, to satisfy the era's thirst for the comforting happy ending instead. Even the Bernstein–Comden–Green musical *Wonderful Town* lacked the ethnic pizzazz of their earlier *On the Town*. It was all pleasant, non-threatening escapist entertainment of a decidedly two-dimensional nature.

West Side Story thus ran counter to 1950s American norms. In many ways it was a radical break with the culture of its times as well as its then-dominant societal self-image. Unlike other hits of the decade (aside from *My Fair Lady*), most shows featured everyday American characters in everyday situations, mostly mooning about their romantic relationships, even as they helped resolve labour strikes or taught small-town kids to play band instruments. It was mostly small-time life that could take place in the Missouri of a Harry Truman or Dwight Eisenhower's Kansas. In sharp contrast, *West Side Story* was set in contemporary slum New York City.

Unlike the pool-playing teens of River City, in *West Side Story* the American youngsters carried switchblades and displayed racism as they fought over turf. The presence of Puerto Rican teens showed abrupt ethnic changes in the American vista, a new generation of immigrants who seemed unwilling to assimilate to American ways – so much for the 1950s depiction of a homogenous, WASP nation. Furthermore, unlike the general respect enjoyed by the adults in other 1950s musicals, here the adults were revealed to be increasingly helpless in the face of youth violence. No flashy uniform or shiny trombones would appease these discontents; violence seemed inevitable. And if 1950s culture preached the goodness, power and effectiveness of democratic America, a far different view of the institutional system is gleaned from Sondheim's mocking 'Officer Krupke', which catalogues how out of touch and ineffective governmental agencies actually were in the face of generational, urban unrest. Similarly, Sondheim's lyrics for 'America' portrayed recent immigrants as questioning the American Dream, surely a first for the Broadway stage and, like 'Officer Krupke', a challenge to how 1950s America generally chose to view itself.

West Side Story also portrayed women differently than other shows of the decade. Though perhaps relatively two-dimensional, and filled out in part by the effusive beauty of Bernstein's music, Maria and Anita (and for that matter the character Anybodys) are not prototypical because they are all rebels. Maria is a teenage, Latina 'good girl', and yet once in love with Tony is willing to break a string of rules: ethnic, traditional, gender, social. Essentially she remains 'good' because she is still guided by romantic love that is epitomized by her and Tony's mock wedding in the bridal shop, where they sing 'One Hand, One Heart'. Perhaps the tragedy of *West Side Story*, in 1950s American eyes, was not so much the racism and gang violence as it was the lost promise of true love. Anita, as Maria's foil, is a passionate spitfire, aggressively sexy and bluntly honest. Unlike the chaste Maria who dances innocently among the mannequins, Anita kicks up her heels as she dares to stand up to the men's authority in 'America'. Though sexual, Anita is not a whore, as demonstrated in the scene where she is almost raped in the soda shop. She is shown as independent and strong, a perfect target for the nativist Jets' intolerant efforts to dominate. Strong women were not unusual on the 1950s musical stage: think Marion the Librarian from *The Music Man* or Babe Williams from *The Pajama Game*. But both of them essentially still operated within their respective WASP societies; Anita is rebelliously independent and decidedly not demure. Anybodys is a gender-bending tomboy who wants to be part of the Jets, the antithesis of the suburban or small-town good girl popularized (or proselytized?) in 1950s mass culture.

Another distinguishing feature of *West Side Story* is its use of language. Sondheim notes how this peculiar language was initiated by Laurents's libretto and that he then elaborated upon it in his lyrics. Much as Abe Burrows (book) and Frank Loesser (lyrics) had elaborated upon Damon Runyan's unique style of Broadway gangster speech to create *Guys and Dolls*' distinctive stage world, so too did Laurents and Sondheim invent a 1950s teenage argot. There are specific 1950s pop culture references to comic books and sci-fi space travel, for instance, along with jazz rhythmic sayings ('from womb to tomb') that encapsulate the American teenager's special, private, in-group world. It is Shakespeare as New York City slang. While that may have resonated with original audiences for the show, as time has passed this has preserved *West Side Story* as somehow timeless. Its artificial language creates a poetic bubble that helps encapsulate and preserve it as its own special world and hence it remains timeless.[20]

When *West Side Story* premiered, audiences proved unresponsive until the song 'America', when they reportedly sat up and took notice. With its lively Latin rhythms, the dance was exhilarating. But it was the lyrics that drove the song. Not only were they clever, but they also demonstrated how sharp differences of opinion existed among the Puerto Rican gang members and their women. Granted the sexually charged subtext of the number, as women challenge the men and vice versa, the pointed word duels also voiced distinctive personalities and encouraged audiences to view the Latin newcomers in a far more complex and sympathetic light, rather than view them as stereotypes. The lyrics allow the audience a mental picture of a foreign land, one with 'tropical breezes' and 'bullets flying' which, whether accurate or not, makes us visitors to their land. This also gives the Sharks an identifiable cultural identity, and not just one serving as faceless strangers. Hence the audience can root for the Puerto Ricans more evenly with the more 'American' Jets, rather than automatically take sides against them. Sondheim achieves all of this using lively wit, making the song as entertaining and fun as it is informative. Since Sondheim's words are intelligent and sharp, so too do we come to view these recent immigrants in those same terms, rather than as ignorant and dangerously incomprehensible. The words encourage us to respect and understand well beyond what would otherwise only be a catchy, foot-stomping, skirt-snapping *tempo du huapango* dance number.

Sondheim may initially have been susceptible to Leonard Bernstein's pressures to write excessively emotional lyrics, akin to his melodies. But if Sondheim made such false steps early on, he gradually gained confidence and with this his artistic footing, writing words to later songs that packed more punch with greater efficiency and theatrical impact.

Sondheim later wrote of his *West Side Story* experience:

> [L]ooking back ... I became aware of how my growing confidence over the two years of writing the show allowed me to improve my work; the later lyrics, like 'Something's Coming,' 'Gee, Officer Krupke' ... have a relaxed tone which is markedly less self-conscious than the earlier ones.[21]

A song like 'Something's Coming' explodes naturally from Tony, unforced and true, yet deliberately incomplete, much like Tony himself, who has no idea what is to come:

> Could be ...
> Who knows? ...
> There's something due any day –
> I will know right away,
> Soon as it shows.
> It may come cannonballing down through the sky,
> Gleam in its eye,
> Bright as a rose.
> Who knows?[22]

The lyrics are urgent and concise, leaving open any possibility thanks to the incomplete sentences and, even when completed, affording only quick glimpses. Tony does not know what will be, only that he will recognize it when he sees it. And he will know before we the audience will. It is beyond his control, happening so suddenly (cannonballing) that he can only react to it when it arrives. But he – and the insistent Bernstein rhythms – believes it will be positive and exhilarating. It will be 'a miracle', 'something good', 'gonna be great!'[23] His enthusiasm feels typical of many youths of the era. Sondheim uses sharp, electric words like 'shock' and 'knock' immediately followed by teenage words that make anything possible, 'catch the moon / one-handed catch' à la Mickey Mantle, blending baseball with myth. Then, as suddenly as the song was upon us, it quickly and unexpectedly evaporates with a lyrical return: 'Who knows?' followed by a hopeful 'Maybe tonight'.[24] The last word, 'tonight', links directly to his balcony scene with Maria, where they, combined, sing the song 'Tonight', thus answering his question of what exactly is coming his way. But as with their counterparts in *Romeo and Juliet*, Tony's connecting with Maria 'tonight' will lead to multiple deaths tomorrow; love followed by death answer the prescient wondering of 'what' in 'Something's Coming'.

Act One ends spectacularly with the gamut of characters simultaneously singing in counterpoint of what 'tonight' means to each of them: love, a rumble, hope, revenge – all things that are realized in Act Two. They are all clearly still kids: aggressive, passionate and seemingly immortal – fuelled by yesterday, alert to tonight, oblivious to tomorrow.

Sondheim ends *West Side Story* by connecting back to the first act's 'Something's Coming'. Tony and Maria tried to escape hate-filled pasts, to create together a loving future. Sadly, their dream dies with Tony in Maria's arms as she sings 'Somewhere'. Here Sondheim inverts the fast approaching 'something' into dark inevitability, building around the repeated yet still elusive word 'some'. The once hoped-for 'something' now becomes a despairing 'somehow, someday' and finally, 'somewhere', as Bernstein's dirge-like evaporating chords match Tony's final breath. The driving youthful energy of 'Something's Coming' has led, at best, to a posthumous reunion for the two lovers at 'some' unknown future time and in 'some' unknown, hoped for better place.

Meantime, 'Gee, Officer Krupke' is the Jets' counterpart to the Shark's song, 'America'. But where 'America' is a can-you-top-this sort of lyric, hence self-consciously clever, the humour of 'Krupke' comes from the gang members' self-conscious awareness of the failure of the social welfare system meant to help them. Through song they provide an astute step-by-step account of systemic dysfunction, mocking it fiercely at every turn. When writing the song, Sondheim particularly relished the chance to end it with the gang giving the cop a defiant 'Fuck you!' But fear of obscenity laws aborted this in favour of Bernstein's suggested alternative, 'Krup you!'[25] which Sondheim acknowledged to be better as it was more 'kidlike' and in keeping with the Jets.[26]

The gang members pass around each verse like a football, tossed from one to the next, each member thus spotlighted, each knowing exactly what happens next in the system. It culminates with them singing the last chorus together, united by a shared familiarity with this institutionalized incompetence. Aside from life on the street, resisting this authority unites them as much as opposing rival gangs. The cop Sergeant Krupke may be the local muscle, but he is only the immediate face of all those whom he represents, in organizational order, according to Sondheim: first the Judge, then the Psychologist, followed by the Social Worker, then finally the Warden. The song then echoes what the boys have no doubt heard, as they pass it amongst themselves to form a summary verbal montage:

Diesel   The trouble is he's crazy.

A-Rab   The trouble is he drinks.

Baby John   The trouble is he's lazy.

Diesel   The trouble is he stinks.

A-Rab   The trouble is he's growing.

Baby John   The trouble is he's grown![27]

The 'answers' swirl and contradict. One shibboleth runs counter to the next: adults proclaiming opinions, not a one bothering to ask the kids themselves. Opinions are not solutions. Frustration leads only – and ultimately – to incarceration. But they will return to the street and the cycle will begin again. It is so sad it is funny. The gang members deride and mock, too cynical for those so young and yet, in Sondheim's hands, the song itself explains the cynicism, making it only natural and inevitable. Besides, if the kids had tried to give honest answers to those in the system, their words would have been overlooked or ignored in favour of proclaimed professional agendas by the powers that be. So the teen gang members are as frustrated with the outcome as their adult supervisors. The song is the result: a litany of discouragement and scorn ... and anger. Yes, it is funny, but it is also caustic, impersonal and cruel. If it were not true, no one would possibly believe it. Their collective experience has only fed their disillusionment and rage, as the song teeters on, careening out of control. Its consequences will soon erupt in the deadly rumble, just around the bend. Bernstein apparently wrote the entire song before Sondheim added a word, yet the lyrics suggest movement and action, not just ideas. There is nothing contrived here; Sondheim uses his cleverness, rather than simply flaunting it, to illuminate and explain restless generational violence. This was an aspect of society that was gaining increasing attention during the 1950s, which no doubt helped to make the show feel extremely relevant to those in attendance.

Gypsy (1959)

Sondheim himself quickly moved on from *West Side Story* to work on *Gypsy*. In fact, he and Laurents began work on it even while doing out-of-town touch-up work on *West Side Story*, before that show opened. Where *West Side Story*'s historical place took years to be established, *Gypsy* quickly gained acclaim as one of the finest musicals ever written.

The show begins in the early 1920s as Momma Rose abandons her father's house to launch her two small daughters into show business. She builds a vaudeville act mostly around daughter June, with Louise filling in. The act does well, and along the way Rose meets a publicity man, Herb, persuading him to join her and help boost the act. Fed up with her pushy mother, June runs off with a boy in the act. Time passes and we see that, rather than cede defeat, Rose has turned to the far less talented Louise. Their bookings get worse even as vaudeville is dying. They end up in Kansas where Rose proposes to Herbie, who wants her to break up the act. When Rose considers booking Louise into a burlesque house as a stripper, Herbie walks out. Louise becomes successful as 'Gypsy Rose Lee' and no longer needs Rose, who, having lost June, Herbie and now Louise, suffers a breakdown done in song. Revivals of the show have offered differing endings, ranging from Louise welcoming her back to Louise rejecting Rose entirely.

The team for *Gypsy* was largely the same as for *West Side Story*. Robbins again envisioned the show while simultaneously directing and doing its choreography; Arthur Laurents again wrote the book and Sondheim the lyrics. Leonard Bernstein's conducting career drew him away and so Jule Styne was recruited to write the score, and Jo Mielziner was brought in to do the stage design. Originally, Sondheim was to do both music and lyrics, but star Ethel Merman had just come off a flop and was nervous about trusting her next project to a still-relative unknown. Sondheim at first bristled, but again consulted with Hammerstein who again urged him to do it. Hammerstein felt that it was a new and critical skill to write for a particular star personality (and voice) and that this experience would in the long run prove especially beneficial to his young protégé. Styne, on the other hand, was an old pro at writing for stars and did prove an outstanding exemplar to Sondheim in what to use, what not and why. If one can hear elements of the future *Sweeney Todd* in Sondheim's work on *West Side Story*, one can certainly hear echoes of *Gypsy* in Sondheim's future show, *Follies*.[28]

Jule Styne was a master of the Broadway hit. He lacked Robbins's and Bernstein's classical emphasis, even though he was a child prodigy. Styne wrote for Hollywood before coming to New York; his song 'Three Coins in the Fountain' had been Oscar nominated. He had already worked with Comden and Green, and would team with them again in the late 1950s, along with their old Revuers chum, Judy Holliday, to create *Bells Are Ringing*. He had also teamed with Jerome Robbins to write some songs for his *Peter Pan*. Styne's skill at writing for stars would again be on display a few years after *Gypsy* when he composed for Barbra Streisand in his show *Funny Girl*. So though he did not share the generational ties to Robbins and Laurents, as Bernstein had, he nevertheless proved in harmony with them as a team, including lyricist Sondheim.

Gypsy was based upon the memoirs of striptease queen Gypsy Rose Lee. It was widely understood that Lee's account was inaccurate and self-serving, but that did not deter Robbins and company. In fact, it gave them greater license to make of it what they would. Gypsy and her sister June Havoc differed greatly on actual events, but both agreed on the large shadow cast by their mother: a ruthless, hard-driving stage mother named Rose Hovick. The collaborative team especially liked that rumours had it that Rose was bisexual, adding to her possibilities as an anti-heroine. Though the show is set in the 1920s and beyond, it spoke effectively to late 1950s New York musical theatre audiences.

It seems an odd collection of characters upon which to base a Broadway show. Though a celebrity, Gypsy Rose Lee was a star of burlesque, a neither conventional nor wholesome livelihood. True, she was brilliant and even later often appeared on television game shows, but her life was unorthodox and she adorned it with myth to heighten its appeal. While the musical bears her name, in the hands of Robbins, Laurents, Sondheim and Styne it centres far more on the character of her mother, created as a star vehicle for that star of Broadway stars, Ethel Merman. With Merman playing Mama Rose, the character Gypsy had little chance to shine, though she needed to do so enough for the show to work, for ruthless, conniving, obsessively driven Rose needs a dramatic surrogate. It appears early on that that job will be filled by talented daughter Baby June, the object of Rose's ambitions and dreams. June eventually runs off with a boy in the act, leaving Rose to zero in instead on the less-talented Louise. Though regularly ignored, Louise functions as Rose's dramatic foil. When Rose's focus centred on show-biz June, Louise was freer to enjoy a more normal life. She is something of a tomboy, but is sweet and innocent and even sings to her pets. It is Rose's relentless insistence that eventually lands them in burlesque, the lowest rung of vaudeville; it is Rose's ongoing pressure that forces Louise's transformation into Gypsy Rose Lee, who removes her clothes while steeling her heart, thereby embodying a complete shift from innocence to cynical knowing. Never having experienced parental love, Gypsy now enjoys public lust instead, so she pushes aside her suddenly clinging, desperate mother in an act of emancipation.

How interesting that in *Gypsy* freedom is only achieved through escape from domesticity. Mama Rose flees her father and her familial responsibilities for a life on the road. But ironically she does so by taking her daughters along with her, which is to say she creates an alternative family model. She is still their mother, ostensibly providing for their welfare. Aside from their travails travelling through space and time on the vaudeville circuit, the only other storyline was Rose's ongoing relationship with Herbie, who becomes her surrogate husband and the girls' surrogate father. So the family is complete. It even survives June's abandonment. Without June, the act downwardly spirals, the last option being to present Louise on a burlesque stage. Herbie can no longer take it and walks out. Thus Rose is rather like Brecht's Mother Courage, whose economic obsession alienates friends and leads her makeshift family into dangers which ultimately destroy it. It is Mother Courage's daughter Katrin who is maternal and courageous, but her mother's antics directly caused her demise. So too is it the case with 'Mama' Rose and daughter Louise. Louise triumphs as Gypsy Rose Lee, but she does so by destroying her true inner self – once marked by sensitivity, generosity and love – turning instead to displaying skin, and only her outer shell.

The musical ultimately shows the means by which Rose realized her own fantasies through her daughter Louise. By hook or by crook, Rose created 'Gypsy'. Rose's narcissism meant that she never really saw either daughter as existing separate from her; robbing each of their own lives, it was then easy for Rose to impose her own identity or desires upon them both. Perhaps early on her dream was dressed up in little girl sugar and spice, wanting to achieve the Shirley Temple-style stardom of child stars. In the end, as the years passed, this veneer is stripped away (fittingly) to reveal Rose's dreams as the tawdry exhibitionist stuff of burlesque instead.

Gypsy portrays Rose's ideal of living a gypsy life. A gypsy was the antithesis of America's 1950s domestic ideal; gypsies travelled from place to place, never having a real home, operating on the fringe of towns, relying on guile to fleece the locals. They dressed extravagantly, enjoyed their exotic roles as outsiders, favoured amoral sensuality rather than the respectable or the responsible, always one step ahead of the law. Theirs was an exciting life of non-conformity and do-as-you-please, rather than one of fitting in sheepishly, keeping one's head down and nose clean. There are strong links between gypsies and actors, as both are seen as wandering performers, generally scorned, distrusted by the status quo. Like gypsies, actors live bohemian lives, which is to say they are free: free to be different, independent, unorthodox, self-expressive and hedonistic. Like another 1950s counter-culture icon, Jack Kerouac, gypsies prefer a life 'On the Road'. Rose's daughters resent living gypsy lives and just wish that 'mama was married', as they favoured settling down and living as a conventional family. But even their protestations cannot sidetrack the freedom and empowerment sought by their freewheeling mother.

As a show business story, *Gypsy* provided its creators with opportunities to utilize 'onstage' lives as well as 'offstage' lives. One wonders where performance starts and ends, which is to say what part of Mama Rose is real and what part a lie? This is a far more complex creative conundrum for Laurents and Sondheim in particular than was found working on *West Side Story*, where the characters are all flat, drawn to fit the needs of the story and little more. Aside from Tony and Maria's rebellion, favouring love over ethnicity, they are all fairly simple and predictable in their actions. They gain their emotional depth largely thanks to the sweep of Bernstein's music; not even Sondheim's lyrics display much real feeling. Audiences may sympathize with these young people's plight, yet, given the story's *Romeo and Juliet* roots, even the outcome can be assumed in advance, so little surprise there either.

Gypsy's characters, on the other hand, are not so readily predictable. Every character in this show has inner conflicts of some sort and takes actions that audiences do not expect. In the case of Herbie, that he stays as long as he does is perhaps as much a surprise to audiences as the fact that he leaves when he does – and why he does. Girly-girl June seems destined for stardom, but escapes to romance; shy tomboy Louise winds up a highly successful sex symbol, cold and calculating. At the centre of it all is that mass of contradictions, Rose. The challenge for the show's creators was to explore these contradictions, truthfully and with detail, while at the same time retaining audience interest and sympathy. This meant acknowledging each character's shortcomings and defining them as recognizable human failings, even those of Rose who becomes increasingly monstrous as the story unfolds. They counterbalanced this by relying upon the show business scenes, both onstage and offstage, to provide relief, while also contextualizing and perhaps justifying the character's poor behaviour. By pursuing a life on the stage, real-life qualities are corrupted; the business of the stage requires this sacrifice, as goodness gives way to expediency and compromise.[29]

A song like 'Small World Isn't It?' could be written for *The Music Man* in its small-town simplicity and seeming candour. The tune is warm and catchy, the sentiments found in Sondheim's words are modest and promise conventional domesticity. It is only that Rose's subsequent actions completely belie this, that she is only interested in a life on the road, not in settling down, that we in retrospect read that song as a sort of sales pitch rather than an opening to true romance. Sentimentality is something that sells, not something actual or to be followed. Sondheim and Styne also make great use of the act's theme song to chart the family's gradual deterioration into seediness: 'Let Me Entertain You' begins as a simple kid's song, a childish appeal for audience approval, an asking for applause, relatively innocent in intention. But as the daughters grow up, the same song takes on other meanings. As a children's song they gradually outgrow it and it comes to be as ill-fitting as a hand-me-down, awkward and tired. In the end it becomes Louise-turned-stripper-Gypsy's theme song, sung as she removes articles of clothing, provocatively one item at a time. So this anthem to childhood efforts to please is similarly transformed into an anything-but-innocent come on, used now to tease and please. The irony here is that it is essentially the same, that what Rose and vaudeville were asking her daughters to do was to capitalize on their attractiveness rather than acknowledge it privately and maternally, without any thought of fame and fortune. So Louise does mature into just who Rose intended all along, and the corresponding loss of innocence was always part of the plan, consciously or not.

For 1950s audiences, a stripper-based biography musical would suggest it had a heavy emphasis on sex, adding to its commercial appeal. If post-Second World War women were chased out of the factories and back into the kitchens, they were also being chased back into their bedrooms. Perhaps it had something to do with the enormous loss of life in the war and the need for the society to replenish lost children, as much as restoring jobs for returning GIs. Even as the culture preached domesticity, homogeneity and suppression, the decade also took delight in an undercurrent of sex. Traditional role models and gender roles became prevalent as WASP society re-established itself. Yet sexuality itself became an obsession. Tennessee Williams became America's wealthiest playwright selling his steamy Southern melodramas to create equally smoldering films, featuring the likes of a sultry Elizabeth Taylor wearing only a slip. So too did William Inge's *Picnic* and *Bus Stop* stir with promises of the forbidden. Marilyn Monroe and her almost comically exaggerated rival, Jayne Mansfield, competed with the lusty Sophia Loren for screen space, even as Hugh Hefner began to publish *Playboy* and race music burst out via Elvis 'the pelvis'. What better than a musical about a famous stripper, one found on the usually respectable and safe Broadway stage?

There are several scenes in *Gypsy* that potentially offer satisfaction to the salacious, though none occur until late in Act Two, thus requiring the audience to return after the intermission. The first is the 'You Gotta Get a Gimmick', in which Louise, about to embark on a life on stage sans clothing, gets instruction from three long-time strippers, each past her prime. Working together, Robbins, Sondheim and Styne set the piece with Louise as an onstage audience, thus parallel to us watching from the house, as each stripper sings her verse and demonstrates her specialty. One plays a bugle between her legs, another flicks on electric lights that flash strategically on her body and the third is a down-on-her-luck classical ballerina, who flits about on toe only to pause for a bump or a grind. It is a homage to show business as much as it is to stripping, as each hearkens back to past fads and forms: nineteenth-century vaudeville, the *Ziegfeld Follies* and even Robbins's background in ballet. What the song is, is funny; what it is not, is sexy.[30]

The second instance of sex is the brief scene where Louise first appears onstage as Gypsy Rose. While she proves to be attractive, as a first-timer she is initially awkward but then increasingly confident as she gets the hang of it. In a sense it echoes the scene in *Show Boat* where Magnolia, abandoned by husband Ravenal, returns to show business after years away and first performs at a New Year's Eve revue, with her father unexpectedly in attendance. What is sexy about this is that Louise is for the first time revealed not only as an attractive young woman, but also as an adult. She gains adulthood before our eyes, losing her innocence in the process. It might be titillating but, if so, it is at a great cost, as we the audience will never again see the young, honestly engaging woman whose life we have witnessed step by step up until now in the show. She opens up physically to the audience but never again reveals her true self, essentially shutting that part of herself down.

The third instance of sex is the show's culminating number, 'Rose's Turn'. The story goes that Robbins was unhappy with this key moment in the show, so he enlisted the help of Sondheim and the two of them found an empty, late-night rehearsal hall in which to work. Together they developed the idea that this would be a flashback number, in which Rose relived her life after being scorned by her now-successful daughter. Sondheim sat at the piano and played bits and pieces of songs that had appeared earlier in the show while Robbins took on the role of Rose, shifting from moment to moment, memory to memory, feeling to feeling, while Sondheim tried to keep up with him. What the two men thereby created was a number of Shakespearean proportions, as Rose took the stage, teetering like Lear between delusion and truth, careening between disappointment and rage, cursing an ungrateful child while grinding her own hips in direct competition with her. Young Gypsy might have the looks, but old Rose outstrips her in pure sexuality and seductive power. Rose is a giantess, doomed by fate to see her sexless daughter take on the mantel that should have been hers all along. Nothing refined or delicate about her, Rose is every bit the earth goddess, overpowering and frightening, the thing itself. She delivers on the sexual promise of the show, though she is middle-aged and anything but attractive.

Gypsy consistently offers sympathy toward the fate of older women in American mass media and culture. The message is clear from the start: only the young can be made stars. Rose abandons her father in order to push her children along in show business; she knows that that is no longer an option for herself. It is not a matter of ability: that she proves in her final number. It is only a matter of looks and age. Similarly, the youthful Louise is shown learning her new craft from older women, those whose lost looks can no longer compensate for limited talent. Once a star, Louise takes on airs, the arrogance of beauty and youth; we never see her age beyond that. Of course *Gypsy* itself capitalized on the real Gypsy Rose Lee's reputation and fame, no doubt a boon to ticket sales. Lee had already been featured two decades earlier in Rodgers and Hart's song 'Zip', part of their *Pal Joey*. Then, as now, celebrity sells. But we never see the 1959 version of Gypsy Rose Lee in *Gypsy*, only her youthful counterpart. Besides, the focus, perhaps the sole purpose for *Gypsy*, was to move away from the daughter and onto her monster of a stage mother, Rose. As they say, 'youth is wasted on the young', so let's take this opportunity to spotlight a woman on the cusp of middle-age decline. One could argue whether this is cruel (as Sondheim often featured monstrous older women characters in his shows) or perhaps kind (as the show's gay creators perhaps sympathized with 1950s American culture's materialistic overemphasis on externals as the primary measure of internal passion, love and truth). Perhaps they viewed themselves as being some sort of gypsies, acting rather than living their everyday lives, refuting charges of deviancy by using their art to challenge then-oppressive norms.

Sondheim took special pleasure that this number forced Ethel Merman to have to 'act' rather than just play herself as she was accustomed to do. Merman took on the challenge and made the most of it. Not only was it perhaps the greatest star turn moment ever written for the Broadway musical stage, but it was also one tailored specially for her. The story goes that immediately after the opening, when it was clearly a hit, Merman, like a little girl, bragged that she was in fact 'acting'.

Sondheim wrote that he was an apprentice shaping lyrics for *West Side Story*, but that he 'came of age' as a lyricist writing *Gypsy*.[31] He had written successfully for young characters in his first two shows; but could he write for older characters, let alone one as protean and dynamic as Mama Rose?

Ethel Merman, as Momma Rose, trumpeted unapologetically in song, shoving everyone forward with her. And Sondheim constructed the lyric superstructure beneath to support her. What was alright for 'some people' was unequivocally not alright for Rose, as in Rose's opening song, 'Some People', Sondheim sculpted a song that clearly differentiated one from the other with each verse until the two collide in the last, with Rose coming out the clear winner: a strong female character in an era that was fast trying to redefine what it was to be a woman.

And the lyricist does not just leave it at that. Rose is complex, as full of charm as she is brass. In the following song, 'Small World', Sondheim has her take a gentler, less direct approach, sidling into the delicate subject matter of marriage by opening with the word 'funny':

> Funny, you're a stranger who's come here,
> Come from another town.
> Funny, I'm a stranger myself here –
> Small world, isn't it?[32]

Where the previous song separated Rose from 'some people' by pointing out her differences from them, here Sondheim reverses her tack by having Rose point out similarities. By linking the two this way, the thinking leads inevitably to linking in marriage. This is not pushy Rose, but rather seductive Rose, as she aims to have her own needs met once again by manipulating others. Yet the audience is as entranced as is Herbie as she moves from business ('we could pool our resources') to a cozy and sweet domesticity:

> Lucky, you're a man who likes children –
> That's an important sign.

> Lucky, I'm a woman with children –
> Small world, isn't it?
> Funny, isn't it?
> Small and funny and fine.[33]

The cleverness here is not in the language or word play, but rather in the character's softly-sold, comfortable arguments. Sondheim happily disappears entirely behind Rose, careful only to show another side of her persona in a natural, entirely convincing manner. Furthermore, he does so in the guise of a middle-aged mother hoping to begin again with a new man. Sondheim had given voice to a pack of juvenile delinquents like Diesel; suddenly he shifts gears and subtly finds words to help construct the far more contradictory essence of stage mother Rose, writing both *West Side Story* and *Gypsy* at roughly the same time.

Yet the twenty-something Sondheim did not abandon youth when writing *Gypsy*. In fact, he explored lost childhood more eloquently in it than he had done in *West Side Story*. But the evolving Sondheim now knew how to create this through demonstration, rather than relying primarily on explanation as he had done before. Sondheim achieved his desired effect mostly through sharp contrasts. If the aim of *Gypsy* is ultimately to explore the loss of innocence, then it was critical to create a memorably defining moment of innocence. Sondheim did this with the most simple of lyrics for the children's song 'Little Lamb', sung by Louise early in the show:

> Little Lamb, little Lamb.
> My birthday is here at last.
> Little lamb, little lamb,
> A birthday goes by so fast.[34]

Louise sings this to her stuffed animal. The song suggests a child both by its simple words and its reference to birthdays. Yet this child is somehow more worldly than first thought, as the last line points to time passing, something no small child would notice or know. Louise sings simple words but from a more knowing perspective, as one looking back rather than as a simple child. Furthermore, that a birthday 'goes by so fast' suggests a sense of loss and disappointment. She is already grieving for her lost childhood with its accompanying innocence. Rather than a 'happy' birthday, she sings to her toy cat:

> ... Ah, why do you look so blue?
> Did somebody paint you like that,
> Or is it your birthday too?[35]

Louise is neglected. Rather than enjoying human contact she is forgotten, left with only the company of her toy creatures. Without maternal attention and validation, Louise is caught somewhere between a remembered childhood and an unknown present as she asks of her fish, 'I wonder how old I am?' and then repeats the same line to her toy lamb.[36]

Louise does not match her mother and sister's entertaining bent. She knows she is 'blue' and that is different from being painted as being blue. One is real and the other not, one internal and sincere, the other an outward show for another's benefit, hence false. Sondheim's lyric also suggests that Louise knows the difference between the two, but that perhaps others, like her mother, do not. Perhaps Rose only responds to the visible appearance but is blind to hidden realities beneath the surface. This would make extra sense given the brash Merman, seemingly all insensitive extrovert, reinforcing that key aspect of the character Rose she would play.

As Louise starts to sing 'Little Lamb' we think it is supposed to be something sung by any child, like the 'Happy Birthday' song. But as it unfolds, we discover it is Louise singing her own private song, expressing her own personal situation and implying with its very simplicity deep emotional wounds peculiar to her own family situation. The child-like nature of the song, and of Louise herself, catches us off-guard, as does her obvious intelligence, sensitivity and profound loneliness. What is even more striking about this is that she sings the song in only a moment alone, as she is otherwise surrounded and occupied by the raucous hustle and bustle of her mother, sister and the very public and busy nature of their show-biz, vaudeville environs. It is a moment of quiet privacy for a girl otherwise overwhelmed by an ongoing avalanche of loud, cynically impersonal, noise.

Sondheim's lyrics for *Gypsy* are consistently natural, never forced, and yet still find ways to sparkle. His wit shines through in the mouths of Louise and Rose in particular, whereas he tends to play it down, fittingly, for characters like Herbie. Though it is tough to pin down as to its exact meaning, who can forget the phrase 'Everything's Coming up Roses' or misunderstand its exhilaration? Or who can miss the daughter's joy in exploring what life would be like 'if mamma was married', or their sense of familial camaraderie in being 'together, wherever we go'?[37]

Sondheim does allow himself one song in which to show off; fittingly, it is a song that celebrates show business itself: 'You Gotta Get a Gimmick'. Just as each aging stripper is given the spotlight in order to strut her stuff, and just as Jerome Robbins similarly indulged when shaping the number's choreography, so too did Sondheim take the opportunity to show off and have fun: 'Mazeppa: Once I was a schlepper / Now I'm Miss Mazeppa / With my Revolution in Dance', or 'Tessie: Dressy Tessie Tura / Is so much more demurer / Than all them other ladies'.[38] As was the case with 'Gee, Officer Krupke', each individual sings of their own experience, but as the song nears its end, they return for snippets that serve to unite them, before singing in unison to further unite them at song's end:

Electra If you wanna make it
Twinkle while you shake it
Tessie If you wanna grind it
Wait till you've refined it
Mazeppa If you wanna bump it
Bump it with a trumpet![39]

It is a lot of fun, and the setting affords more freedom, but the song may be faulted because of its inferred references to things beyond each woman's ken. What does Mazeppa know of the nineteenth-century star Mazeppa, for example? The original was Jewish, and this stripper version uses the Yiddish 'schlepper', but that seems an unlikely purposeful homage. Furthermore, her mention of a 'Revolution in Dance' is highbrow and modernist, more akin to an Isadora Duncan than to an aging burlesque queen. Similarly, Sondheim has Tessie use the highbrow word 'demurer', followed by an ungrammatical 'all them other ladies'. Her character echoes a one-time modern dancer, but her words suggest she hung around ladies without ever really being one herself. It all seems to culminate with the rhyme of 'bump it' with 'trumpet', again funny and crude, but, perhaps more significantly, the words call attention to themselves more than they seem natural. One could finally argue that the chosen words and references are entirely appropriate given that they so neatly match characters so deliberately overdrawn.

Perhaps Sondheim's best work in *Gypsy* is the song 'Rose's Turn'. He provides a detailed account of how he constructed the number in improvisational fashion late at night, onstage, lit only with a ghost light, while Jerome Robbins acted out Rose doing a strip number. It was a last-minute replacement for a ballet Robbins had envisioned but lacked the time to execute, hence the song. Sondheim suggested it could be made up of 'fragments of all the songs associated with her and the people in her life: the songs we'd heard all evening, colliding in an extended surreal medley'.[40]

The number opens with Rose taking the place of Louise, with her stripper's familiar 'Here she is, boys!' before launching into a fragment of 'Let Me Entertain You', which is then elaborated to show Rose to be better at this than her daughter, bragging 'Well, I got it!'[41] But this suddenly zags into an echo of 'Some People' which unexpectedly dissolves into a moment of self-pity, 'You either have it – / Or you've had it.' She quickly regroups, and the word 'momma' takes on a sexual meaning at first, with 'Momma's gonna show it to ya!' that begins a list of ten lines, each starting with the word 'Momma'. If you remove the word 'Momma' that begins each line, you get a progression of her condition, as she is:

... talkin' loud
... doin' fine!
... getting' hot
... goin' strong
... moving' on!

But then it unexpectedly turns dark: 'all alone'. Then she refutes it as she tries to recover:

... doesn't care
... lettin' loose
... got the stuff
... lettin' go –[42]

But letting go again leads to being alone, and her breakdown begins lyrically as she can no longer get past even that first word, stuttering when she tries to say 'Momma'. She then rallies to begin this litany again, but mixes stutters in with her collapsing boasts, ending with 'momma's gotta let go!'[43]

What is missing from the above is the repetition of the word 'Momma' itself, with each line. Yes, it started out as a sexual boast, à la Sophie Tucker, but it is also the trigger word, repeated over and over as she breaks, as if she herself was a child calling out repeatedly – and desperately – for her own mother. It is also Rose as mother who is supposed to have children, but both of whose daughters have abandoned her. Without her daughters, is she still a mother? If she is no longer a mother, is show business all she has left? If so, given her wild ambitions at the start of the play, she has done nothing but spiral downward, now reduced to aping burlesque. A woman's sexuality begins the piece; a woman having given birth (hence a mother) is the middle motif; a childless mother can boast about her sexual prowess, but can she really compete against Gypsy Rose Lee, who is a younger version of herself? Can she let go, or was she let go by her strip-star daughter? What has she left? Her narcissism turns her then to the past, to account for the years lost where she gave all to her children and supposedly kept nothing for herself, now seen as too old and discarded, 'they take the bows and you're battin' zero!'[44]

The tone shifts again, echoing early days with 'I had a dream', where she first claimed she did it all for June, then denies self-interest to the long-gone Herbie, then once more takes credit, 'And if it wasn't for me then where would you be / Miss Gypsy Rose Lee?' Angry, resentful, she then demands the time back, 'Well, someone tell me, when is it my turn?'[45]

Where before she echoed the word 'Momma', she now echoes 'Everything's coming up Rose' – not 'roses' but rather her name, 'Rose' immediately followed by an endless string of 'For me!' to end the number.[46] So 'Momma' gives way to 'Everything's ... Rose' before the final veil is removed to uncover her ugly, underlying truth, that it always was only about Rose herself. She is raging that her surrogacy resulted in her being a second banana to her daughter, not comprehending that that was the inevitable result of her vicarious ambition. Had Louise/Gypsy not rejected her, then perhaps she could have maintained the charade, along with its lie of being a loving mother rather than a self-serving parent. If Louise pushes her out, then Rose is now free to roar the truth of her supreme selfishness. It is not quite an anagnorisis, however, as Rose is still unable to see that she is responsible for Louise's behaviour, that she created out of her one faithful daughter a monster much like she herself, damaged and incapable of loving, only able to vaunt publically her sexuality. Rose may be King Lear, raging against the storm about ungrateful children, but she is also Medea, slaughtering them in the name of her own frustration and rejection. She cannot even blame others; all she can see is herself, as Sondheim ends the number with the repeated word 'me'.[47]

'Rose's Turn' is a *tour de force* display of lyrical mastery and unlike anything previously heard in a musical. Sondheim traces the subtle emotional shifts and turns of a character the exact moment they are experiencing it, through words. Each word counts. Each is a device in creating the context of that particular character, in that particular situation, at that moment in time. Sondheim still loves clever word play, but his genius is in making each moment work. Each word builds to each phrase; each phrase to each line; each line adds up to each song, just as each steadily and collectively builds to shape a person going through a pivotal, recognizable experience in their life. While the words (and later the accompanying music) matter, Sondheim is ultimately recreating the human experience, the workings of the mind and of the heart, with little storms that collectively build, through the course of a song, through the course of an entire musical, to form storms that smash, crash and roar with a wonderfully evocative theatricality.

Conclusion

The creative teams for *West Side Story* and for *Gypsy* had much in common. Though Styne was a decade older and Sondheim a decade younger than their collaborative counterparts, like the vast majority of musical theatre creators they were all Jews. Except for Styne, Comden and Green, all were gay men. It has been said that the reasons why Jerome Robbins named names to HUAC was because he was frightened about being exposed as gay, hence destroying his career, and because HUAC's muscle-bound tactics made him frightened as a Jew. Other musical writing teams of the era did not so challenge accepted norms: certainly not Alan Jay Lerner and Frederick Loewe, Richard Adler and Jerry Ross or Frank Loesser.

Oscar Hammerstein certainly introduced a liberal worldview into his shows, but would only go so far. When *Finian's Rainbow* premiered and proved a hit despite its underlying far-left politics, Hammerstein famously wrote to Yip Harburg, applauding it and suggesting it said what he himself had not said but wanted to say. In other words, Hammerstein could not – or would not – go to such political extremes in his own work, favouring reform to revolution, not willing to upset the status quo. This ensured that Rodgers and Hammerstein shows preserved their national and hence commercial appeal. American soldiers might find romance with Polynesian women in *South Pacific*, but they learn to overcome their bigotry and triumph at the end by sharing soup, an ultimate reassuring statement of American domesticity and middle-class values. In other words, in the end Nellie overcomes her prejudices as Emile succumbs to wholesome Americana.

In contrast, both *West Side Story* and *Gypsy* portray another side of American life, one far less wholesome and yet perhaps more 'real'. Both musicals portray those relegated to the fringe of American society, and do so with great sympathy and understanding. The average 1950s middle-class American would do all they could to avoid the neighbourhood and denizens found in *West Side Story*, preferring to retreat to the warmth and safety of suburban homes instead. Puerto Ricans were people of colour, and Tony and Maria's love was forbidden because it was biracial, as much as anything else. This was shown at a time when the civil rights movement was in its infancy but on the rise. Only three years earlier, the landmark *Brown v. Board of Education* ruling had been handed down by the Supreme Court, and *West Side Story* opened the same year that Lyndon Johnson engineered the Civil Rights Act of 1957. The creators of *West Side Story* were all Jews, sympathetic to such change, at odds with the dominant culture. Remember that just as the dark-skinned Maria held the dying light-skinned Tony in her arms at show's end, so too was this originally supposed to be a Jewish 'Maria' holding a dying Irish 'Tony' in her arms. They thereby matched Shakespeare's tragedy to a Bernstein dirge to touch audience's hearts, but just beyond this impassioned lament they portrayed characters reconciling their ethnic differences, urging 1950s America to similarly overcome its racism.[48]

Similarly, Rose in *Gypsy* is deliberately escaping domestic roles and society when she flees with her daughters to pursue a life in vaudeville. No respectable mother would dream of doing so, especially in the Eisenhower decade. Indeed, *Gypsy* portrays a string of marginalized characters struggling to survive, not always nice or good and all of whom would be considered outcasts by the then-dominant culture. That the collaborative team did so successfully – both artistically and commercially – while somehow depicting those characters as triumphant, even in moments of great loss, not only attests to their talent, but also, I would suggest, to the fact that they personally operated on the fringes of American society. While Jerome Robbins cowered before HUAC, Arthur Laurents never apologized for being Jewish or gay. And while Sondheim kept his personal preferences private, he too ultimately defined himself as a gay, Jewish male. The same was ultimately true of Bernstein as well. This is not to create a litany of identities but rather to make the point that, living in a decade of conformity, they differed in this respect from many of their peers, and perhaps explains their shared affinity for creating musicals that offered an alternative view of society, and that, if so, they did this with a sensitivity born of empathy.[49]

Note also that both *West Side Story* and *Gypsy* remain among the few classic shows to enjoy repeated Broadway revivals. Though written against the backdrop of the 1950s, beyond their artistic excellence, both shows speak to concerns that transcend their era and continue to speak to us today: *West Side* Story with its concerns with urban gang violence, immigration and diversity; *Gypsy* with its issues of women's rights, media imagery, self-image and commodification.

While many still applaud *Gypsy* as a masterpiece, it lost out to the more conventional *The Sound of Music* for Best Musical Tony Award for 1959. This presaged how Sondheim's later groundbreaking masterpiece, *Sunday in the Park with George*, lost out on the 1984 Tony Award to Jerry Herman's far more conventional musical, aside from its subject matter, *La Cage Aux Follies*.

With his roots firmly planted in the soil of Oscar Hammerstein's experience and approach to musical theatre, which dated back to the 1920s, Stephen Sondheim was a standard bearer of the book musical and those elements that formed its Golden Age. That Sondheim continued to write successful musicals into the 1990s, and beyond, highlights his role as a torchbearer of that form, continuing to practice its teachings successfully. It is also true, as we see in his 1950s work, that Sondheim simultaneously championed subject matter and sensibilities that ran counter to the conservative culture with which Broadway is usually associated. As such, he embodied the twentieth-century American musical and set the tone for the twenty-first to follow.

Armed with a rich background and legacy, Sondheim was uniquely positioned to blossom forth creatively in the 1970s. He was forty years old when *Company* premiered, harkening a new type of musical. His collaborations with Bernstein, Robbins, Laurents and Styne had provided a bedrock sense of how musicals operate, from which he could now develop more ground-breaking works. Many point to *Company* as being the first 'concept' musical, which is to say one built as a montage rather than in narrative structure; yet Sondheim had personally witnessed a precursor of this a quarter-century earlier with old mentor Hammerstein's efforts (with Rodgers) to create *Allegro*. Sondheim's verbal felicity was matched only by his sharp discipline, trying to make every word count.

Unlike most 1950s composers or lyricists, Sondheim anticipated the cultural sensibilities of the 1960s and 1970s. Where theirs was often sentimental and emotional, Sondheim's eye was far more sceptical and critical, favouring irony and insights, more cynical than benign. Like Bernstein, he wanted his music to match his observations so that singing a Sondheim song meant going through the given character's thoughts and feelings, moment by moment, in excruciating detail. It was not indulgently emotional but it was scrupulous in recreating the human experience, pains and pleasures, thoughts and second thoughts. Look at a song such as 'Every Day a Little Death' from *A Little Night Music* (1973), where two women sing of two men, say similar words and yet voice strikingly different meanings, stinging for both and yet wise in their contrasts. Its ironies are witty, its insights devastating and its music haunting.

Yet even as Sondheim is a twentieth-century musical theatre composer and lyricist, strict in his understandings of what works and what does not, he consistently sought to stretch the definition of what that might be. He did not bring his own personal issues to bear but rather sought to recreate the experience of others, with which he occasionally identified. Yet while his approach to his work might resemble that of the pointillist artist George Seurat, there is no sense that Sondheim confuses himself with Seurat. Perhaps Sondheim differs from subsequent generations of musical makers whose works seem determined to project themselves, with their own stories and identity issues, in this ability that he has to himself erase his work. If so, then perhaps we could define Sondheim as being essentially conservative in his approach.

If Hammerstein defines the form of Sondheim's work, his subject matter owes more to Robbins and Laurents. Sometimes Sondheim favoured light material as fodder for his shows, such as *A Funny thing Happened on the Way to the Forum* (1962) or *A Little Night Music*, but for the most part he dwelt with those on the fringe, challenging the dominant culture rather than endorsing it. His characters are often unhappy, having compromised the ethical in the name of ambition, or, worse, have even been mass murderers or assassins. So even as he carries on the aesthetic teachings of Oscar Hammerstein, he has forged ahead, using the musical, with its safe guise as escapist entertainment, as a vehicle to question and challenge societal norms and thereby clearing space in the culture for all those who see beyond, for all those who differ.

5

Alice Childress: *Florence* (1949), *Gold Through the Trees* (1952) and *Trouble in Mind* (1955)

Soyica Diggs-Colbert

Introduction

Alice Childress's original contribution to American drama garnered the distinction of being the first play by an African-American woman to receive a professional production in New York City (*Gold Through the Trees*). Some sources also designate her the first woman to win an Obie Award,[1] and in 1972 she became the first African-American woman to direct (co-directed with Joseph Papp) an Off-Broadway play, when *Wedding Band: A Love/Hate Story in Black and White* premiered at the New York Shakespeare Festival.

Her early life and career shaped the world that she creates on stage. Childress was born in 1916 in South Carolina and later moved to New York where she lived with her maternal grandmother. Although formally uneducated, Childress's grandmother introduced her to the world of art, taking her to galleries and churches and encouraging her use of imagination. Her grandmother told her to write down stories about the people on their street and imagine the types of lives being lived all around her. The focus on the lives and experiences of everyday people that distinguishes Childress's drama draws from her grandmother's first creative writing assignments.

Childress never graduated from high school because she was forced to begin working when her grandmother died. Her unconventional arts education, however, persisted. In 1941, Childress joined the American Negro Theatre (ANT). Organized with a mission akin to W. E. B. Du Bois's theory of a black theatre for and of the black community, ANT operated for its first five years in the basement of the 135th Street branch of the New York Library, now the Schomburg Center for Research in Black Culture. ANT became a training ground for Childress and others, including Ruby Dee, Ossie Davis, Harry Belafonte and Sidney Poitier. As a member of ANT, Childress learned how to play all the roles in a theatre: playwriting, directing, managing, acting and serving as a stagehand. Childress's first big break came as an actor. She played the role of Blanche in the American version of Philip Yordon's *Anna Lucasta*. The play went on to Broadway, and Childress garnered a Tony nomination for her performance.

Childress's theatre

Writing in the wake of Second World War, in the midst of the Cold War and during the burgeoning civil rights movement, Alice Childress's work presents the political, social and artistic challenges of being an intersectionalist black feminist artist before third-wave feminism.[2] The Second World War ushered in an economic boom that coincided with the administration of the GI Bill. The bill made low-interest mortgage loans available to veterans, drastically expanding the pool of US homeowners and the middle class. The dream-like quality of home ownership became a reality for more Americans and emerged as the backdrop for Lorraine Hansberry's *A Raisin in the Sun* (1959). Childress's drama of the 1950s – *Florence* (1949), *Gold Through the Trees* (1952) and *Trouble in Mind* (1955) – does not take place in the domestic sphere; instead, it examines how public spaces communicate the possibilities and limitations of post-Second World War US democracy and class ascension. The setting of her plays shifts attention to her characters as workers and their experience of the public sphere, which is divided along class, race and gender lines. Unfettered loyalty to democracy and its spread internationally became a difficult proposition for Childress, understanding the uneven distribution of resources in the United States. In addition to struggling with the ideological limitations of aligning oneself with the capitalism of the United States, Childress's work also takes up the contemporary social context of the civil rights movement, which also called into question the limitations and hypocrisy of US democracy.

Criticism of Childress's drama often focuses on the groundbreaking nature of her characterizations, building plays around the lives of working-class black women. La Vinia Delois Jennings's biography, *Alice Childress*, argues that Childress's woman-centred theatre distinguishes her from her contemporaries. In the introduction to Childress's selected plays, Kathy Perkins makes a similar point, saying that 'Childress's plays concentrate on the struggles and triumphs of the black poor and working classes. She called herself a "liberation writer" and created strong, compassionate, often militant female characters who resisted socioeconomic conditions.'[3] In *The Other Blacklist: The African American Literary and Cultural Left of the 1950s*, Mary Helen Washington offers a corrective to interpretations of mid-twentieth-century black writers that do not account for their class politics and involvement with the Communist Party. Washington makes the case that leftist organizations supported Childress's drama, particularly the play *Gold Through the Trees*, and influenced her thought. I have argued in 'Dialectical Dialogues: Performing Blackness in the Drama of Alice Childress' that Childress's drama anticipates the critiques that third-wave feminists make of the masculinist leadership and agenda promoted during the civil rights movement.[4] Here, I examine the specific ways Childress's drama of the 1950s depicts class, race and gender-based forms of oppression as interconnected, and therefore offers an 'intersectionalist' feminist point of view. Legal scholar Kimberlé Crenshaw coined the term 'intersectionality' in 1989 to describe how the experience of being a woman of colour requires attending to the simultaneity of being, in her case, black and a woman.[5] Childress's drama disrupts renderings of art as a reflection of contemporary social contexts of the 1950s in which race-based modes of oppression dominated national conversations, and demonstrates the ways that art may serve an anticipatory, future-oriented, world-making function.

Florence (1949)

Alice Childress's drama reflects and responds to the political and aesthetic contexts of the 1950s, presenting characters and situations that engage with the burgeoning civil rights movement as an international movement for racial, gender and class equality. In 1949, after years of finding limited roles for a black woman to play, Childress wrote her first play, *Florence*. The ANT first produced *Florence* in 1949 in Harlem at St Mark's on 125th Street in a small loft space.

The Committee for the Negro in the Arts (CNA) also produced the play the following year at Club Baron on Lenox Avenue. Childress directed the CNA production as part of an evening titled Just a Little Simple, which also featured Childress's adaptation of Langston Hughes's *Simple Speaks His Mind*. In October 1950, the leftist periodical *Masses and Mainstream* published *Florence*.

The play, set in a segregated train station, depicts an encounter between Mrs Whitney, a black woman and the mother of the titular character, and a white woman named Mrs Carter. At the rise of the play, Marge (Florence's sister) and Mrs Whitney, called Mama in the play, enter the segregated train station. Marge has come to see Mama off on her journey to bring Florence home. The conversation between Marge and Mama suggests Florence left the South for Harlem to pursue a career as an actor after a group of vigilantes murdered her husband for attempting to vote. As part of her pursuit, Florence leaves her son in the care of her sister. Although Florence has had some minimal success working in the theatre (we learn later she has also appeared in a film), as far as her sister knows, Florence has only been able to gain employment as a stagehand. Her limited success has left her in dire financial straits, and, in order to make ends meet, she has requested that her family send money. Instead of sending money, Mama has decided to travel to New York to bring Florence home.

Although the play opens with the recounting of the personal tragedy that led Florence to chase her dreams, it carefully situates Florence's experience within a larger structure of inequality that limits the life chances and opportunities of black people in general. The set creates a division not only along racial lines but gender as well. Demonstrating the interworking of race and gender division, the stage directions focus on the race and gender separate space of the rest room.[6] Within moments we learn the black women's rest room is inoperable and if Mama needs to use the facilities, she must use the black men's rest room. The inclusion of an intersectional problem as part of a play set in a segregated train station demonstrates how Childress's drama, on the one hand, engages with the central social context of the civil rights movement, and on the other hand, anticipates the third-wave feminism of the late twentieth century. Although segregation focuses on racial difference as the primary social distinction, Childress's drama also calls attention to the operation of segregation along gender lines. The operation of segregation, creating not only racial but also gender hierarchies, ingrains its force through the set.

The opening scene returns to the context of segregation through Marge and Mama's discussion of Florence's state of mind, and, according to Marge, errant exercise of privilege. Marge charges that Florence 'must think she's white' because she (1) attempts to work in a segregated clothing store, (2) moved to New York to pursue an acting career and (3) left her son in the care of relatives.[7] Marge's estimation of how certain modes of behaviour install racial identity misnames the complex web of intersecting identity formations that perpetuate and restrict black women's behaviour in the 1950s. On the heels of the Second World War, the idea of men leaving children in the care of women is not only acceptable, but also a part of nation building. Although it may seem incommensurate to liken Florence's choice to leave the South and pursue acting with the decision to fight in the armed services, both actions serve to normalize gender relations, creating expectations about the role of a mother versus a father. The important distinction, however, is that other women fill in the parental gap so that Florence can pursue her career. Therefore, her actions do not dislocate childcare as women's work, but rather call attention to the possibility of women performing other types of labour as well. The idea that identity is created through a set of actions governed by the individual's choices within a pre-existing social context does not emerge until the late twentieth century. While Marge's comment does not express the expansive philosophical shift encapsulated in understanding identity as socially constructed rather than biologically determined, she does, nonetheless, give voice to latent understandings of difference as an arbitrary forestalling of certain social privileges. She also articulates the way understandings of race create belief systems that secure race, class and gender hierarchies.

Florence's purportedly errant way of thinking functions as a threat to Marge because it stresses the family's already precarious financial position and troubles the social relationships that Marge understands as immutable. So even as Marge's language allows for a post-structuralist rendering of identity, she sees such a formulation as a fantasy. The play, however, establishes the tension between fixed notions of race, expressed in the mapping of space and behaviours, and shifting ideas and beliefs about race in order to trouble the restrictions Marge places on black womanhood. Childress's stage becomes the setting to rethink the limited roles black women play in the social sphere. The play suggests that the limitations are not a result of inherent difference, but because of the roles available to them.

Along with rendering arbitrary and variable the spatial restrictions that support racial difference as an essential difference, *Florence* also shows how words and language serve to install blackness as a contested category. Once Marge departs, Mrs Carter enters the stage with an air of superiority. She addresses the porter, a 50-year-old black man, as 'boy' and instructs him to tend to her bags. As the porter leaves, he tells Mama he will help with her bags too, and she responds 'Thank you, sir.'[8] The form of address has significance because it alerts the audience to the operation of race at the intersection of gender formation, and demonstrates how Mrs Carter asserts her white privilege by denying the porter access to the category of manhood. The function of naming makes available and forecloses certain forms of identity, so it is equally important that Mama calls the porter 'sir', establishing her ability to name and disrupt Mrs Carter's authority.

The shifts in assignation introduce the contestation between Mama and Mrs Carter over how to define blackness. Mrs Carter understands blackness as fundamentally a tragic category. In an effort to demonstrate her investment in racial inclusion, Mrs Carter explains to Mama that she travelled to the South to visit her brother. She explains that her brother recently finished a novel about a character who aspires to be an attorney, but has one flaw – blackness. Given the immutability of blackness, the character commits suicide. Mrs Carter offers the story as a means to connect with Mama, but instead the story produces confusion. Mama begins to describe people that she knows that have the physical characteristics to pass for white but identify as black. She challenges Mrs Carter's assumption that death is a better option than being black. She also finds perplexing Mrs Carter's assertion that, if given the chance, a black person would rather identify as white. Mama's counter-narrative serves to disrupt the presumed value of whiteness and Mrs Carter's claim to progressivism.

Mama also serves to correct some of Mrs Carter's presumptions about black people that fit phenotypical standards for blackness. When Mrs Carter learns that Florence is a performer, she immediately assumes she is a singer. Mama quickly dispels yet another racial assumption and explains that her daughter is a struggling actress. Mrs Carter seems to empathize with Florence's situation since she too works as an actor. After describing her difficulty in finding work, even given her wide network of connections, Mama asks Mrs Carter if she will help Florence find a job. Although Mrs Carter seems to understand that Florence has acted and aspires to continue working in theatre and film, she tells Mama that she has a job for Florence – as a maid for her friend. The conversation reveals a stunning incident of misrecognition that disrupts the interracial alliance. Although Mama tells Mrs Carter that Florence is an actor, Mrs Carter can only understand Florence as a singer or a maid. Mrs Carter's assumption places Florence's race and gender identity in relation to class, and renders blackness in perpetual service to whiteness. She refuses to reconcile blackness with the professional space that she occupies. The utter lack of recognition serves as the dramatic catalyst in the play, which encourages Mama to cancel her trip to New York. The refusal to understand Florence's identity based on her actions also clarifies how the construction of identity requires not only an actor, but also a willing audience. Childress stages the encounter not for Mrs Carter to see her bias, but for the audience to recognize how it misrecognizes black people.

As mentioned previously, the contestation between Mama and Mrs Carter takes place in a segregated train station, which draws attention to how spatial dynamics reinforce essentialist notions of race and support racial hierarchies. When Mrs Carter first meets Mama, she specifies that she is from the North not the South. She suggests that her philanthropic activities demonstrate her liberalism, and in so doing she maps ideological investments onto geographic locations. Certainly, the labour conditions of the North and South in the early and mid-twentieth century inform the ways that race functions. Florence moves to New York to pursue acting because it functions as the centre of the black art world. Nevertheless, Mrs Carter proves that she enjoys the benefits of segregation, which may function differently in the North but yields the same outcome of oppression.

Similar to Mrs Carter's attempts to regulate the black characters and blackness through her use of language, the play demonstrates how the characters' traversal of the train station amounts to a negotiation of power. Throughout the play the porter, Mrs Carter and Mama all find themselves on the 'wrong' side of the station. The movement shows the arbitrariness of distinguishing the seating for white and black passengers. It also calls attention to the ability of individuals to reclaim space. By the end of the play, Mrs Carter has shifted to the 'coloured' side to address Mama. Mrs Carter's proximity to Mama creates intimacy and danger. By the time Mrs Carter moves to the coloured side, Mama has already asked her to help find Florence a job. Mrs Carter reveals that the job she can offer is being a maid, and Mama, according to the stage directions, '*reaches out, clutches Mrs. Carter's wrist almost pulling her off balance*'.[9] Once Mama realizes what she had done, she admonishes, 'You better get over on the other side of that rail. It's against the law for you to be over here with me.'[10] Segregation law functions to protect and benefit white people, but Mama deploys the law to create personal space. Mama sends Mrs Carter back to her side, not to reinstall the order of segregation, but to demonstrate how she decides to manipulate the law after demonstrating its permeability. The final gesture of the play, Mama touching the railing that separates the sides of the station, shows how her choice to send Florence the money rather than require she return home chips away at the physical and ideological structures that support race, gender and class hierarchies. The gesture aligns material manifestations of the law (separate bathrooms and benches) with performed ones.

In *Florence*, Childress demonstrates how segregation informs racial perceptions that function in tandem with class and gender expectations of what qualifies as black women's labour, how women interact within a segregated world and how family structures operate along gender lines. *Florence* specifies the ways that racial segregation limits the possibilities for a black woman working in the performing arts. The play depicts the impossibility of Mama and Mrs Carter coming to an understanding, because the experiences of Mama and Florence work in relationship to the narratives Mrs Carter has been told, rather than the lived experiences of the people around her. The miscues play out through the women's dialogue and appear in the setting of the play. The realism that Childress deploys in *Florence* and returns to in *Trouble in Mind* serves as a mechanism to rethink the social drama of the 1950s. Childress's work distinctively distils the complexity of racial segregation as imbricated in gender and class hierarchies, and offers avenues for characters to address discrimination through speech acts and choreography.

Gold Through the Trees (1952)

In many ways Childress's drama speaks to such contemporary African-American writers as Richard Wright and Ann Petry. Similar to both Petry and Wright, Childress's drama reflects the conditions of racial domination for the working poor. Just as Wright sought to depict the downfall of an average young black man in his 1940 novel *Native Son*, Childress's drama features the quotidian struggles of average working-class black people rather than the triumphs of heroes and heroines. *Native Son* (which Wright adapted for the stage with Paul Green in 1941) depicts the social forces that transform the 20-year-old black protagonist, Bigger Thomas, into a murderer. Living on the South Side of Chicago, the book opens with Bigger cornering and beating a rat to death, a symbolic representation of his eventual fate. The social landscape of Petry's *The Street* (1946), set in Harlem, resonates with the world Bigger Thomas experiences but does not prove as detrimental for the female protagonist, Lutie Johnson, who struggles to raise her son, given limited resources and opportunities. The world depicted in the work of Wright, Petry and Childress focuses on how social manifestations of race impact on the lives of average black Americans.

At the same time, Childress also considers the impact of the Cold War on aesthetic practices, and how it limits the stories a playwright tells. In *Gold Through the Trees*, Childress presents a sketch drama that draws from the formal attributes of a musical and a pageant. CNA produced *Gold Through the Trees* at Club Baron. The production, directed by Childress and Clarice Taylor, ran from 7 April to 28 May 1952. In a review of the play for *Freedom*, Lorraine Hansberry writes that 'Alice Childress seems to know more about language and drama than most people who write for theatre today, and the result is that whatever its little weaknesses, *Gold Through the Trees* is probably the most worthwhile and entertaining show currently running in New York.'[11]

Gold Through the Trees links the mid-twentieth-century policing of black men to an international history of racial violence that has a damaging effect on mothers and women. In so doing, it engages with the Cold War battle between the United States and Russia over the geographic scope of the civil rights movement. As Mary Helen Washington explains:

> By keeping the focus on U.S. race problems as rooted in colonialism and imperialism [an international perspective], the radical Left refused to sanction the State Department's propaganda that racism was rooted in individual prejudices and needed only a larger dose of American democracy for its total annihilation.[12]

The United States sought to limit the scope of the civil rights movement to the domestic sphere, while activists and participants saw the movement as tied to international struggles for black freedom. The organization of Childress's play suggests a relationship between the transatlantic slave trade, the abolitionist movement, contemporary practices of policing and the anti-apartheid movement in South Africa.

The play opens with a 'sequence' that features 'a woman of Ur ... 2,500 years B.C.' who details an origins story intersecting the Middle East, Asia, Africa and Europe, which led to fundamental advances in philosophical and religious knowledge. The play establishes knowledge production as an international rather than European phenomenon, and therefore creates an epistemological basis for the other scenes of the play. The opening sequence also specifies that a woman's voice is central to the beginnings of knowledge. In the scene, which consists of a monologue, she states:

> I watched Teshup on his throne at Tel Halaf. I saw the waters cover the city of Ur ... I heard Memnon's statue singing on the west bank of the Nile ... I stood with King Khafra and watched the life blood flow from the men and women who built the great Sphinx of Giza ... I watched Pontius Pilate dip his hands in the basin of the water ... I stood by the wall of Plato's academy ... I, the eternal woman.[13]

The 'thousands'-year history established in the opening sequence functions in a similar way to W. E. B. Du Bois's *The Star of Ethiopia* (1913), in that it offers a version of history that foregrounds the contribution of Africa to the making of world knowledge.

In the *African American Theatrical Body: Performance, Reception, and the Stage*, I examine how Du Bois tailors the attributes of the pageant form to offer a sweeping depiction of black history. Pageants usually consist of narratives primarily told through movement and song and organized through scenes. Pageants function differently from musicals in that they are often produced by community members, focus on distilling local histories and use an outline or sketch of scenes rather than a detailed script, leaving room for improvisation in each performance. Du Bois's pageant *The Star of Ethiopia*, however, sought to tell the history of the black world and therefore exceeded the characteristic historical and geographic scope of American pageants in the early twentieth century. It did, nonetheless, cohere to the use of community members as a part of the production, and the impetus toward education. *Gold Through the Trees* follows the impulse toward education but does not follow the convention of using community members as a part of the production. As Perkins details in the production history that introduces *Gold Through the Trees* in the selected plays collection that she edited, '*Gold Through the Trees* is considered the first professionally produced play written by an African American woman – professionally produced, in the sense that it had Equity actors.'[14] Even though the use of community members enabled the participants to engage in the act of making history, the epistemological impact of Childress's play aligns with the goals of Du Bois's *Star of Ethiopia*.[15]

After establishing an intersecting basis of knowledge production, the play moves to the west coast of Africa to focus on a sequence of events that provide the building blocks for racial inequality in the twentieth century. Once again, the sequence 'Africa Wounded' focuses on the perspective of women. The scene depicts a bloody battle that results in 'broken shield and spears' and 'the blood' of combatants covering the land.[16] The Queen discovers through the conversation with an Old Woman that the King is not dead but that he has been captured. The Old Woman explains, 'The king and his brother and many more they took in chains. All the young and beautiful sons of our women. The strong and lovely daughters, torn from their mothers. Only the weak and old are left behind.'[17] The Old Woman also suggests that enemy combatants introduced the word 'slave' to her lexicon. Although forms of slavery pre-dated the transatlantic slave trade, the emphasis on how the Old Woman and Queen come to understand the new condition suggests the shaping force of transatlantic slavery on racial formations that emerge alongside gender identities and within international contexts. The focus on the women left behind also demonstrates the way slavery shaped not just the enslaved, but also the structures of families and communities.

Although the play makes reference to the brutality of slavery, it does not focus attention on the experience of the enslaved, but shifts attention to the sacrifices women make to gain freedom. The third sequence, 'Stranger in a Strange Land', which ends Act One, is set in 1850s Cape May, NJ. The sequence engages with a familiar figure of the abolitionist movement, Harriet Tubman. It does not detail her harrowing experiences as a conductor on the Underground Railroad, but instead focuses on her work as a washerwoman with two other women to gain money to support abolitionism. The sequence resists the hagiography that often emerges in telling the stories of a great man or woman, and instead focuses on the sacrifices a group of women make to support the movement. The two women that join Harriet, Celia and Lennie, question the impact individual sacrifice will have on the collective good. Celia inquires, 'how much can we get like this? Maybe if everybody worked and gave their money to the underground it would mean something. This way I just can't see it, but I believe in freedom and I understand.'[18] Celia also complains of her weary condition. The reservations of Celia and Lennie contextualize the heroism often associated with Tubman to (1) demonstrate the ways other women contributed to the abolitionist movement and (2) reveal the human frailties that coincide with activism. The women's labour as washerwomen is not separate from but necessary to Tubman's role as a conductor on the Underground Railroad.

In popular depictions of Tubman, she often appears in masculinist roles, holding a gun and participating in the physical labour of evading slave catchers. Tubman's ability to appear as a hero in Childress's drama relies on her participation in the prototypical labour of women among women. The depiction adds value to 'women's work', aligning it with the mythology of 'a Moses named Tubman'.[19] In depicting Tubman as a washerwoman, Childress also aligns the abolitionist figure with the playwright's experiences of working as a domestic while developing her theatre practice with ANT. In addition, the play demonstrates the quotidian yet subversive practices that facilitate political movements. Washington explains:

> The civil disobedience of these three women [Harriet, Celia and Lennie] may certainly have been a disguised reference to Childress's own underground work, since by 1952, according to her friend and leading communist Herbert Aptheker, who had gone into hiding, Childress too had crossed the line into subversive and illegal activity. Aptheker told me in an interview that during the worst days of the McCarthy period Childress let him use her uptown apartment for meetings with underground communists. This could have meant a jail term for Childress. Since this is not mentioned in her files, I conclude that the FBI never discovered the full extent of Childress's radical politics.[20]

Maintaining the play's emphasis on women's points of view, Act Two opens with an unnamed woman giving a monologue about losing her son. The speech details the great effort the speaker and her husband took to protect their son from harm throughout childhood. Eventually, as the son matures, his parents can no longer shield him from the strife that attends racism and poverty.

The speech functions as a lament of the mother's inability to function in one of the primary roles of a parent: as a protector. The scene suggests that racism and poverty preclude black parents from functioning in certain roles, and that the exclusion from motherhood produces a melancholic state, or perpetual form of mourning. The final words of the speech situate the speaker within a collective of mothers:

> I have some sisters ... they lost their sons too ... and they don't wander about looking as I do ... They are supposed to be wiser ... The doctor says I am sick ... He is wrong I am just lonely and tired ... tired of searching and asking ... I hope you never lose your boy.[21]

The language of diagnosis and perpetual searching without finding further evidences the structure of melancholia. At the same time, the assertion of a common state of loss demonstrates the way black womanhood operates in relationship to the denial of the maternal. The scene demonstrates how racialism affects women and the familial, communal and social roles they play.

The opening scene of the second act, which consists of a mother's lament, ends with a verse from the children's lullaby 'Bye Baby Bunting' to reinforce the contradictory moods of black motherhood. The words 'Bye Baby Bunting / Daddy's gone a-hunting / To buy a little rabbit skin / To wrap the baby bunting in' soothe the baby and show how the parents of the child work together to provide for their son, keeping him warm and safe.[22] The soothing sound of the lullaby shifts to the tragic-comedy of the blues in the next sequence, 'Martinsville Blues'. The sequence contains a song that recalls seven black men (Frank Hairston, Jr, age twenty; Booker T. Milner, age twenty-two; Howard Lee Hariston, age twenty; James Luther Hairston, age twenty-two; John Claybon Taylor, age twenty-three; Francis DeSales Grayson, age thirty-eight; Joe Henry Hampton, age twenty-one) from Martinsville, VA, being executed in 1951 for raping a white woman. The execution marked the largest mass execution for rape that had been reported. Although unsuccessful, the case served as a battleground for civil rights activism. The NAACP provided a defence in all seven cases and appealed the convictions. The defence questioned the constitutionality of Virginia state law, which stipulated that only black men could be executed for rape.

The song 'Martinsville Blues' focuses on the execution rather than the trial, in order to memorialize the loss of seven young men. The singer cries out to his mother, singing 'Mother, oh Mother / It's so hard to bear / Got to give up the life you gave me / To that mean old electric chair.'[23] The call and response between the first two sequences in Act Two reinforces how Childress's drama places women at the centre. Even in 'Martinsville Blues' the structure of the men's song works in relationship to the opening monologue to recalibrate the history of the Martinsville Seven to a family tragedy rather than a male-centred narrative. At the same time, the song focuses on the individuals lost, in an effort to personalize the civil rights' history. The stage directions indicate that the final line of the song will speak *'the names of the first four to die and then the next three and finally the seven names in order'*.[24] The movement from general to specific deepens the trauma of the woman in the opening monologue, clarifying that the common experience does not mitigate the impact of losing a child.

The final scene of the play begins with the omnipresent Woman from the opening scene, offering a centuries-long history of domination that sets the stage for the colonization of Africa and mid-twentieth-century black freedom struggles. The majority of the scene is set in South Africa in 1952, and links the burgeoning anti-apartheid movement there to global black independence and civil rights movements, through the Woman's opening and the conversation that follows among native South Africans, John, Ola and Burney. John explains how a strategy of civil disobedience has developed in response to laws 'that are undemocratic, unjust, and against the rights of man'.[25] The resistance, which includes riding 'the city transportation', travelling freely and striking, resonates with practices conducted in the United States to oppose segregation. The reference to striking also calls attention to how labour practices inform civil rights and serve as a primary point of entry for 1950s black freedom movements.

John references the events that led him to join the resistance, which includes his six months of forced labour, resulting from a protest with the Transvall [sic] mineworkers. The harsh punishment – six months' compulsory labour for protesting – reveals the connection between labour practices and racial hierarchies. Burney explains the goals of the movement, saying, 'What we want is a decent world, where poverty is not a means to wealth, where ignorance is not used to prove race superiority, where sickness and death are not a part of our mines.'[26] As with the US civil rights movement, the interrelated goals of workers' rights and the elimination of racial hierarchies served as the basis for resistance to South African apartheid. Linking the goals in the final scene of the play, *Gold Through the Trees* reinforces Childress's intersectional feminism, and her investment in depicting the black freedom movements in the United States as part of an international movement.

Although, as Washington argues, Childress's participation in 1950s international black workers' rights movements has been largely unexplored, one need only look at the characters, scenarios and themes in her plays to get a sense of the pressing issues of her day. The scenes that organize *Gold Through the Trees* offer a long history of black freedom struggles that disrupt the temporal constraints of Childress's realist drama. The formal attributes of the play, however, call attention to an aspect of her art and work that sought to foreground women's roles and voices, not only in the burgeoning modern US civil rights movement, but also in the formation of black freedom struggles, from the struggle for emancipation to desegregation. Women's points of view give insight into the interrelation between struggles for racial, gender and class equality because women often function at the intersection of public and private social struggles. To foreground the work and contribution of women meant rethinking the representation of the modern civil rights movement and the form such representation could take.

Trouble in Mind (1955)

Childress's interest in giving voice to everyday women that contributed to the civil rights movement also emerged in the column she wrote for Paul Robeson's newspaper, *Freedom*. According to Washington, 'from 1951 to 1955, the period of the high Cold War, she contributed a regular – and, in some instances, procommunist – column to Paul Robeson's international-socialist newspaper, *Freedom*, maintaining close ties with Robeson even when many others were running fast to distance themselves from him'.[27] Childress's column, structured like a dramatic monologue, consisted of letters from a black domestic named Mildred to her friend Marge. The witty and irreverent letters draw attention to the daily interactions, or what a twenty-first-century audience would call microaggressions, that underpin racial hierarchies.

Her interest in representing the political contributions of working-class black women emerged alongside her development as an artist and activist. Washington argues:

> The institutions that Childress was closely associated with during the fifties – *Masses & Mainstream*, Club Baron, the Jefferson School of Social Science, *Freedom*, Sojourners for Truth and Justice, the American Negro Theatre, the committee for the Negro in the Arts – constituted a major part of the Harlem Left, a cultural front that shaped Childress's personal and public life and continued in Harlem throughout the 1950s, long after the 'official' Popular Front was considered dead.[28]

Washington's analysis of Childress furthers her claim that black artists participated in leftist labour movement activities during the Cold War. Although popular perceptions of the civil rights movement depict racial equality as its primary goal, as evidenced by the 1963 March on Washington for Jobs and Freedom, the movement also focused on workers' rights. Washington contends that the elision of black artists from histories of the left during the Cold War stems from the competing interests of artists and activists, including Childress, to expose US democracy's shortcomings and avoid appearing 'un-American'.

Paul Robeson functioned as a primary example of the penalties for associating with the Communist Party. Washington explains that 'during this political moment in the 1950s black writers and intellectuals were being intimidated, arrested, interrogated, indicted, jailed, deported, and blacklisted'.[29] During the period, the State Department revoked the passports of Robeson and W. E. B. Du Bois, severely curtailing Robeson's ability to earn a living as an internationally touring musician.

Although the FBI also kept a file detailing Childress's association with leftist organizations such as the CNA and Robeson's periodical, *Freedom*, the direct impact on Childress of the Bureau's surveillance is less clear. Washington argues that Childress maintained an ambiguous relationship with the Communist Party to maintain her opportunities as an artist. Nevertheless, based on the organizations that she collaborated with (*Masses & Mainstream*, Club Baron, the Jefferson School of Social Science and Sojourners for Truth and Justice), her political investments in advocating workers', women's and civil rights are clear.[30]

The Cold War backlash shaped Childress's work as well, informing the characterization and contexts of her 1955 play *Trouble in Mind*. The play depicts a rehearsal for the play *Chaos in Belleville*, which explores the lynching of a young black man who attempts to vote. The cast includes white and black actors of different ages. The central character, Wiletta Mayer, must negotiate the demands made of her personally and professionally to work in show business, but in the case of this performance, the demands prove too much. Wiletta is a middle-aged actress who yearns to be in the spotlight. As a result, she develops a professional persona that ingratiates her to white directors. As the cast members arrive in the opening scene of the play for a rehearsal, Wiletta introduces herself to John, a man young enough to be her son, and begins to offer him unsolicited advice about how to get along as a black actor with the play's white director, Al Manners. She explains:

> **Wiletta** Laugh! Laugh at everything they say, makes 'em feel superior.
>
> **John** Why do they need to feel superior?
>
> **Wiletta** You gonna sit there and pretend you don't know why?
>
> ...
>
> **Wiletta** We laugh and dispute him. [*She illustrates*] 'Oh, now, Mr. Manners, it ain't that bad!' ... White folks can't stand unhappy Negroes ... so laugh, laugh when it ain't funny at all.
>
> **John** Sounds kind of Uncle Tommish.
>
> **Wiletta** You callin' me a 'Tom'?[31]

The exchange illustrates Wiletta's willingness to appear servile in order to comfort the white director. Her scene of instruction seems to distinguish her from the strong female characters of Childress's *Florence* and *Gold Through the Trees*. Wiletta advises John to make a social sacrifice rather than a material one in order to put the director at ease and advance his career. The plot, however, challenges the willingness to acquiesce that characterizes Wiletta in the opening scene.

Once the entire cast has arrived, Manners begins rehearsal using what he characterizes as an unconventional rehearsal method that will solicit the actors' true feelings about the racial dynamics depicted in *Chaos in Belleville*. Manners begins with the white ingénue, Judy Sears. He instructs her to walk downstage, and although she studied acting at Yale, she walks upstage. As Manners teaches her stage directions, he throws a crumpled-up piece of paper on the floor in frustration. The stage directions indicate, '*Judy starts to pick up the paper*', but Manners admonishes, 'Hold your position! Wiletta pick up the paper!'[32] Exercising a bit of chivalry, the two black male actors, John and Sheldon, move to pick up the paper and Manners barks, 'I asked Wiletta!'[33] Shocked out of her obsequiousness, she responds, 'Well hell! I ain't the damn janitor!' And then, according to the stage directions, '*Trying to check her temper*', 'I ... well, I ... shucks ... I ... damn.'[34] Before Wiletta has a chance to make a decision about how to respond, Manners calls the scene to reveal that his direction was an improvisation geared towards tapping into the actors' emotions. Although Wiletta instructs John to go along with the director's belittlement, when confronted with a task that makes her physically and emotionally vulnerable to the rest of the cast, she refuses to comply.

The tension between Wiletta and Manners contextualizes Wiletta's earlier conversation with John as a description of survival strategies that emerge during the social contexts of the Cold War and modern civil rights movement. The characterization and social references in the play explicate the tension between Wiletta's instruction to John and her response to Manners's orders. Just as John finds Wiletta's advice – 'Laugh! Laugh at everything they say' – Tommish, he is astounded that Sheldon, an older black male character actor, does not know what the word 'chaos' means, or that Wiletta and Millie, a black actor '*about thirty-five years old*', complain about the racism of the theatre in front of Judy.[35] John's point of view reflects a generational shift in educational opportunities and an understanding of race and racism that does not restrict his social interactions in the same ways as the other characters.

Trouble in Mind references the civil rights movement and the House Un-American Activities Committee (HUAC) hearings but does not focus attention there. When Millie enters the stage, she carries a newspaper and comments regarding school desegregation in Little Rock, Arkansas: 'Look at 'em! Throwin' stones at little children, got to call out the militia to go to school.'[36] The conversation does not dwell on Millie's comment, which functions as more of an aside than a point of discussion. Similarly, Sheldon mentions that he is looking for a new apartment, and the director's white assistant, Eddie, suggests Sheldon consider his apartment building. Sheldon inquires if the building is integrated and when Eddie realizes that the building does not have any black residents, he changes the subject. Finally, Bill – the leading man in *Chaos in Belleville* – and Manners have an inconspicuous conversation about people being named: a subtle reference to the HUAC proceedings. Sheldon interjects, 'I sang on a program once with Millie, to help somebody that was in trouble ... but later on I heard they was tryin' to overthrow the gov'ment.'[37] The stage directions indicate that Sheldon's comment embarrasses Manners, Eddie and Bill, so they change the conversation. The asides and delicate references mark a distinct change from the clear, and in moments, didactic political message of *Gold Through the Trees*. The shift in tone, however, captures the fear of reprisal for being named a communist.

Even though the play-within-the-play, *Chaos in Belleville*, addresses the struggle for equal voting rights, *Trouble in Mind* focuses on the stereotypical roles black actors must play in order to work in professional theatres. Manners describes *Chaos in Belleville* as a play about the contemporary civil rights movement. The plot of *Chaos in Belleville* depicts the lynching of Eddie's character for attempting to vote, and the play features Bill's character giving a speech about moderation. In the 1950s, the US federal government often responded to the demands of civil rights activism with calls for moderation and patience. Although President Dwight D. Eisenhower sent federal troops to protect students in Little Rock, he was reluctant to enforce the Supreme Court's ruling in *Brown v. Board of Education*. *Trouble in Mind* establishes a shift in Childress's political tone that emerges alongside the weak federal support of the civil rights movement and the televised airings of the HUAC hearings in 1954. Although the play does not offer the same overt politics of *Gold Through the Trees*, it concludes that moderation, either in representational politics or governmental ones, will do more harm than good. The play ultimately affirms Childress's commitment to intersectional feminism, but demonstrates the ways her social contexts informed the tone and shape of her work.

Trouble in Mind premiered on 3 November 1955 at the Greenwich Mews Theatre in New York City. As Perkins details, based on an interview with the playwright, the production of the play mirrored the dynamic depicted in the play. Perkins explains that 'Childress had similar problems of "interpretation" with her own white producer when he threatened to cancel the Off-Broadway run if she did not end the play happily. According to Childress, happy endings were expected in the commercial theatre at this time.'[38] Childress ultimately regretted acquiescing to the producer, by ending the play with reconciliation between the director and the cast.[39]

Childress's commitment to depicting strong women characters persists in *Trouble in Mind*, as does the concern in *Florence* over white women facilitating black women's oppression. *Trouble in Mind* depicts antagonism between Judy and Millie, to reveal how race produces competition among women that facilitates patriarchy and racism. The antagonism begins when Millie learns that Judy will play the role of the Southern landowner's daughter, a type of role with emotional depth that Millie longs to play. The role calls for Judy to function as an intermediary between her father and the black characters. Meanwhile, Millie complains, 'wish I get to wear some decent clothes sometime. Only chance I get to dress up is offstage. I'll wear them baggy cotton dresses but damn if I'll wear another bandana.' She continues, 'Last show I was in, I wouldn't even tell my relatives. All I did was shout "Lord, have mercy!" for almost two hours every night.'[40] Judy is not personally to blame for the flat, stereotypical roles that Millie plays, but she does reinforce the structural hierarchies of the theatre, which map along gender and race lines.

In a rehearsal scene, Judy demonstrates concern over perpetuating racist language, but is unable to understand Millie's larger critique of how racial bias informs the characterization throughout the play. In the scene, Judy hesitates when the script calls for her to say the words 'darkies' and 'niggers'. The director briefly discusses her concern and then decides to move on with the rehearsal, concluding that the language represents the character's point of view. Judy stops rehearsal again because she feels Millie reacting negatively to her character. She passively asks Manners to intervene, questioning, 'She *is* their friend, right? It's just that I feel reactions and ...'[41] Once again, Manners halts rehearsal to address Judy's concern. Manners ultimately dismisses her complaint, so her behaviour reinforces the disciplinary power of the white male director, and an opportunity is missed by Judy and Millie to have a conversation about their mutual grievances. *Trouble in Mind* and *Florence* suggest the limits of interracial conflict resolution among women in the mid-twentieth century. Although *Trouble in Mind* offers the problem of coalitions among women as fundamental to the perpetuation of racial inequality, it does not provide the opportunity for women to come together. Such spaces and conversations become the work of the third-wave feminists, but Childress's attention to such dynamics anticipates the importance of understanding how gender differences facilitate racial hierarchies.

Trouble in Mind also considers the ways intraracial conflict across gender lines positions black women as facilitators of violence against black men. In *Chaos in Belleville*, Wiletta's character must decide how to manage the social upheaval John's character (Job) – Wiletta's son in the play – causes after he attempts to vote. The script indicates that Wiletta instructs Job to surrender to Judge Willis so that he can be safe from the lynch mob in the county jail. Job's death, however, is inevitable. Wiletta laments, 'The writer wants the damn white man to be the hero – and I'm the villain.'[42] Wiletta tries to explain that the idea of a black mother entrusting her son's life to a white judge contradicts the social logic of US race histories. Instead of surrendering Job, Wiletta suggests changing the script to Wiletta's character instructing Job to run. The shift in the script addresses the implausibility of the scene.

Although Mannners first feigns interest in Wiletta's critique, his investment in the social relations that *Chaos in Belleville* affirm overrides his ability to render thoughtful black characters. Exasperated by Wiletta's accusation – 'You are a prejudiced man, a prejudiced racist'[43] – Manners fires back, saying, 'Don't compare yourself to me! What goes for my son doesn't necessarily go for yours! Don't compare him [points to John] ... with three strikes against him, don't compare him with my son, they've got nothing in common ... not a goddam thing!'[44] The differentiation that Manners articulates quiets the cast and results in him cancelling rehearsal for the rest of the day. It also clarifies the limits of moderate approaches to civil rights issues. Although *Chaos in*

Belleville attempts to present sympathetic black characters, it falls far short of depicting human ones. Moreover, it presents the dehumanization as a function of intraracial and intergenerational conflict rather than the structural racism that an uneven access to citizenship produces. This means that although the white characters in *Chaos in Belleville* attempt to intervene for the black characters, the structure of the plot implies that a black person attempting to exercise the civil right to vote is committing a capital offence. The structure disqualifies the black characters from acting as citizens.

Although much of *Trouble in Mind* takes a more subtle approach than *Gold Through the Trees,* its meditation on black motherhood makes a stronger statement because it not only demonstrates black mothers' inability to shield their sons from state violence, but also contemplates how representational politics place black women as perpetrators of the violence. *Gold Through the Trees* links the mother's inability to save her son from execution to a long history of state authorized racial violence, from slavery to colonialism to executions. Through *Chaos in Belleville*, conversely, *Trouble in Mind* depicts black women's backwardness and inability to mother as the cause of black men placing themselves in precarious situations that result in state sanctions. The emphasis shifts from the social structures that produce anti-black violence to choices black people make. Wiletta's decision to defy the script reveals to the audience of *Trouble in Mind* the ways representational politics reinforce structural racism, but her decision does not cause a structural change to the theatre world imagined in the play. The play ends with the presumption that Manners will fire Wiletta. In the final scene, she stands alone on stage and recites Psalm 133. She finally has her moment as a thoughtful figure in the spotlight, but it must occur outside of *Chaos in Belleville.*

Although the emphasis and form of Childress's work shifts throughout the 1950s, her investment in rendering complex black women characters persists. Her focus on the lives of average black women, who experience the world as a result of their gender, class and racial positions, provides the opportunity to show how such perspectives could transform the social settings of the play. Although Childress's characters, for the most part, do not succeed in making structural change, they offer a point of view from which the imaginative and constitutive visions of third-wave feminists unfold.

6

Jerome Lawrence and Robert E. Lee: *Inherit the Wind* (1955), *Auntie Mame* (1956) and *The Gang's All Here* (1959)

Alan Woods

Introduction

Jerome Lawrence and his writing partner of more than half a century, Robert E. Lee, established a record as creators of theatrical work virtually unmatched in mid-twentieth-century American theatre.[1] At least one of their more than 39 plays is in constant performance somewhere in the world, virtually every week of every year – a statement which has been essentially true since their theatrical debut in 1949 with the book and lyrics for the musical *Look, Ma, I'm Dancin'!*[2] Their most produced plays include the perennials *Inherit the Wind* (first produced 1955), *Auntie Mame* (1956) and its musical adaptation *Mame!* (1966), and a later work, *The Night Thoreau Spent in Jail* (1970). Their record of constant production is matched only by Thornton Wilder's *Our Town*, the plays of their contemporaries Arthur Miller and Tennessee Williams, and a writer from toward the end of their careers, Neil Simon.

A proud Ohio Buckeye, Jerome Lawrence (who was born in 1915 in Cleveland) first wrote for the Hillel Players as a student at Ohio State University in the late 1930s. After graduation, Lawrence wrote and directed for CBS in both Hollywood and New York. Robert E. Lee (who was born in Elyria in 1918, and whom Lawrence never quite let forget that he attended Ohio Wesleyan University in nearby Delaware, Ohio, rather than Ohio State) wrote and directed for the advertising agency Young and Rubicam, and was often on CBS radio as well. The pair knew of each other's work, and numerous friends suggested they meet. This, they finally accomplished in January 1942, in New York, and immediately decided to form a writing partnership. Their first collaboration was a script, 'Inside a Kid's Head', which was performed on the experimental radio programme *Columbia Workshop* and later widely anthologized.[3] The new team was a success and by the spring of 1942 they relocated to Los Angeles, with plans to break into writing for motion pictures in addition to radio. However, the war intervened and by July of 1942 the pair were among the founders of the Armed Forces Radio Service, writing and directing numerous scripts – 60 for *Mail Call* and 162 for *Yarns For Yanks*, among many more. They also began their first writing for the legitimate theatre, creating a script that was considered by the Theatre Guild, at the time a major production company for quality drama, but they eventually passed on this particular play.

After the war, Lawrence and Lee returned to civilian life, and, having met composer Hugh Martin, were asked to write a scene for a musical he was starting to plan with choreographer Jerome Robbins – a major figure in the American musical theatre world. The musical was to star comedienne Nancy Walker, who had had a personal success in Martin's 1942 musical, *Best Foot Forward*. The scene was written and approved and the pair were hired to write the show, now titled *Look, Ma, I'm Dancin'!* While Lawrence moved to New York and took an apartment to work on the script, Lee stayed in Los Angeles, less sure the production was actually going to happen. As he suspected, it seemed to stall, as is often the case with new work by young writers. Then veteran director

George Abbott became interested in the script, and the show was suddenly in rehearsal.

Look, Ma, I'm Dancin'! featured Walker as a Texas beer heiress who funded a ballet company and insisted on performing, turning into a comically bumbling ballerina in the process. With Harold Lang and Herbert Ross, both well-known Broadway musical artists in the cast, the show opened on 29 January 1948 to praising reviews and a strong box office. It was a major hit of that winter season, even given a feature spread in *Life* magazine. An unseasonably hot spring negatively affected box-office sales – in the days before the air conditioning of Broadway theatres was able to make audiences comfortable even in the humid heat of a mid-town New York summer – and the show closed in mid-July, having made a small profit. Shortly after, Lee would marry Janet Waldo, a radio actress then best known for playing Corliss Archer (she would later become equally well known as the voice of Judy Jetson, Penelope Pitstop and many others).

Lawrence and Lee returned to primarily radio work, producing hundreds of scripts for such series as *Favorite Story* (for which a celebrity selected a story that the writers then dramatized), *Halls of Ivy*, *Young Love* and *The Dinah Shore Show*. The writers' own favourite story involved an actual historical event: the election of a cow as Ohio State's Homecoming Queen in 1926. It was a prank by a group of Agriculture College students who nominated 'Maudine Ormsby' and then got her elected.[4] Among the major writers for network radio, Lawrence and Lee wrote, directed and produced 299 broadcasts of musical theatre works for the weekly series *The Railroad Hour* between 1948 and 1954, including the scripts and lyrics for 60 original musicals. They also published four short musicals with the music publisher Harms, but these ventures seemed short lived. They had yet to make their big breakthrough on the stage.

Inherit the Wind (1955)

Lawrence and Lee returned to the live theatre with the script for *Inherit the Wind*, which was first produced at Margo Jones's Theatre '55 in Dallas, and then moved to Broadway once its potential was recognized. Its tremendous success on Broadway would lead the pair to focus on writing for the stage almost exclusively from 1955 through to the late 1970s, when they would become champions for the then-emerging regional theatre movement. Margo Jones's pioneering work in regional theatre was to have an enormous impact on later developments, as professional regional theatres gradually augmented (and in some places replaced) the theatres housing touring productions sent 'on the road' from New York. Jones's work was among the inspirations for the support Lawrence and Lee were to provide decades later for the American Playwrights' Theatre a similar solution for the limited resources then available to playwrights outside the commercial Broadway stage.[5]

In returning to the Broadway stage, Lawrence and Lee were returning to what had become the epicentre of the American theatre world and one of the major centres for professional theatre around the globe.[6] American theatre had thrived at a national level in the second half of the nineteenth century and first half of the twentieth, but by the immediate post-Second World War years, the regional circuits that had fed this began to disappear, and theatre had become centred increasingly in New York. By the mid-1950s, the theatrical community was estimated to stand at 20,000 people, now centred in New York – including performers, designers, stagehands, publicity managers, theatre staff (including ushers) and so forth.[7] The creation of theatre work was generally regarded as the work of skilled craftspeople working collaboratively, a point made by Richard Hummler in the show business paper *Variety*.[8] In short, the day of the highly acclaimed individual artist being credited with creation seemed over for a time. That it would return was inevitable, but with few exceptions the theatrical scene of the 1950s was, as Hummler suggests, primarily collaborative.

Lawrence and Lee seemed to embrace the theatrical zeitgeist of the period as they ventured forward with their 'collaborative' script for *Inherit the Wind*, a script in which they had also collaborated with actual history, as they invented much of the dialogue and changed several facts for dramatic impact – what the playwrights called 'factual fiction or fictional fact'.[9] They were also lucky enough to have their work translated by an expert team of theatre practitioners. Herman Shumlin both directed and produced, and brought in well-known star Paul Muni, returning to the New York stage for the first time in six years, as Drummond, Ed Begley as Brady and a young Tony Randall as Hornbeck.[10] Both Muni and Begley won Tony Awards for their performances. Also, upcoming stage designer Peter Larkin was asked to create the set, and his ingenious two-level staging aptly conveyed the idea of an entire country town and won him his second Tony Award.

The famous Scopes 'Monkey Trial', in which a high school teacher was tried in 1925 for having defied an old Tennessee state law against the teaching of evolution, provided the source material for the play. Famed turn-of-the-twentieth century orator (and three-time presidential candidate, albeit always unsuccessful) William Jennings Bryan (1860–1925) led the prosecution at the trial, while Clarence Darrow (1857–1938), well known as a founding member of the American Civil Liberties Union and for having defended Leopold and Loeb, the 'thrill killers' of a teenaged boy the previous year, was the defence attorney. John Thomas Scopes (1900–70) was convicted (although the conviction was later reversed on a technicality). The trial attracted national attention, with many reporters travelling to Dayton, Tennessee, to provide coverage (and, indeed, the town leaders later admitted the whole brouhaha had been created to attract publicity to the town).[11]

Ironically enough, Lawrence and Lee chose to dramatize the Scopes trial in order to address what was for them, in the early 1950s, the burning issue of freedom of speech. The men were aghast at the 'witch hunting' hearings of the US Congress's House Committee on Un-American Activities, encouraged most famously by Senator Joseph R. McCarthy of Wisconsin. McCarthy seemed to find anti-Americans – most of whom he identified as communists – everywhere he looked. Although they were not personally involved, and had not been called before HUAC, the writing duo was certainly aware of the effects of such red-baiting tactics and the effect of these on the artistic community. Lawrence and Lee were politically progressive, and, wanting to mount a spirited defence of and demand for free speech, searched for an historical event that had taken place within a court setting that could substitute for the HUAC hearings. In this quest, they were inspired by Maxwell Anderson's use of poetic and dramatic licence in drawing upon the Sacco-Vanzetti case for his 1935 drama, *Winterset*, and his earlier fictionalizing of history in 1933's *Mary of Scotland*, for which Anderson also created scenarios that never actually happened.[12]

They chose the Scopes trial because they believed evolution was, by 1954, thoroughly accepted, and through the format of such a trial they could offer a view of the philosophy and impetus behind the HUAC hearings, with their similar agenda to restrict free thought in a nation supposedly founded on such freedoms. After all, there had been little outcry from Sportin' Life's questioning of the veracity of biblical tales in 'It Ain't Necessarily So' in 1935's *Porgy and Bess* (though perhaps the racial controversy surrounding the musical had overshadowed this aspect). The playwrights had assumed that the timely issue of civil rights would be readily apparent, and audiences and critics would focus upon the schoolteacher's right to speak. However, they did not foresee the surging popularity of creationism from religious fundamentalists, which would continue to grow through the development of mega churches and conservative preachers to spread their views through radio and television.[13] Such groups were outraged by what they saw as the playwrights' deliberate ignoring of historical fact, and pointed out several misstatements regarding the conduct of the trial and the people involved. Obviously, such criticisms ignored the playwrights' own words in the introduction to the published text, in which they clearly state that the play 'does not pretend to be journalism. It is theatre.'[14] The playwrights had freely adapted the events to create a more effective theatrical piece, using the Scopes trial as inspiration rather than as source material. The play and its characters, by the playwrights' own admission, bear little resemblance to the events or people involved in the Scopes trial and are truly their own creation.

Among the script's many strengths is its use of stage spectacle, but in this instance not the Broadway theatre's typically lavish spectacle of scenery and costuming – though that sort of spectacle would be part of the appeal of the next Lawrence and Lee play, *Auntie Mame*. In *Inherit the Wind*, the spectacle is created by the large number of actors – twenty-two in the premiere Dallas production, tripled to sixty-five in New York – so that crowds literally filled the stage space – the town square – in the first act for the excited mob welcoming Brady to the fictional town of Hillsboro (in an unnamed state somewhere in mid-America to keep it as representative as possible). The community is an integral part of the playwrights' vision, as their opening stage direction makes clear:

> *In and around the Hillsboro Courthouse. The foreground is the actual courtroom, with jury box, judge's bench and a scattering of trial-scarred chairs and counsel tables. On a raked level above it are the courthouse square, Main Street, and the converging streets of the town. This is not so much a literal view of Hillsboro as it is an impression of a sleepy, obscure country town about to be vigorously awakened.*
>
> *It is important to the concept of the play that the town is visible always, looming there, as much on trial as the defendant. The crowd is equally important, so the court becomes an arena.*[15]

The large cast was also essential in the frenzy of the prayer meeting scene that closed the first scene of Act Two, culminating in the Reverend Brown's calling down curses first on Cates, then on his own daughter Rachel, for defending Cates, followed by Brady defending her and citing the verse from the Book of Proverbs that gives the play its title: 'He that troubleth his own house ... shall inherit the wind' (Prov. 11.29).

Focusing in on one of the era's newly recognized demographics, the play opens with two young teenagers, Howard and Melinda. To Melinda's shock and horror, Howard brings up evolution, and we are shown right away the central conflict in the 'mouths of the young'. It is for the future of these youths that truths must be told, and it will be made clear later on that knowledge of evolution has not harmed Howard or made him forget his ten commandments. Rachel Brown heads to the jail to visit the local schoolteacher with whom she is in love, Bert Cates, who has been arrested for teaching the theory of evolution. A relatively minor case has become a media event due to the principles involved, and two big-name lawyers have been called in to prosecute and defend. Outside the courthouse, Rachel's father, Reverend Brown, is overseeing the raising of a banner urging people to 'Read your Bible'. A crowd gathers, at one point bursting into 'Gimme That Old Time Religion' as they wait for Brady, and E. K. Hornbeck, a journalist covering the trial, looks on with withering cynicism.

Matthew Harrison Brady, renowned orator and politician, will be the prosecuting attorney at Cates's trial, and he will argue that creationism is the only explanation for the world, and to deny this, as science does, is sinful. Brady has come not to prosecute Cates so much as defend the state statute against teaching evolution and the 'Living Truth of the Scriptures'.[16] He views this as a fight to maintain people's belief in the Bible and God. We are in no doubt that this is a real battle, as on his arrival the townspeople confer on Brady the honorary title of Colonel in the State Militia. Drummond is a known agnostic, with a reputation for defending even the knowingly guilty and freeing them by exposing inequities in the laws they have broken. Brady warns, 'He'll try to make us forget the lawbreaker and put the law on trial.'[17] But Drummond will view this as a trial about the right to think, thus setting personal liberty against the laws of the land.

The town views Henry Drummond as satanic next to the evangelical Brady, with one young girl crying out 'It's the Devil!!' as Drummond enters Dayton.[18] This is a Bible-belt town and they see his defence of Cates as a personal attack on their faith. These old-fashioned townsfolk are mostly creationists, and in many ways it becomes the town itself that is on trial, for being backward thinking. But Drummond will not denigrate the Bible, as he makes this an argument about the right to free speech. Both attorneys understand that this is a landmark case that will influence the education of future generations. Meantime, we witness Brady overeating, despite his wife's warnings. Brady is overweight, and this is partly what kills him in the end, and it is a symbol of his overindulgence in everything, including his own opinion at the expense of others. Hornbeck shares his opinions with Rachel in support of Cates and his view of Brady as a relic of a bygone era.

As the trial begins, various potential jurors are questioned and it becomes apparent that this will be a politically charged, communally divisive event. Drummond removes his coat, due to the heat, revealing lavender suspenders. Brady attempts to mock him for being 'big city fashionable', until Drummond explains he bought them in Brady's own small Nebraska home town – the world is clearly changing however much some want it to remain the same. In the aftermath of the trial session, there is an announcement that a prayer meeting will be held to which Drummond strongly objects. His insistence that the banner and prayer meeting are unfairly prejudicial, and they should at least give equal time and publicity to Darwin, is dismissed by the judge as preposterous. With the same apparent prejudice, the judge will also accept Brady's objection that all of Drummond's scientific witnesses, there to prove the reality of evolution, are 'Irrelevant, immaterial, inadmissible'.[19] But the truth is, technically he is right, for the state law does not allow such views to be spoken, regardless of whether they are correct or false. The initially calm tone of the prayer meeting rises toward hysteria, as Reverend Brown calls down curses on Cates and then, when Rachel protests, on his own daughter. He depicts the extremes of religious bigotry, which can turn on its own kith and kin. Even Brady feels he has gone too far, calling for moderation and forgiveness as better paths for the faithful. When Brady and Drummond finally have a moment alone, Brady asks why they have grown so far apart when they were once close, and Drummond explains, 'All motion is relative. Perhaps it is *you* who have moved away – by standing still.'[20] Lawrence and Lee ensure we see Drummond as representing the future and the march of progress, while Brady, though not a terrible man, can only represent a more limited past.

The trial itself is a direct contest between Brady and Drummond, as both criticize everything the other says and does to try to find an opening, like two prizefighters sparring. Unable to maintain his cross-examination of Howard due to repeated sustained objections from Brady, Drummond still sneaks in a speech advocating truth above morality. Brady has Rachel take the stand and relate various opinions Cates has shared with her regarding recent events and the state of his own religious beliefs. Reverend Brown's rigid intolerance is further revealed as we learn how he had preached that one of Cates's students, who had drowned, did not die in a state of grace because he had never been baptized and that his soul was writhing in hellfire – an opinion against which Cates vociferously objects. Brady unfairly twists Cates's private musings to Rachel about the relationship of God and man into a declaration that God does not exist, and Rachel dissolves into tears. Cates protests, pointing out that these were private conversations and just questioning ideas rather than asserting any facts. Drummond, showing a kindness we see little of from the self-professed Christians, allows Rachel to leave the stand without cross-examination.

Just as HUAC often refused to allow those brought before them to defend themselves, Brady and the Judge will not allow Drummond to call any scientists to testify in Cates's defence, so Drummond changes tactics and calls on Brady to become a witness. Not allowed to ask about Darwin, the Judge does allow questions about the Bible. By drawing attention to such improbable tales as Jonah and the whale, and the creation of the world in just six days, Drummond demonstrates that the Bible should not be taken as literal truth, but as allegorical. Pointing out that if God gave man the ability to reason, it should not be blasphemy to question the Bible, and Drummond begins to draw the spectators to his viewpoint and a realization that science and religion need not be diametrically opposed. Tricked by his own sense of righteous self-importance, Brady is led by Drummond into asserting that God speaks to him personally – which is why his views must be the only ones allowable – and when teased about such a pompous claim, also contradictorily admits that 'each man is a free agent'.[21] This is a statement on which Drummond seizes to defend his client's right to free speech. This rhetorical victory sends Brady into a manic recitation of biblical passages that allows both Drummond and the audience to mock him, as he is dismissed from the witness stand. The scene ends as Brady collapses and his wife rushes to comfort him.

Act Three reveals the main characters waiting for the verdict, and it is clear that despite his exposure of Brady, Drummond does not expect victory. He compares the jury system to a horse race, and implies Brady is like a toy horse he had been given as a child, that turned out to be rotten underneath the paint, and poorly constructed. Drummond urges Cates to always look behind the surface and, if something is based on lies, to show it up, whatever the cost. That the playwrights have made it fairly clear to the audience that Cates has done nothing genuinely wrong, the jury's guilty verdict is meant to parallel the likely truth that most of those condemned (arrested, fined or blacklisted) by HUAC were similarly only guilty of having held unpopular viewpoints rather than having done anything truly criminal. The court finds Cates unanimously guilty, but it is a pyrrhic victory, because he is only given a minimal fine and low bond, and will most likely win on appeal to the Supreme Court. The verdict is a further mockery of justice as the Judge was pressured to impose such a light punishment by the town's Mayor, who is fearful of a media backlash should Cates be too severely sentenced. Brady objects to such leniency, but is overruled.

The Judge adjourns the trial, but Brady pulls out a large sheaf of papers and starts making a speech as everyone is leaving. However, he has been discredited and no one is prepared to listen. As he shouts to be heard, he suddenly collapses and is carried away. Confused, Cates asks Drummond if he won or lost, and Drummond informs him that he won by bringing national attention to a bad law. Hornbeck also says his newspaper will pay Cates's bail to keep him out of jail. After Rachel enters, to tell Cates she has left her father's house and is willing to have a more open mind, the Judge returns with the news that Brady has died. Hornbeck and Drummond disagree over Brady's worth, with Drummond defending his old opponent and accusing Hornbeck of being too cynical and unfairly critical of religious belief, pointing out that Brady had the same rights as Cates to believe whatever he wanted.

Cates has undeniably broken the law, which is why he must be found guilty, but the law is shown to be unjust. Our sympathy for Cates is automatic, because he is not grandstanding or trying to cause trouble, but is a meek and ordinary man, in looks and intellect. He simply felt it ridiculous not to say what he knew to be a scientific truth. Cates pays a price for his stance, as he loses his job and lodgings, and his life will be hard, but as Drummond points out, he has made it easier for the next person to stand up for what he believes, so has done justice a good turn. He is also rewarded by the love of Rachel as they leave town together to start a new life. Left alone, Drummond picks up two books that have been left – the Bible and Cates's copy of Darwin – weighing them against each other. Drummond's efforts had been to prove that it is possible to believe in the Bible and science simultaneously, as one does not necessarily negate the other. As he leaves with copies of both Darwin and the Bible in his briefcase, he underlines this understanding.

Inherit the Wind addresses a major concern of the playwrights: the right of the individual to personal fulfilment and the expression of an individualized approach to life. The right to personal goals, regardless of the conformist pressures of the society surrounding every person, was a cardinal principle deeply held by both writers, and that concern can be seen underlying the major characters' strengths and flaws in *Inherit the Wind*. And although critical attention (and that of most audiences) is focused substantially on the contest between Brady and Drummond, the playwrights also provide an audience surrogate in the character of Rachel. Her journey from her horror at Cates's espousal of Darwinian evolution to acceptance of it (and Cates), and then her realization that her journey will take her away from Hillsboro and the conformist repression of free thinking that her father and his congregation personify, are both a call to the acceptance of progress and, perhaps, even a subtle nod to the growing strength of women.

The play's second major theme, the need to speak truth to power, is fully articulated in the 'Golden Dancer' speech near the beginning of Act Three. Drummond remembers a wooden rocking horse he was fixated on from the age of seven after seeing it in the window of the local general store, strongly believing, 'If I had Golden Dancer I'd have everything in the world that I wanted.' It was all golden, with purple spots, and in the child's vision a spectacular and glamorous toy. Eventually his parents, having scrimped and saved grocery money and worked overtime for months, bought it for him as a surprise gift. Drummond then sounds a cautionary note:

> ... I woke up in the morning and there was Golden Dancer at the foot of my bed! ... I jumped into the saddle and started to rock – (*Almost in a whisper*) And it *broke*! It split in two! The wood was rotten, the whole thing was put together with spit and sealing wax! All shine and no substance! (*Turning to Cates.*) Bert, whenever you see something bright, shining, perfect-seeming – all gold, with purple spots – look behind the paint! And if it's a lie – show it up for what it really is![22]

The speech stands by itself and, indeed, is often used by student actors for scene work and as an audition piece. It forms the heart of the play inasmuch as it is a call to all those witnessing the way the rights of the individual were being trampled upon in America by their own government – with its enforced loyalty oaths, FBI surveillance and congressional investigations – to speak out and shame those doing the trampling.

Lawrence and Lee's emphasis on the need for free expression is present in each of the major plays created by the playwrights through the rest of their careers, both in texts they jointly co-authored as well as in those each wrote singly. *Inherit the Wind* was released as a film by United Artists in 1960 with great success, starring Spencer Tracy, Fredric March and Gene Kelly. Melvyn Douglas and Ed Begley starred in a *Hallmark Hall of Fame* television version in 1965 on NBC TV, while a later 1988 NBC version starred Jason Robards and Kirk Douglas, with a script rewritten by John Gay with some changes that the original writers did not approve (such as turning Brady into a Jimmy Swaggert-type evangelist). Despite Lawrence and Lee's misgivings, both Robards and the production won Emmy Awards the following year.

Auntie Mame (1956)

After *Inherit the Wind*, Lawrence and Lee had equally great success with *Auntie Mame* (1956). The play was adapted from a highly successful selection of comic vignettes by Patrick Dennis, published in 1955.[23] Just as with *Inherit the Wind*, the couple developed their characters far beyond their source material, in this case creating many of Mame's more memorable lines. Rather than construct a typical well-made play, they crafted what appears on the surface a rather loose, episodic celebration of life, but it is one that is causally logical and carefully structured. Producers Robert Fryer and Lawrence Carr approached Rosalind Russell to star in the Broadway production; Russell had returned to the stage with great success in 1953 in the musical *Wonderful Town*, after many years as a film star. Both Dennis and Russell loved the script. Dennis felt it captured the spirit of the book but took on its own dynamic, and was anything but a safe, conventional play, while Russell called it a 'revue without music' and something of a theatrical 'freak'.[24]

Lawrence and Lee wanted Mame to represent the new kind of multi-layered and multi-talented person they saw emerging in a society being sped forward by advances in communication and mobility. Their play, with multiple sets showing Mame's constant redecoration of her Manhattan apartment, follows her coping with the unexpected arrival, in the midst of a wild party, of her recently-orphaned nephew, Patrick, accompanied by his nurse, Norah. The party's guests include Vera Charles, a self-important actress, and Radcliffe, described as a 'He-type She' (and a clear reference to celebrated English author/icon Radcliffe Hall, author of the classic lesbian novel *The Well of Loneliness*).[25] Vera's deadpan cynicism serves as a well-crafted comic foil for Mame's sunnier humour, and Vera's constant drunken state provides its own running gag throughout the play.

Much humour is found in Mame's constant party-giving, while she simultaneously attempts to become a model middle-class, maternal figure raising a small child. Her placing Patrick in a 'progressive' school run by a sometime lover, Ralph Devine, allows satire of such educational experimentation (which includes the nudity of all concerned), while the periodic intrusion of Mr Babcock, a conservative bank trustee assigned as trustee to the estate of Patrick's father, contrasts the bohemian and free-thinking lifestyle at Mame's with Babcock's rigid morality. Thus the playwrights satirize the upper class's conformism as well as their weakness for 'fads'. Just as Mame will later save Patrick from a narrow life of bigotry and stultifying convention, in the first act we see the need to care for Patrick as saving Mame from an empty, dilettante life of hedonism.

As the play progresses, Mame loses her fortune and tries to join the workforce. She is humorously inefficient as both a telephone switchboard operator, who gets tangled up in her own wires, and as a Macy's salesperson at the roller skate counter, who is unable to fill out a sales slip. She gets fired from both positions, but before leaving Macy's had caught the eye of a rich Southerner, Beauregard Jackson Pickett Burnside. He follows her home and soon proposes marriage. Next, Mame has to deal with his Southern relatives (whose clichéd characterizations entirely meet a mid-1950s New York theatre audience's preconception of the cultural norms of the American South – as, of course, does Beau's name and that of his family's plantation: Peckerwood). The central event for her encounter with the family is a foxhunt, at which Mame rides down the fox, eventually revealing, only to young Patrick, that she got stuck in the saddle and couldn't stop the horse! She winds up being extolled by the oblivious Southern gentry for her horse-riding prowess. Her courage and free spirit again win her the day.

Mame's secretary, Agnes Gooch, serves the plot by being sent off by Mame to various events, and whose unmarried pregnancy upsets the very proper and uptight family of Gloria Upson, the vacuous debutante to whom Patrick has become engaged. The party her parents host for Patrick, Gloria and Mame serves to provide additional satire as Mame sees the thoroughly conservative, middle-class life toward which Patrick is heading. Mame throws her own gathering to celebrate the engagement, with her agenda being to break up the match. This provides Lawrence and Lee with many humorous digs as the outrageous people from the first act reappear, and Mame's agent, Lindsay, arrives with the page proofs of her autobiography. The delighted guests read portions aloud, to the shock and horror of the Upsons, who are finally, utterly dismayed at the news that the house next to theirs – which in the earlier scene has been established as just over the line in their subdivision restricting any other than Caucasian Anglo-Saxons from purchasing – has been bought by Mame and donated as a Home for Refugee Jewish Children.[26]

Mame's party makes Patrick realize just how disastrous a marriage to Gloria would be, and so he winds up with the commonsensical Pegeen Ryan, the interior decorator who has been working on Mame's apartment. In the play's final scene, set several years later, Mame is in India, having married Lindsay after Beau's unfortunate death. She returns to New York and lures Patrick and Pegeen's son, Michael, with tales of India. Pegeen refuses to let Michael travel with Mame, which causes Michael to say, 'You know what your problem is, Mom? You don't live. LIVE!' and to the horror of his parents, comically repeats the tag line we had earlier heard Mame declare, 'Life is a banquet, and most poor sons-of-bitches are starving to death!'[27] As the play ends, we see Mame repeating her insistence that one must expose oneself to life's complexities that we saw in her first scene with young Patrick, as she gives Michael a pad, telling him to write down words he doesn't understand. This precisely mirrors her earlier actions with Patrick as she excitedly declares, again, 'What times we're going to have.'[28]

As was the case with *Inherit the Wind*, *Auntie Mame* demonstrates an emphasis on the development of the individual. Indeed, much of the action (and the play's humour) is driven by Mame's attempt to transform herself into a sweetly maternal maiden aunt, despite being constantly interrupted by figures from her wild life. Mame's constant efforts to change were shown by the play's construction: many short scenes, often with lavishly spectacular settings provided by Oliver Smith and costumes by Noel Taylor, that create a kaleidoscopic view of Mame's life, and young Patrick's bewildered fascination. The playwrights also created vividly theatrical moments, as when, in the final moments of the last scene in

Act One, Beau's relatives line up at the proscenium line, staring into the audience as if watching the foxhunt in which Mame's horse runs away with her. Despite the wild horse, Mame manages to triumph and to capture the fox as well.

Patrick growing into young adulthood is handled by having the beginning scenes of Act Two follow Mame and Beau on their eight-year-long honeymoon tour across the world, culminating with avid photographer Beau backing up to take another snapshot of Mame, and falling off the Matterhorn in the process. The potentially anti-comic sequence that would show Mame as sorrowing widow is relieved by the introduction of secretary Agnes Gooch, whose change from timid mouse to libidinous and (unwed) pregnant mouse, after being paired by Mame with the dashing Brian O'Bannion, provides a richly comic (and, in 1956, daring) subplot. Also, the grown-up Patrick's engagement to Gloria Upson gives opportunities to poke fun at repressed suburbanites, again a favourite target for the self-consciously sophisticated Broadway audiences of the time.

The rapid pace and multiple scenes of the play led many original reviewers to see the play as episodic and not really logically progressive. Repeated productions, and the eventual musical adaptation, have demonstrated the falsity of that evaluation; the comedy is indeed carefully structured and developed through thoroughly detailed character relationships. And as is often the case with theatrical productions, the play's performers gained much of the credit for its initial success, particularly Russell and Peggy Cass as Gooch. It took a while for critics to recognize the strengths of the script, as opposed to the power of the excellent production it received. Indeed, John Chapman, the critic for the *New York Daily News*, wrote some three years after the play opened:

> Did it ever occur to you that a critic could be wrong once in a while? It has to me.
>
> For example, take the night of Oct. 31, 1956, when 'Auntie Mame' opened. While admitting that I had one wonderful time, I wrote, 'The only reason for seeing the comedy is Rosalind Russell ...'
>
> My apologies to the adaptors of Patrick Dennis' novel, Jerome Lawrence and Robert E. Lee. They must have wrought better than I thought, for 'Auntie Mame' is actress-proof. Anybody could play it, and almost everybody has.[29]

And *Auntie Mame* has proven, over the years, a thoroughly reliable vehicle, particularly for maturing female performers seeking a starring stage engagement. *Auntie Mame* was filmed with Russell and Cass, and released by Warner Brothers in 1958. It went on to become a cult favourite, with midnight screenings at the 10th Street Cinema in New York and the Tiffany Theatre in Los Angeles for many years.

The Gang's All Here (1959)

While *The Gang's All Here* is produced less frequently than the other major plays of Lawrence and Lee, it too focuses on serious issues, especially as it deals with political corruption and on the need for a political candidate to fiercely preserve the ability to speak clearly and forthrightly. Just like *Inherit the Wind*, for which Lawrence and Lee chose events from the past around which to build their plot, *The Gang's All Here* was also a play very much of its time, containing clear political concerns for its era. The effects of advertising and new electronic media on politics of the 1950s were apparent, as information previously kept in the backroom began to disseminate far more freely. Lawrence and Lee wanted to expose the increasing difficulties any United States president might experience in running for and maintaining the office in the face of this lessening of privacy. The need to be scrupulously open, honest and aware was more important than ever.

The action follows a presidential candidate, Griffith P. Hastings, into the White House, despite his being a relatively weak contender. Beginning at a Chicago hotel with the delegates caught in a primary gridlock between two other lacklustre presidential candidates, we meet a group of 'backroom boys' swapping favours and jostling for votes. The group seems dominated by the evidently shrewd Rafferty, who remains calm and aloof. After one of the 'gang', Charles Webster, who is supposedly supporting the nomination of the Massachusetts governor, cynically declares they need to get going or '[a] complete stranger could slip in – some grass roots amateur with nobody behind him but the people',[30] Rafferty finally puts forward Hastings, a politician he has been advising for some time, as such a potentially new candidate: 'He's got what people vote for.'[31] What that turns out to be are his good looks, a splendid head of hair and piercing eyes, and the fact that 'he never forgets a friend'.[32]

The men are worried that Hastings's wife has too much control over him, but Rafferty soon gets his colleagues' support, including Webster, especially with the suggestion of some comfortable government positions as payback: Webster is offered the head of the Veterans' Bureau. Hastings initially declines; he likes being in the Senate, viewing it as 'the greatest club in the world',[33] and is both reluctant and fearful to take on the responsibility of president. However, after Rafferty and Webster have assured his wife, Frances, that no commitments have been made to secure his nomination, and the governor (with whom they have yet to speak) has agreed to be vice president, she persuades Hastings to take it on. He easily wins the vote and is sworn in, and we next see them moving into the White House.

The selling of the candidate despite his shortcomings is clearly depicted. Hastings is not a bad person – he is just unsuited to the position, with little understanding of the work of government and too many skeletons in the closet. This is partly why Rafferty and his group have selected him, as they feel this will better allow them to manipulate him into giving them what they want: power and money. Once elected, the play follows his efforts to govern fairly, handicapped by this corrupt group of advisors and his own ignorance of what is going on around him. He is clearly out of his depth when talking policy, and Hastings is only happy when playing cards and drinking with his buddies, who are all given lucrative posts, despite his wife's objections. Rafferty tricks his way into being offered Attorney General and gets his friend Joshua Loomis named Minister of the Interior. Hastings does form a bond with Bruce Bellingham, one of the interim secretaries, who decides to stay on to try and protect his president, but the corruption is too much for him. While the others ensnare Hastings in their schemes, not even playing poker with him honestly, but giving up hands to let him win to flatter him, Bellingham tries to get him to report on them. A mix of cowardice and mistaken loyalty prevents Hastings from doing so until too late.

Hastings's final betrayal by Rafferty, who tries to blackmail him with knowledge of his mistress and illegitimate child, eventually leads Hastings to commit suicide (with poison) at the play's climax rather than face public disgrace and potential impeachment for the incriminating documents they had tricked him into signing, including one that had signed away public oil leases for private sale. Lawrence and Lee partially intended for the play to operate as a cautionary tale against acting in such a way as to allow oneself to become so compromised. At least before he died Hastings sent the press a message regarding his demand for Rafferty's resignation and an insistence that his other 'friends' should be investigated. The play provides detailed examination of the manipulation of public opinion during political conventions in national elections, as well as the difficulties of governing from the White House, especially when it is uncertain who can be trusted.

We learn that Webster has created a scheme through his administration of the Veterans' Bureau by which he has a company deliver supplies that are then rejected and sent back to the company for a kickback, and then the government gets charged for new supplies. Also, we watch as Rafferty gets Hastings – who has been softened up first with a few drinks – to sign an unread document, with assurances he has checked it over, which we know will sign government oil over to Loomis's control. This particular exchange brings to mind the 1921–2 Teapot Dome scandal, during Warren G. Harding's term as president, during which oil reserves were transferred to the Department of the Interior and then sold to private ownership.[34] Rafferty is the lead villain and organizer of all the corruption, not even ashamed of what he has done, as he refuses to see his schemes as a moral issue, but merely how politics operate to ensure those involved get sufficient funds to keep them interested. But he is not given the last word. True to form, the play is not entirely cynical and offers some glimmers of hope in the erstwhile Arthur Anderson, who works hard as Secretary of State, and the reluctance of some of Hastings's friends to get involved. We also have the young idealist Bruce Bellingham, who tries to save Hastings from himself, and even after failing insists he will keep trying to fight the corruption: 'Somebody in politics has to give a damn,' he tells the president, '[a]nd I give a damn.'[35]

Lawrence and Lee only loosely based the play around the career of President Harding – like the playwrights, an Ohio native – who was generally considered to have been something of an amiable hack who just followed the party line. He had swept the general election of 1920 through a campaign largely conducted from his front porch in Ohio, an election many felt he had won due more to image than any record of service or accomplishment. Many of his cronies were found to be corrupt and his presidency had been fraught with scandals also in the Veterans' Bureau, as well as concerns over oil leases and other instances of greed at the public's expense. While Harding officially died of a heart attack, there were rumours regarding the timeliness of his death in the face of such scandals, and the playwrights have Hastings swallow poison and insist to his wife there be no autopsy to make it look like natural causes. Suggesting that the real facts would have been greeted as too outrageous to be true, Lawrence and Lee again adapted historical 'facts' to dramatic purposes. The play must have seemed a pretty safe bet for Kermit Bloomgarden Productions, particularly in a season leading up to a national election in which politics would be on everyone's mind, and as a play by the authors of the major hits *Inherit the Wind* and *Auntie Mame*.

However, the play was not a success in its initial Broadway run, despite the presence of major performers such as Melvyn Douglas as Hastings and E. G. Marshall as Rafferty. It was possible that Douglas had made Hastings too likable, and audiences had missed much of the social criticism behind the election of such an unsuitable candidate. Even while the effects of advertising and television coverage on election results were already very apparent, as were reports of corrupt underlings in the later years of Dwight D. Eisenhower's administration, Eisenhower's eight years of governing had not been nearly as venal as the graft we see in the play, and audiences seemed unwilling to accept such a negative view of politicians.

The play opened in October of 1959, just as the 1960 presidential campaign was kicking off, with potential candidates testing the water. Voters were feeling mostly positive toward politicians and political campaigns – cynicism would come later. However, the playwrights were interested in writing

> ... about the Presidency. Not about a president ... about the man, the office, the father-image, the godhead we send to 1600 Pennsylvania Avenue. [We wanted to w]rite about the 'public solitude' this man faces, the problems he grapples with, personal, emotional, moral, spiritual.[36]

Their implicit warning against electing a president based on looks and image rather than character would become far more relevant as time passed.

Conclusion

All in all, Jerome Lawrence and Robert E. Lee were playwrights both of their time, reflecting the practice and pattern of theatre production in the 1950s through to the 1980s, as well as looking forward to future – and changing – patterns as American theatre became truly national and centred not in New York but across the country. As professional, commercially successful (and viable) writers, their work clearly reflects the theatrical conventions of their times as well. In none of the major plays is the illusion of the fourth wall ever violated, and the plays adhere, for the most part, to the theatrical realism dominant in those years, including the occasional shorthand of a stereotyped character (as, for example, Ito, Mame's Asian houseboy). There is no sign in their work that they were influenced by the experimental work becoming more prominent mostly toward the later end of this period, notably the Theatre of the Absurd (Artaud, Ionesco, Genet and others), political drama as exemplified by the plays of Bertolt Brecht (actively championed by Columbia University professor and critic Eric Bentley) or the highly publicized minimalist work of Samuel Beckett (himself deeply influenced by James Joyce).

However, although they eschewed such experimentation themselves, staying firmly within the context of the realistic performance style perhaps best exemplified by the Method acting espoused by Stella Adler and Lee Strasberg and his Actors' Studio, they were still voices for change in both the theatre and the society in which they lived. As Norman Cousins suggests, 'Great playwrights are both teachers and social philosophers. They open the minds of people to important truths, enabling them to make useful connections with their fellow human beings.'[37] That Lawrence and Lee were able to transmit their concerns with an underlying optimism made their message more palatable. As Cousins concludes, Lawrence and Lee were 'constantly involved in the drama of the surrounding world. The slightest vibrations are picked up on their antennae. They respond to whispers and not just to explosions.'[38] Constantly vigilant against the forces of censorship and limitation they saw endangering a country that had been based upon freedom, their plays spoke out in opposition to such restraints, both politically and privately. The longevity of their plays is testament to their quality, for their plays are able to entertain and provoke thought. Through their drama, Lawrence and Lee were able to offer insight into the political and social systems of the times for which they were written, but also for times to come.

Looking beyond Broadway and, ultimately, beyond the commercial theatre itself, the playwrights recognized the broadening scope of theatrical performance at all levels, lending their celebrity and authority to the newer developments that continue to shape the theatre into the present century. Their own work has survived its creators and bids fair to continue to hold the stage for the foreseeable future. It is significant that their major works remain in constant production at all levels – from professional theatres, community theatres, academic high school and college drama groups to informal social groups that gather to read plays aloud. Their works also appeal outside America. Virtually not a week goes by without a Lawrence and Lee play in performance somewhere, both in the United States and across the globe, on every continent. The writers made an important, and lasting, impact, as their work has joined the international repertoire. What is perhaps the most quoted line from *Auntie Mame* is manifestly the playwrights' own credo: 'Life is a banquet, and most poor sons-of-bitches are *starving* to death! Live!'[39] Lawrence and Lee provided the sustenance for the theatre's own banquet, celebrating life in all its entangled – and in the playwrights' views – glorious relationships.

Afterword

Susan C. W. Abbotson

William Inge

Inge's success in the 1950s brought him financial comfort, but never psychological ease. After four amazing successes, one after the other, he was easily the most successful playwright of the decade, perhaps making him the most obvious target for an up and coming new critic, Robert Brustein, looking to cause an impact. The resulting essay Brustein wrote for *Harper's* in 1958,[1] in which he eviscerated Inge as a playwright, unfairly reducing his plays to preachy endorsements of family life in which women tame free-living men through symbolic emasculations, has been seen by most scholars as the first nail in Inge's coffin, and the decline from public grace began almost immediately, beginning with 1959's *A Loss of Roses*, which closed after twenty-five performances.

With Oedipal issues at its core, the play depicts widow Helen Baird and her 21-year-old son Kenny, who seduces their neighbour, Lila, who works at a seedy nightclub, and then rejects her. The production was problematic: Inge's preferred director, Elia Kazan, had not been available, so Inge inexpertly took on the role of producer, and they had had to make casting changes late in rehearsal. Everyone involved, including Inge in hindsight, felt the opening should have been postponed. While not every critic disliked the play, the majority, including Brooks Atkinson from the *New York Times*, saw it as 'lacking the color of life of its predecessors' and Brustein continued to snipe.[2] The play is gloomier than his previous offerings and located in the city rather than a small Midwestern town, and critics seemed reluctant to accept this change of tone or location in his work. However, the movie rights had been sold prior to its being written and would eventually appear much changed as *The Stripper* in 1963, although this also failed to garner critical favour, even with a happier ending and Joanne Woodward playing Lila. Inge would win an Academy Award for his 1961 original screenplay *Splendor in the Grass*, but would not have another successful Broadway production in his lifetime.

Many who worked with Inge spoke of an internalized anger in him that would on rare occasions burst free, though never at other people.[3] Some of this anger seemed to leak into his later work, as characterizations grew harsher and uglier, providing the core of darkness that so upset his critics. Also, while his message continued to be the need for acceptance, in the age of rebellion that the 1960s had become, his plays seemed out of step for the times. In 1963, despite a newspaper strike that delayed reviews, he opened *Natural Affection*. It presented another love triangle, this time among mother, son and the mother's new lover. It contained far stronger language and violence than previous works, with the son murdering a neighbour in cold blood at the finale. Critics appeared shocked, not knowing with whom they should sympathize, viewing Inge as out of his depth in such lurid material, and apparently craving his more compassionate characters of old. It was another flop, closing after thirty-six performances. In his preface to the play, Inge explained, 'I wanted to expose some of the atmosphere in our lives that creates violence.'[4] He was writing more brutal and sordid plays for what he saw as desperate and irrational times. His later work teems with the dread of urban violence, brushes with failure or suicide and the perils of lost celebrity. Characters increasingly drink, take drugs and kill or assault others, while still searching for love.

While it is possible, especially in hindsight, to see homosexual aspects in several of his characters, when Inge began to write, such elements were deliberately vague, given that homosexuality was still illegal. He had written two short plays, 'The Boy in the Basement' and the satirical 'The Tiny Closet' in the 1950s, which dealt with the topic more openly, but did not publish them until 1962, significantly, perhaps, after the death of both of his parents. His father had died in 1954 and his mother in 1958. This 1962 volume, Summer Brave *and Eleven Short Plays*, contained not only his preferred version of *Picnic* in which Madge, for him, more realistically, stays home, but also a number of experimental pieces, mostly character studies, that show his interest in other techniques and themes. It seems clear that he was keen to experiment beyond simple realism, and he was becoming more willing to address homosexual themes. As he told Digby Diehl in 1967:

> I think any creative person who is going to survive more than one decade or so has to find himself anew periodically because he has to change with the times. I know the kind of play that was being done in the fifties has no audience now. And I know I don't have the same kind of approach to writing as I did in the fifties.[5]

His last Broadway attempt was 1966's *Where's Daddy?* Set in New York, satirizing psychoanalysis, absurdist principles, television advertising, method acting and Samuel Beckett, it depicts a husband struggling to accept new fatherhood, being urged to do so by the openly homosexual Pinky Pinkerton, who offers a strong defence of marriage and family as a preferred way of life. It also contained references to male prostitution and suicide, and the nicest people in the show were the helpful black neighbours. Again, it seemed that most critics did not know what to make of it, so they made it into another flop; although Richard Watts Jr seemed to recognize its possibilities, declaring, 'Mr. Inge is back with a wise and winning comedy.'[6] It closed after twenty-two performances.

After his work on *Dark at the Top of the Stairs*, Kazan had urged Inge to create a film for him to direct, and the playwright was eager to comply with *Splendor in the Grass* – a tale of sexual frustration about two young people in love who have disapproving families. He leaves town and finds another girl; she remains behind, attempts suicide and ends up with another man. As had happened with 1956's *Baby Doll*, Kazan was able to translate Hollywood censorship of some of the racier scenes into a box-office success, and Warren Beatty would become a star, but Inge was unhappy with changes Kazan had made to his script, and they would not work together again. After *Splendor*, Inge adapted James Leo Herlihy's novel *All Fall Down* (1962) for the screen. This also starred Beatty, and was about two brothers affected by an overprotective mother. This was more familiar Inge terrain, and several critics thought his version better than the original book. In 1964, Inge moved permanently to the West Coast, a sign of his changing allegiances. However, after working a long time on his next movie, *Bus Riley's*

Back in Town, when it finally opened in 1965 it had been changed so radically from his original screenplay that Inge had his name removed from the credits, using the pseudonym Walter Gage.

While many contemporary critics suggested Inge was simply writing bad material, it may be closer to the truth to say he was just writing differently, and audiences could not accept the change. Also, poor luck and judgement in the presentation of his later plays, especially, led to lacklustre or ill-timed productions. Into the 1960s, Inge displayed a growing concern with negative criticism and his own fall from grace, but the driving necessity to face reality, keep on living and never give up continued to imbue much of his work, even as the challenges against this possibility seemed to have grown. Voss astutely describes Inge's core message throughout his work as being 'we all need the courage to accept what life brings us, adapt our lives to life's realities, and proceed to find as much light and love as we can'.[7]

While popular legend has it that Inge turned his back on dramatic writing, a glance at the numerous unpublished manuscripts that abound in the Inge Collection at Independence Community College in Kansas would suggest otherwise. As he withdrew further from the world in later life, Inge became an avid watcher of television. While his foray into movies, as with stage plays, began with huge success and then dwindled, his papers contain many treatments for possible television series, such as *Complex*, a series in which each episode would take place in a different apartment in a large city apartment complex. An understanding that television might be the future home of good drama was something many of his peers, aside from Paddy Chayefsky, did not consider. Sadly, his loss of reputation prevented any of these from being picked up. His one television production was for an episode for *Bob Hope Presents the Chrysler Theatre* called 'Out on the Outskirts of Town'. It screened in 1964 to little applause, and Inge was sorely disappointed at the way it had been so quickly thrown together.

One of Inge's last produced plays was *The Last Pad*, a stark piece about a group of inmates on death row. Initially performed Off-Broadway in 1970, it attracted little attention. The same year he published his first novel, *Good Luck, Miss Wyckhoff*, about a lonely schoolteacher who has an illicit affair with a black student. Having 'failed' with plays and the big and small screen, Inge tried his hand at fiction. His second novel, largely autobiographical, *My Son is a*

Splendid Driver, came out in 1971. While the first sold around 12,000 copies in hard cover, the second only managed 8,000, and his third, *The Boy at the Circus*, never found publication. This, and numerous other manuscripts can be found in the William Inge Archives at Independence Community College. Continuing to battle a deepening depression, Inge was hospitalized for an overdose of barbiturates on 2 June 1973. He signed himself out three days later and returned home. Though having arranged with his friend, playwright William Gibson, to move back East for psychiatric treatment, he was unable to survive the night and committed suicide on the night of 10 June, by monoxide poisoning in his garage in Los Angeles.

On his death, Inge was much mourned, but commentators generally viewed his demise as a natural outcome. Paul L. Montgomery's *New York Times* announcement described a 'bright career turned to ashes' and Inge as a man 'ill and depressed for some time', while Brooks Atkinson opined that Inge had 'lost his gift of seeing the living truths' and judged that 'For all practical purposes his career was over.'[8] But as Clurman suggests, 'Fault was found with Inge for not measuring up to standards he never set himself.'[9] In his introduction to *Dark at the Top of the Stairs*, Tennessee Williams insightfully suggested that Inge created plays that were 'at first deceptively smooth on the surface, then suddenly but subtly penetrating'.[10] Unfortunately, in Inge's later years, no one was willing to look beneath that surface.

Inge was a man who fully understood, as Ralph Voss puts it, 'loneliness and frustration and fear',[11] but he was also the man Tennessee Williams once described, who rather than focusing on the 'Dark at the top of the stairs', could embrace the complete opposite, so that his work might reveal 'an odyssey in which the stairs rise from darkness to light through something remarkably fine and gallant in his own nature'.[12] It is, perhaps, this aspect of his legacy to which we need to pay more attention. As Harold Clurman wrote in 1974, 'I am convinced Inge was underestimated.'[13] With the theatrical excesses of the following decades, Inge soon slipped from the public notice, though his plays have never gone out of print. The William Inge Festival, begun in 1982 in his hometown of Independence to celebrate and remember this extraordinary writer, has since become an annual event at which both a living American playwright is honoured and the work of Inge is revived and explored.[14]

Stephen Sondheim

While Sondheim developed a reputation as an elegant and startling lyricist during the 1950s, he was not content to be solely writing words and wished to write music, too. Despite acclaim, the 1957 stage production of *West Side Story* had not been a major hit and would not attract a large fan base until after the movie release in 1961. During the 1960s Sondheim's reputation as both lyricist and composer would grow as he began to set the musical theatre world on fire with his controversial innovations in terms of style (linguistic and melodic), content and structure. Working against the winning format established by Sondheim's mentor, Oscar Hammerstein, and his contemporaries, by which musicals were built around a plot (usually a love story) with naturalistic sets, he created musicals built around an idea that controls and shapes everything else. Several of his early musicals fared poorly, likely because they were ahead of their time, but the theatre world would slowly catch up, and revivals are frequent and have fared well, along with a series of revues based upon his work.[15] Sondheim had an artistic vision for how musicals should be written, as a serious art form with substantive content, and once shared it would transform musical theatre of the future.

Working against the saccharine attitude so common to the genre, Sondheim refused to see musicals as trivial entertainment, reassuring, complacent or sentimental. His work would disturb and challenge rather than placate. His selection of material strives beyond simplistic, predictable romantic comedy, his characters are far less cheery and attractive and his music and lyrics are complex, daring and challenging. Uncaring of commercial success and striking at the foundations of how previous musicals were constructed, he also altered how songs were used: 'Not enough songwriters understand the function of a song in a play,' Sondheim explains. 'They write songs in which the character explains himself. This is self-defeating. A song should reveal the character to the audience, but the character does not have enough self-knowledge to describe himself in these terms.'[16] Sondheim's music often uses difficult intervals and dissonant harmonies. He avoids stock patterns, unless creating a satirical pastiche, and dislikes the reprises and repetitions that make other show tunes so instantly memorable, but his concern was never about creating 'hits' but rather whole musicals. His efforts would help re-energize the Broadway musical and forever change the genre.

Sondheim was determined to use songs in different ways, and his first produced musical for which he composed the entire score came in 1962: *A Funny Thing Happened on the Way to the Forum*. It ran for 964 performances and won six Tony Awards, including Best Musical, but Sondheim was not directly nominated. Sondheim describes it as the 'direct antithesis of the Rodgers and Hammerstein school. The songs could be removed from the show and it wouldn't make any difference.'[17] In Hammerstein's model, songs were designed to move along the action, but while Sondheim's songs helped pace the show and prevent it from becoming too relentless, in this case they were no longer needed for dramatic purposes. Intricately constructed, *Forum* had initial difficulties getting produced as investors missed its satirical heart and saw its differences as negatives. Based on the work of the Roman comic playwright Plautus, its complex plot told the tale of a slave striving for his freedom. But where were the dancing and multiple costume changes, and why was it so broadly farcical? A 1996 revival would run for a further 715 performances and win its star, Nathan Lane, another Tony.

Sondheim's next effort, *Anyone Can Whistle* (1964), was filled with pastiche numbers to satirize traditional musical comedy expectations, and at one point they had the cast seated as if an audience to laugh and applaud the spectators (similar to what Peter Brook did in his production of *Marat/Sade* that same year). A wild plot about a mayoress trying to pull a scam amid a confusing array of characters, many from the local asylum, was almost as chaotic as the production, which was fraught with upsets and dissents. In hindsight, Sondheim felt they had packed too much in and tried to be too clever, which audiences had found off-putting and confusing. It closed after nine performances, but would later become a cult favourite, and although most critics reviled it, *Morning Telegraph*'s Whitney Bolton discerned it was offering something different. 'The new musical,' he wrote, 'is not a perfect musical commentary by several chalks, but it is a bright first step toward a more enlightened and cerebral musical theatre, a musical theatre in which that kind of show can say something about its times and the mores of those times.'[18]

Sondheim's next project returned him to solely lyrics as a favour to Richard Rodgers, who needed someone to work with on *Do I Hear a Waltz?* (1965) – a musical version of Arthur Laurents's *The Time of the Cuckoo* (1952). For this tangled tale of love affairs between tourists and locals in Venice, Sondheim was not keen about what seemed a more traditional project; it never fully came together and was reviewed poorly. A similar fate befell a television project for which Sondheim wrote the score – an episode in ABC's *Stage 67* series, 'Evening Primrose' (1966) – although the plot was more unusual. Demonstrating Sondheim's attraction to the bizarre, this 'horror musical' related the story of a man, played by Anthony Perkins, hiding from the outside world in a department store, only to find it already occupied by hermits who have had a similar idea.

Sondheim's next musical, and his first in a series produced by Harold Prince, would be the one that best defined the 'concept' musical toward which he was striving. Centring on character and theme rather than plot, in a kind of comic Brechtian inversion, *Company* (1970) uses songs to interrupt the story, sung by characters outside the scene. It was an ensemble piece with a slight plot that was more interested in explicating character than narrative; even the choreography by Michael Bennett was character driven. While not intended as a 'statement' piece, based on a series of short plays by George Furth, it nonetheless explores the difficulties of relationships and commitment in an increasingly dehumanizing society. Dispensing with a chorus, it included many lengthy and complex songs with a lot of subtext that are less show tunes than music that is an intrinsic part of the show, and critics tended to admire the craft but dislike the experience. They objected to unlikable characters and the show's bleak outlook, and felt it was too cerebral. After the lead was changed to a more likable and comic character, the musical became a hit, running for 690 performances and winning six of its twelve Tony nominations, including Best Musical, and Best Music and Best Lyrics for Sondheim.[19] As Mel Gussow suggested, '*Company* is an original, unconventional work, which may be why some in the audience seemed restless. Perhaps they expected to be glad-handed by a typical Broadway hit, instead of confronted with irony, taste, and wit – rare commodities in the musical theatre.'[20]

Continuing in an experimental vein, *Follies* (1971) is built around the concept of a reunion in a crumbling Broadway theatre of a group of past Follies dancers, centring on the disillusionment of two couples involved. Avoiding incident, it uses ghost characters to shadow the leads and help play out their memories. Because it was more cinematic in its lighting, sound and movement, initial reviews were bewildered by its complexity. After dropping several numbers, simplifying the staging and adding clarifying dialogue it came together more smoothly, and while reviews remained mixed, Sondheim again won Tony Awards for Music and Lyrics,[21] and it ran for 522 performances.

For the more traditionally plotted romantic 'operetta', *A Little Night Music* (1973), Sondheim decided to compose most of the score in waltz time. But characters sang inner monologues rather than to each other, and critics found it cold and cerebral. However, despite its lack of sentimental emotion, Clive Barnes declared it a triumph for Sondheim: 'Heady, civilized, sophisticated, and enchanting', with 'an orgy of plaintively memorable waltzes' and 'breathtaking lyrics'. 'Good God!' he concludes, 'an adult musical!'[22] A happier conclusion and not as disturbingly tense or cynical, this production was the first of Sondheim's to pay back the investors, running for 601 performances and winning him his third set of Tony Awards.[23]

Not all of Sondheim's concept musicals were so successful. *Pacific Overtures* (1976), about the Westernization and decline of Japanese civilization, drew on Kabuki theatre, created a Western equivalent of Japanese musical styles with minor keys and employed simpler haiku-style lyrics. But while critics recognized its difference, they did not recommend the experience. It took 18 months to find enough Asian-looking actors to cast the show, but it only ran for 193 performances. Despite its dark, gothic vibe, *Sweeney Todd* (1979) fared better. Though not an opera, it uses music beyond the songs to keep tension mounting, and breaks new ground in its balance between farce and melodrama; it is both comic musical and horror movie. While some critics were uneasy, as they felt pulled to sympathize with a pair of villains who murdered people and baked them into pies, they had to admit to the musical's creativity and energy. It ran for 558 performances, won eight of the nine Tony Awards for which it was nominated, including Best Musical and Best Score, and the 2007 movie version directed by Tim Burton, with Johnny Depp, grossed over $150 million worldwide.

The reverse chronology plot about a trio of theatre people in *Merrily We Roll Along* (1981), perhaps inspired by Harold Pinter's similarly constructed *Betrayal* (1978), confused audiences and critics, and it closed after sixteen performances. The decision to use young, inexperienced actors was partly responsible, as the complex polyphony of Sondheim's vocal parts is not easy to grasp, but the composer felt discouraged until persuaded by James Lapine to engage in a new, more experimental project. *Sunday in the Park with George* (1984) ran for 540 performances and won Sondheim the Pulitzer Prize for Drama. The first act works toward recreating on stage the design of pointillist Georges Seurat's famous painting *A Sunday Afternoon on the Island of La Grand Jatte* (1884). The second act leaps forward a hundred years to depict Seurat's great-grandson, a sculptor, returning to the island to seek inspiration. Tony Straige's innovative staging combined live actors with inanimate art, and the music was as rhythmically complex as pointillism itself. While reviews were not unanimous, and most of that year's Tony Awards went to the more traditional *La Cage Aux Folles*, Jack Kroll opined that 'Sondheim's score is original even for him ... To say that this show breaks new ground is not enough; it also breaks new sky, new water, new flesh and new spirit.'[24]

Three years later, Sondheim introduced his fractured fairy tale, *Into the Woods* (1987), which ran for 765 performances and was made into an award-winning movie with Meryl Streep in 2014, for which he wrote some new songs. Its embedded commentary on the questing myths of childhood and the importance of community and responsibility made it a popular show around the country, frequently produced in regional theatres. The rhapsodic *Passion* (1994), about the obsessive love of a colonel's ailing cousin for a young soldier, after only 280 performances became the shortest-running show to win a Tony for Best Musical. In 1997, Sondheim's early unproduced work, *Saturday Night*, about young men getting in and out of trouble, finally found production. In 2004, an earlier comic piece done at Yale University in 1974 called *The Frogs* was brought to Broadway, and *Assassins*, about real or imaginary attempts at presidential assassination in a carnivalesque atmosphere, which had originally run Off-Broadway in 1990, won a Tony for Best Revival. A story of two brothers moving from Gold Rush to 1920s Florida real-estate boom formed the background for *Roadshow* in 2008 (originally tried out as *Bounce* in 2003), and in 2014 a new reverse chronology project with David Ives was announced, titled *All Together Now*. For a writer who has often referred to himself as lazy, Sondheim remains prolific into his 80s. Starting as early as 1973 with *Sondheim: A Musical Tribute*, there have been several tributes to Sondheim's work. This conveys the tremendous respect he has built within American musical theatre. Several performers, including Barbara Wood, Elaine Stritch, Patti Lupone and Mandy Patinkin, have mounted shows based solely on his songs, and Barbra Streisand's best-selling album of Broadway tunes featured six of his songs. He has also written crosswords for *New York* magazine, written soundtracks and songs for movies (the one for *Dick Tracy* [1990] won an Oscar) and been involved in many other projects, including several Off-Broadway experiments, and lyrics, songs or music for many other shows. There are film or television versions of many of his musicals, and while his attempt at a non-musical screenplay, for *The Last of Sheila* (1973), and a non-musical play, *Getting Away with Murder* (1996), did not do well (both murder mysteries), they pay testament to his delight in puzzles and love of the slightly macabre. To celebrate his 80th birthday, the Stephen Sondheim Theatre was named on Broadway in 2010, and in 2014 he was awarded the Presidential Medal of Freedom.

Theatre producer David Merrick (who produced *Gypsy*) views Sondheim as 'without doubt the world's greatest lyricist'.[25] Writing about Sondheim's lyric-writing contributions to the theatre, music critic John Wilson describes a 'depth, range and consistency far beyond that of any previous lyric writer for the Broadway theatre'. More than clever or inspirational, what Wilson sees as key to Sondheim's writing is the 'individual completeness' that each song has 'within itself that goes beyond the superficialities of style', even when Sondheim is writing pastiche. 'He is, in effect, a summation and an elevation of all the lyric writing that has gone before him.'[26] Sondheim changed the texture of American musicals as profoundly as Hammerstein had done before him, and as Joanne Gordon asserts, 'His work has redefined the genre and as a result the gulf that separated "serious," "legitimate" theatre from the musical theatre has effectively been bridged.'[27]

Alice Childress

Although Childress did less acting after the 1950s, she continued to write not only plays, but also fiction and essays, becoming a driving force in African-American literature. Though not all of her work was published or produced, she wrote nearly twenty plays, mostly focused on racial inequities and issues of social justice. As a playwright, her work stretches over four decades, and there are fifty boxes of archival material held at the New York Public Library for the Performing Arts. Her work centres on those she sees as disadvantaged, both black and white, and mostly female: the losers of life who are too often overlooked, or as Childress would suggest, 'the have-nots in a *have* society, those seldom singled out by mass media, except as a source material for derogatory human and/or condescending clinical, social analysis'.[28]

As Doris Abramson explained in 1969, 'Alice Childress has been, from the beginning, a crusader and a writer who resists compromise. She tries to write about Negro problems as honestly as she can.'[29] Childress's fearless experimentation and scorn of commercialism and sentimentality were inspirational and encouraging to those writing feminist drama, and black theatre in particular. The honesty of her work consistently showed audiences and readers a previously unseen side of African-American life, and the effects of poverty in the wealthiest nation on earth. Challenging racism and sexism and their effects, her writing is most powerful for its focus on people as self-actualizing individuals, for Childress wished to affirm human value and dignity, regardless of status, and regardless of providing ideal exempla for black America.

Prior to producing her first major drama of the 1960s, Childress made her final appearance on Broadway in a short-lived gritty urban drama by Warren Miller, *The Cool World*, alongside James Earl Jones. *Wedding Band: A Love/Hate Story in Black and White* was completed in 1962. Set in South Carolina during the First World War, it deals with a forbidden interracial love affair between a seamstress, Julia, and Herman, a German merchant. Unable to legally marry, they pretend they are wed, and she passes for white. Despised by the black community, she is also hated by Herman's white family, even though she tends to his sick mother, and this unfairness ultimately causes her to explode in anger. After Herman dies from a heart attack, she realizes she has no widow's rights, and tries to rekindle her affinity to the black community.

Due to the scandalous nature of its material and the stark realism it presented, it was impossible for Childress to get *Wedding Band* produced in New York, but Ossie Davis was able to mount a production at the University of Michigan in Ann Arbor, with Ruby Dee in the role of Julia. It was not until 1972 that *Wedding Band* played in New York, at the New York Shakespeare Festival, with Dee repeating her role as Julia. Childress co-directed with Joseph Papp, making her the first African-American woman to direct an Off-Broadway play, and the play ran for 175 performances. Critics universally raved about how it showed blacks as individuals yearning for a better life, rather than as caricatures.

In 1974, Papp produced and directed a television version of 'Wedding Band' for *ABC Theatre*, with Ruby Dee again as Julia. Unlike the stage version that focuses on the backyard community and the central character of Julia finding her 'black self', due to Papp's insistence, the television version focused more on the central relationship between Julia and Herman. Some Southern affiliate stations refused to carry the nationally televised broadcasts due to its interracial romance and 'frank' language, but Eileen Heckart was nominated for an Emmy for her portrayal of Herman's bitterly racist mother.

Throughout the 1960s, Childress was clearly an established voice. In 1965, she was featured in the BBC presentation *The Negro in the American Theatre*. She was then named scholar-in-residence for Harvard University at the Radcliffe Institute for Advanced Study from 1966 to 1968. Her 1969 *New York Times* article responding to the question 'Can Black and White Artists Still Work Together?' insisted that American theatre was still predominantly white and segregated, but that having blacks on stage alongside whites could not represent any kind of assimilation. But since '[t]heatre serves as the mirror of life experience and reflects only what looks into it' and 'everyone yearns to see their own image once in a while', it is imperative that black theatre and plays about blacks gain more support. Pointing out that '*In the past 40 years only 18 plays by black writers have been presented on Broadway*' (original italics), she asserts her intention to keep writing despite the difficulties of getting work produced.[30] It was hard for black artists to get not just mainstream production, but also publication: *Trouble in Mind* was not formally published until a revised edition in 1971, and *Wedding Band* had to wait until 1973.

In 1968, Childress had appeared in the film *Up Tight*, about the Black Power movement after the assassination of Martin Luther King, Jr. Shortly afterward she and her husband, composer Nathan Woodard, created *Young Martin Luther King, Jr.*, a biographical musical for children, telling the King story from his marriage to the Montgomery bus boycott. While it was very factual, Childress infused King with humour to assure children's interest. This was first produced in 1969 as part of a series of plays called 'Prelude to Greatness', presented to Long Island schools. In 1970, she wrote *The World On a Hill*, set on a Caribbean island where a wealthy white woman and her son reassess their lives after an encounter with a poor West Indian youth, for publication in a Macmillan collection marketed to schools, called *Plays to Remember*. Another play, *The African Garden* (1971), was never produced and only a short scene from it ever published.[31] It depicts another young character, Simon, seeking connection with a sympathetic adult in the form of Ashley, who has arrived in Harlem, shortly after a 1960s riot, in search of his African heritage.

Her interest in creating younger characters, as well as reaching out to a younger audience, was becoming evident. Recognizing the importance of reaching black youths in particular, she wrote several dramatic pieces for children, including the short plays *When the Rattlesnake Sounds* (1975), a fictionalized story of Harriet Tubman working in a laundry and helping the cause of abolition, and *Let's Hear It for the Queen* (1976), which offers a feminist spin on the 'Queen of Hearts' nursery rhyme, picking up from where it ends. All of the characters in this play have different ethnic backgrounds, a multicultural twist unique for its time. These did not remain long in print, and it would be through her adolescent novels that she would have the greatest impact.

A Hero Ain't Nothin' but a Sandwich, about a 13-year-old heroin addict, but told from the shifting point of view of a variety of characters connected to the central protagonist, drew much attention. Reviewed as groundbreaking, and winning several major awards, it revolutionized writing for young adults with its hard-hitting realism regarding the lives of urban youths. In 1978 this would be turned into a successful movie based on Childress's screenplay. The book was banned as offensive by many libraries for its language and dark situations, but was widely read. In 1979, Childress received a Pulitzer nomination for her adult book *A Short Walk*, a fictional biography of a mulatto woman trying to survive in 1940s Harlem. More adolescent novels followed, including *Rainbow Jordan* (1981), about the struggles of a poor, black, foster child, and *Those Other People* (1989), which deals with racism, homophobia and sexual molestation.

For adults, in 1969, Childress had crafted a short play, *String*, loosely based on a Guy de Maupassant story. About a poor vagrant who is unfairly suspected of having stolen a wallet, it played Off-Broadway at the Negro Ensemble Company as part of an evening of one-acts, alongside plays by Derek Walcott and Ted Shine. A longer work, *Wine in the Wilderness*, was produced for television in 1971. This was about a Harlem woman, 'Tommy', fighting the limitations of poverty. Burned out of her apartment during African-American riots, she is befriended by an artist looking for a model of a grass roots woman, ignorant and unattractive, for his triptych. Attracted to him, she becomes disillusioned on discovering the reasons for his selection. It premièred on WGBH's series *On Being Black*, produced by Luther James. Several stations refused to carry the telecast, including the entire state of Alabama, because of its inflammatory language and radical themes.

The next year, *Mojo: A Black Love Story*, produced at Harlem's New Heritage Theatre, shows Irene, after discovering she has cancer, visiting her former husband, Teddy, before going for treatment. As they relate their past we see they still have feelings for each other, but have both struggled with their ethnicity to find dignity and hope. Teddy is now with a white girl and Irene confesses to discovering she was pregnant after the divorce, and to having the child adopted. While Childress addresses the sexual and social tensions growing in black communities as a result of the black liberationist movement, the play is unlike many of the angry African-American protest plays of that period, as it explores more deeply the personal black experience of love.

An attempt at opera at the start of the 1970s, *The Sun Like Gold*, a dramatization of the life of Harriet Tubman, with music by Ulysses Kay, never found production, but two more of the musicals she created with Woodard did. One was a 1977 piece, *Sea Island Song*, about the Gullah-speaking people from South Carolina and Georgia. Commissioned by South Carolina Arts, it lay unproduced,[32] but retitled *Gullah* and now featuring a graduate student in anthropology studying African culture in the region, it was produced at the University of Massachusetts, Amherst's Hampden Theatre in 1984, when Childress became an Artist-in-Residence. The plot centres on the student's discovery and drive to defend the local Gullah people from exploitation by commercial developers.

Childress's third co-written musical was after her friend, the actress Clarice Taylor, asked her to pen something based on the life of vaudeville comedienne Jackie 'Moms' Mabley in which Taylor could star. *Moms: A Praise Play for a Black Comedienne* was first produced in 1986, and had a short run Off-Broadway at the start of 1987. Taylor, wanting to mount the play again later that year, 'reworked' it with playwright Ben Caldwell and retitled it *Moms: The First Lady of Comedy*, giving no credit to Childress. Childress won her subsequent copyright infringement case against the production.

While theatre histories make only passing mention of Childress, she was in the forefront of important developments in that medium, as acknowledged in 1980 when she was given the Paul Robeson Award for Outstanding Contributions to the Performing Arts. Also, in 1990, her many accomplishments were celebrated at the Langston Hughes Festival 'Tribute to Alice Childress' at the City College of New York. Ruby Dee hosted the event, which featured presentations and performances by Woodie King, Jr, James V. Hatch, Vinie Burrows and playwright J. E. Franklin. Throughout her career, Childress was deeply concerned over the lack of attention given to black women in all fields of entertainment, and much of her writing was to offer a corrective. Not only did she create better roles for women, but she also detailed the compromises people make in order to survive, and acknowledged those living on the margins of society. Her work helped raise awareness about equal rights, women's opportunities and the importance of art and storytelling in society. While she wrote in many genres, she began with drama, and its conventions influenced all of her subsequent writing, which is all extremely character driven and visual. She left behind a body of work that continues to be admired for its frank treatment of racial issues.

Childress was also highly active in a mix of professional writing, political and social organizations and committees throughout her life, which included travels to Russia and China. In her later years, Childress lectured at Fisk University and Radcliffe, and archives show that she was working on a variety of teleplays, mostly featuring black female protagonists, both fictional and real, such as Paul Laurence Dunbar's character Patsy Barnes, as well as Bessie Smith, Hattie McDaniel and Fannie Lou Hamer. There are also files for *Bricks Without Straw* (1983), a mini-series about Booker T. Washington and his wife Olivia proposed by New Image Productions. None of these appear to have been produced. Childress died in 1994 of complications from cancer, while still working on a piece about her great-grandmother, Ani, who at only 12 years old had been abandoned after emancipation until rescued and offered a home by a white woman, Anna Campbell.

Jerome Lawrence and Robert E. Lee

Clearly compatible, Jerome Lawrence and Robert E. Lee worked together for over half a century, and aside from numerous radio dramas and several screenplays for television and film, created around forty plays and musicals. Alan Woods points out that 'Alone among theatre writers of the 1950s and 1960s, Lawrence and Lee moved freely and successfully – from serious drama to comedy to musical comedy.'[33] Where Lawrence was always the more politically involved, Lee had a fascination with how things worked, and their collaborations appear seamless, with they themselves unable to recall who contributed what. In a 1992 interview, Lawrence suggested that 'Almost [all] if not all of our plays share the theme of the dignity of every individual mind, and that mind's life-long battle against limitation and censorship.'[34] Storytellers rather than sermonizers, somewhat inspired by Maxwell Anderson's fictionalized histories, they routinely called on historical events to pass commentary on contemporary happenings, focusing on issues of injustice and often showing a prescience regarding future occurrences. Norman Cousins suggests that like Oscar Hammerstein and Rodgers, they gave 'a common touch to elegant ideas'.[35] Like the musical duo, this led to commercial success that has sometimes overshadowed the craft, complexity and social engagement of their work.

All too often it has been assumed that they simply recreated past events, or adapted the material of others with little of their own input, but nothing could be further from the truth. Both passionately believed that theatre should be of consequence and deal with ideas and issues of social significance. While overlooked by most scholars, their plays contain significant socio-political commentary to make them worthy of further study. However, their tremendous success of the 1950s would not be repeated, except perhaps for the movie versions of *Mame* and *Inherit the Wind*,[36] and *The Night Thoreau Spent in Jail*, which was never mounted on Broadway but became a popular play to produce at regional and community theatres, with over seventy-five productions in 1970 alone; it also became a classroom staple alongside *Inherit the Wind* and has been produced around the world.

Just over a month after *The Gang's All Here* opened in 1959, the duo produced *Only in America*, loosely based on essays by Jewish Southern essayist Harry Golden, but with a lot of their own invention. With understanding and humour, the play explores bigotry as it relates to race, HUAC and Golden's secret past as an ex-convict, but becomes a celebration of American potential. It depicts Golden's success as a first-generation immigrant and the rise of Helen, a black graduate from Cornell, from scrubbing floors to a secretarial position with Golden. They used a similar episodic design to *Auntie Mame*, with Golden's consistent drive for social justice and appreciation of his immigrant roots to provide a through line. However, critics found the protagonist a less engaging character than Mame, and complained that the play lacked tension and narrative. Apparently unready to regard its intrinsic messages regarding civil rights and racial equality, their hostile reaction closed the play after only twenty-eight performances (although a West Coast production that shortly followed ran for nearly a year and then toured). Lawrence and Lee's next two Broadway plays would fare even worse.

A Call on Kuprin (1961) was adapted from Maurice Edelman's fictional novel about the Soviet–American space race. It thoughtfully explored concepts of patriotism and the responsibilities and role of scientists. A poorly timed opening, with the wrong lead actor, gained mixed reviews for the production, and it only lasted for twelve performances. Its inclusion, prior to news of any manned flights into space, of a Russian cosmonaut sent into orbit and subsequently lost was also upstaged during tryouts by the surprise launch of a real cosmonaut into space – Yuri Gagarin – who in safely returning made the play feel suddenly outdated. Somewhat based on Eva Perón, *Diamond Orchid* (1965) explored the abuses of power in its depiction of an ambitious, greedy and unscrupulous Latin-American woman, Felitia, who helps her colonel lover take over his country. Unusually pessimistic for the duo, in its suggestion that the social conditions that produced Felitia could not be prevented from creating more such tyrants, and berated by critics for what they felt was an incomplete script, it closed after only five performances.[37] Like *Kuprin*, production demands had led to its creation being rushed and again poorly cast. It had also been costly to produce, making its subsequent failure a major blow. Perhaps recognizing that the economics of Broadway seemed now only suited to musicals, they switched genres.

A 1948 musical, for which they had written the book *Look, Ma, I'm Dancin'!*, was about a wealthy woman who sponsors the tour of a ballet company so that she can dance in it. Directed by George Abbott with scenic design by Oliver Smith, it had only a modest run of 188 performances, and 1956's *Shangri-La*, based on James Hilton's novel, for which they wrote book and lyrics, had closed after only twenty-one. However, their adaptation of their second biggest hit of the 1950s, *Auntie Mame*, into the musical *Mame* did far better, totalling 1,508 performances (more than doubling those of the original play) and winning three of its eight Tony nominations, including Best Actress for Angela Lansbury in the lead. Jerry Harman wrote the score, and would do so again for 1969's *Dear World*, an adaptation of Jean Giraudoux's *The Madwoman of Chaillot* (1945). This whimsical story about an aging eccentric wanting to thwart corporate plans to turn Paris into an oilfield was not the usual musical narrative of its time; it was not very successful, closing after only 132 performances, although Lansbury would again win a Tony for Best Actress. It has fared better in revival productions at smaller venues.

Their experiences of the 1960s led Lawrence and Lee to reject the growing commercialism of Broadway that seemed to devalue and displace more serious drama, or anything that appeared to be different. During the 1950s it had become harder to make a profit from any play in New York as production costs mounted and lucrative touring opportunities to make up deficits dried up with the increased popularity of film and television. Not wishing to produce Off-Broadway or join the burgeoning Off-Off-Broadway scene, Lawrence and Lee eventually gave up on Broadway altogether.

In 1965 they founded American Playwrights Theatre at Ohio State University, as testament to their belief that the future development of meaningful drama in the United States would belong to a professional regional theatre rather than the overly capitalized Broadway arena. The group lasted for fifteen years, and while it supported many new plays and playwrights, its biggest success was Lawrence and Lee's *The Night Thoreau Spent in Jail*, which opened at Ohio State in 1969 and transferred to Washington DC's Arena Stage the following year. Depicting Thoreau's resistance to the Mexican War was intended as a protest against America's then involvement in Vietnam, but it is also an exploration of personal choice, conscience and citizenship. We are not served a chronological narrative, but witness Thoreau recalling various events from his past life while he waits in jail for refusing to pay the poll tax levied to finance the war.

Other collaborations had slighter impact. *The Incomparable Max* (1971), based on Max Beerbohm's *Seven Men*, combines the stories of Enoch Soames, a poet who makes a pact with the devil to see his future, and A. V. Laider, a palmist who makes an ambiguous prediction of death. The show only lasted for twenty-three performances in New York, as critics disliked the meta-theatrical way the character of Beerbohm had been included. *Jabberwock: Improbabilities Lived and Imagined by James Thurber in the Fictional City of Columbus* (1972) was written to open the Thurber Theatre at Ohio State University. With little scenery but plenty of imagination, the play takes us through the formative years of James Thurber during the First World War, and introduces us to his equally inventive mother.

When the other was not interested in a project, Lawrence and Lee did occasionally work solo, such as with Lawrence's one-act play *Live Spelled Backwards ...* (1966) and Lee's *Ten Days That Shook the World* (1973), based on socialist journalist John Reed's book about the 1917 Russian October Revolution, and a chancel drama, *Sounding Brass* (1975), which was performed at the Reformed Church, Bronxville, New York. In collaboration, other works of the 1970s were a screenplay for the television drama *Lincoln, The Unwilling Warrior* (1975), for NBC, and another musical, *Actor* (1977), based on the life of Paul Muni and broadcast on *Hollywood Television Theatre*, and *First Monday in October* (1978). This last, a fictional plot about the problems faced by the first woman to be appointed to the US Supreme Court, three years before that would be the case, has at its core a key concern of the playwrights: the stark dangers that lie behind any kind of censorship. It did well in a limited run that was extended, and led to a subsequent tour. It was also made into a movie in 1981 for which Lawrence and Lee wrote the screenplay.

In 1990, the couple were inducted into the national Theater Hall of Fame, the same year they were named Fellows of the American College Theater Festival at the Kennedy Center. Their final collaboration, prior to Lee's death in 1994, was *Whisper in the Mind*. It examines scientific rationalism and the power of the mind through Benjamin Franklin's confrontations with Dr Anton Mesmer in 1784, and posits that good ideas can go awry when not pursued in the right manner. Written in 1990, it first appeared at Arizona State University, and a revised version was produced at Missouri Repertory Theatre in 1994. As Woods suggests, despite a paucity of scholarly interest, the couple's plays 'survive because they deal with ideas and provide more than an evening's entertainment: they provide food for thought as well, dealing with some of the major conflicts of our time'.[38]

Documents: Popular Writings from the 1950s

From 'The Spirit of the Age' in *Company Manners* by Leo Kronenberger (1955)

(By kind permission of John Kronenberger)

... What are the striking, the special, the so-to-speak symbolic qualities of our time? What – if, indeed, manners makyth man – are our predominating manners? Wherein does 1954 differ from 1902 or 1854 or 36 B.C.? I shan't pretend to say; but I shall at least speculate.

From among many possible descriptive labels, I shall use but two; and one I shall borrow. Mr. Auden a few years ago spoke of our age as the Age of Anxiety. An age that may be said to have begun with the concept of the inferiority complex, and that vibrates angrily now with the menace of the H bomb, will hardly bring serenity. An age that saw a totalitarian regime bring on a catastrophic war, that has produced in turn further fighting and a barely nominal peace, is not likely to be an age of reassurance. It must be the cry of almost every age that it was born a little too late, or too soon. But the people of this age do have some cause for thinking that they have been assaulted and disrupted beyond the common measure. Freud – to go no farther – has forced them to have quite unprecedented and often highly unpleasant opinions of themselves, their fathers, their mothers, their wives, their children. The key figure of the age has been, of course, the psychoanalyst, who has not been a very well-understood figure, either. The general public has been led to regard him as a combination of priest and Pinkerton operative, so that the general public has been led to form romantically sinister opinions about him. The huge way in which he looms, moreover, is to this extent a liability: it is a reminder that we may be, each of us, far from well: the man who symbolizes the cure also emphasizes the ailment. No doubt he is there to tell us that we have nothing to fear but fear, but also to point out how many odd identities, how many artful disguises, fear can have. I am so far from optimistic about today's world or tomorrow's as to be hopelessly unsure where safety, let alone salvation, lies; but there is a form of pessimism that is part of our current psychology that I consider unfortunate.

... Beyond the fact that ours has been genuinely an age of crises, it is one of anxiety because we have begun to face unpleasant facts about the universe. In the first flush of these revelations we tended to become more cynical and amoral, but equally to become more tolerant. The manners of the 1920s, complicated by that social phenomenon known as Prohibition, became rebellious by intent and unrepressed by circumstance: there seems to be a terrible misunderstanding on the part of a great many people to the effect that when you cease to believe you may cease to behave. The manners of the 1930s, complicated by that pressure known as Social Consciousness, became at once very doctrinaire and very careless: there were presumably no two ways of doing the things that mattered, and it did not matter how you did the rest. Yet the depression years of the '30s, plagued though they were by want and menaced though they were by war, were perhaps less an age of anxiety than this is, because the '30s felt that the coming explosion would be a thunderstorm to clear the air. Today the worst kind of perplexity is added to anxiety: the future, which a while back we were all plotting, however desperately, like a game of chess, has now become something we can only gamble on, like a game of roulette.

And this is, I think, very much the Age of Anxiety, the age of the neurosis, because along with so much that weighs on our minds there is perhaps even more that grates on our nerves. Has there ever been an age so rife with neurotic sensibility, with that state of near shudders, or near hysteria, or near nausea, much of it induced by trifles, which used to belong to people who were at once ill-adjusted and overcivilized? Has there ever before been such an assortment of people who have found such an assortment of things to set their teeth on edge? I am not speaking of the Horace Walpoles or the

Hedda Gablers, the squeamish exquisites or frustrated neurotics who inhabit every age. Most people of breeding have always been 'jarred' by clashing colours, or scratchy pens, or rasping voices: they were neurotic, that is, to the degree that they were 'aesthetic.' But now, and by the thousands, and with no assurance whatever that the edgier the teeth the more *raffiné* the taste, people are quirky, jumpy, jittery, inwardly tense. And since, in far too many cases, we cannot set this down to their being overbred, we can only conclude that they are overburdened. They are reacting to the pressures of a world, in itself insecure, with too aggressive techniques.

Physically, mechanically, modern life is on the whole a very superior mode of existence. It is noisy, very noisy in big cities, but it has always been very noisy in big cities; the rumble of moving carts, the din of street criers and bell ringers during the seemingly idyllic times assaulted the ear quite as unpleasantly as honking horns and screaming sirens and blasting and riveting today. Life is dirty, very dirty in big cities, but consider the coal smoke and exposed garbage of past times, not to speak of the days when housewives poured their slops out of upstairs windows, and ditches choked with dead dogs and refuse ran down the middle of the streets. Consider the stenches that were ubiquitous for centuries and have been outlawed, really, only in our own time. Most of all, consider how much better our nerves *should* be, living as we do in an age of comparative courtesy. It is true that the high breeding and distinguished manners of a small special class have all but vanished and that ours is an age of extremely sloppy behavior. But it is not what most past periods have been – ages of extremely arrogant, of appallingly rude behavior. The Augustan Age that boasts a reputation for perfect breeding and supreme urbanity was in general the most highhanded, quarrelsome, insulting, slanderous, straight-out downright rude age – that one could well conceive.

... On the other hand, we can hardly not put in evidence that archfoe of stability and serenity – speed; we can hardly doubt that all the rush, the hurry, the headlongness of life has told on our nerves in America. It is not a difference in passion, any more than a difference in plumbing, that really distinguishes our life from that of our ancestors; it is a difference in pace. We not only travel faster than we used to, in subways rather than sedan chairs, in planes rather than on horseback. We eat much faster than we used to; we talk much faster than we used to – so much that the drawl, which once we thought rather charming, is nowadays apt to set those aforementioned teeth on edge. Certainly we get bored and blasé much faster than we used to: we have lost much of the wide-eyed interest in things that earlier ages had, but even more we have lost the capacity to *remain* absorbed. The public that waited from month to month in a pleasurably wild suspense for the new installment of a novel by Richardson or Dickens, and waited with such intensity that the matter of Clarissa Harlowe's virtue became something like a national crisis – such a public remains incomprehensible to us who, in the same space of time, would more likely encounter Clarissa in a magazine serial, as a novel between covers, as a *Reader's Digest* abridgment, as a comic strip, as a play – and very possibly as a plagiarism.

And what counts more in this age of anxiety than our eating or talking or traveling or tiring of things faster than we used to is the fact that we now succeed or fail much faster than we used to. Fame was once built like furniture – slowly, painstakingly, expensively; but then it lasted a lifetime. Once people did not simply read novels, they read novelists; the new Meredith or Hardy, even the new Wells or Mrs. Wharton, was a kind of obligation even when it failed to be an event. People were faithful to their matinee idols during half a lifetime; they grew old, indissolubly bound to Julia Marlowe or John Drew, as one grows old with one's wife or one's husband, for better for worse, for richer for poorer. Today the few bobby-sockers who are not shamelessly fickle are flagrantly polyandrous. Byron had, of all writers, the most dazzlingly meteoric rise to fame, and even Byron was left a little breathless by waking up one morning to find himself famous. But on any morning these days whole segments of the population wake up to find themselves famous, while, to keep matters shipshape, whole contingents of celebrities wake up to find themselves forgotten. Consider only that portion of the population that has not yet attained the age of twelve. There was a time, and a fairly recent one, when you could probably count on the fingers of one hand all the famous people in the world under the age of twelve: a musical child prodigy like Hoffman or Elman, a ten-year-old boy at Harvard, a boy king, a child princess, a Daisy Ashford or a Charley Ross. Now we have movie children who earn a million dollars before you can say Jack Robinson or they can say cat; we have little Quiz Kids and other prodigies of every description, many of them past their peak at nine and all washed up at fourteen.

Yet the comic and satiric aspects of all this, beyond being themselves a little crude, must give way before the real implication of such rocketing success and plummeting failure. Certainly in these days success is almost without distinction, as failure is without dignity; certainly, too, success must leave one quite as anxious as failure. For how much pride is to be had in the winning, and how much permanence goes with what is won? The technique of winning is so shoddy, the terms of winning are so ignoble, the tenure of winning is so brief; and the specter of the has-been – a shameful rather than a pitiable sight today – brings a sudden chill even to our sunlit moments.

Among many other slogans that might partly express the spirit of the age I would add to Mr. Auden's just one of my own – and one at the strict level of manners, which of course his is not. The perturbations of our time go far deeper than the mores know how to explain. But on the surface of life, where we can only guess at times how sick people are by how strangely they act, or infer their anxieties from their absurdities, perhaps our age is more than anything else the Age of Publicity. In terms of affecting our lives today, I think the only man fit to be compared with Sigmund Freud or Karl Marx is P. T. Barnum. After Barnum, life was to have all the charlatanry of the old-time circus, though much less of the charm. After him, it would be folly to think that good wine needs no bush. After him, things that had customarily been done for pleasure were to be done for pay; after him, there was to be less and less privacy in life, and so less and less feeling that privacy is a desirable thing. After Barnum came the press agent and the stooge, the chatter column, the gossip columnist; and Oscar Wilde's remark that there is one thing worse than being talked about and that is not being talked about became more and more true as it became more and more trite. After Barnum – two or three generations after Barnum – people were married at the top of Ferris wheels, and spent their wedding nights in department-store show windows, and gave birth to children under klieg lights, and threw tremendous parties to celebrate their divorce. For Barnum had triumphed, ballyhoo had triumphed, at any rate in America; and with it we have seen something not so much vanish as become tawdry and besmirched. Along with Barnum's celebrated cynicism about the birth rate there was his humor about, say, the Grand Egress; there was his vitality, his sense of the gaudy, his knack for the unexpected. And all this has persisted into our own time, and we still offer our own version of it today – dressing up celebrities, dressing up nonentities, in anything from adjectives to leopard skins. And we do it all in a style to prove that there is still plenty of slapdash colour in American life, still plenty of energy and ingenuity and exuberance. The trouble with us in America isn't that the poetry of life has turned to prose, but that it has turned to advertising copy.

And in an age of publicity, technique becomes all-important: the proper presentation, as the advertising world describes it; the proper packaging, as the mercantile world describes it; the phrase that will linger; the face you won't forget. Philistia, furthermore, swallows it all, loves it, imitates it. A man named Turner recently told me he had named his baby son Tommy, not as you might suppose because the alliteration pleased him, but because 'Tommy Turner' is an easy name to remember and 'that would prove very useful in business.' But the very publicity that dictates our habits destroys our thinking. For the great conspiracy of our time is that nobody shall be forced, shall even be permitted, to learn the truth about anything, or the beauty or value of anything, *at first hand*: that we shall all be veritable kings in the sense that we have tasters, and veritable princelings in the sense that we have whipping boys; and that people couldn't be more willing to do our reading for us if we were blind; or more eager to cut up our culture into little pieces for us if we were babies. The directions for becoming cultured are, as it were, right on the box and are as simple and plain as the directions for baking a cake. The wonder of our age is that everything is labeled and spotlighted, preshrunk, predigested, passed on by experts. The trouble with our age is that it is all signposts and no destination.

... Ours is pre-eminently an age of publicity because it is so well equipped to publicize: one advertising agency, one radio or TV station can do in a day what once upon a time took months. And with everything publicized so nimbly, and packaged so smartly, and swallowed so painlessly, the outer sophistication is greater today, the enameling is smoother. No doubt people of taste and sensibility always think that their age is pre-eminently vulgar; and so is ours. Yet we may wonder whether, in the primary sense, this is so true of our own time; we can hardly help noticing that what might be called a pristine vulgarity is largely outlawed, largely gone. Gone is the worst of the Gilded Age, as expressed in mere

Bigness and Muchness and Thickness and Richness and Newness. It was too oppressive, too indigestible. We have invented streamlining, and we have learned to put our faith in the specialist. The Age of the Specialist is folded into the Age of Publicity and could hardly exist outside it. Ours is not so much an age of vulgarity as of vulgarization; everything is tampered with or touched up, or adulterated or watered down, in an effort to make it palatable, in an effort to make it pay.

What we need for cultural health today is what we needed and got for our physical health nearly half a century ago: Pure Food & Drug Laws concerning thought and feeling. But it is very much a question whether we shall get them. The problem in any case – even divorcing it from the far vaster one of world politics and economics – the problem in the world of manners, on the plane of culture, is immensely difficult, involving as it does all the impurity, the pull-two-ways by which we live and by which we have perhaps immoderately prospered. It might be more horrifying, but it would be far simpler, if America were completely soulless and visionless, were altogether materialistic. It is a good deal more complicated because we are of so mixed a composition, so bifocal an outlook, serving God and Mammon both, and both at the same time.

From 'Introduction' to *The Power of Positive Thinking* by Norman Vincent Peale (1952)

This book is written to suggest techniques and to give examples which demonstrate that you do not need to be defeated by anything, that you can have peace of mind, improved health, and a never-ceasing flow of energy. In short, that your life can be full of joy and satisfaction. Of this I have no doubt at all for I have watched countless persons learn and apply a system of simple procedures that has brought about the foregoing benefits in their lives. These assertions, which may appear extravagant, are based on bona-fide demonstrations in actual human experience.

Altogether too many people are defeated by the everyday problems of life. They go struggling, perhaps even whining, though their days with a sense of dull resentment at what they consider the 'bad breaks' life has given them. In a sense there may be such a thing as 'the breaks' in this life, but there is also a spirit and method by which we can control and even determine those breaks. It is a pity that people should let themselves be defeated by the problems, cares, and difficulties of human existence, and it is also quite unnecessary.

In saying this I certainly do not ignore or minimize the hardships and tragedies of the world, but neither do I allow them to dominate. You can permit obstacles to control your mind to the point where they are uppermost and thus become the dominating factors to your thought pattern. By learning how to cast them from the mind, by refusing to become mentally subservient to them, and by channeling spiritual power through your thoughts, you can rise above obstacles which ordinarily might defeat you. By methods I shall outline, obstacles are simply not permitted to destroy your happiness and well-being. You need be defeated only if you are willing to be. This book teaches you how to 'will' not to be.

The purpose of this book is a very direct and simple one. It makes no pretense to literary excellence nor does it seek to demonstrate any unusual scholarship on my part. This is simply a practical, direct-action, personal-improvement manual. It is written with the sole objective of helping the reader achieve a happy, satisfying, and worthwhile life. I thoroughly and enthusiastically believe in certain demonstrated and effective principles which, when practiced, produce a victorious life. My aim is to set them forth in this volume in a logical, simple, and understandable manner so that the reader, feeling a sense of need, may learn a practical method by which he can build himself, with God's help, the kind of life he desires.

If you read this book thoughtfully, carefully absorbing its teachings, and if you will sincerely and persistently practice the principles and formulas set forth herein, you can experience an amazing improvement within yourself. By using the techniques outlined here you can modify or change the circumstances in which you now live, assuming control over them rather than continuing to be directed by them. Your relations with other people will improve. You will become a more popular, esteemed, and well-liked individual. By mastering these principles, you will enjoy a delightful new sense of well-being. You may attain a degree of health not hither known by you and experience a new and keen pleasure in living. You will become a person of greater usefulness and will wield an expanded influence.

From *The Bride's Cookbook* by Poppy Cannon (1954)

'A Word to the Wives'

To the Bride we bring this book ... to the Bride, to the man she loves, and to the friends who come within the shining circle.

Here is a cookbook (if we must use that stodgy word for so romantic a volume) which is different from all others since it combines tenderness with information ... romance with practicality ... the most up-to-the-minute news of ready foods, along with much age-old and ageless wisdom which is not necessarily culinary.

This book is devoted to the principle that the Bride, aided by the canner, the baker, the ready-mix and frozen-food maker, may right from the start equal and even excel the ladies who win blue ribbons at the County Fair.

... This is a very different book because it is based on a new theory: that some of the best meals of our time are whizzed together in a matter of minutes, often with the sketchiest of equipment and by the most blissfully untutored impresarios, i.e., Brides with flowers in their hair and only half an eye on what's bubbling. In this book the can opener, the mix, and frozen food take their place among the immemorial little gods of hearth and household.

With this book the Bride can discover how to cook meals that are not only adequate but entrancing ... and do it with little of the real work of cooking. No longer plagued by kitchen-maid chores, which have been taken over by the food manufacturer, she soon becomes an artist at her stove, adept in the realms of cookless cookery, where a dash of herbs, a splash of wine, an unusual garnish, may lift the ready soup, the frozen stew, the prepared cake mix, from just plain food to a social art. Some are basic, starting from scratch, but scarcely a one is orthodox, and *none* is difficult. All of the recipes are easy to prepare, alluring to look upon, good to eat.

From *The Crack in the Picture Window* by John Keats (1956)

For literally nothing down – other than a simple two per cent and a promise to pay, and pay, and pay until the end of your life – you, too, like a man I'm going to call John Drone, can find a box of your own in one of the fresh-air slums we're building around the edges of America's cities. There's room for all in any price range, for even while you read this, whole square miles of identical boxes are spreading like gangrene throughout New England, across the Denver prairie, around Los Angeles, Chicago, Washington, New York, Miami – everywhere. In any one of these new neighborhoods, be it Hartford or Philadelphia, you can be certain all other houses will be precisely like yours, inhabited by people whose age, income, number of children, problems, habits, conversation, dress, possessions and perhaps even blood type are also precisely like yours. In any one of these neighborhoods it is possible to make enemies of the folks next door with unbelievable speed. If you buy a small house, you are assured your children will leave you perhaps even sooner than they should, for at once they will learn never to associate home with pleasure. In short, ladies and gentlemen, we offer here for your inspection facts relative to today's housing developments – developments conceived in error, nurtured by greed, corroding everything they touch. They destroy established cities and trade patterns, pose dangerous problems for the areas they invade, and actually drive mad myriads of housewives shut up in them.

These facts are well known to responsible economists, sociologists, psychiatrists, city managers and bankers, and certainly must be suspected by the people who live in the suburban developments, yet there's no end in sight to the construction. Indeed, Washington's planners exult whenever a contractor vomits up five thousand new houses on a rural tract that might better have remained in hay, for they see in this little besides thousands of new sales of labor, goods, carpenters, plasterers, plumbers, electricians, well-diggers, bricklayers, truck drivers, foremen and day laborers. Then come the new householders, followed by their needs. A shopping centre and supermarket are hurriedly built, and into this pours another army of clerical and sales personnel, butchers, bakers, janitors, auto dealers, restaurateurs, waitresses, door-to-door salesmen, mail carriers, rookie cops, firemen, schoolteachers, medicine men of various degrees – the whole ruck and stew of civilization's auxiliaries. Thus, with every new development, jobs are born, money is earned, money is spent, and pretty soon everyone can afford a new television set, and Washington calls this prosperity.

... First of all, a housing development cannot be called a community, for that word implies a balanced society of men, women and children wherein work and pleasure are found and the needs of all the society's members are served. Housing developments offer no employment and as a general rule lack recreational areas, churches, schools, or other cohesive influences.

A second present and future national danger lies in the fact that developments are creating stratified societies of singular monotony in a nation whose triumph to date has depended on its lack of a stratified society, on the diversity of its individuals. Yet today it is possible to drive through the various developments that surround one of our cities and tell at a glance the differing social strata.

Here is the $10,000 development – two bedrooms, low-priced cars, average income $75 a week after taxes, three children, average food budget $25 weekly; jobs vary from bus driver to house painter. Here is the $13,950 house – three bedrooms, available to foremen and successful newspapermen, medium-priced cars, two and a half children per average home; men's shoes cost $12 to $20 at this level. Next is the $17, 450 split level, especially designed for split personalities, upper-medium cars; liquor bill is $25 weekly; inmates take fly-now-pay-later air rides to Europe.

From *The Vanishing Adolescent* by Edgar Z. Friedenberg (1959)

Adolescence is not simply a physical process; there is more to it than sexual maturation. It is also – and primarily – a social process, whose fundamental task is clear and stable self-identification.

This process may be frustrated and emptied of meaning in a society which, like our own, is hostile to clarity and vividness. Our culture impedes the clear definition of any faithful self-image – indeed, of any clear image whatsoever. We do not break images;

there are few iconoclasts among us. Instead, we blur and soften them. The resulting pliability gives life in our society its familiar, plastic texture. It also makes adolescence more difficult, more dangerous, and more troublesome to the adolescent and to society itself. And it makes adolescence rarer. Fewer youngsters really dare to go through with it; they merely undergo puberty and simulate maturity.

There has recently been growing concern about this; adults have noticed the change and gravely remark the emergence of a beat and silent generation. On the whole, we don't like it; and even those of us who find a convenience would rather not be credited with having brought it about. Rather, we treat our silent, alienated, or apathetic youth as problems, as psychological or social aberrations from the normal course of adolescence. This evasion, however comforting, is unreal. It is the fully human adolescent – the adolescent who faces life with love and defiance – who has become aberrant.

Real adolescents are vanishing. I do not suppose they will become extinct, but they are certainly struggling to carry a disproportionate load of our common humanity. Many are holding back, and some are getting crushed. My purpose, in this book, is to show why this is so, and what I think we are losing.

From *100 Things You Should Know About Communism and Education* (1951)

(This is the opening extract from one of a series of pamphlets produced by HUAC about the threat and effect of communism on the US.)

1 What is Communism?

   A conspiracy to conquer and rule the world by any means, legal or illegal, in peace or in war.

2 Is it aimed at me?

   Right between the eyes.

3 What do Communists want?

   To rule your mind and your body from the cradle to the grave.

Extracts from House Committee on Un-American Activities hearings 1952–1956

From the statement and affidavit of Elia Kazan to HUAC, 9 April 1952

I have come to the conclusion that I did wrong to withhold those names before, because secrecy serves the Communists, and is exactly what they want. The American people need the facts and all the facts about all aspects of Communism in order to deal with it wisely and effectively. It is my obligation as a citizen to tell you everything I know.

Although I answered all other questions which were put before me before, the naming of these people makes it possible for me to volunteer a detailed description of my own activities and of the general activity which I witnessed. I have attempted to set these down as carefully and fully as my memory allows. In doing so, I have necessarily repeated portions of my former testimony, but I believe that by so doing I have made a more complete picture than if I omitted it.

... I was a member of the Communist Party from sometime in the summer of 1934 until the late winter or early spring of 1936, when I severed all connection with it permanently.

I want to reiterate that in those years, to my eyes, there was no clear opposition of national interests between the United States and Russia. It was not even clear to me that the American Communist Party was taking its orders from the Kremlin and acting as a Russian agency in this country. On the contrary, it seemed to me at that time that the Party had at heart the cause of the poor and unemployed people whom I saw on the streets about me. I felt that by joining, I was going to help them, I was going to fight Hitler, and, strange as it seems today, I felt that I was acting for the good of the American people.

Kazan then gives the Committee several names and relates the activities that caused him to break with the Party:

I had enough regimentation, enough of being told what to think and say and do, enough of their habitual violation of the daily practices of democracy to which I was accustomed. The last straw came when I was invited to go through a typical Communist scene of crawling and apologizing and admitting the error of my ways. The invitation came from a Communist functionary brought in for the occasion ... He made a vituperative analysis of my conduct in refusing to fall in with the Party line and plan for the Group Theater, and he invited my repentance. My fellow members looked at him as if he were an oracle. I have not seen him since, either.

That was the night I quit them. I had had enough anyway. I had had a taste of police-state living and did not like it. Instead of working honestly for the good of the American people, I had found that I was being used to put power in the hands of people for whom, individually and as a group, I felt nothing but contempt, and for whose standard of conduct I felt a genuine horror.

From the statement of Edward G Robinson to HUAC, 30 April 1952

It is a serious matter to have one's loyalty questioned. Life is less dear to me than my loyalty to democracy and the United States. I ask favours of no one. All I ask is that the record be kept straight and that I be permitted to live free of false charges. I readily concede that I have been used, and that I have [been] mistaken regarding certain associations which I regret, but I have not been disloyal or dishonest.

I would like to find some way to put at rest the ever-recurring innuendoes concerning my loyalty. Surely there must be some way for a person falsely accused of disloyalty to clear his name once and for all. It is for this purpose that I come again voluntarily before this Committee to testify under oath. What more can I do? Anyone who understands the history of the political activity of Hollywood will appreciate the fact that innocent, sincere persons were used by Communists to whom honesty and sincerity are as foreign as the Soviet Union is to America. I was duped and used. I was lied to. But, I repeat, I acted from good motives, and I have never knowingly aided Communists or any Communist causes.

... I have been fighting them and their ideology in my own way. I just finished appearing in close to two hundred and fifty performances of *Darkness at Noon* all over the country. It is, perhaps, the strongest indictment of Communism ever presented.

From the intended statement of Paul Robeson to HUAC, 12 June 1956 (the Committee would not allow it to be read or accepted for the record)

It is a sad and bitter commentary on the state of civil liberties in America that the very forces of reaction, typified by Representative Francis Walter and his Senate counterparts, who have denied me access to the lecture podium, the concert hall, the opera house, and the dramatic stage, now hale me before a committee of inquisition in order to hear what I have to say. It is obvious that those who are trying to gag me here and abroad will scarcely grant me the freedom to express myself fully in a hearing controlled by them.

It would be more fitting for me to question Walter [James] Eastland and [John Foster] Dulles than for them to question me, for it is they who should be called to account for their conduct, not I. Why does Walter not investigate the truly 'un-American' activities of Eastland and his gang, to whom the Constitution is a scrap of paper when invoked by the Negro people and to whom defiance of the Supreme Court is a racial duty? And how can Eastland pretend concern over the internal security of our country while he supports the most brutal assaults on fifteen million Americans by the White Citizens' Councils and the Ku Klux Klan? When will Dulles explain his reckless irresponsible 'brink of war' policy by which the world might have been destroyed?

... My travels to sing and act and speak cannot possibly harm the American people. In the past I have won friends for the real America among the millions before whom I have performed – not for Walter, not for Dulles, not for Eastland, not for the racists who disgrace our country's name – but friends for the American Negro, our workers, our farmers, our artists.

By continuing the struggle at home and abroad for peace and friendship with all of the world's people, for an end to colonialism, for full citizenship for Negro Americans, for a world in which art and culture may abound, I intend to continue to win friends for the best in American life.

From the testimony of Arthur Miller to HUAC, 21 June 1956

> **Mr. Arens** Tell us, if you please, sir, about these meetings with the Communist Party writers which you said you attended in New York City ... Can you tell us who was there when you walked into the room?
>
> **Mr. Miller** Mr. Chairman, I understand the philosophy behind this question and I want you to understand mine. When I say this, I want you to understand that I am not protecting the Communists or the Communist Party. I am trying to and will protect my sense of myself. I could not use the name of another person and bring trouble on him. These were writers, poets, as far as I could see, and the life of a writer, despite what it sometimes seems, is pretty tough. I wouldn't make it any tougher for anybody. I ask you not to ask me that question. (*The witness confers with his counsel.*) I will tell you anything about myself, as I have.
>
> **Mr. Arens** These were Communist Party meetings, were they not?
>
> **Mr. Miller** I will be perfectly frank with you in anything relating to my activities. I take the responsibility for everything I have ever done, but I cannot take the responsibility for another human being ...
>
> **Mr. Arens** Mr. Chairman, I respectfully suggest that the witness be ordered and directed to answer the question as to who it was that he saw at these meetings.
>
> **Mr. Jackson** May I say that moral scruples, however laudable, do not constitute legal reason for refusing to answer the question. I certainly endorse the request for direction.
>
> **The Chairman** You are directed to answer the question Mr. Miller ...
>
> **Mr. Scherer** There is a question before the witness; namely, to give the names of those individuals who were present at this Communist Party meeting of Communist Writers. There is a direction on the part of the Chairman to answer that

question. Now, so that the record may be clear, I think we should say to the witness – Witness, would you listen?

Mr. Miller Yes.

Mr. Scherer We do not accept the reasons you gave for refusing to answer the question, and it is the opinion of the committee that, if you do not answer the question, you are placing yourself in contempt. (*The witness confers with his counsel.*) That is an admonition that this committee must give you in compliance with the decision of the Supreme Court. Now, Mr. Chairman, I ask that you direct the witness to answer the question.

The Chairman He has been directed to answer the question, and he gave us an answer that we just do not accept.

Mr. Arens Was Arnaud d'Usseau chairman of this meeting of Communist Party writers which took place in 1947 at which you were in attendance?

Mr. Miller All I can say, sir, is that my conscience will not permit me to use the name of another person. (*The witness confers with his counsel.*) And that my counsel advises me that there is no relevance between this question and the question of whether I should have a passport or there should be passport legislation in 1956.

Mr. Arens Mr. Chairman, I respectfully suggest that the witness be ordered and directed to answer the question as to whether or not Arnaud d'Usseau was chairman of the meeting of the Communist Party writers in New York in 1947 at which you were in attendance.

The Chairman You are directed to answer the question.

Mr. Miller I have given you my answer, sir …

Mr. Jackson I am not satisfied with that. That is entirely too vague. What I want is a positive statement as to whether or not you will answer that question. (*The witness confers with his counsel.*)

Mr. Miller Sir, I believe I have given you the answer that I must give.

Theatre in the 1950s

From 'The Innocence of Arthur Miller' in *The Dramatic Event* by Eric Bentley (1954)

The theatre is provincial. Few events on Broadway have any importance whatsoever except to that small section of the community – neither the élite nor a cross section – that sees Broadway plays. A play by an Arthur Miller or a Tennessee Williams is an exception. Such a play is not only better than the majority; it belongs in the mainstream of our culture. Such an author has something to say about America that is worth discussing. In *The Crucible*, Mr. Miller says something that *has* to be discussed. Nor am I limiting my interest to the intellectual sphere. One sits before this play with anything but intellectual detachment. At a moment when we are all being 'investigated,' or imagining that we shall be, it is vastly disturbing to see indignant images of investigation on the other side of the footlights. Why, one wonders, aren't there dozens of plays each season offering such a critical account of the state of play by an author, like Mr. Miller, who is neither an infant, a fool, a swindler, is enough to bring tears to the eyes.

... There has been some debate as to whether this story of seventeenth-century Salem 'really' refers to our current 'witch hunt' yet since no one is interested in anything *but* this reference, I pass on the real point at issue, which is: the validity of the parallel. It is true in that people today are being persecuted on quite chimerical grounds. It is untrue in that communism is not, to put it mildly, merely a chimera. The word communism is used to cover, first, the politics of Marx, second, the politics of the Soviet Union, and, third, the activities of all liberals as they seem to illiberal illiterates. Since Mr. Miller's argument bears only on the third use of the word, its scope is limited. Indeed, the analogy between 'red-baiting' and witch hunting can seem complete only to communists, for only to them is the menace of communism as fictitious as the menace of witches. The non-communist will look for certain reservations and provisos. In *The Crucible*, there are none.

From 'West Side Story' in *The Theater In Spite of Itself* by Walter Kerr (1963)

The dances in *West Side Story* came up like geysers through the floor of the city.

The curtain rose on a silence, and a pause. It was the last silence, almost the last pause. Against an empty-eyed background of warehouse windows five or six blue-jacketed young delinquents, with the tribal mark 'Jets' scrawled across their taut shoulders, were lounging, waiting for the first whisper of violence.

Their impatience came to life in their fingers. A snapping rhythm began to tap out a warning of mayhem to come. Knees began to itch, and move, under the lazy, overcast midsummer sky in Puerto Rican New York.

The Sharks – equally young, equally sick with very old hatreds – appeared from the alleyways in twos and threes. There was a sneer, a hiss, a tempting and tantalizing thrust of an arm, and then – with a screeching downbeat from the orchestra pit – the sorry and meaningless frenzy was on. From this moment the show rode with a catastrophic roar over the spider-web fire escapes, the shadowed trestles, and the plain dirt battlegrounds of a big-city feud.

Choreographer Jerome Robbins did not run out of his original explosive life-force. Though the essential images were always the same – two spitting groups of people advancing with bared teeth and clawed fists upon one another – there was fresh excitement in the next debacle, and the next. When a gang leader advised his cohorts to play it 'Cool,' the intolerable tension between an effort at control and the instinctive drives of these potential killers worked on the theater with pressure-cooker menace. When the knives came out, and bodies flew wildly through space under buttermilk clouds, the sheer release was breath-taking.

Again and again there was the striking use of suppressed sound: the rustle of feet being thrust as quietly as possible into toeholds on a wire-barrier, the clap of a hand on a leather-clad shoulder as a too-eager Shark was halted in mid-flight. Casual shoulders converged, backs rose in arches alley cats might have envied, stealthy feet slipped sideways into circling pools of hostility until, from a single swift upthrust at the heart of the cauldron, an explosion of venom could roar outward to the wings.

This constant pendulum-swing of pressure and release became the fundamental visual and dramatic pattern of the entertainment. Mr. Robbins' Polish-American Romeo and his Puerto Rican Juliet first met at a gymnasium dance that was going badly: the rival street gangs were already brushing elbows as they warily circled the social floor, waiting for the one grating exchange that would give them the right to act.

As the waiting approached fever pitch, there was a sharp inhalation. Out of opposite corners on a swiftly darkened stage came the spellbound lovers, eyes riveted upon one another. As they met, the silhouetted enemies behind them subtly changed footwork: a mocking, insidiously mincing minuet echoed the lovers' mood without for a moment ceasing to threaten them. The figure of the dance was romantic, but a Satanic rigidity infected its grace. The moment was stretched taut: a longing couple, a coiled crowd. Then restlessness reasserted itself: knees bent with more emphasis, elbows unlocked and jabbed the air, a picture that had had temporary shape and control broke open toward stomping rebellion. Chaos was coming; the lovers would be lost in it.

The dissolves that carried us – via a rainfall of streamers or a nightmare of spinning fences – from tiny Puerto Rican rooms to garishly lighted alleys were everywhere ingenious, but nowhere more so than in the transition that swept us into the free stage and the extended melodic line of Leonard Bernstein's 'Somewhere.' ... *West Side Story* ... was an utterly serious musical play that, in its ambition and partial achievement, created fresh new demands of its own – specifically, for an emotional recognition and character penetration that would match the sober urgency of its orchestration and its dancing ... [I]t was a remarkable piece of work to come from a Broadway tradition that is generally thought of as merely giddy.

Extracts from 'For a Negro Theatre' by Alice Childress (*Masses and Mainstream*, February 1951)

Several months ago Theodore Ward and I had a heated though friendly discussion concerning Negro Theatre. He claimed that there was a definite need for such a theatre while I held to the idea that a Negro theatre sounded as though it might be a Jim Crow institution. Since that day I have given much thought to everything he said on that occasion and I believe that now I have an understanding of what he meant.

The word theatre is derived from the Greek, meaning to see or view. One obvious function of a Negro people's theatre is to give us the opportunity of seeing and viewing the Negro people.

Today in America the Negro actor attends drama schools which, like the public schools, take little interest in the cultural or historical background of the Negro people. The Negro actors, scenic designers, playwrights, directors, are taught only the techniques developed by the white artist. We certainly need and feel an appreciation for this technique. But certainly too there should be additional instruction which would advance the white as well as the Negro actor and playwright in his knowledge of the Negro people's culture. What Negro director or actor today is capable of portraying an African on the stage? Most of us can only 'suggest' an African because we have been divorced through education from much of our cultural heritage.

In the drama class the Negro student usually does white roles taken from popular plays. He occasionally does a Negro part also taken from a popular Broadway play, while the white actors, for the most part, never do a Negro role.

The Negro artist has to turn within himself for guidance when he portrays his own people. But even this is of little help in the face of the director who is also searching for his concept of the Negro character.

Where is the truth? Where are the schools that will teach us Negro art forms? We must create them and devote time, study and research toward the understanding and projection of Negro culture.

We must not only examine African art, but turn our eyes toward our neighbors, the community, the domestic workers, porters, laborers, white-collar workers, churches, lodges and institutions. We must look closely and search for the understanding which will enable us to depict the Negro people.

I have learned that I must watch my people in railroad stations, in restaurants, in the fields and tenements, at the factory wheels, in the stores, on the subway. I have watched and found that there is none so blind as he who will not see.

My people walk in beauty, their feet singing along the pavement; my people walk as if their feet hurt, in hand-me-down shoes; some of my people walk in shoes with bunion pockets, shoes with slits cut for the relief of corns; and the children walk on feet that are growing out of their shoes; and my people walk without shoes.

My people move so gently and jostle rudely; they step gingerly, they walk hard; they move along with abandon and show defiance and there are some who move timidly.

I love them all but I love most those who walk as they would walk, caring nothing for impressions or fears or suppressions ... those who walk with a confident walk. These things we must learn to duplicate.

... Yes, we need a Negro people's theatre but it must not be a little theatre. Its work is too heavy, its task is too large to be anything other than a great movement. It must be powerful enough to inspire, lift, and eventually create a complete desire for the liberation of all oppressed peoples.

The Negro people's theatre must not condemn what it does not understand. We must seek out every artistic expression and if it does not conform to our present mode of production, we must examine it closely to see if it is a new form or some vague whispering from the past. We must be the guide and light the way to all that we may glean the precious stuff from that which is useless. We must be patient and, above all, ever-searching. We should, in this second half of the century, plan to turn out the largest crop of Negro artists in the entire history of America. Our voices must be heard around the world. The Negro people's theatre must study and teach not only what has been taught before but found and establish a new approach to study of the Negro in the theatre, dance and arts.

From 'Monkeying with the Scopes Trial' by Henry Hewes (*Saturday Review*, 1955)

The Scopes trial of 1925 was a deliberate affair. It was instigated by the American Civil Liberties Union, which asked for a volunteer to defy the Tennessee law against teaching evolution in the schools. In this way a stupid law was rendered ineffective by its being held up to public ridicule.

In their new play, *Inherit the Wind*, Jerome Lawrence and Robert E. Lee have chosen not to present the history of the Scopes trial exactly as it was, but rather to reshape its details so that it would illustrate the larger point it proved. Thus, the play's sympathetic villain, Matt Brady (drawn after William Jennings Bryan), is a personalization of what fanaticism can lead to in the most well-intentioned of men. Its malcontent, E. K. Hornbeck (patterned on H. L. Menken), becomes a frightening portrait of the cruel dry dust that can result from absolute skepticism and immoderate brilliance. And its hero, Henry Drummond (based on Clarence Darrow), balances within one man the rebelliousness and unswerving logic of a Menken with the compassionate warmth of a Bryan. The plot and palely-sketched other characters are incidental to this trio of richly-written studies.

... Since this production is so strongly pictorial, it is most fortunate in having the best setting of the season. Peter Larkin's two-level arrangement creates an entire country town which emerges as much the play's central character as any in the cast ... [and] lifts the play from a trial melodrama to a mural drama that tries to suggest the pathos of the smalltowner's struggle with orthodoxy, and the hope for progress in the Biblical phrase 'He that troubleth his own house shall inherit the wind; and the fool shall be servant to the wise in heart.'

NOTES

1 Introduction to the 1950s

1 For a fuller discussion of this tendency to mythologize, see Mary Caputi, *A Kindler, Gentler America: Melancholia and the Mythical 1950s* (Wisconsin: University of Minnesota Press, 2005).

2 James Gilbert, *A Cycle of Outrage: America's Reaction to the Juvenile Delinquent in the 1950s* (New York: Oxford University Press, 1986), 6.

3 Darryl Jones, Elizabeth McCarthy and Bernice M. Murphy, *It Came From the 1950s! Popular Culture, Popular Anxieties* (New York: Palgrave Macmillan, 2011), 5.

4 In the early 1950s, Sears Roebuck ceased publication of their regional catalogues on the grounds that tastes had become national.

5 In just the first half of the decade American personal wealth almost tripled. Landon Y. Jones, *Great Expectations: America and the Baby Boom Generation* (New York: Coward, McCann, and Geoghegan, 1980), 20.

6 'U.S. Again Is Subdued by Davy', *Life* 38 (17) (25 April 1955): 27.

7 Andrew Hurley, *Diners, Bowling Alleys and Trailer Parks: Chasing the American Dream in the Postwar Consumer Culture* (New York: Basic, 2001), 282.

8 Food preservation technology designed for the troops during the war was given upscale packaging and remarketed to the populace. Magazines and cookbooks featuring menus and recipes increased interest. For example, Poppy Cannon's popular *Can-Opener Cookbook* (1952).

9 Laura Shapiro, *Something from the Oven: Reinventing Dinner in 1950s America* (New York: Viking, 2004), 15.

10 Elaine Tyler May, *Homeward Bound: American Families in the*

Cold War Era (New York: Basic, 1988), 5, 8. One other increase for the period was also in the number of 'shotgun weddings', suggesting that many of those marriages were the result of premarital sex.

11   Alan Petigny, *The Permissive Society: America, 1941–1965* (New York: Cambridge University Press, 2009), 255.
12   May, *Homeward*, 151.
13   Petigny, *Permissive,* 103.
14   Ironically, the increased social stigma against homosexuality during the 1950s was balanced against a similar rise in gay enclaves and bars. While the conservative drift of society may have slowed rebellion, seeds were being planted for the future.
15   See Joanne Meyerowitz, *Not June Cleaver: Women and Gender in Post War America 1945–1960* (Philadelphia: Temple University Press, 1994).
16   Publically, the 1950s saw modest political gender gains, with a rise in female senators and women at state-level positions. Many states withdrew restrictions on women serving in juries, and greater percentages of women voted. There were also more women pursuing higher education. Petigny, *Permissive*, 159–63.
17   Jones, McCarthy, Murphy, *It Came From*, 54.
18   Thomas Maier, *Dr. Spock: An American Life* (New York: Harcourt, Brace, 1998), 202, 468.
19   Robert H. Bremner and Gary W. Reichard, eds, *Reshaping America: Society and Institutions 1945–1960* (Columbus: Ohio State University Press, 1982), ix.
20   May, *Homeward*, 117.
21   Bremner and Reichard, *Reshaping,* x.
22   Ibid., x–xi.
23   See Arthur Bestor, *Educational Wastelands* (1953), or Rudolph Flesch, *Why Johnny Can't Read* (1955).
24   See David Reisman, *The Lonely Crowd: A Study of the Changing American Character* (1950), or John Keats, *The Crack in the Picture Window* (1956).
25   Wini Breines, 'Domineering Mothers in the 1950s', *Women's Studies International Forum* 8 (6) (1985): 601–8.
26   Gilbert, *A Cycle*, 63.
27   See Erik Erickson, *Childhood and Society* (1950), who coins the term 'identity crisis' and advocates against too strict parenting, or

Edgar Z. Friedenberg, *The Vanishing Adolescent* (1959), who urges accommodation between generations rather than antagonism.

28   'A New $10 Billion Power: The US Teenage Consumer', *Life* 47 (9) (31 August 1959): 78–85.

29   Glenn Altschuler, *All Shook Up: How Rock 'n' Roll Changed America* (New York: Oxford University Press, 2003), 37.

30   Mary L. Dudziak, *Cold War Civil Rights: Race and the Image of American Democracy* (Princeton, NJ: Princeton University Press, 2002), 111.

31   See Mike Gross, 'US Now a "Musical Democracy" as Result of Disk Spread: Lomax', *Variety*, 25 March 1959: 58.

32   Susan J. Douglas, *Listening In: Radio and the American Imagination* (New York: Times, 1999), 227. Millions more were made on 'fan' products; Elvis alone had over 50 items with his imprint, including lipstick!

33   Mitch Miller, who became the chief of Columbia's pop singles division in 1950, was lionized as a genius; by 1953 he had produced over 50 hits and between 1950 and 1956 was associated with records that sold around 80 million copies. See Albin J. Zak III, *I Don't Sound Like Nobody: Remaking Music in 1950s America* (Ann Arbor: University of Michigan Press, 2010), 49.

34   Often 'black' hits were re-recorded by white singers for greater distribution, and black songwriters were frequently pressured into signing away their rights in order to get airtime. Thus, rock and roll was a mixed blessing; on the one hand it offered integration and greater respect as black music, styles and values entered the mainstream, but on the other hand it was also a form of theft.

35   Zak, *I Don't Sound*, 6. Not all were enamoured of Elvis, many viewing him as an archetypal juvenile delinquent, at least until he got cleaned up and joined the army in 1958.

36   Journalists Jack Lait and Lee Mortimer betray their inherent racism as they describe the new teen music 'with tom-toms and hot jive and ritualistic orgies of erotic dancing, weed-smoking and mass media, with African jungle background' (*USA Confidential*. New York: Crown, 1952, 37). But many found the energy of rock and roll unsettling, and suspected it was a prime motivator of juvenile delinquency.

37   The first Best Vocalist winners of the new Grammy awards for music were Perry Como (1958), Frank Sinatra (1959) and Ella Fitzgerald (1958 and 1959).

38 See Lionel Trilling, *The Liberal Imagination* (1950), or Joseph Wood Krutch, *Is the Common Man Too Common?* (1954). Trilling called for greater psychological subtly in writing over what he saw as a growing dogmatic social realism. Krutch feared that a capitalist democracy would lead to a debasement of taste, in which mass media and the desire for conformity might reduce the desire for excellence. Such fears were compounded when 238 writers were banned from US libraries in 1954 as 'too subversive'.

39 Susan Sessions Rugh, *The Golden Age of American Family Vacations* (Lawrence: University Press of Kansas, 2008), 19.

40 According to National Park Service data (https://irma.nps.gov/Stats/ [accessed 17 March 2017]) visitors to the parks almost tripled from 1946 to 1956, when they reached 61.6 million, initiating Mission 66, a ten-year plan to upgrade increasingly overwhelmed park facilities.

41 *National Recreation Survey* (Washington, DC: Outdoor Recreation Resources Review Commission, 1962), 56–7.

42 'Bingo is Getting too Big', *Reader's Digest* (March 1955): 102.

43 Petigny, *Permissive*, 191.

44 Having made the phrase 'rock 'n' roll' famous, Freed would appear in movies of that genre, then switched to television in 1957 to host *The Big Beat*. This would be eclipsed by Dick Clark's *American Bandstand* after Freed fell foul of a payola scandal in the 1960s.

45 Altschuler, *All Shook Up*, 15.

46 Charles Aaronson, ed., *The 1960 International Television Almanac* (New York: Quigley, 1959), 9A, 14A.

47 As an outlier, the popular show *The Honeymooners*, in its depiction of a more lower-class life, suggests audiences may have been more open to variety than the networks supposed.

48 Rugh, *Golden Age*, 92.

49 Ibid.

50 'Indies' accounted for only 1 per cent of film output in 1951, but by 1958 this had risen to 50 per cent and they had been responsible for three Best Picture Oscars. Thomas P. Doherty, *Teenagers and Teenpics: The Juvenalization of American Movies in the 1950s* (Philadelphia: Temple University Press, 2002), 22.

51 See Christopher H. Sterling and Timothy Haight, *The Mass Media* (New York: Prager, 1978).

52 'Film Future: GI Baby Boom', *Variety* (5 March 1958): 1, points out that 13–21-year-old movie goers had risen from 19.6 million

in 1952 to 22.4 million in 1958, a number that was expected to continue to rise.

53 Other gimmicks include 'nurses' handing out life insurance policies to audience members in case they died of fright while watching *Macabre* (1958), and the director, William Castle, hired actors to collapse in the theatres during the show. For his next film, *The Tingler* (1959), he had movie seats wired to give audience members a mild tingling shock.
54 Petigny, *Permissive*, 21.
55 May, *Homeward*, 27.
56 Petigny, *Permissive*, 24
57 Ibid., 25.
58 Quoted in James Killian, *Sputnik, Scientists, and Eisenhower* (Cambridge, MA: MIT Press, 1977), 8.

2 American Theatre in the 1950s

1 Albert Wertheim, 'The McCarthy Era and the American Theatre', *Theatre Journal* 34 (2) (May 1982): 211.
2 Playbill for *Picnic*, 13 April 1953, n.p.
3 Christopher Bigsby, *Modern American Drama: 1945–2000* (New York: Cambridge University Press, 2000), x.
4 John Gassner, *Theatre at the Crossroads: Plays and Playwrights of the Mid-Century American Stage* (New York: Holt, Rinehart and Winston, 1960), xiv.
5 It is not insignificant that many of this decade's playwrights were themselves undergoing psychoanalysis.
6 David W. Sievers, *Freud on Broadway* (New York: Cooper Square, 1970), 451.
7 *Galileo* had been presented Off-Broadway in 1947.
8 All numbers taken from http://www.ibdb.com (accessed 17 March 2016).
9 Bruce McConachie, *American Theatre in the Culture of the Cold War: Producing and Contesting Containment 1947–1962* (Iowa City: University of Iowa Press, 2003), 1.
10 Ibid., xi.
11 George Jean Nathan, *Theatre in the Fifties* (New York: Knopf, 1953), 36.

12 Bigsby, *Modern American Drama*, 31.
13 Ibid., 21.
14 Ibid., 23.
15 Gassner, 66.
16 Arthur Miller, 'What Makes Plays Endure?', in *The Theatre Essays of Arthur Miller*, ed. Robert A. Martin and Steve Centola (New York: DaCapo Press, 1996), 260.
17 Bigsby, *Modern American Drama*, 73.
18 See *The Theatre Essays of Arthur Miller* and *Echoes Down the Corridor*, ed. Steve Centola (New York: Viking, 2000).
19 Arthur Miller, 'Introduction to the *Collected Plays*', in *Theatre Essays*, 122–3.
20 Brooks Atkinson, 'Early Williams', *New York Times*, 22 November 1956, 49. David Krasner, *American Drama 1945–2000* (Malden, MA: Blackwell, 2006), 44.
21 Brooks Atkinson, 'At the Theatre', *New York Times*, 5 February 1951, 33.
22 John Lahr, *Tennessee Williams: Mad Pilgrimage of the Flesh* (New York: Norton, 2014), 258.
23 Elia Kazan, 'Notes on *Camino Real*', Elia Kazan Collection, Cinema Archives, Weslyan University.
24 Walter Kerr, '*Camino Real*', *New York Herald Tribune*, 20 March 1953, 12.
25 One of his student plays from 1938, *Not About Nightingales,* had featured Queen, a homosexual convict obsessed with his image, but that was not produced until 1998.
26 Gassner, 82.
27 Thomas P. Adler, *American Drama, 1940–1960: A Critical History* (New York: Twayne, 1994), 85.
28 Ibid., 104.
29 Weales, 106.
30 Alan Woods, 'Introduction', in *Selected Plays of Jerome Lawrence and Robert E. Lee* by Jerome Lawrence and Robert E. Lee (Columbus: Ohio State University Press, 1995), xxi.
31 Adler, *American Drama*, 123.
32 John Clum, *Paddy Chayefsky* (Boston: Twayne, 1976), 70.
33 Weales, 177.

34 Harold Clurman, *Lies Like Truth* (New York: Macmillan, 1958), 64.
35 McConachie, 232.
36 Elizabeth S. Kim, 'Asian-American Drama', in *Companion to American Drama*, ed. Jackson R. Bryer and Mary C. Hartig (New York: Facts on File, 2004), 35.
37 Ibid., 35.
38 McConachie, 38.
39 Bigsby, *Modern American Drama*, 72.
40 David Savran, *Communists, Cowboys and Queers* (Minneapolis: University of Minnesota Press, 1992), 91–2.
41 The opening night performance of which brought the young James Dean to the attention of Kazan.
42 Frank Rich, 'Introduction', in *Mielziner: Master of Modern Stage Design* by Mary C. Henderson (New York: Backstage Books, 2001), 6.
43 McConachie, 91.
44 John Kendrik, http://www.musicals101.com/1950bway.htm (accessed 17 March 2016).
45 He would remain active well past his centennial year, helping to revise the libretto of a 1994 revival of *Damn Yankees* shortly before his death at the age of 107.
46 Kendrik, musicals101.com.
47 Brooks Atkinson, 'Six Vital Stage Sets', *New York Times*, 11 April 1954, 24.
48 Where Meyerhold worked toward a propagandist, communal theatre, stripped down to appeal to the lowest common denominator, Aronson was less political and more concerned with designs that could uplift the actors rather than dominate or overpower them.
49 Quoted in Frank Rich and Lisa Aronson, *The Theatre Art of Boris Aronson* (New York: Knopf, 1987), 7.
50 Ibid., 99.
51 Ibid., 129.
52 Ibid., 141.
53 'Broadway's Busy Jeremiah: Oliver Smith, Scenic Designer, Laments State of Stage Active Schedule', *New York Times*, 28 April 1957, X3

54 Mary C. Henderson, *Mielziner: Master of Modern Stage Design* (New York: Backstage Books, 2001), 142.
55 Brooks Atkinson, '*Guys and Dolls*: Broadway Rat-Race Based on Some Damon Runyan Characters', *New York Times*, 3 December 1950, X1.
56 Ibid.
57 Atkinson, 'Six Vital Stage Sets', 24.
58 Brooks Atkinson, 'Theatre: Savage Satire: *Miss Lonelyhearts* is Staged at Music Box', *New York Times*, 4 October 1957, 26.
59 Brooks Atkinson, 'At the Theatre', *New York Times*, 30 December 1953, 17.
60 Brooks Atkinson, '*Flower Drum Song* Opens at St. James', *New York Times*, 2 December 1958, 44.
61 Atkinson, 'Six Vital Stage Sets', 24.
62 Ibid.
63 Brooks Atkinson, 'Drama on Coast: Report on Arena Staging of *Inherit the Wind* and Other Productions', *New York Times*, 23 March 1958, X1.
64 Brooks Atkinson, '*No Time for Sergeants* Makes the Audience Roar', *New York Times*, 6 November 1955, X1.
65 Eric Bentley, *Thirty Years of Treason* (New York: Viking, 1971), 947.
66 Larry Ceplair and Steven Englund, *The Inquisition in Hollywood: Politics in the Film Community 1930–1960* (Garden City, NY: Anchor/Doubleday, 1980), 371. Ceplair and Englund further suggest the pointlessness of these 'show' trials, by explaining that out of the 902 names offered by the 58 'friendly' witnesses, HUAC already had almost 700 (371–2).
67 Wertheim, 212. Wertheim was referring to plays such as *Member of the Wedding*, *Tea and Sympathy* and *Picnic*, which makes his definition somewhat debatable as each of these plays, when closely examined, offer more complexity than a simple melodrama.
68 Brenda Murphy, *Congressional Theatre: Dramatizing McCarthyism on Stage, Film, and Television* (New York: Cambridge University Press, 1999), 2–3.
69 See Wertheim, 215–16.
70 See Wertheim, 213.
71 Murphy, 247.

72 Ibid., 250–1.
73 Ibid., 3.
74 Ibid., 162, 184.
75 Quoted in Ellen Schrecker, *The Age of McCarthyism: A Brief History with Documents* (Boston: Bedford Books, 1994), 201–2.
76 Thomas Adler, *Robert Anderson* (Boston: Twayne, 1978), 72.
77 Brooks Atkinson, 'At the Theatre', *New York Times*, 23 January 1953, 15.
78 Arthur Miller, 'Preface to an Adaptation of Ibsen's *An Enemy of the People*', in *Theatre Essays*, 17.
79 Adler, *American Drama*, 74.
80 Murphy, 156.
81 John Arden, in *Arthur Miller and Company*, ed. C. W. E. Bigsby (London: Methuen, 1990), 92.
82 Stephen J. Whitfield, *The Culture of the Cold War* (Baltimore: Johns Hopkins University Press, 1991), 113.
83 Michael Gazzo's *Hatful of Rain*, in which the wife, Celia, informs the police about her husband's drug use to try to save him from himself, is another example of a play that tries to gain sympathy for the informer and imply righteousness is on their side.
84 Adler, *American Drama*, 80.
85 Harry J. Elam, 'African-American Drama', in *Companion to American Drama*, ed. Jackson R. Bryer and Mary C. Hartig (New York: Facts on File, 2004), 8.
86 Childress would also be the first black women to direct an Off-Broadway play, although that would not occur until 1972, alongside Joseph Papp, for a production of *Wedding Band*.
87 Quoted in Kathy A. Perkins, 'Introduction', *Selected Plays* by Alice Childress (Evanston, IL: Northwestern University Press, 2011), xxi.
88 Lorraine Hansberry, 'Alice Childress' Acting Brightens a Fine Off-Broadway Theatre Piece', *Freedom* 3 (9) (1953): 7.
89 See Kathlene McDonald, *Feminism, the Left, and Postwar Literary Culture* (Jackson: University Press of Mississippi, 2012), 65.
90 Alice Childress, 'Knowing the Human Condition', in *Black American Literature and Humanism*, ed. Baxter Miller (Lexington: University of Kentucky Press, 1981), 10.
91 McConachie, 190.
92 James Baldwin, 'Sweet Lorraine', in *To Be Young, Gifted and Black*

by Lorraine Hansberry (New York: New American Library, 1969), xii.
93 Krasner, 59.
94 All three also became successful movies during the 1950s.
95 Ethan Mordden, *Coming Up Roses: The Broadway Musical in the 1950s* (New York: Oxford University Press, 1998), 27.
96 *Cinderella* (1957) was created expressly for television, and although a successful broadcast reaching more than 107 million viewers, would not be produced on Broadway until 2003.
97 Kendrik, http://www.musicals101.com/1950bway.htm (accessed 8 August 2015)
98 Mark Steyn, *Broadway Babies Say Goodnight: Musicals Then and Now* (New York: Routledge, 1999), 119.
99 Thomas A. Greenfield, *Broadway: An Encyclopedia of Theatre and American Culture*, Vol. 1 (Santa Barbara, CA: Greenwood, 2010), xxxviii.
100 Timothy D. Taylor, *The Sounds of Capitalism* (Chicago: University of Chicago Press, 2012), 128.
101 Andrea Most, *Theatrical Liberalism: Jews and Popular Entertainment in America* (New York: New York University Press, 2013), 89.
102 Quoted in Craig Zadan, *Sondheim and Co.* (New York: Harper & Row, 1989), 12.
103 Ibid., 25.
104 Ibid., 28.
105 Ibid., 230.
106 Ibid., 62–3.
107 Paddy Chayefsky, *Television Plays* (New York: Simon and Schuster, 1955), 132.
108 Clum, 35.
109 Weales, 70.
110 Off-Broadway theatres stood between 5th and 9th Avenues from 34th to 56th Street, and commonly seated 199–299 people.
111 This was necessary at a period when many of the key publications that influenced public opinion, including the *New Yorker*, still did not send their drama critics to review Off-Broadway productions.
112 Quoted in Milly Barranger, *Theatre: A Way of Seeing* (New York: Cengage, 2014), 63.

113 Quoted in Arnold Aronson, *American Avant-garde Theatre: A History* (New York: Psychology Press, 2000), 55.
114 Quoted in Michael Patterson, *The Oxford Guide to Plays* (Oxford: Oxford University Press), 91.
115 Henry Hewes, 'Miracle on Fourteenth Street', *Saturday Review of Literature*, 26 September 1959, 27.
116 Ruby Cohn, *New American Dramatists: 1960–1980* (New York: Petersen-Macmillan, 1982). Quoted in http://bingweb.binghamton.edu/~ccarpen/1950.htm (accessed 17 March 2016).
117 Allan Krapow, 'A statement', in *Physical Theatres: A Critical Reader*, ed. John Keefe and Simon Murray (New York: Routledge, 2007), 108.
118 Gwen Orel, 'Regional Theatres', in *Broadway: An Encyclopedia of Theatre and American Culture*, Vol. 2, ed. Thomas A. Greenfield (Santa Barbara, CA: Greenwood, 2010), 530.
119 Robert Edward Gard and Gertrude S. Burley, *Community Theatre: Idea and Achievement* (Westport, CT: Greenwood, 1959).
120 Robert Edward Gard, Marston Balch and Pauline B. Temkin, *Theatre in America* (Madison, WI: Dembar Educational Research Services, 1968), 40.
121 Nellie McCaslin, *Historical Guide to Children's Theatre in America* (Westport, CT: Greenwood, 1987), 21.
122 Ibid.

3 William Inge

1 Ralph Voss, *A Life of William Inge: The Strains of Triumph* (Lawrence: University Press of Kansas, 1989), 21.
2 Robert Alan Aurthur, 'Hanging Out', *Esquire* (November 1973): 42.
3 Ralph Voss, 'William Inge at 100', presented at William Inge Theatre Festival on 17 April 2013.
4 Arthur F. McClure, *William Inge: A Bibliography* (Boston: Garland, 1982), xiv.
5 Voss, *Life of William Inge*, 79.
6 Gilbert Millstein, 'The Dark at the Top of William Inge', *Esquire* (August 1958): 63.

7   Voss, *Life of William Inge*, 83.
8   John Simon, 'The "Sheba" of Queens', *New York* (9 September 1974): 67.
9   Voss, *Life of William Inge*, 118.
10 Brooks Atkinson, 'At the Theatre', *New York Times*, 20 February 1953, 14.
11 This was Newman's Broadway debut and he would shortly after get his first film contract.
12 Inge asserts this in a 1967 interview with Digby Diehl, although he further insists that Virgil's desire has never been consummated. See *Behind the Scenes: Theatre and Film Interviews from the Transatlantic Review*, ed. Joseph J. McCrindle (New York: Holt, Rinehart and Winston, 1971), 114.
13 Brooks Atkinson, 'Theatre: *Bus Stop*', *New York Times*, 3 March 1955, 23.
14 Brooks Atkinson, 'The Theatre: Illuminations by Inge', *New York Times*, 6 December 1957, 38.
15 Voss, *Life of William Inge*, 51.
16 Quoted in Patrick Pacheco, 'Sam Gold Works to Revive *Picnic* – and William Inge's Standing', *Los Angeles Times*, 12 January 2013, http://articles.latimes.com/2013/jan/12/entertainment/la-et-cm-inge-picnic-20130112 (accessed 9 April, 2015).
17 Jeff Johnson, *William Inge and the Subversion of Gender* (Jefferson, NC: McFarland, 2005), 20.
18 David W. Sievers, *Freud on Broadway* (New York: Cooper Square, 1970), 356.
19 While Tarzan movies had been popular for several decades, they reached their peak in the 1950s, during which ten Tarzan movies were produced.
20 R. Baird Shuman, *William Inge*, rev. edn (New York: Twayne, 1982), 1–2.
21 McClure, *William Inge*, xv.
22 Although Alcoholics Anonymous was formed in 1935, the dissemination of its ideas took time, and it was not until the 1950s that it became well enough known for its membership to expand.
23 Even when Doc hears Turk's laughter and understands this means that Marie and Turk have slept together, two pages later Inge still includes a direction that '*DOC is mystified, trying to figure it all out.*' Inge, *Four Plays*, 46.

24 Inge, *Four Plays*, 33–4.
25 Ibid., 56.
26 Ibid., 5, 7.
27 Ibid., 11, 38.
28 For this, Inge invents the satirical *TABOO!* show, with an announcer asking over driving tom-toms, 'Won't you join me? ... Won't you leave behind your routine, the dull cares that make up your day-to-day existence, the little worries, the uncertainties, the confusions of the work-a-day world and follow me where pagan spirits hold sway, where lithe natives dance on a moon-enchanted isle ...' Ibid., 22.
29 Ibid., 57.
30 Ibid., 50.
31 Ibid., 42.
32 Ibid., 52.
33 Ibid., 75.
34 Ibid., 147.
35 Ibid., 75.
36 In Inge's original script, Hal was even less likeable, but at the urging of the director, lines were added to the Broadway production of the play to make him a more acceptable hero.
37 Inge, *Four Plays*, 120.
38 Ibid., 132.
39 Ibid., 79, 101.
40 Ibid., 79.
41 Ibid., 155.
42 Ibid., 187.
43 Ibid., 188.
44 Ibid., 200.
45 Ibid., 157.
46 Ibid., 178.
47 Ibid., 183–4.
48 Ibid., 219.
49 Ibid., 183.
50 Ibid., 155.
51 Ibid., 219.

52   Ibid., 161.
53   Ibid., 225.
54   Ibid.
55   Ibid., 257. The effects of childhood trauma were an increasingly popular line of inquiry in the enthusiasm for psychotherapy of the 1950s.
56   Ibid., 234.
57   Ibid., 294.
58   Ibid., 271.
59   Ibid., 234.
60   While Inge seems to have Sonny orate Hamlet's 'To be or not to be' speech before the party as a foreshadowing of Sammy's fate – by which he decides not to suffer the 'slings and arrows' anymore – it may also be a reference to Sonny's similarity to Hamlet as an Oedipal figure – a popular reading of the play in the 1950s after Ernest Jones's *Hamlet and Oedipus* (1949).
61   Inge, *Four Plays*, 303.
62   Ibid., 233.
63   Albert Wertheim, 'American Theatre in the 1950s and Inge's Plays', in *William Inge: Essays and Reminiscences on the Plays and the Man,* ed. Jackson Bryer and Mary Hartig (Jefferson, NC: McFarland, 2014), 17.
64   Robert Patrick, 'The Inside-Outsider', *William Inge: Essays and Reminiscences*, 28. See also Jeff Johnson, *William Inge and the Subversion of Gender* (Jefferson, NC: McFarland, 2005), for a fuller study of these tropes.
65   William Inge, 'Foreword', *Four Plays* (New York: Grove, 1958), vi.
66   Ibid., vii.
67   Voss, *Life of William Inge*, 31, 49.

4 Stephen Sondheim

1   Meryle Secrest, *Stephen Sondheim: A Life* (New York: Vintage Books, 1999).
2   Ibid., 98–112.
3   Craig Zadan, *Sondheim & Company* (New York: Da Capo Press, 1994), 12–14.

4   Secrest, *Stephen Sondheim*, 56.
5   Stephen Sondheim, *Finishing the Hat* (New York: Knopf, 2010), xix, and elsewhere throughout the book.
6   Amanda Vaill, *Somewhere: The Life of Jerome Robbins* (New York: Broadway Books, 2006), 80–110.
7   Carol J. Oja, *Bernstein Meets Broadway: Collaborative Art in a Time of War* (New York: Oxford University Press, 2014), 15.
8   Ibid., 103–15.
9   Vaill, *Somewhere*, 215–20.
10 *Leonard Bernstein: Reaching for the Note*. Directed and written by Susan Lacy. American Masters documentary, 1998, DVD. This includes an interview with Sondheim in which he characterizes the music of *Candide* in contrast to *West Side Story*.
11 Sondheim, *Finishing the Hat*, 51.
12 Arthur Laurents, *Original Story: A Memoir of Broadway and Hollywood* (New York: Applause Books, 2000). This book covers Laurents's early years, both personally and professionally. Some additional insights and information by him appear in his follow-up biography, *The Rest of the Story: A Life Completed* (New York: Applause Books, 2012).
13 Zadan, *Sondheim & Company*, 11–25.
14 YouTube's showing of the BBC's *Prom: Stephen Sondheim at 80* Concert, 1:14 into the programme.
15 Sondheim, *Finishing the Hat*. Sondheim describes working collaboratively in detail, especially the chapters on *West Side Story* and *Gypsy*. He makes it clear there that he viewed his work on those two shows as learning experiences through which he honed his craft. For Sondheim's respect for Laurents's dramaturgy, see Zadan, *Sondheim & Company*, 28.
16 Ibid., 55.
17 Ibid., 49–50 notes how and why Robbins was disliked when working on *West Side Story*. This portrait of him differs from the more playful Robbins working on *On the Town* as portrayed in Oja, *Bernstein Meets Broadway*.
18 See also *Leonard Bernstein: Reaching for the Note*.
19 On Laurents's directing of the revival, see *The Rest of the Story*, 157–60; on the show as a failure in its creator's eyes, see Zadan, *Sondheim & Company*, 26–30.
20 Sondheim, *Finishing the Hat*, 33.

21 Ibid., 32.
22 Ibid., 35.
23 Ibid.
24 Ibid.
25 Ibid., 50–2.
26 Ibid., 52.
27 Ibid., 51.
28 See Sondheim, *Finishing the Hat*, 56, on Hammerstein's encouraging Sondheim to write only lyrics, to learn to write for Ethel Merman and hence other stars. For more on Styne, see Max Wilk, *They're Playing Our Song* (New York: Atheneum, 1973).
29 Sondheim, *Finishing the Hat*, 56–7. Sondheim tells of how early on working on *Gypsy* Arthur Laurents insisted Sondheim accompany him to watch Lee Strasburg teach at his Actor's Studio and that Sondheim was embarrassed by the experience. Still, it demonstrates Laurents's influence and intent to add depth to *Gypsy*'s characterizations. It also situates *Gypsy* as being a part of this larger movement toward realism and emotional depth found in the post-Second World War years.
30 For commentary on Robbins's work on this scene and its humour, see *Jerome Robbins: Something to Dance About*. Directed by Judy Kinberg and written by Amanda Vaill. American Masters documentary, 2008, DVD. This DVD also includes an interview with Sondheim in which he recounts the story of how he and Robbins worked together in the rehearsal hall to create the number 'Rose's Turn'.
31 Sondheim, *Finishing the Hat*, 55.
32 Ibid., 60.
33 Ibid.
34 Ibid., 63.
35 Ibid.
36 Ibid.
37 Ibid., 69.
38 Ibid., 71.
39 Ibid.
40 Ibid., 77.
41 Ibid., 75.
42 Ibid.

43 Ibid.
44 Ibid.
45 Ibid.
46 Ibid.
47 Ibid.
48 Note how the original stage version had the light-skinned, Italian Carol Lawrence and the Jewish Larry Kert as Maria and Tony, but in the film version, initially directed by Robbins, Natalie Wood's make-up is noticeably and deliberately dark in colour, heightening the racial dimensions of the show.
49 For Laurents, see *Original Story*, 29; for Robbins, see Vaill, *Somewhere*, 215–19.

5 Alice Childress

1 See Kathy A. Perkins's 'Introduction' in *Selected Plays: Alice Childress* (Evanston, IL: Northwestern University Press, 2011), x, where she notes that she has not located any evidence that Childress won an Obie Award, although La Vinia Delois Jennings's biography, *Alice Childress* (New York: Twayne, 1995), 7, names Childress as the first woman playwright to receive an Obie Award.
2 'Intersectional third-wave feminism', also known as women of colour feminism, is traditionally understood as emerging in the late twentieth century as a critique of mid-twentieth-century second-wave feminism's focus on middle-class white women. Third-wave feminism accounts for multiple kinds of feminists rather than a singular feminist point of view. It also acknowledges the way other modes of identification, including race, class and sexual orientation, inform feminist practices and politics.
3 Perkins, 'Introduction', xi.
4 For more on how late twentieth-century black writers respond to the male-centred representation of the civil rights movement, see Erica R. Edwards, *Charisma and the Fictions of Black Leadership* (Minneapolis: University of Minnesota Press, 2012), and Robert J. Patterson, *Exodus Politics* (Charlottesville: University of Virginia Press, 2013).
5 Kimberlé Crenshaw, 'Demarginalizing the Intersection of Race and Sex: A Black Feminist Critique of Antidiscrimination Doctrine', *University of Chicago Legal Forum* (1989): 140.

6   Jennings makes a similar point about the function of the rest room, *Alice Childress*, 22.
7   Alice Childress, *Selected Plays: Alice Childress* (Evanston, IL: Northwestern University Press, 2011), 8.
8   Ibid.
9   Ibid., 20.
10 Ibid.
11 Quoted in Childress, *Selected Plays*, xxi. Jennings also notes that Hansberry's review is the first review of an original work by Childress, *Alice Childress*, 6.
12 Mary Helen Washington, *The Other Blacklist: The African American Literary and Cultural Left of the 1950s* (New York: Columbia University Press, 2014), 20.
13 Childress, *Selected Plays*, 25–6.
14 Ibid., 24.
15 Mary Helen Washington recounts comparisons of the formal attributes of *Gold Through the Trees* with Langston Hughes's *Don't You Want to Be Free* (1938), 'which combined dramatic historical narrative, leftist politics, and African American music', 136.
16 Childress, *Selected Plays*, 27.
17 Ibid., 28.
18 Ibid., 32.
19 Ibid., 30.
20 Washington, *The Other Blacklist*, 137.
21 Childress, *Selected Plays*, 37.
22 Ibid., 38.
23 Ibid.
24 Ibid., 39.
25 Ibid., 44.
26 Ibid., 43.
27 Washington, *The Other Blacklist*, 124.
28 Ibid., 126.
29 Ibid., 11.
30 For more detailed analysis of Childress's involvement in leftist organizations, see Washington, *The Other Blacklist*, 126–32.
31 Childress, *Selected Plays*, 53.

32 Ibid., 65.
33 Ibid.
34 Ibid.
35 Ibid., 54.
36 Ibid., 55.
37 Ibid., 86.
38 Perkins, 'Introduction', xxiv.
39 See Kathlene McDonald, *Feminism, the Left, and Postwar Literary Culture* (Jackson: University Press of Mississippi, 2012), 65.
40 Childress, *Selected Plays*, 57.
41 Ibid., 70.
42 Ibid., 106.
43 Ibid., 107.
44 Ibid., 109.

6 Jerome Lawrence and Robert E. Lee

1 All details of the lives and careers of Jerome Lawrence and Robert E. Lee are taken from *The Selected Plays of Jerome Lawrence and Robert E. Lee*, ed. Alan Woods (Columbus: Ohio State University Press, 1995).
2 A show that the writers later referred to as a 'nervous success'.
3 Several of the anthologies are listed in Lawrence and Lee, *Selected Plays*, xxiii, fn. 4, including Ernest H. Winter, ed., *Happenings* (Toronto: Thomas Nelson and Sons, 1969).
4 See http://library.osu.edu/blogs/archives/2015/10/09/how-a-world-record-holding-holstein-became-homecoming-queen/ (accessed 17 March 2016).
5 Lawrence E. Fink, 'The American Playwrights Theatre: Creating a Partnership Between Commercial and Educational Theatre as an Alternative to Broadway in the 1960s and 1970s', dissertation, Ohio State University, 1993.
6 The American theatre had been a truly national phenomenon in the nineteenth century and the first half of the twentieth; although New York was certainly an important centre, and, for many theatrical artists, to appear on a New York stage was a clear signal of arrival, there were also major theatre centres in major cities across the

country, often with chains of playhouses in smaller cities in their region. It was entirely possible for a performer to have a major career entirely outside of New York, as did a number of major figures who remain generally unknown to those who focus on the Broadway stage for their knowledge of theatre's history: performers such as Thomas W. Keene, Mademoiselle Hortense Rhea and Frederick B. Warde. See Alan Woods, 'Mademoiselle Rhea: An American Bernhardt?', *Theatre Survey* 21 (1980): 129–44, and Woods, 'Frederick B. Warde: America's Greatest Forgotten Tragedian', *Educational Theatre Journal* 19 (1977): 333–44, among others. It has been estimated that a star, even one centred in a local theatre, could play a single role for up to two years in relatively small local performance circuits during this period. See, for example, Vera Mowry Roberts, '"Lady-managers" in Nineteenth-Century American Theatre', in *The American Stage: Social and Economic Issues from the Colonial Period to the Present*, ed. Ron Engle and Tice L. Miller (Cambridge and New York: Cambridge University Press, 1983), 30–46.

7 Brooks Atkinson, *Broadway*, rev. edn (New York: Macmillan, 1974), 432.

8 Richard Hummler, 'Anybody here remember collaboration? Once common practice, now defunct', *Variety* (19 December 1988/3 January 1989): 39, 42.

9 Alan Woods, 'General Introduction', in Lawrence and Lee, *Selected Plays*, xx.

10 The production features in a book by one of the stage managers, David Clive's *Theatre Tales (Pre-Andrew Lloyd Webber)* (New York: Writer's Showcase, 2001), 88–104. He also provides a full description of the touring company, starring Melvyn Douglas, who had taken over the role of Drummond from Muni for a few months on Broadway while Muni was out having eye surgery, 108–23.

11 The discussions and arrangements to bring attention to the town, through putting Scopes on trial, are covered by Douglas O. Linder in 'State v. John Scopes ("The Monkey Trial")', http://law2.umkc.edu/faculty/projects/ftrials/scopes/evolut.htm (accessed 17 March 2016).

12 For a more detailed background on what inspired Lawrence and Lee to write the play, see their explanation in '*Inherit the Wind*: The Genesis and Exodus of the Play', *Theatre Arts* (August 1957): 33, 94.

13 For more detailed information on this trend, which has grown exponentially with the emergence of multi-channel cable television

in the last decade of the twentieth century and the first two decades of the twenty-first, see Megan Mujllen, *The Rise of Cable Programming in the United States: Revolution or Evolution?* (Austin: University of Texas Press, 2003). By 2015, a search of social media revealed more than a dozen websites excoriating the playwrights for their factual errors; for examples, see the listings at www.creation.com and www.answersingenesis.org (both accessed 17 March 2016). See also Edward J. Larson, *Summer for the Gods: The Scopes Trial and America's Continuing Debate Over Science and Religion* (New York: Basic Books, 2006).

14 Lawrence and Lee, *Selected Plays*, 9.
15 Ibid., 15.
16 Ibid., 22.
17 Ibid., 25.
18 Ibid., 28. Just as Arthur Miller depicted in his earlier play, *The Crucible* (1953), those who feel they are in the right, rather than open rational dialogue, automatically demonize anyone against them: it happened with the earlier opposition against Puritan theocracy, as it would with supposed communists against patriotic Americans, and here with believers in evolution versus creationists.
19 Ibid., 48.
20 Ibid., 43.
21 Ibid., 56.
22 Ibid., 60.
23 Patrick Dennis, *Auntie Mame* (New York: Vanguard Press, 1955). 'Patrick Dennis' was a pseudonym (one of several) employed by writer Edward Everett Tanner III (1921–76).
24 Lawrence and Lee, *Selected Plays*, 78.
25 For Hall, see http://www.egs.edu/library/radclyffe-hall/biography/ (accessed 17 March 2016).
26 Ibid., 162.
27 Ibid., 164.
28 Ibid., 92, 165.
29 'Some Matters of Opinion', *New York Sunday News*, 15 June 1959, sec. 3: 1. Ellipses in original. Both Greer Garson and Beatrice Lillie played Mame on Broadway during its long run, and Lillie later opened the play in London. Constance Bennett, Sylvia Sidney and Eve Arden were also seen on Broadway as Mame.

30 Lawrence and Lee, *Selected Plays*, 182.
31 Ibid., 184.
32 Ibid., 186.
33 Ibid., 189.
34 See Laton McCartney, *The Teapot Dome Scandal: How Big Oil Bought the Harding White House and Tried to Steal the Country* (New York: Random House, 2008).
35 Lawrence and Lee, *Selected Plays*, 230.
36 Lawrence and Lee, 'The Gang is Almost Here', typescript, Lawrence and Lee Collection 8:10, Jerome Lawrence and Robert E. Lee Theatre Research Institute, Ohio State University Libraries.
37 Norman Cousins, 'Foreword', in Lawrence and Lee, *Selected Plays*, vii.
38 Ibid.
39 *Auntie Mame*, Lawrence and Lee, *Selected Plays*, 144.

7 Afterword

1 Robert Brustein, 'The Men-Taming Women of William Inge', *Harper's* (November 1958): 52–7.
2 Brooks Atkinson, 'Theatre: *Loss of Roses*: New Inge Play Bows at O'Neill', *New York Times*, 30 November 1959, 27, and Robert Brustein, 'Theatre: *Loss of Roses*', *New Republic*, 21 December 1959, 23, in which he declared the play to be 'uninspired and not worth seeing'.
3 See Ralph Voss, *A Life of William Inge: The Strains of Triumph* (Lawrence: University Press of Kansas, 1989), 162–3.
4 William Inge, *Natural Affection* (New York: Random House, 1963), ix.
5 Digby Diehl, 'Interview with William Inge', in *Behind the Scenes: Theatre and Film Interviews from the Transatlantic Review*, ed. Joseph McCrindle (New York: Holt, Rinehart and Winston, 1971), 108.
6 Richard Watts Jr, 'Two on the Aisle: Happy Return of William Inge', *New York Theatre Critics' Reviews* 27 (1966): 347.
7 Voss, *Life of William Inge*, 275.

8   Paul L. Montgomery, 'William Inge, Playwright, Is Dead', *New York Times*, 11 June 1973, 1, and Brooks Atkinson, 'A Haunted Playwright', *New York Times*, 11 June 1973, 38.
9   Harold Clurman, 'A Review of *Overnight*', *The Nation*, 3 August 1974, 92.
10 Tennessee Williams, 'Introduction', in *Dark at the Top of the Stairs* by William Inge (New York: Random House, 1958), viii.
11 Voss, *Life of William Inge*, 273.
12 Quoted in Montgomery, 'Playwright, Is Dead', 38.
13 Harold Clurman, '*Overnight*', 92.
14 See http://ingecentre.org for more details (accessed 17 March 2016).
15 *Gypsy*, in particular, continues to do well; in 1989 with Tyne Daly, the production ran for 581 performances and won Tony Awards for Best Revival and for Daly as Best Actress in a Musical. Bernadette Peters's 2003 production ran for 451 performances and Patti Lupone's 2008 one for 332, and she also won a Tony, making Rose an obvious landmark role for women.
16 Quoted in John S. Wilson, 'Everything's Coming Up Sondheim', *Theatre Arts* (June 1962): 64.
17 Quoted in Craig Zadan, *Sondheim and Co.* (New York: Harper & Row, 1989), 68.
18 Ibid., 94.
19 The show was also a huge hit in London, garnering some of the most positive reviews ever given to a musical there, and its 2006 Broadway revival won a Tony for Best Revival.
20 Mel Gussow, '*Company* Anew: Larry Kert Assumes Role of Batchelor', *New York Times*, 29 July 1970, 31.
21 It won seven out of its eleven nominations.
22 Clive Barnes, 'The Theatre: *A Little Night Music*', *New York Times*, 26 February 1973, 26.
23 Judy Collins's later success with 'Bring in the Clowns' from *A Little Night Music* proved Sondheim's material could produce a hit and won him one of his eight Grammy awards.
24 Jack Kroll, 'Sondheim Paints a Picture', *Newsweek*, 14 May 1984, 83.
25 Quoted in Zadan, *Sondheim and Co.*, 35.

26 John S. Wilson, 'Getting Lyrical Over *Night Music*: Pop', *New York Times*, 22 April, 1973, 126.
27 Joanne Gordon, *Art Isn't Easy: The Theatre of Stephen Sondheim* (New York: Da Capo Press, 1992), 18.
28 Alice Childress, 'A Candle in a Gale Wind', in *Black Women Writers (1950–1980): A Critical Evaluation*, ed. Mari Evans (New York: Doubleday, 1984), 112.
29 Doris E. Abramson, *Negro Playwrights in the American Theatre: 1925–1959* (New York: Columbia University Press, 1969), 190.
30 Alice Childress, 'But I Do My Thing', *New York Times*, 2 February 1969, D9.
31 Alice Childress, 'Scene from *The African Garden*', in *Black Scenes*, ed. Alice Childress (Garden City, NY: Doubleday, 1971), 137–45.
32 Another unproduced piece she wrote with Woodard was *Behind Every Door: A Light Opera for a Working Lady* (1984–5), although it was a finalist in a contest sponsored by the New York Shakespeare Festival.
33 Alan Woods, 'General Introduction', in *Selected Plays of Jerome Lawrence and Robert E. Lee*, ed. Alan Woods (Columbus: Ohio State University Press, 1995), xix.
34 Nena Couch, 'An Interview with Jerome Lawrence and Robert E. Lee', *Studies in American Drama 1945 to the Present* 7 (1) (1992): 14.
35 Norman Cousins, 'Foreword', *Selected Plays*, viii.
36 *Mame* was filmed with Lucille Ball in 1974 to disappointing reviews. *Inherit the Wind* has so far been filmed four times: in 1960 with Spencer Tracy and Fredric March; in 1965 with Melvyn Douglas and Ed Begley; in 1988 with Kirk Douglas and Jason Robards; and in 1999 with Jack Lemmon and George C. Scott; several of these productions won awards. Aside from numerous regional, school and community theatre productions, it has also been revived twice on Broadway, first in a disappointing production in 1996 with George C. Scott and Charles Durning, but then to greater success in 2007 with Brian Dennehy and Christopher Plummer. Michael Kuchwara reported that it was 'still an unabashed crowd pleaser' ('*Inherit the Wind* Crackles with Drama', *Associated Press*, 12 April 2007).
37 As Jerome Lawrence explained to Alan Woods in a personal correspondence dated 14 March 1993, a friend suggested to the playwrights after the opening performance that 'This should have

been a musical.' It would take Andrew Lloyd Webber and Tim Rice 11 more years to come to the same conclusion with the creation of *Evita*.

38   Alan Woods, 'General Introduction', *Selected Plays*, ix.

BIBLIOGRAPHY

Books on the 1950s

Altschuler, Glenn. *All Shook Up: How Rock 'n' Roll Changed America.* New York: Oxford University Press, 2003.

Boddy, William. *Fifties Television: The Industry and Its Critics.* Urbana: University of Illinois Press, 1990.

Bremner, Robert H. and Gary W. Reichard, eds. *Reshaping America: Society and Institutions 1945–1960.* Columbus: Ohio State University Press, 1982.

Cohen, Lizbeth. *A Consumer's Republic: The Politics of Mass Consumption in Postwar America.* New York: Vintage, 2003.

Cuordileone, Kyle A. *Manhood and American Political Culture in the Cold War.* New York: Routledge, 1998.

Doherty, Thomas P. *Teenagers and Teenpics: The Juvenalization of American Movies in the 1950s.* Philadelphia: Temple University Press, 2002.

Dudziak, Mary L. *Cold War Civil Rights: Race and the Image of American Democracy.* Princeton, NJ: Princeton University Press, 2000.

Emmons, Caroline S., ed. *Cold War and McCarthy Era: People and Perspectives.* Santa Barbara, CA: ABC-CLIO, 2010.

Gilbert, James. *A Cycle of Outrage: America's Reaction to the Juvenile Delinquent in the 1950s.* New York: Oxford University Press, 1986.

Halberstam, David. *The Fifties.* New York: Villard, 1993.

Harvey, Brett. *The Fifties: A Women's Oral History.* New York: HarperCollins, 1993.

Hurley, Andrew. *Diners, Bowling Alleys and Trailer Parks: Chasing the American Dream in the Postwar Consumer Culture.* New York: Basic Books, 2001.

Johnson, David K. *The Lavender Scare: The Cold War Persecution of Gays and Lesbians in the Federal Government.* Chicago: University of Chicago Press, 2004.

Jones, Darryl, Elizabeth McCarthy and Bernice M. Murphy, eds. *It Came*

from the 1950s! Popular Culture, Popular Anxieties. New York: Palgrave Macmillan, 2011.
Lev, Peter, ed. History of the American Cinema. Vol 7, Transforming the Screen 1950–1959. New York: Charles Scribner's Sons, 2003.
Marling, Karal Ann. As Seen on TV: The Visual Culture of Everyday Life in the 1950s. Cambridge, MA: Harvard University Press, 1994.
May, Elaine Tyler. Homeward Bound: American Families in the Cold War Era. New York: Basic, 1988.
McCarthy, Anna. The Citizen Machine: Governing by Television in 1950s America. New York: New Press, 2010.
Meyerowitz, Joanne. Not June Cleaver: Women and Gender in Postwar America 1945–1960. Philadelphia: Temple University Press, 1994.
Miller, Douglas T. and Marion Nowak. The Fifties: The Way We Really Were. Garden City, NY: Doubleday, 1977.
Petigny, Alan. The Permissive Society: America, 1941–1965. New York: Cambridge University Press, 2009.
Rugh, Susan Sessions. The Golden Age of American Family Vacations. Lawrence: University Press of Kansas, 2008.
Schrecker, Ellen. The Age of McCarthyism: A Brief History with Documents. Boston: Bedford Books, 1994.
Shapiro, Laura. Something from the Oven: Reinventing Dinner in 1950s America. New York: Viking, 2004.
Spigel, Lynn. Make Room for TV: Television and the Family Ideal in Postwar America. Chicago: University of Chicago Press, 1992.
Spring, Dawn. Advertising in the Age of Persuasion: Building Brand America 1941–1961. New York: Palgrave Macmillan, 2011.
Whitfield, Stephen J. The Culture of the Cold War. Baltimore: Johns Hopkins University Press, 1991.
Zak III, Albin J. I Don't Sound Like Nobody: Remaking Music in 1950s America. Ann Arbor: University of Michigan Press, 2010.

Books on American theatre

Aronson, Arnold. American Avant-Garde Theatre: A History. New York: Psychology Press, 2000.
Bean, Annemarie. A Sourcebook of African-American Performance: Plays, People, Movements. New York: Routledge, 1999.
Bigsby, Christopher. A Critical Introduction to Twentieth-Century American Drama, 3 vols. New York: Cambridge University Press, 1985.

Bigsby, Christopher. *Modern American Drama 1945–2000*. New York: Cambridge University Press, 2000.
Block, Geoffrey. *Enchanted Evenings: The Broadway Musical from Show Boat to Sondheim*. Oxford: Oxford University Press, 1997.
Bordman, Gerald M. *American Theatre: A Chronicle of Comedy and Drama, 1930–1969*. New York: Oxford University Press, 1996.
Brown-Guillory, Elizabeth. *Their Place on the Stage: Black Women Playwrights in America*. Westport, CT: Praeger, 1990.
Bryer, Jackson R. and Richard Allan Davison, eds. *The Art of the American Musical: Conversations with the Creators*. New Brunswick: Rutgers University Press, 2005.
Bryer, Jackson R. and Mary C. Hartig, eds. *Companion to American Drama*. New York: Facts on File, 2003.
Butsch, Richard. *The Making of American Audiences: From Stage to Television, 1750–1990*. Cambridge: Cambridge University Press, 2000.
Clurman, Harold. *Lies Like Truth*. New York: Macmillan, 1958.
Devlin, Albert J. and Marlene J. Devlin, eds. *The Selected Letters of Elia Kazan*. New York: Knopf, 2014.
Durham, Weldon B. *American Theatre Companies, 1931–1986*. Westport, CT: Greenwood, 1989.
Elam, Harry J. and David Krasner, eds. *African-American Performance and Theatre History: A Critical Reader*. New York: Oxford University Press, 2001.
Freeman, Morris. *American Drama in Social Context*. Carbondale: Southern Illinois University Press, 1971.
Gard, Robert Edward and Gertrude S. Burley. *Community Theatre: Idea and Achievement*. Westport, CT: Greenwood, 1959.
Greenfield, Thomas A. *Broadway: An Encyclopedia of Theatre and American Culture*, 2 vols. Santa Barbara, CA: Greenwood, 2010.
Harvell, Tony A. *Latin American Dramatists since 1945: A Bio-Bibliographical Guide*. Westport, CT: Praeger, 2003.
Henderson, Mary. *Mielziner: Master of Modern Stage Design*. New York: Back Stage Books, 2001.
Hill, Errol G. and James V. Hatch. *A History of African American Theatre*. Cambridge: Cambridge University Press, 2006.
Houchin, John H. *Censorship of the American Theatre in the Twentieth Century*. Cambridge: Cambridge University Press, 2009.
Kazan, Elia. *Kazan on Directing*. New York: Vintage, 1999.
Kolin, Philip K. and Colby H. Kullman. *Speaking on Stage: Interviews with Contemporary American Playwrights*. Tuscaloosa: University of Alabama Press, 1996.

Krasner, David. *American Drama 1945–2000: An Introduction*. Malden, MA: Blackwell, 2006.

Krasner, David. *A Companion to 20th Century American Drama*. Malden, MA: Blackwell, 2007.

Lewis, Allan. *American Plays and Playwrights of the Contemporary Theatre*. Revised edition. New York: Crown, 1970.

Marsh-Lockett, Carol P., ed. *Black Women Playwrights: Visions on the American Stage*. New York: Psychology Press, 1999.

McCaslin, Nellie. *Historical Guide to Children's Theatre in America*. Westport, CT: Greenwood, 1987.

Meserve, Walter J. *An Outline History of American Drama*. Totowa, NJ: Littlefield, Adams, 1965.

Mielziner, Jo. *Designing for the Theatre: A Memoir and a Portfolio*. New York: Atheneum, 1965.

Most, Andrea. *Theatrical Liberalism: Jews and Popular Entertainment in America*. New York: New York University Press, 2013.

Murphy, Brenda. *The Cambridge Companion to American Women Playwrights*. New York: Cambridge University Press, 1999.

Murphy, Brenda. *Tennessee Williams and Elia Kazan: A Collaboration in the Theatre*. Cambridge: Cambridge University Press, 2006.

Rice, Elmer. *The Living Theatre*. New York: Heinmann, 1959.

Rich, Frank and Lisa Aronson. *The Theatre Art of Boris Aronson*. New York: Knopf, 1987.

Salem, James M. *A Guide to Critical Reviews, Part I: American Drama, 1909–1982*, 3rd edn. Metuchen, NJ: Scarecrow, 1984.

Saxon, Theresa. *American Theatre: History, Context, Form*. Edinburgh: Edinburgh University Press, 2011.

Shiach, Don. *American Drama 1900–1990*. Cambridge: Cambridge University Press, 2000.

Sievers, W. David. *Freud on Broadway: A History of Psychoanalysis and the American Drama*. New York: Cooper Square, 1970.

Smith, Susan Harris. *American Drama: The Bastard Art*. New York: Cambridge University Press, 2006.

Stanlake, Christy. *Native American Drama: A Critical Perspective*. Cambridge: Cambridge University Press, 2010.

Watt, Stephen and Gary A. Richardson. *American Drama: Colonial to Contemporary*. Boston: Heinle & Heinle, 1994.

Wilk, Max. *They're Playing Our Song*. New York: Atheneum, 1973.

Williams, Dana A. *Contemporary African American Female Playwrights: An Annotated Biography*. Westport, CT: Greenwood, 1998.

Wilmer, S. E. *Theatre, Society and the Nation: Staging American Identities*. Cambridge: Cambridge University Press, 2008.

Wilmeth, Don B. *The Cambridge Guide to American Theatre*.
  Cambridge: Cambridge University Press, 2007.
Wilmeth, Don B. and Christopher Bigsby. *The Cambridge History of
  American Theatre*, 3 vols. Cambridge: Cambridge University Press,
  2006.
Young, Harvey. *The Cambridge Companion to African American
  Theatre*. Cambridge: Cambridge University Press, 2012.
Ziegler, John Wesley. *Regional Theatre: The Revolutionary Stage*.
  Minneapolis: University of Minnesota Press, 1973.

Books on 1950s American theatre

Adler, Thomas P. *American Drama, 1940–1960: A Critical History*. New
  York: Twayne, 1997.
Bentley, Eric. *Thirty Years of Treason*. New York: Viking, 1971.
Carpenter, Charles. *Dramatists and the Bomb: American and British
  Playwrights Confront the Nuclear Age, 1945–1964*. Westport, CT:
  Praeger, 1999.
Elsom, John. *Cold War Theatre*. New York: Routledge, 1992.
Gassner, John. *Theatre at the Crossroads: Plays and Playwrights of
  the Mid-Century American Stage*. New York: Holt, Rinehart and
  Winston, 1960.
Harris, Richard H. *Modern Drama in America and England, 1950–1970*.
  Detroit: Gale, 1982.
Jackson, Lawrence P. *The Indignant Generation: A Narrative History
  of African American Writers and Critics, 1934–1960*. Princeton, NJ:
  Princeton University Press, 2011.
Kabatchnik, Amnon. *Blood on the Stage, 1950–1975: Milestone Plays
  of Crime, Mystery, and Detection*. Lanham, MD: Scarecrow Press,
  2011.
Laurents, Arthur. *Original Story: A Memoir of Broadway and
  Hollywood*. New York: Applause Books, 2000.
Laurents, Arthur. *Mainly on Directing: Gypsy, West Side Story, and
  Other Musicals*. New York: Borzoi, 2009.
McConachie, Bruce A. *American Theatre in the Culture of the Cold
  War: Producing and Contesting Containment, 1947–1962*. Iowa City:
  University of Iowa Press, 2003.
McDonald, Kathlene. *Feminism, the Left, and Postwar Literary Culture*.
  Jackson: University Press of Mississippi, 2012.
Mordden, Ethan. *Coming Up Roses: The Broadway Musical in the
  1950s*. New York: Oxford University Press, 1998.

Murphy, Brenda. *Congressional Theatre: Dramatizing McCarthyism on Stage, Film, and Television*. New York: Cambridge University Press, 2003.
Nathan, George Jean. *Theatre in the Fifties*. New York: Knopf, 1953.
Perucci, Tony. *Paul Robeson and the Cold War Performance Complex: Race, Madness, Activism*. Ann Arbor: University of Michigan Press, 2012.
Vaill, Amanda. *Somewhere: The Life of Jerome Robbins*. New York: Broadway Books, 2006.
Washington, Mary Helen. *The Other Blacklist: The African American Literary and Cultural Left of the 1950s*. New York: Columbia University Press, 2014.

Playwright bibliographies

Alice Childress

Primary

Childress, Alice. 'For a Negro Theatre'. *Masses and Mainstream* 4 (February 1951): 61–4.
Childress, Alice. 'The World on a Hill'. In *Plays to Remember*, ed. Henry B. Maloney, 103–25. Toronto: Macmillan, 1968.
Childress, Alice. *When the Rattlesnake Sounds*. New York: Coward, McCann and Geoghegan, 1975.
Childress, Alice. *Let's Hear It for the Queen*. New York: Coward, McCann and Geoghegan, 1976.
Childress, Alice. 'A Candle in a Gale Wind'. In *Black Women Writers (1950–1980): A Critical Evaluation*, ed. Mari Evans, 111–16. Garden City, NY: Anchor Press, 1984.
Childress, Alice. *Moms: A Praise Play for a Black Comedienne*. New York: Flora Roberts, 1993.
Childress, Alice. *Mojo and String*. New York: Dramatists Play Service, 1998.
Childress, Alice. *Like One of the Family: Conversations from a Domestic's Life*. Boston: Beacon Press, 2001.
Childress, Alice. *Selected Plays*. Evanston, IL: Northwestern University Press, 2011.

Secondary

Austin, Gayle. 'Alice Childress: Black Woman Playwright as Feminist Critic'. *Southern Quarterly* 25 (Spring 1987): 53–62.

Betsko, Kathleen and Rachel Koenig. 'Alice Childress', *Interviews with Contemporary Women Playwrights*, edited by Kathleen Betsko and Rachel Koening, 62–74. New York: William Morrow, 1987.

Bower, Martha Gilman. *Color Struck under the Gaze: The Pathology of Being in the Plays of Johnson, Hurston, Childress, Hansberry, and Kennedy*. Westport, CT: Greenwood Press, 2003.

Diggs, Soyica. 'Dialectical Dialogues: Performing Blackness in the Drama of Alice Childress'. In *Contemporary African American Women Playwrights: A Casebook*, ed. Philip Kolin, 28–46. New York: Routledge, 2007.

Hay, Samuel A. 'Alice Childress's Dramatic Structure'. In *Black Women Writers (1950–1980): A Critical Evaluation*, ed. Mari Evans, 117–28. New York: Doubleday, 1984.

Jennings, La Vinia Delois. *Alice Childress*. New York: Twayne. 1995.

Maguire, Roberta. 'Alice Childress'. In *The Playwright's Art: Conversations with Contemporary American Playwrights*, ed. Jackson Bryer, 48–69. New Brunswick, NJ: Rutger's University Press, 1995.

William Inge

Primary

Inge, William. *Four Plays by William Inge*. New York: Random House, 1958.

Inge, William. *Loss of Roses*. New York: Random House, 1960.

Inge, William. *Splendor in the Grass: A Screenplay*. New York: Bantam Books, 1961.

Inge, William. *Summer Brave and Eleven Short Plays*. New York: Random House, 1962.

Inge, William. *Natural Affection*. New York: Random House, 1963.

Inge, William. *Where's Daddy?* New York: Random House, 1966.

Inge, William. *A Complex Evening: Six Short Plays by William Inge*. Independence, KS: Independence Community College Press, 2009.

Secondary

Bryer, Jackson and Mary Hartig, eds. *William Inge: Essays and Reminiscences on the Plays and the Man*. Jefferson, NC: McFarland, 2014.

Johnson, Jeff. *William Inge and the Subversion of Gender*. Jefferson, NC: McFarland, 2005.
McClure, Arthur F. *Memories of Splendor: The Midwestern World of William Inge*. Topeka: Kansas State Historical Society, 1989.
McClure, Arthur F. and C. David Rice, eds. *A Bibliographical Guide to the Works of William Inge (1913–1973)*. Lewiston, NY: Edwin Mellen Press, 1991.
Shuman, R. Baird. *William Inge*. Revised edition. New York: Twayne, 1982.
Voss, Ralph. *A Life of William Inge: The Strains of Triumph*. Lawrence: University Press of Kansas, 1989.

Jerome Lawrence and Robert E. Lee

Primary

Lawrence, Jerome and Robert E. Lee. 'The Angels Weep'. *Studies in American Drama 1945 to the Present* 7 (1) (1992): 19–87.
Lawrence, Jerome and Robert E. Lee. *Selected Plays of Jerome Lawrence and Robert E. Lee*, ed. Alan Woods. Columbus: Ohio State University Press, 1995.
Lawrence, Jerome, Robert E. Lee and James Thurber. *Jabberwock: Improbabilities Lived and Imagined by James Thurber in the Fictional City of Columbus, Ohio*. New York: Samuel French, 1974.

Secondary

Guterman, Gad. 'Field Tripping: The Power of *Inherit the Wind*'. *Theatre Journal* 60 (4) (December 2008): 563–83.
Johnson, Bruce E. *Lawrence and Lee's* Inherit the Wind: *A Critical Commentary*. New York: Monarch, 1979.
Mancini, Candace. *Freedom of Thought in Jerome Lawrence and Robert Edwin Lee's* Inherit the Wind. Detroit: Greenhaven Press, 2011.
Studies in American Drama 1945 to the Present 7 (1) (1992). (Special issue on Lawrence and Lee that contains an interview, an extensive bibliography and a previously unpublished play, *The Angels Weep*, a prequel to *Inherit the Wind*, featuring Henry Drummond earlier in his career.)

Stephen Sondheim

Primary

Sondheim, Stephen. *Finishing the Hat: Collected Lyrics (1954–1981) with Attendant Comments, Principles, Heresies, Grudges, Whines and Anecdotes.* New York: Knopf, 2010.
Sondheim, Stephen. *Look, I Made a Hat: Collected Lyrics (1981–2011) with Attendant Comments, Amplifications, Dogmas, Harangues, Digressions, Anecdotes and Miscellany.* New York: Knopf, 2011.

Secondary

Banfield, Stephen. *Sondheim's Broadway Musicals.* Ann Arbor: University of Michigan Press, 1993.
Citron, Stephen. *Sondheim and Lloyd-Webber: The New Musical.* New York: Oxford University Press, 2001.
Garebian, Keith. *The Making of Gypsy.* New York: Mosaic Press, 1998.
Gordon, Joanne. *Art Isn't Easy: The Theatre of Stephen Sondheim.* New York: Da Capo Press, 1992.
Gordon, Joanne, ed. *Stephen Sondheim: A Casebook.* New York: Garland, 1997.
Gottfried, Martin. *Sondheim.* New York: Harry N. Abrams, 2000.
Horowitz, Mark Eden. *Sondheim on Music: Minor Details and Major Decisions.* Lanham, MD: Scarecrow Press, 2003.
MacKenzie, Gina Masucci. *The Theatre of the Real: Yeats, Beckett, and Sondheim.* Columbus: Ohio State University Press, 2008.
Secrest, Meryle. *Stephen Sondheim: A Life.* New York: Knopf, 1998.
Swayne, Steve. *How Sondheim Found His Sound.* Ann Arbor: University of Michigan Press, 2007.
Zadan, Craig. *Sondheim and Co.* New York: Harper & Row, 1989.

Web resources

http://www.americantheatre.org/ (accessed 8 August 2015)
http://bingweb.binghamton.edu/~ccarpen/1950.htm (accessed 8 August 2015)
http://www.ibdb.com (accessed 8 August 2015)
http://www.theatrehistory.com/american/index.html (accessed 8 August 2015)

INDEX

$64,000 Question, The (TV series) 29

Aaron, Hank 23
Abbott, George 57, 59, 85, 191, 229
ABC Theatre (TV series) 223
Abel, Lionel 44, 93
  Absalom 44, 93
Abramson, Doris 222
Actor's Equity 55, 81, 92, 96, 176
Actors Studio 58, 209, 272 n.29
Actor's Workshop of San Francisco 95–6
Adler, Richard 85, 86, 160
  Damn Yankees 41, 43, 59, 85, 140, 263 n.45
  Pajama Game, The 41, 43, 59, 85, 140, 141
  see also Ross, Jerry
Adler, Stella 58, 209
Adler, Thomas 50, 52, 76, 77, 78
Adventures of Harriet and Ozzie, The (TV series) 28
Adventures of Rin Tin Tin, The (TV Series) 28
advertising 1, 3, 6, 26–7, 32, 87, 190, 238
  effects of 205, 208
  in plays 44, 57, 213
Affairs of State (Verneuil) 41
Agee, James 20
  Death in the Family, A 20

Albee, Edward 54, 94
  Zoo Story, The 94
Alcoholics Anonymous (AA) 103, 107–9, 268 n.22
alcoholism 21, 34, 101, 103, 105, 118, 125, 129, 212
  in plays 103–5, 107–9, 114–15, 125
Aleichem, Sholem 89
Alison's House (Glaspell) 90
All About Eve (film) 30
All–American Girls Professional Basketball 23
Alley Theater 95–6
American Ballet Theatre 133
American Bandstand (TV series) 28
American Civil Liberties Union 193, 254
American Community Theatre Association 96
American Dream, The 2, 10, 11, 45, 80, 84, 141
American in Paris, An (film) 30
American National Theatre and Academy (ANTA) 54, 93
American Negro Theatre (ANT) 166, 168, 177, 181
American Player's Theatre 192, 230
American Psychology Society 33
Americans at Work (TV series) 27

American Theatre Association 96, 97
Anderson, Maxwell 61, 75, 193, 227
  Anne of the Thousand Days 67
  Barefoot in Athens 75
  Knickerbocker Holiday 61
  Mary of Scotland 90, 193
  Winterset 193
Anderson, Robert 53, 56, 76
  Tea and Sympathy 42, 53–4, 56, 62, 68, 76, 264 n.67
Andersonville (Kantor) 20
Anniversary Waltz (Chodorov; Fields) 42
Anouilh, Jean 42, 76
  Lark, The 69, 76
  see also Hellman, Lillian
Anski, S.
  Dybbuk, The 52
anti-intellectualism 2, 19, 75
anti-Semitism 16, 119
Aptheker, Herbert 177
Archibald, William 67
  Innocents, The 50, 67
architecture 22–3
  set design 66, 70
Arden, John 77
Ardrey, Robert 73
  Shadow of Heroes 73
  Sing Me No Lullaby 73
Arena Stage 95–6, 230
Aronson, Boris 54, 57, 60, 62, 63–6, 69, 263 n.48
Around the World in 80 Days (film) 30
art 21–2
Artaud, Antonin 94, 95, 209
Arthur Godfrey's Talent Scouts (TV series) 29
Artists Theatre 93
Ashbery, John 93

Asimov, Isaac 20
  Foundation 20
  I, Robot 20
As the World Turns (TV series) 28
Atkinson, Brooks 48, 63, 67–71, 77, 102, 211, 215
atomic power 10, 12–14, 28–30, 32, 39, 46, 54, 72, 105, 139
Atomic Submarine (film) 32
Auden, W. H. 233, 237
Aurthur, Robert Alan 90, 100
  Man is Ten Feet Tall, A 90
Autry, Gene 28
Axelrod, George 51
  Seven Year Itch, The 41, 51
  Will Success Spoil Rock Hunter? 51, 70
Ayers, Lemuel 62

Babbitt, Milton 127
Back to the Future (film) 1
Bad Seed, The (March) 19
Baker, Carroll 62
Baker, Word 44
Balanchine, George 133
Baldwin, James 21, 83
  Go Tell it on the Mountain 21
  Notes of a Native Son 21
Balsam, Martin 90
Baltimore Colts 23
Barnes, Clive 219
beat generation 21, 244
Beatty, Warren 58, 103, 213
Beck, Julian 93–4
Beckett, Samuel 42, 46, 94, 209, 213
  Endgame 42
  Krapp's Last Tape 94
  Waiting for Godot 42
Beerbohm, Max 230
  Seven Men 230
Beetle Bailey (cartoon) 33

INDEX

Begley, Ed 193, 200, 280 n.36
Behan, Brendan 44
  Quare Fellow, The 44
Behind the Great Wall (film) 30
Belafonte, Harry 166
Bellow, Saul 21
Ben Hur (film) 30
Bennett, Michael 218
Benny, Jack 28
Bentley, Eric 71, 209, 250
Berkey, Ralph 78
Berle, Milton 28
Berlin, Irving 84
  Annie Get Your Gun 61
  Call Me Madam 59
Bernstein, Leonard 87, 133–6,
  138–42, 146–7, 150, 162
  Candide 70, 76, 88, 135, 271
  n.10
  On the Town 70, 132–4, 138,
  271 n. 17
  Sondheim and 88, 128, 131,
  136, 138–9, 142–5, 161,
  163
  West Side Story 52, 59–61,
  127–8, 131, 134–46,
  154–5, 157, 160
    design of 70, 136, 138–9,
    149–50
    impact 86, 137, 140–2,
    147, 162, 216, 251–2
    race 55–6, 87–8, 134–5,
    139–42, 161–2
  Wonderful Town 43, 59, 60,
  88, 134, 140, 203
  see also Comden, Betty; Green,
  Adolph; Hellman, Lillian;
  Sondheim, Stephen
Berry, Chuck 19
Bigsby, Christopher 40, 46–7,
  56
Bishop, Elizabeth 20
Blackboard Jungle, The (film) 31

blacklisting 14–15, 72–3, 181,
  198
Blackmer, Sidney 101
Black Power 80, 224
Blau, Herbert 95
Blue Denim (Herlihy; Noble) 61
Bock, Jerry 89
  Fiddler on the Roof 42, 66,
  89, 132
  Fiorello 59, 89
  see also Harnick, Sheldon
Bolton, Whitney 217
Boone, Pat 19, 31
Booth, Shirley 58, 101
Bradbury, Ray 20
  Farenheit 451 20
  Illustrated Man, The 20
  Martian Chronicles, The 20
Branch, William 54, 79
  In Splendid Error 79
  Medal for Willie, A 79
Brando, Marlon 31, 32, 57, 58,
  62, 105
Brecht, Bertolt 42, 77, 93–4, 130,
  148, 209, 218
  Good Woman of Setzuan, The
  42
  Mother Courage 148
  Threepenny Opera, The 93
  see also Weill, Kurt
Breen, Joseph 30
Bridge on the River Kwai, The
  (Film) 30
Brook, Peter 217
Brooks, Gwendolyn 20
Brown, Jim 23
Brown, John 79
Brown v. Board of Education 17,
  161, 184
Brustein, Robert 211, 278 n.2
Bryan, William Jennings 193, 255
Brynner, Yul 85
Burley, Gertrude 96

Burney, (US Surgeon General) Leroy 37
Burroughs, William 21
  Naked Lunch 21
Burrows, Abe 142
  Guys and Dolls 31, 41, 43, 60, 67–8, 70, 86, 142
  see also Loesser, Frank
Burrows, Vinnie 226
Burstyn, Ellen 104
Burton, Tim 219
Bwana Devil (film) 30
Byrd, Harry 17

Cabaret (Ebb; Kander) 51, 66
Caesar, Sid 28
Café Crown (Kraft) 62
Caffè Cino 94
Cage, John 95
Caldwell, Ben 226
  Moms: The First Lady of Comedy 226
  see also Taylor, Clarice
Calvacade of America (TV series) 27
Cannon, Poppy 241
  Bride's Cookbook, The 241
Capote, Truman 62
  Grass Harp, The 62
  House of Flowers (Arlen) 60
Capp, Al 33
Captain Video (TV series) 28
cars 2, 4, 23–4, 27, 35, 243
  hot rods 24–5, 30–1, 105
Casablanca (film) 128
Cass, Peggy 204–5
Cassidy, Hopalong 28
Caulfield, Holden 19
censorship 19, 210, 213, 227, 231
Chaikin, Joseph 93
Chapman, John 88, 204
Chapman, Robert 56, 74
  Billy Budd 43, 56, 74
  see also Coxe, Louis
Chayefsky, Paddy 52–3, 90–2, 214
  Bachelor Party, The 91
  Marty 30, 90, 91
  Middle of the Night 52, 61
  Mother, The 91–2
  Printer's Measure 91
  Tenth Man, The 42, 52
Chekhov, Anton 61, 93
  Cherry Orchard, The 61
Children's Theatre 96–7
Children's Theatre Committee 97
Childress, Alice 54, 80–2, 165–87, 222–6, 252–4, 265 n.86
  African Garden, The 224
  Bricks Without Straw (TV series) 226
  Florence 81, 166, 168–73, 182, 185–6
  Gold Through the Trees 81–2, 166–7, 173–80, 182, 184, 187
  Gullah 226
  Hear It for the Queen 224
  Hero Ain't Nothin' but a Sandwich, A (novel) 224
  Just a Little Simple 81, 168
  Like One of the Family (novel) 81
  Mojo: A Black Love Story 225
  Moms: A Praise Play for a Black Comedienne 226
  Rainbow Jordan (novel) 225
  Sea Island Song 225–6
  Short Walk, A (novel) 225
  String 225
  Sun Like Gold, The 225
  Those Other People (novel) 225
  Trouble in Mind 81–2, 166, 173, 180–7, 223–4

Wedding Band: A Love/Hate Story in Black and White 165, 222–4, 265 n.86
When the Rattlesnake Sounds 224
Wine in the Wilderness 225
World On a Hill, The 223
Young Martin Luther King Jr. 224
see also Woodard, Nathan
China 14, 15, 73, 227
Chorpenning, Charlotte 97
Christie, Agatha 41
Witness for the Prosecution 41, 62
Cino, Joseph 94
Circle-in-the-Square 93
civil rights 1, 15–17, 39, 73, 79–80, 140, 161, 180, 184, 273 n.4
Civil Rights Act (1957) 16, 161
in plays 73–81, 166–9, 174, 176–87, 193–4, 228, 247
Cleveland Browns 23
Clift, Montgomery 134
Clooney, Rosemary 19
Clum, John 52, 91
Clurman, Harold 53, 64, 102, 215
Cocktail Party, The (Eliot) 43
Cohn, Ruby 94
Cold War, The 13–14, 28, 54, 139, 166, 180–3
concerns 14, 72, 174
impact 9, 23, 45, 105, 174, 182–3
Cole, Nat King 19
Columbia Workshop 190
Comden, Betty 131, 133–4, 136, 140, 147, 160
Bells Are Ringing 59, 140, 147

On the Town 70, 132–4, 138, 271 n.17
Wonderful Town 43, 59, 60, 88, 134, 140, 201
see also Bernstein, Leonard; Green, Adolph; Styne, Jules
comics (print) 6, 12, 32–3, 142, 236
Committee for the Negro in the Arts (CNA) 80, 168, 174, 181
communism 8, 11, 13–16, 49, 71–5, 184, 244–50, 277 n.18
abroad 12–13, 15–16, 63, 74, 139
fears of 2, 14–16, 31, 39, 73–4, 78
HUAC 14–15, 71–3, 184, 245–9
in America 13–16, 73, 177, 180–1, 193, 244–50
in plays 73–4
Communist Party 13, 16, 167, 181, 245–6, 248–9
community theatre 96–7, 210, 228, 280 n.36
Como, Perry 19, 259 n.37
Consul, The (Menotti) 43
Coogan, Jackie 120
Cooper, Gary 32
Court Theatre (Chicago) 95
Cousins, Norman 209–10, 227
Coxe Louis 56, 74, 77
Billy Budd 43, 56, 74
Witchfinders, The 77
see also Chapman, John
Crawford, Cheryl 58
Crenshaw, Kimberlé 167
Crosby, Bing 32
Cukor, George 135

Dallas Theatre Center 95
Dante, Alighieri 115, 117

Darrow, Clarence 193, 255
Davidson, Bill 24
Davis, Ossie 54, 72, 166, 223
   Alice in Wonder 72
   Big Deal, The 72
Day, Doris 32
Day the Earth Stood Still, The (film) 30
Dean, James 31, 57–8, 62, 263 n.41
Dee, Ruby 83, 166, 223, 226
Dee, Sandra 31
Defense Advanced Research Projects Agency (DARPA) 34–5
De Kooning, Willem 21
   Police Gazette 21
   Woman 1 21
Delinquents, The (film) 30
De Maupassant, Guy 225
DeMille, Agnes 59
Denker, Henry 78
Dennis, Patrick 201, 204
Dennis the Menace (cartoon) 33
Depp, Johnny 219
Depression, The 13, 45, 96, 234
desegregation 2, 17–18, 180, 184
   see also segregation
Desperate Hours, The (Hayes) 43, 60
Detroit Lions 23
Dial 'M' for Murder (Knott) 71
Diehl, Digby 213, 262 n.12
Dig (magazine) 33
Dinah Shore Show, The (radio series) 191
diners 3, 22, 114
Disney 5, 24, 29
   Adventures of Davy Crockett, The (TV series) 5, 29
   Dumbo (film) 29
   Man and the Moon (TV programme) 29
   Mickey Mouse 29
   Our Friend, the Atom (TV programme) 29
   Survival in Nature (TV programme) 29
Donehue, Vincent J. 60
Don't Knock the Rock (film) 30
Douglas, Kirk 201, 280 n.36
Douglas, Melvyn 200, 208, 276 n.10, 280 n.36
Douglass, Frederick 79
Dragnet (TV series) 29
Dragstrip Girl (film) 30
Drake, Alfred 58
Dramatists Guild 55
Du Bois, Raoul Penè 60
Du Bois, W. E. B. 166, 175–6, 181
   Star of Ethiopia 175–6
Dunbar, Paul Laurence 226
Duncan, Isadora 157
Dunnock, Mildred 58
Dürrenmatt, Friedrich 42
   Visit, The 42, 43
D'Usseau, Arnaud 249

Edelman, Maurice 227
   Call on Kuprin, A 227
Eisenhower, Dwight D. 10, 15–17, 34–5, 48, 74, 140, 162, 184, 208
Eisenhower, Mamie 26
Elam, Harry J. 79
Ellison, Ralph 21
Everly Brothers 19
Explorer 35

Face the Nation (TV series) 27
Fashion 12, 25–6, 33, 116
Fast, Howard 73
Father Knows Best (TV series) 1, 28
Fats Domino 19

INDEX

Faulkner, William 20
  Fable, A 20
Favorite Story (radio series)
Federal Aid Highway Acts 16
Federal Bureau of Investigation
  (FBI) 81–2, 177, 181, 200
Federal Housing Authority 11
Ferber, Edna 19
  Giant 19
Ferrer, José 60
Fichandler, Zelda 95
Fifth Season, The (Regan) 42
film 6, 29–32, 55, 58, 70, 109,
  128, 135, 224, 227, 230,
  260 n.50, 261 n.53
  Kazan and 62–3, 78, 213
  musicals 61, 70, 86, 139, 221
  plays 61, 68, 101, 151, 200,
    205, 273 n.48, 280 n.36
  television 26–7, 29, 90, 200–1
  see also movies
First World War 13, 20, 139, 222,
  230
Firth, George 137
Fitzgerald, Ella 19, 259 n.37
Flash, The (comic) 33
Fly, The (film) 30
Fonda, Henry 58
Food and Drug Administration,
  The (FDA) 34
Foote, Horton 54, 90
  Trip to Bountiful, The 90
Forbidden Planet (film) 30
Ford, Glenn 32
Ford Foundation 95–6
Fosse, Bob 59, 85
Fourposter, The (De Hartog) 42,
  43, 60
Frank, Anne 53
  *Anne Frank: The Diary of a
    Young Girl* 20
Franklin, Benjamin 231
Franklin J. E. 226

Freed, Alan 26, 260 n.44
Freedom (magazine) 81, 174,
  180–1
Freud, Sigmund 34, 233, 237
Friedan, Betty 7
  Feminine Mystique, The 7
Friedenberg, Edgar Z. 243
  Vanishing Adolescent, The
    243–4
Fryer, Robert 201
Fuchs, Klaus 13
Furth, George 218

Galileo 75
Gard, Robert 96
Gargarin, Yuri 229
Gassner, John 40, 47, 49
Gay, John 201
Gazzara, Ben 58
Gazzo, Michael 54, 78
  Hatful of Rain 54, 78, 265
    n.83
Gelber, Jack 54, 93–4
  Apple, The 94
  Connection, The 53, 93–4
Gelbert, Larry 136–7
Genet, Jean 209
Gibbs, Wolcott 56, 64
  Season in the Sun 56, 60, 64
G I Bill 2, 10, 166
Gibson, William 52, 215
  Miracle Worker, The 41, 52
  Two for the Seesaw 41, 52
Gide, André 56
Gidget (film) 31
Gigi (film) 30
Gilbert, James 1
Ginsberg, Alan 21
  Howl 21
Giraudoux, Jean 42, 229
  Madwoman of Chaillot, The
    229
  Ondine 60, 70

Goetz, Augustus 56
   Immoralist, The 56
Goetz, Ruth 56
   Immoralist, The 56
Go Johnny Go! (film) 30
Golden Apple, The (La Touche; Moross) 43
Golden, Harry 228
Goldman, James 137
Good Housekeeping (magazine) 32
Goodrich, Frances 53
   Diary of Anne Frank, The 42, 43, 53–4, 65–6, 102
   see also Hackett, Albert
Gordon, Joanne 221
Gossett, Louis, Jr. 79
Grable, Betty 32
Graham, (Reverend) Billy 8
Grant, Cary 32
Great Depression, The
   see Depression, The
Greatest Show on Earth, The (film) 30
Green, Adolph 131, 133–4, 136, 140, 147, 160
   On the Town 70, 132–4, 138, 271 n.17
   Wonderful Town 43, 59, 60, 88, 134, 140, 201
   Bells Are Ringing 59, 140, 147
   see also Bernstein, Leonard; Comden, Betty; Styne, Jules
Greenfield, Thomas 86
Green Lantern (comic) 33
Green, Paul 173
   Native Son (Wright) 173
Grotowski, Jerzy 95
Group Theater 57–8, 61, 62, 64, 246
Guggenheim Museum 22
Guiding Light (TV series) 28
Gunsmoke (TV series) 28

Gussow, Mel 218
Guthrie, A. B. 20
   Way West, The 20
Guthrie, Tyrone 60
Guzman, Jacob Arbenz 16

Hackett, Albert 53
   Diary of Anne Frank, The 42, 43, 53–4, 65–6, 102
   see also Goodrich, Frances
Hagen, Uta 58, 62, 76
Haley, Bill 18
Hall, Radcliffe 201
Halls of Ivy (radio series) 191
Hamer, Fannie Lou 227
Hammerstein, Oscar, II 55, 84–7, 131–2, 161, 221, 227
   Allegro 128–9, 163
   Carousel 84, 132
   Cinderella 86, 266 n.96
   Flower Drum Song 55, 70, 85
   King and I, The 31, 41, 43, 55, 59, 60, 67, 84–5, 132, 134
   Me and Juliet 85
   Oklahoma! 59, 62, 70, 84, 129, 131, 132
   Pipe Dream 85
   Show Boat 131, 152
   Sondheim and 87, 127–30, 136, 138, 147, 162–4, 216–7, 272 n.28
   Sound of Music, The 41, 70, 84–5, 89, 129, 132, 162
   South Pacific 43, 60, 61, 67, 84, 132, 161
   see also Kern, Jerome; Rodgers, Richard
Hansberry, Lorraine 53–4, 80–4, 166, 174, 274 n.11
   Raisin in the Sun, A 43, 53, 80, 82–4, 166
Hans Christian Anderson (film) 86

INDEX

Happy Birthday (Loos) 61
Happy Days (TV series) 1
Happy Time, The (Taylor) 41, 62
Harburg, Yip 161
   Finian's Rainbow (Lane) 161
   Jamaica (Arlen) 62, 70
Harding, Warren G. 207–8
Hardy Boys, The (TV series) 21
Harnick, Sheldon 89
   Fiddler on the Roof 42, 66, 89, 132
   Fiorello 59, 89
   see also Bock, Jerry
Harris, Jed 65
Harris, Julie 51, 58, 62
Hart, Lorenz 131, 153
   By Jupiter 61
   Connecticut Yankee, A 130
   I Married an Angel 61
   Pal Joey 43, 153
   see also Rodgers, Richard
Hart, Moss 60, 61
   You Can't Take It with You 90
   see also Kaufman, George S.
Hatch, James V. 226
Hayes, Helen 58, 61
Hayward, Susan 32
Hear It Now (radio) 27
Heckart, Eileen 102, 223
Hefner, Hugh 151
Hellman, Lillian 76, 88, 135
   Candide 70, 76, 88, 135, 271 n.10
   Children's Hour 76
   Lark, The 69, 76
   see also Anouilh, Jean; Bernstein, Leonard
Hemingway, Ernest 20
   Old Man and the Sea, The 20
Hepburn, Audrey 58
Herman, Jerry 162
   La Cage Aux Follies 162, 220
   Hello Dolly 42

   Mame! 189, 228, 280 n.36
   see also Lawrence, Jerome; Lee, Robert E.
Hersey, John 20
   Wall, The 20
Hewes, Henry 94, 254–5
Hi and Lois (cartoon) 33
Hildegard 105
Hilton, James 229
   Shangri-La 229
Hiss, Alger 13
Hitler, Adolf 14, 245
Hogan, Ben 23
Holden, William 32, 102, 135
Holliday, Judy 133, 147
Holly, Buddy 19
Hollywood Ten 14
Holocaust, The 20, 46
homophobia 48, 50, 56, 103, 117, 225, 258 n.14
homosexuality 15, 19, 39, 100, 103, 127, 134–5, 153, 160, 162
   in plays 44–5, 48–50, 54, 56, 102, 117, 123, 212–13, 262 n.25, 268 n.12
Hope, Bob 32
Hopper, Edward 65
   Nighthawks at the Diner 65
Horne, Lena 62
Hot Cars (film) 30
Hot Rod (magazine) 33
Hot Rod Girl (film) 30
Hot Rod Rumble (film) 30
House of Wax (film) 30
House Un-American Activities Committee (HUAC) 14–15, 29, 39, 132, 139, 244–9
   hearings 14, 71–2, 78, 184, 245–9, 264 n.66
   in plays 71–8, 135, 183–4, 193–4, 197–8, 228
   Kazan and 63, 78, 245–6

Miller and 47, 77–8, 248–50
Robbins and 134, 138, 160, 162
Howard, Sidney 86
  Silver Cord, The 90
  They Knew What They Wanted 86
Howdy Doody Show, The (TV series) 28
HUAC *see* House Un-American Activities Committee
Hudson, Rock 32
Hughes, Langston 81, 168, 274 n.15
  Simple Speaks His Mind 81, 168
  Simply Heaven 81
Hummler, Richard 192

Ibsen, Henrik 77
I Love Lucy (TV series) 28, 90
Industry on Parade (TV series) 27
Inge, William 50–1, 56, 99–125, 151, 211–15
  All Fall Down (film) 213
  Boy at the Circus, The (novel) 215
  'Boy in the Basement, The' 212
  Bus Riley's Back in Town (film) 213–14
  Bus Stop 50, 56, 61, 65, 102, 104–5, 114–18, 122–5, 151
  Come Back, Little Sheba 50, 101, 104–10, 123–5
  Complex (TV series) 214
  Dark at the Top of the Stairs, The 50, 62, 102, 104, 119–25, 213, 215
  Farther Off from Heaven 101, 102
  Front Porch, The 101
  Good Luck, Miss Wyckhoff (novel) 214–15
  Last Pad, The 214
  Loss of Roses, The 65, 103, 211–12
  My Son is a Splendid Driver (novel) 214–15
  Natural Affection 212
  'Out on the Outskirts of Town' 214
  'People in the Wind' 102
  Picnic 68, 101–2, 104–5, 110–14, 116, 122–5, 212, 264 n.67
    film 61, 102, 151
    success of 43, 50, 60, 61, 102
  Splendor in the Grass (film) 103, 212–13
  Stripper, The (film) 103, 211–12
  Summer Brave 102, 212
  'Tiny Closet, The' 212
  Where's Daddy? 213
  Williams and 50, 100–1, 104, 123, 215
Inquisition, The (Spanish) 75, 76
In the Summer House (Bowles) 70
Invasion of the Body Snatchers (film) 30
Invisible Man, The (Ellison) 21
Ionesco, Eugène 42, 93, 209
  Chairs, The 42
  Lesson, The 42
Irving, Jules 95
Isherwood, Christopher 51
Ives, David 137, 221

Jack Benny Show, The (TV series) 90
Jackson, Andrew 130
Jackson, Shirley 20
  Haunting of Hill House, The 21
James, Henry 67

Turn of the Screw, The 67
James, Luther 225
Jennings, La Vinia Delois 167
Jim Crow laws 16, 80, 253
Joan of Arc 69, 75–6
Johns, Jasper 22
   False Start 22
   Three Flags 22
Johnson, Greer 80
   Mrs. Patterson 80
   see also Sebree, Charles
Johnson, Jeff 105
Johnson, Lyndon 161
Jones, James 19
   From Here to Eternity 19, 30
Jones, James Earl 222
Jones, Margo 95, 101, 191–2
Jones, Robert Edmond 66
Joyce, James 209
Julius Caesar (film) 105
Junior League, The 97
juvenile delinquency 2, 12, 259
   n.35, 259 n.36
   in plays 30–1, 88, 91, 137–8,
     140–1, 145–6, 155, 162,
     251
Juvenile Jungle (film) 30

Kabuki 219
Kahn, Louis 22
Kanin, Garson 65
Kantor, MacKinlay 20
Kaprow, Allan 94–5
   18 Happenings in 6 Parts 94–5
Kaufman, George S. 60
   Silk Stockings 59, 140
   You Can't Take it with You 90
   see also Hart, Moss; Porter,
     Cole
Kaye, Danny 86
Kaye, Nora 135
Kay, Ulysses 225
   Sun Like Gold, The 225

   see also Childress, Alice
Kazan, Elia 58, 61, 211, 263 n.41
   director 48–9, 54, 57, 60–3,
     66, 213
   Miller and 57, 62–3, 78
   testimony 63, 78, 245–6
Keats, John 242
   *Crack in the Picture Window,
     The* 242
Keller, Helen 52
Kelly, Gene 200
Kelly Walt 33
Kendrick, John 59, 85
Kern, Jerome 131
   Show Boat 131, 152
   see also Hammerstein, Oscar, II
Kerouac, Jack 21, 149
   On the Road 21
Kerr, Walter 49, 251
Kim, Elizabeth S. 52
Kind Sir (Krasna) 61
King, Martin Luther, Jr. 17, 224
Kingsley, Sidney 74
   Darkness at Noon 43, 74, 247
King, Woodie, Jr. 226
Kinsey, Alfred 6, 105
   *Sexual Behavior in the Human
     Female* 6
   *Sexual Behavior in the Human
     Male* 105
Kismet (Borodin; Forrest; Wright)
   43, 140
Kitt, Eartha 80
Klee, Paul 65
Koestler, Arthur 74
Korea 9, 15, 55, 78–9
Kraft, Hy S. 62
Krasner, David 48, 83
Kroll, Jack 220
Kronenberger, Louis 233
   Company Manners 233–9
Krutch, Joseph Wood 19, 260
   n.38

Ku Klux Klan 16, 247
Kunitz, Stanley 20

Ladd, Alan 32
Ladies Professional Golf
    Association 23
LaGuardia, Fiorello H. 89
Lahr, John 49
Lancaster, Burt 103, 105
Lane, Nathan 217
Lang, Harold 191
Lansbury, Angela 229
Lapine, James 137, 220
Larkin, Peter 60, 62–3, 70–1,
    193, 255
Lassie (TV series) 28
Laurents, Arthur 51–2, 88–9,
    128, 131, 135–9, 142,
    146–9, 161–4, 272 n.29
  Bird Cage, The 64
  Do I Hear A Waltz? 129, 131,
    132, 218
  Gypsy 59, 61, 131, 137,
    146–62
    design of 68, 146–54
    impact 52, 87–8, 128, 137,
      146, 272 n.29, 279 n.15
  Home of the Brave 135
  Time of the Cuckoo, The 52,
    218
  West Side Story 52, 59–61,
    127–8, 131, 134–46,
    154–5, 157, 160
    design of 70, 136, 138–9,
      149–50
    impact 86, 137, 140–2,
      147, 162, 216, 251–2
    race 55–6, 87–8, 134–5,
      139–42, 161–2
  see also Bernstein, Leonard;
    Sondheim, Stephen; Styne,
    Jules
Lavender Scare 15

Lawrence, Carol 138, 201
Lawrence, Jerome 51, 71, 73–4,
    189–210, 227–31
  Actor 231
  Auntie Mame 41, 51, 70, 189,
    194, 201–5, 208–10, 228
  Call on Kuprin, A 228–9
  Dear World 229
  Diamond Orchid 229
  First Monday in October 231
  Gang's All Here, The 73–4,
    205–9, 228
  Incomparable Max, The 230
  Inherit the Wind 191–201,
    203, 205, 208, 254–5
    achievements 41, 43, 51,
      60, 71, 191–2, 228
    free speech 51, 73–4,
      193–200
  'Inside a Kid's Head' 190
  *Jabberwock: Improbabilities
    Lived and Imagined by
    James Thurber in the
    Fictional City of Columbus*
    230
  *Lincoln, The Unwilling
    Warrior* (TV programme)
    230
  Live Spelled Backwards ... 230
  Look, Ma, I'm Dancing! 135,
    189–91, 229
  Mame! 189, 228
  *Night Thoreau Spent in Jail,
    The* 189, 228, 230
  Only in America 71, 228
  Shangri-La (Warren) 71, 229
  Whisper in the Mind 231
  see also Herman, Jerry; Lee,
    Richard E.; Martin, Hugh
League of New York Theaters 55
Leave It to Beaver (TV series) 1,
    28

INDEX

Lee, Gypsy Rose 146–9, 152–3, 159
Lee, Robert E. 51, 71, 73–4, 189–210, 227–31
  Actor 231
  Auntie Mame 41, 51, 70, 189, 194, 201–5, 208–10, 228
  Call on Kuprin, A 228–9
  Dear World 229
  Diamond Orchid 229
  First Monday in October 231
  Gang's All Here, The 73–4, 205–9, 228
  Incomparable Max, The 230
  Inherit the Wind 191–201, 203, 205, 208, 254–5
    achievements 41, 43, 51, 60, 71, 191–2, 228
    free speech 51, 73–4, 193–200
  'Inside a Kid's Head' 190
  Jabberwock: Improbabilities Lived and Imagined by James Thurber in the Fictional City of Columbus 230
  Lincoln, The Unwilling Warrior (TV programme) 230
  Look, Ma, I'm Dancing! 135, 189–91, 229
  Mame! 189, 228
  Night Thoreau Spent in Jail, The 189, 228, 230
  Only in America 71, 228
  Shangri-La (Warren) 71, 229
  Sounding Brass 230
  Ten Days That Shook the World 230
  Whisper in the Mind 231
  see also Herman, Jerry; Jerome Lawrence; Martin, Hugh
Leonowens, Anna 85

Leopold, Nathan 193
Lerner, Alan Jay 85, 140, 160
  Brigadoon 61, 70, 85
  My Fair Lady 41, 42, 43, 60, 70, 85, 140
  Paint Your Wagon 70, 85
  see also Loewe, Frederick
Levittown 11
Levitt, Saul 75
  Andersonville Trial, The 75
Levitt, William 11, 22
Lewis, Jerry 32
Lewis, Jerry Lee 19
Lewis, Robert 58, 61–2
Life with Father (Crouse; Lindsay) 42
Li'l Abner (cartoon) 33
Lincoln Center 69
Lippa, Louis 44
  House Remembered, A 44
Little Richard 19
Little Theatre Movement 95, 96
Living Theatre 93–4
Loeb, Richard 193
Loesser, Frank 86, 87, 142, 160
  Guys and Dolls 31, 41, 43, 60, 67–8, 70, 86, 142
  Most Happy Fella, The 43, 86
  Where's Charley? 86
  see also Burrows, Abe
Loewe, Frederick 85, 140, 160
  Brigadoon 61, 70, 85
  My Fair Lady 41, 42, 43, 60, 70, 85, 140
  Paint Your Wagon 70, 85
  see also Lerner, Alan Jay
Logan, Josh 57, 59, 61–2, 68, 102
  Mister Roberts (Heggen) 61
  Wisteria Trees, The 61, 68
Lomax, Alan 18
Lone Ranger 28
Look Homeward Angel (Frings)
Loren, Sophia 151

Lost Weekend, The (film/book) 109
loyalty oaths 10, 14, 200
Lunt, Alfred 60
Lupone, Patti 221, 279 n.15

Mabley, Jackie 226
MacArthur, (General) Douglas 15
McCarthyism 15, 39, 48, 72, 76, 78, 132, 135, 177
McCarthy, Joseph 15, 47, 76, 78, 193
McCaslin, Nellie 97
McClure, Arthur 100, 106
McConachie, Bruce 44, 54, 56, 58, 82–3
McCullers, Carson 53, 101, 105
  Ballad of the Sad Café, The 105
  Member of the Wedding, A 43, 53, 101, 264 n.67
McDaniel, Hattie 227
McGuire, Dorothy 103
MacLeish, Archibald 20, 53
  J. B. 43, 53–4, 60, 62–3, 65–6
McNeill, Claudia 83
MAD (magazine) 33
magazines 6–7, 32–3, 108, 191, 221, 236, 257 n.8
Magnificent Ambersons, The (TV programme) 90
Mail Call (radio series) 190
Mailer, Norman 21
Make Room for Daddy (TV series) 28, 90
Malden, Karl 62
Malina, Judith 93–4
Maltz, Albert 73
  Morrison Case, The 73
Mann, Daniel 101
Mann, Theodore 93
Man on a Tightrope (film) 63
Mansfield, Jayne 151

Marat/Sade (Weiss) 217
March, Fredric 200, 280 n.36
Marciano, Rocky 23
Marshall, E. G. 208
Martin, Dean 19, 32
Martin, Hugh 190
  Best Foot Forward (Blane) 190
  Look, Ma, I'm Dancing 135, 189–91, 229
  see also Lawrence, Jerome; Lee, Robert E.
Martin, Mary 58, 59, 71, 86
Martinsville Seven 178–9
Marxism 54, 250
Masses and Mainstream 168, 181, 182, 252–4
Maverick (TV series) 28
Mays, Willie 23
Mazeppa 157
Medea 160
Meet the Press (TV series) 27
Meighan, Thomas 120
Melville, Herman 56
Menken, H. L. 255
Menninger, William C. 21
  How to Be a Successful Teenager 21
Merman, Ethel 58, 68, 88, 146, 148, 153–4, 156, 272 n.28
Merrick, David 221
Merrill, Bob
  Funny Girl 147
  New Girl in Town 47, 59
  Take Me Along 47
  see also Styne, Jules
Merrill, James 93
Mesmer, Dr. Anton 231
Messel, Oliver 60
Metalious, Grace 21
  Peyton Place 21
Method acting 57–8, 61, 209
Meyerhold, Vsevolod 64, 263 n.48

INDEX

Michener, James 19
  Hawaii 19
Mielziner, Jo 57, 60–3, 66–70, 102, 146
Mies van der Rohe, Ludwig 22
Mighty Mouse 28
Miller, Arthur xi, 47–8, 57, 65, 92, 190, 250
  All My Sons 62
  Collected Plays 47–8
  Crucible, The 43–4, 47, 65, 76–8, 102, 250
  Death of a Salesman 47, 57, 62, 66–7
  Enemy of the People, An (Ibsen) 42, 62, 77
  HUAC 47, 76–8, 248–9, 250
  Kazan and 57, 62–3, 78
  Memory of Two Mondays 47, 65
  View from the Bridge 47, 65, 78
Miller, J. P. 90
  Days of Wine and Roses 90
Miller, Warren 222
  Cool World, The 222
Milwaukee Repertory Theatre 95
Miranda, Lin-Manuel 139
  Hamilton 130
Mitchell, Loften 79–80
  Land Beyond the River, A 79–80
Modern Teen (magazine) 33
Monroe, Marilyn 32, 33, 47, 58, 78, 103, 151
Montalban, Ricardo 62
Montgomery, Paul L. 215
Montgomery, Robert 60
Moon is Blue, The (Herbert) *41*
Moore, Marianne 20
Morrden, Ethan 84
Morse Players 101
Mosaddegh, Mohanned 16

Mosel, Tad 90
  Other People's Houses 90
Most, Andrea 88
Motherwell, Robert 21–2
  Elegy to the Spanish Republic 22
movies 1, 6, 8, 24, 28–32, 44, 213–14, 221, 224, 231, 268 n.19
  HUAC and 14, 29, 72, 264 n.66
  musicals 31, 88, 216, 219–21, 266 n.94, 273 n.48
  plays into 48, 51, 63, 101–3, 211, 228, 231
  teen 3, 5, 12, 30–2, 260 n.44, 260 n.52
  television and 31, 52, 90–1
  see also films
Muni, Paul 192–3, 231, 276 n.10
Murphy, Brenda 72, 74, 75–6, 77
Murrow, Edward R. 15, 27
music 3, 6, 17–19, 55, 87, 259 n.37
  classical 87, 113, 127, 132–3, 139, 147
  industry of 18, 36, 259 n.33, 259 n.34
  popular 12, 17–19, 28, 31, 105, 151, 259 n.36

Nabokov, Vladimir 19, 118
  Lolita 19, 118
Nancy Drew 21
Nash, N. Richard 90
  Rainmaker, The 90
Nathan, George Jean 45
National Aeronautic Space Administration (NASA) 35
National Airlines 35
National Association for the Advancement of Colored People (NAACP) 17, 55, 178

National Defense Education Act 35
National Education Association
  (NEA) 10
Nazis 75, 85
Negro Actor's Guild 55
Negro Ensemble Company 225
*Negro in the American Theatre,
  The* (BBC; TV programme)
  223
New Deal 15–16
New England Theatre Guild for
  Children 97
Newman, Paul 58, 90, 102, 268
  n.11
New Playwright's Theatre 72
newspapers 26, 32–3, 43–4, 81,
  180, 212
New York City Ballet 59
New York Philharmonic 87
New York Shakespeare Festival
  165, 223, 280 n.32
New York Yankees 23
Nixon, Richard 3, 11, 15
No Time for Sergeants (Levin) 42,
  60, 71
nuclear
  family 1, 120
  fears 2, 10, 12–13, 29–32, 39,
    72, 105, 234
  power 28, 31–2, 35

O'Brien, Herbert R. 39
O'Casey, Sean 62
  Shadow of a Gunman 62–3
O'Connor, Flannery 20
  *Good Man is Hard to Find,
    A* 20
Odets, Clifford 64
  Country Girl, The 60, 64
Oenslager, Donald 60
Off-Broadway 40, 44, 48–9, 73,
  79, 92–4, 230, 266 n.110,
  266 n.111

Childress and 82, 165, 185,
  223, 225–6, 265 n.86
plays on 44, 46, 48–9, 72–3,
  93–4, 214, 220–1, 261 n.7
Off-Off-Broadway 40, 94–6, 230
O'Hara, Frank 93
Oja, Carol J. 133
Omnibus (TV series) 27, 90
*100 Things You Should Know
  About Communism and
  Education* 244
O'Neill, Eugene xi, 44, 46–7, 92
  Ah, Wilderness 47
  Anna Christie 47
  Iceman Cometh, The 44, 46
  Long Day's Journey Into Night
    43, 46
  Moon for the Misbegotten 46
  Touch of the Poet, A 46
Open Theatre 93–4
Orel, Gwen 95
Osato, Sono 133
Osborn, Paul 55, 61
  On Borrowed Time 61
  Point of No Return 43
  World of Suzie Wong, The 55,
    61, 68

Palmer, Arnold 23
Paper Bag Players (New York) 97
Papp, Joseph 93, 165, 223, 265
  n.86
Parks, Rosa 17
Patrick, John 53, 55
  Teahouse of the August Moon
    (play) 41, 43, 53, 55, 60,
    62, 70
Patrick, Robert 123
Peale, Norman Vincent 8, 19, 239
  *Power of Positive Thinking,
    The* 8, 19, 239–41
Peanuts (cartoon) 33
Perkins, Anthony 218

Perkins, Kathy 167, 175, 185
Peron, Evita 229
Perry Joe 23
Perry Mason (TV series) 29
Peter Pan (Charlap; Leigh) 59, 71, 86, 140, 147
Peterson, Louis 54, 79–80
  Take a Giant Step 79–80
Petigny, Alan 6
Petry, Ann 173–4
  Street, The 173–4
Philco-Goodyear Television Playhouse (TV series) 90, 91
Phil Silvers Show, The (TV series) 28, 90
Phoenix Theatre 76, 93
Picasso, Pablo 21, 105
Pinter, Harold 220
  Betrayal 220
Pirandello, Luigi 93
Plain and Fancy (Hague; Horwitt) 140
Plautus 217
Playboy (magazine) 33, 151
Playhouse 90 (TV series) 28, 90
Playhouse of Stars (TV series) 90
Plume de Ma Tante, La (Blanche; Calvi; Parker) 1, 43
Pogo (cartoon) 33
Poitier, Sidney 83, 166
Pollock, Jackson 21
  Autumn Rhythm (Number 30) 21
  Convergence 20
Porgy and Bess (Gershwin; Hayward) 194
Porter, Cole 84
  Can-Can 41, 68
  Kiss Me Kate 62
  Silk Stockings 59, 140
  see also Kaufman, George S.
Presley, Elvis 18, 26, 31, 151, 259 n.32, 259 n.35

Preston, Robert 103
Prince, Harold 130, 218
Provincetown Playhouse 94
Psychoanalysis (comic) 33
Pulitzer Prize Playhouse (TV series) 28, 90

Quinn, Anthony 62
Quintero, José 93
Quo Vadis (film) 30

racism 16, 21, 161, 174, 259 n.36
  in plays 79, 84, 140–1, 177–87, 222–5
  radio 4, 6, 26–8, 35–6, 44, 72, 194, 238
    drama 28, 44–5, 92, 108, 135, 190–1, 227
    music 18, 26–7, 29, 105
    talk 18, 27, 100
Railroad Show, The (radio series) 191
Randall, Tony 193
Rand, Ayn 21
  Atlas Shrugged 21
Randle, Bill 26
Rauschenberg, Robert 22
  Bed 22
  Canyon 22
Ray, Johnny 19
Reader's Digest (magazine) 33, 236
Rebel Without a Cause (film) 31
Redford, Robert 135
Redhead (Fields; Hague) 43
Red Scare 31, 71, 132
Red Skelton Show, The (TV series)
Reed, John 230
Revvers, The 133, 147
Reynolds, Debbie 32
Richards, Lloyd 83

Richardson, Jack 94
    Gallows Humor 94
    Prodigal, The 30, 94
Rich, Frank 57, 66
Richter, Conrad 20
    Town, The 20
Robards, Jason, Jr. 47, 58, 201, 280 n.36
Robbins, Jerome 128, 131–6, 138–9, 147–8, 163–4, 271 n.17
    choreography 59, 61, 88, 132–4, 139, 146, 152, 157–8, 190, 251–2
    director 57, 59, 86, 88, 132, 138, 146, 152, 272 n.30, 273 n.48
    'Fancy Free' 133
Robe, The (film) 30
Robert Montgomery Presents (TV series) 28, 90
Robeson, Paul 72, 81, 180, 181, 247–8
Robinson, Edward G. 246–7
Robinson, Jackie 23
Robinson, Sugar Ray 23
Rock Around the Clock (film) 31
Rodgers, Jimmie 19
Rodgers, Richard 84, 87, 128–32, 153, 161, 217–18, 227
    Allegro 128–9, 163
    By Jupiter 61
    Carousel 84, 132
    Cinderella 86, 266 n.96
    Connecticut Yankee, A 130
    Do I Hear A Waltz? 129, 131, 132, 218
    Flower Drum Song 55, 70, 85
    I Married an Angel 61
    King and I, The 31, 41, 43, 55, 59, 60, 67, 84–5, 132, 134
    Me and Juliet 85

Oklahoma! 59, 62, 70, 84
Pal Joey 43, 153
Pipe Dream 85
Sound of Music, The 41, 70, 84–5, 89, 162
South Pacific 43, 60, 61, 67, 84, 132, 161
see also Hammerstein, Oscar, II; Hart, Lorenz; Laurents, Arthur; Sondheim, Stephen
Roethke, Theodore 20
Rogers, Buck 28
Rogers, Carl 34
Rome, Harold 61, 85–6
    Destry Rides Again 70, 86
    Fanny 61, 68, 85–6
    Wish You Were Here
Roosevelt, Franklin D. 102
Rosenberg, Ethel 13
Rosenberg, Julius 13
Rose, Reginald 90–1
    Crime in the Street 91
    Dino 91
    Twelve Angry Men 90, 91
Ross, Herbert 191
Ross, Jerry 85, 160
    Damn Yankees 41, 43, 59, 85, 140, 263 n.45
    Pajama Game, The 41, 43, 59, 85, 140, 141
    see also Adler, Richard
Rothko, Mark 22
    Four Darks in Red 22
    Number 61 (Rust and Blue) 22
Roth, Philip 21
Runyon, Damon 86, 142
Russell, Bertrand 10
Russell, Rosalind 201, 204–5
Russia 13, 63, 89, 174, 227, 228, 230, 245
    see also Soviet Union

Saarinen, Eero 22, 69

INDEX

Sacco-Vanzetti case 193
Saint, Eva Marie 90
St. Louis Star Times 100
Saint of Bleeker Street, The
  (Menotti) 43
Salem witchtrials 75, 77, 250
Salinger, J. D. 19
  Catcher in the Rye, The 19
Salk Institute 22
Salk, Jonas 37
Sandburg, Carl 20
San Francisco Mime Troupe 97
Savran, David 56
Schiller, Friedrich 93
Science and Mechanics (magazine)
  32
Scopes, John Thomas 193–4,
  254–5
Scott, Randolph 32
Schulberg, Budd 78
  On the Waterfront 30, 63, 78
Seagram Building 22
Search for Tomorrow (TV series)
  27
Season in the Sun (Gibbs) 56, 60,
  64
Sebree, Charles 80
  Mrs. Patterson 80
  see also Johnson, Greer
Second World War 12–13, 79–80,
  95, 135, 192, 233–4
  affect on families 5, 169
  affect on women 25, 151, 169
  depictions 20, 53
  impact 40, 45, 55, 96, 139,
    166–7, 169, 272 n.29
See It Now (TV series) 27
segregation 17, 79–81, 83, 168–9,
  172–3, 179, 222, 223 *see
  also* desegregation
Serling, Rod 90, 92
  Requiem for a Heavyweight 90
  Twilight Zone (TV series) 92

Seurat, George 163–4, 220
  *Sunday Afternoon on the
  Island of La Grand Jatte,
  A* 220
Seuss, Dr. 21
  Cat in a Hat, The 21
  Horton Hear a Who! 21
  *How the Grinch Stole
  Christmas* 21
Shafer, Peter 137
Shake, Rattle, and Roll (film) 30
Shakespeare in the Park 93
Shakespeare, William 67, 77, 88,
  104, 118, 134, 137, 142,
  152, 161
  Hamlet 270 n.60
  King Lear 153, 160
  Romeo and Juliet 114, 134,
    144, 150, 252
Shaw, George Bernard 10, 76, 85,
  140
  Pygmalion 85, 140
  Saint Joan 76
Sherman Anti-Trust Act 29
Sherwood, Robert E.:
  Abe Lincoln in Illinois 90
Shine, Ted 225
Shore, Dinah 19, 28
Shrevelove, Burt 128, 136
Shrike, The (Kramm) 43, 60
Shumlin, Herman 192
Shurman, R. Baird 106
Sievers, David 40, 105
Simon, John 101
Simon, Neil 92, 190
Sinatra, Frank 32, 259 n.37
Skelton, Red 28
Sleepy Hollow (Battista; Lessner;
  Maloney) 67
Smith Act 73
Smith, Bessie 227
Smith, Oliver 60, 63, 66, 69–70,
  133, 203, 229

Sneider, Vern 53
  Teahouse of the August Moon
    (novel) 53
Socrates 75
Sojourners for Truth and Justice
  80, 181, 182
Sondheim, Stephen 52, 55, 66,
  87–9, 127–64, 216–21
  All Together Now 221
  Anyone Can Whistle 217
  Assassins 164, 220
  Bounce 220
  Company 129, 163, 218
  Dick Tracy (film score) 221
  Do I Hear A Waltz? 129, 131,
    132, 218
  'Evening Primrose' (TV
    programme) 218
  Follies 147, 218–19
  Frogs, The 220
  Funny Thing Happened on the
    Way to the Forum, A 129,
    164, 217
  Getting Away with Murder
    (play) 221
  Gypsy 59, 61, 131, 137,
    146–62
    design of 68, 146–54
    impact 52, 87–8, 128, 137,
      146, 272 n.29, 279
      n.15
  Into the Woods 220
  Last of Sheila, The (film) 221
  Little Night Music, A 163–4,
    219
  Merrily We Roll Along 220
  Pacific Overtures 219
  Passion 220
  Roadshow 220–1
  Saturday Night (Epstein) 128,
    220
  Sondheim: A Musical Tribute
    221
  Sunday in the Park with
    George 162, 220
  Sweeney Todd 147, 164, 219
  West Side Story 52, 59–61,
    127–8, 131, 134–46,
    154–5, 157, 160
    design of 70, 136, 138–9,
      149–50
    impact 86, 137, 140–2,
      147, 162, 216, 251–2
    race 55–6, 87–8, 134–5,
      139–42, 161–2
    see also Bernstein, Leonard;
      Laurents, Arthur; Rodgers,
      Richard; Styne, Jules
Soviet Union 10, 13–14, 35, 228,
  246, 250 see also Russia
Spigelgass, Leonard 55
  Majority of One 55, 60
Spock, (Dr.) Benjamin 8
  Common Sense Book of Baby
    and Child Care 8
Sports 23, 25
Sports Illustrated (magazine) 33
Sputnik 10, 32, 35
Stage 67 (TV series) 218
Stalag 17 (Bevan; Trzcinski) 60
Stalin, Joseph 10, 13, 63, 74, 139
Stanislavsky, Constantin 57, 58,
  63–4
Stanley, Kim 58
Stapleton, Maureen 58
Steiger, Rod 62
Steinbeck, John 19
  East of Eden 19, 63
Stevens, Wallace 20
Stevenson, Adlai 15
Stewart, James 32
Strasberg, Lee 58, 209, 272 n.29
Strauss, Levi 26
Streep, Meryl 220
Streisand, Barbra 135, 147, 221
Strindberg, August 93

Stritch, Elaine 221
Studio One (TV series) 28, 90
Styne, Jules 131, 146–8, 150, 152, 160–3
  Bells Are Ringing 59, 140, 147
  Funny Girl 147
  Gypsy 59, 61, 131, 137, 146–62
    design of 68, 146–54
    impact 52, 87–8, 128, 137, 146, 272 n.29, 279 n.15
  High Button Shoes 62
  'Three Coins in the Fountain' 147
  see also Comden, Betty; Green, Adolph; Laurents, Arthur; Merrill, Bob; Sondheim, Stephen
Sullivan, Annie 52
Sullivan, Ed 28
Sunrise at Campobello (Schary) 43, 60, 102
Superman 28
Supreme Court 17, 29, 161, 184, 198, 231, 247, 249
Swaggert, Jimmy 201
Swanson, Gloria 120

Tabori, George 62
  Flight Into Egypt 62
Tales from the Crypt (comic) 33
Talmudge, Norma 120
Tarzan 105, 268 n.19
Taylor, Clarice 174, 226
  Moms: The First Lady of Comedy 226
  see also Caldwell, Ben
Taylor, Elizabeth 32, 151
Taylor, Noel 203
Taylor, Robert Lewis 20
Taylor, Timothy 87
Teapot Dome scandal 207
Teenage Crime Wave (film) 30

Teenage Dance Party (TV series) 28
teenagers 12, 21, 25–6, 28, 31, 33, 142, 259 n.36
  crime 30–1, 91, 137
  gangs 91, 134, 137–9, 141–2, 144–5, 162, 251
  in plays 114, 119, 123, 134, 137, 139, 141–5, 162, 195, 251
Teen Hop (TV series) 28
Teen World (magazine) 33
Television 3–5, 24, 26–31, 35–6, 70–2, 140, 194, 230, 238, 243
  influence of 1, 3, 5–6, 45, 18, 20, 26–9, 45, 89, 92, 208, 288–9 n.13
  in plays 72, 105, 108, 116, 213
  news 27, 32, 35, 44
  plays on 28, 52, 54, 86, 89–92, 200–1, 221, 223, 225
  series and shows 1, 5, 26–9, 75, 86, 92, 105, 147–8, 260 n.44, 266 n.96
  writers 45, 52, 54, 90–2, 128, 214, 218, 227, 230–1
Teller, Edward 35
Temple, Shirley 149
Ten Commandments, The (film) 30
Texaco Star Theatre (TV series) 28
Theatre de Lys 93
Theater '47/'55 (Dallas) 95, 101, 191
Theatre Guild 76, 101, 190
Theatre of the Absurd 209
Them! (film) 30
Thing from Another World, The (film) 30

Thirty Pieces of Silver (Fast) 73
Three for Tonight (Schumann; Wells) 43
Thurber, James 230
Till, Emmett 17
Time Limit! (Denker; Berkey) 78
Tobacco Road (Kirkland) 42
Toulouse-Lautrec, Henri de 68
Tracy, Spencer 200, 280 n. 36
Travels of Jaime McPheeters, The (Taylor) 20
Tree Grows in Brooklyn, A (Fields; Schwartz) 59, 67
Trilling, Lionel 19, 260 n.38
Trip to Chinatown, A (Hoyt) 133
Truman, Harry S. 14, 27, 140
Tubman, Harriet 176–7, 224, 225
Tucker, Sophie 159
Tufts University Magic Circle 97
Tupperware 7
TV dinners 5
TV Guide (magazine) 27
Twain, Mark 10
Tynan, Kenneth 66, 94

Uncle Tom's Cabin (Stowe) 134
Underground Railroad 176–7
Up Tight (film) 224
Uris, Leon 19
   Exodus 19
U.S. Steel Hour, The (TV series) 90

Valentino, Rudolph 120
Van Allen, James 35
Vance, Nina 95
Van Druten, John 51, 56, 73
   Bell, Book and Candle 51, 73
   I Am a Camera 43, 51, 56, 65
Vanguard 35
Verdon, Gwen 58
Vidal, Gore 21, 54, 90
   Visit to a Small Planet, A 54, 70, 90

Vietnam 55, 79, 230
Viva Zapata! (film) 63
Voltaire 135
Voss, Ralph 99–103, 125, 214–15

Walcott, Derek 225
Waldo, Janet 191
Walker, Nancy 190–1
Wallach, Eli 58, 62
Wandering Jew 121
Ward, Theodore 252
Ward, Winifred 97
War of the Satellites (film) 32
Warren, Robert Penn 20
Washington, Booker T. 227
Washington, Mary Helen 167, 174, 177, 180–1
Watts, Richard, Jr. 213
Wayne, John 32
Way We Were, The (film) 135
Weales, Gerald 51, 53, 92
Weidman, John 137
Weill, Kurt 61, 93
   Knickerbocker Holiday 61
   Threepenny Opera, The 93
   see also Brecht, Betolt
Weird Science (comic) 32
Weisel, Elie 20
   Night 20
Wertham, Fredric 12
   Seduction of the Innocent 12
Wertheim, Albert 123
West, Nathaniel 69
   Miss Lonelyhearts 69
Wheeler, Hugh 137
When Peggy Sue Got Married (film) 1
White, E. B. 21
   Charlotte's Web 21
Whitfield, Steven 78
Whyte, William H. 9
   Organization Man, The 9
Wilbur, Richard 20, 135

INDEX

Wilder, Thornton 62, 92, 190
  Matchmaker, The 60
  Our Town 90, 190
  Skin of Our Teeth, The 62
Wild One, The (film) 31
William Inge Festival 215
Williams, Tennessee 48–50, 63, 92
  Baby Doll (film) 63, 213
  Battle of Angels 49
  Camino Real 48–9, 62
  Cat on a Hot Tin Roof 42–3, 48–9, 56, 62, 69
  Garden District 48
  Glass Menagerie, The 101
  homosexuality and 48–9, 56, 123
  Inge and 50, 100–1, 104, 123, 215
  Orpheus Descending 8–9, 65
  Rose Tattoo, The 43, 48, 60, 64–5
  Something Unspoken 48
  stature xi, 48, 57, 151, 190, 250
  Streetcar Named Desire, A 57, 62–3, 66–7
  Suddenly Last Summer 48–9
  Summer and Smoke 67
  Sweet Bird of Youth 48–9, 62, 69
Wilson, John 221
Wilson, Meredith 86
  Music Man, The 41, 43, 86, 140–1, 150
Wilson, Sloan 21
  Man in the Grey Flannel Suit, The 21
Winters, Shelley 58
Wirz, (Captain) John 75
Wise, Brownie 7

Witham, Barry 72
Wood, Audrey 101
Wood, Barbara 221
Wood, Natalie 62
Woodard, Nathan 224, 225, 280 n.32
  Gullah 226
  Moms: A Praise Play for a Black Comedienne 226
  Sea Island Song 225–6
  Young Martin Luther King Jr. 224
  see also Childress, Alice
Woods, Alan 51, 227, 231
Woodward, Joanne 90, 212
working women 7, 25, 113–14, 124, 167–9, 171–3, 176–7, 180–2, 202–3, 258 n.16
  discrimination toward 2, 7, 12, 107–8, 182–3
  housewives 5–7, 22, 27, 106–9, 119, 242
Wouk, Herman 20, 74
  Caine Mutiny, The (film) 20
  Caine Mutiny Court-Martial, The (play) 43, 74–5
Wright, Frank Lloyd 22
Wright, Richard 173–4
  Native Son 173–4

Yarns for Yanks (radio series) 190
Yordan, Philip 166
  Anna Lucasta 166
You Can Survive (pamphlet) 12
Young Audiences (New York) 97
Young Love (radio series) 191

Zak, Albin J. 18
Ziegfeld Follies 152
Zorba (film) 66

www.ingramcontent.com/pod-product-compliance
Lightning Source LLC
Chambersburg PA
CBHW070014010526
44117CB00011B/1571